Windows® 10

3rd Edition

by Andy Rathbone

for
dummies®
A Wiley Brand

Windows® 10 For Dummies®, 3rd Edition

Published by **John Wiley & Sons, Inc.**, 111 River Street, Hoboken, NJ 07030-5774, www.wiley.com

Copyright © 2018 by John Wiley & Sons, Inc., Hoboken, New Jersey

Media and software compilation copyright © 2018 by John Wiley & Sons, Inc. All rights reserved.

Published simultaneously in Canada.

For general information on our other products and services, please contact our Customer Care Department within the U.S. at 877-762-2974, outside the U.S. at 317-572-3993, or fax 317-572-4002. For technical support, please visit https://hub.wiley.com/community/support/dummies.

Wiley publishes in a variety of print and electronic formats and by print-on-demand. Some material included with standard print versions of this book may not be included in e-books or in print-on-demand. If this book refers to media such as a CD or DVD that is not included in the version you purchased, you may download this material at http://booksupport.wiley.com. For more information about Wiley products, visit www.wiley.com.

Library of Congress Control Number: 2018938744

ISBN: 978-1-119-47086-1; ISBN (ePDF): 978-1-119-47090-8; ISBN (ePub): 978-1-119-47091-5

Manufactured in the United States of America

C10017482_020720

Contents at a Glance

Table of Contents

Introduction

Welcome to *Windows 10 For Dummies,* the world's best-selling book about the newest — and supposedly last — Windows version, Windows 10!

This book's popularity probably boils down to this simple fact: Some people want to be Windows whizzes. They love interacting with dialog boxes. Some randomly press keys in the hope of discovering hidden, undocumented features. A few memorize long strings of computer commands while washing their hair.

And you? Well, you're no dummy, that's for sure. But when it comes to Windows and computers, the fascination just isn't there. You want to get your work done, stop, and move on to something more important. You have no intention of changing, and there's nothing wrong with that.

TIP

HOW I WROTE THIS BOOK

How did this book arrive in your hands so quickly after Microsoft released its latest big update? No, I didn't crank it out in two weeks. While building Windows 10, Microsoft shipped early releases to people who signed up for its Windows Insider's program (https://insider.windows.com). This gave Microsoft a way to test new features before shipping them to the public. And it gave me a chance to write about features before they were released.

I spent many months poring over early releases, writing up sections of the book in advance. Then, when Microsoft released its final, approved version to the Windows Insider members, I went over every section, screenshot, and step-by-step instruction to make sure the book's instructions matched Microsoft's final release.

A few weeks later, when Microsoft released the final version of Windows to the public, the publisher was able to release this book, as well.

That's where this book comes in handy. Instead of making you a whiz at Windows, it merely dishes out chunks of useful computing information when you need them. Instead of becoming a Windows expert, you'll know just enough to get by quickly, cleanly, and with a minimum of pain so that you can move on to the more pleasant things in life.

And you'll be able to do that whether you're dealing with a touchscreen tablet, laptop, or desktop computer.

About This Book

Don't try to read this book in one sitting; there's no need. Instead, treat this book like a dictionary or an encyclopedia. Turn to the page with the information you need and say, "Ah, so that's what they're talking about." Then put down the book and move on.

Don't bother trying to memorize all the Windows jargon, such as Select the Menu Item from the Drop-Down List Box. Leave that stuff for the computer enthusiasts. In fact, if anything technical comes up in a chapter, a road sign warns you well in advance. Depending on your mood, you can either slow down to read it or speed on around it.

Instead of fancy computer jargon, this book covers subjects like these, all discussed in plain English:

>> Keeping your computer safe and secure

>> Making sense of the Windows 10 Start menu

>> Finding, starting, and closing programs and apps

>> Locating the file you saved or downloaded yesterday

>> Setting up a computer or tablet for the whole family to share

>> Copying information to and from a disc or flash drive

>> Saving and sharing files from your smartphone or digital camera

>> Printing or scanning your work

>> Creating a network between two or more computers to share the Internet, files, or a printer

>> Fixing Windows when it's misbehaving

There's nothing to memorize and nothing to learn. Just turn to the right page, read the brief explanation, and get back to work. Unlike other books, this one enables you to bypass the technical hoopla and still complete your work.

How to Use This Book

Windows 10 will most definitely leave you scratching your head at some point. It's the most complicated version of Windows ever released to the public, so take pride in the fact that you're strong enough to persevere.

When something in Windows leaves you stumped, use this book as a reference. Find the troublesome topic in this book's table of contents or index. The table of contents lists chapter and section titles and page numbers. The index lists topics and page numbers. Page through the table of contents or index to the spot that deals with that particular bit of computer obscurity, read only what you have to, close the book, and apply what you've read.

If you're feeling adventurous and want to find out more, read a little further in the bulleted items below each section. You can find a few completely voluntary extra details, tips, or cross-references to check out. There's no pressure, though. You aren't forced to discover anything that you don't want to or that you simply don't have time for.

If you have to type something into the computer, you'll see easy-to-follow bold text like this:

Type **Media Player** into the Search box.

In the preceding example, you type the words *Media Player* and then press the keyboard's Enter key. Typing words into a computer can be confusing, so a description follows that explains what you should be seeing on the screen.

When I describe a key combination you should press, I describe it like this:

Press Ctrl+B.

That means to hold down your keyboard's Control key while pressing your keyboard's B key. (That's the shortcut key combination that applies bold formatting to selected text.)

Whenever I describe an email address or filename, I present it this way:

```
notepad.exe
```

And website addresses appear like this:

```
www.andyrathbone.com
```

This book doesn't wimp out by saying, "For further information, consult your manual." Windows doesn't even come with a manual. This book also doesn't contain information about running specific Windows software packages, such as Microsoft Office. Windows is complicated enough on its own! Luckily, other For Dummies books mercifully explain most popular software packages.

Don't feel abandoned, though. This book covers Windows in plenty of detail for you to get the job done. Plus, if you have questions or comments about *Windows 10 For Dummies,* feel free to drop me a line on my website at www.andyrathbone.com. I answer a reader's question each week, either personally or online.

Finally, keep in mind that this book is a *reference.* It's not designed to teach you how to use Windows like an expert, heaven forbid. Instead, this book dishes out enough bite-sized chunks of information so that you don't *have* to learn Windows.

Touchscreen Owners Aren't Left Out

Although Windows 10 comes preinstalled on all new Windows desktop PCs and laptops, Microsoft also aims Windows 10 at owners of *touchscreens.* Tablets, phones, and some laptops and desktop monitors come with screens you can control by touching them with your fingers.

If you're a new touchscreen owner, don't worry. This book explains where you need to touch, slide, or tap your fingers in all the appropriate places.

If you find yourself scratching your head over explanations aimed at mouse owners, remember these three touchscreen rules:

» **When told to *click,* you should *tap.*** Quickly touching and releasing your finger on a button is the same as clicking it with a mouse.

» **When told to double-click, *tap twice.*** Two touches in rapid succession does the trick.

>> **When told to *right-click* something, *hold down your finger on the item.* Then, when an icon appears, *lift your finger.*** The right-click menu appears onscreen. (That's what would have happened if you'd right-clicked the item with a mouse.) While you're looking at the pop-up menu, tap any of its listed items to have Windows carry out your bidding.

REMEMBER

If you find touchscreens to be cumbersome while you're sitting at a desk, you can always add a mouse and keyboard to your touchscreen tablet. They work just fine. In fact, a mouse and keyboard almost always work better than fingers on the Windows desktop, even in Windows 10. (They're almost mandatory on small Windows tablets.)

And What about You?

Chances are good that you already own Windows 10, or you're thinking about upgrading. You know what *you* want to do with your computer. The problem lies in making the *computer* do what you want it to do. You've gotten by one way or another, perhaps with the help of a computer guru — for instance, a friend at the office, a relative, or perhaps a neighbor's teenager.

But when your computer guru isn't around, this book can be a substitute during your times of need.

Icons Used in This Book

It just takes a glance at Windows to notice its *icons*, which are little push-button pictures for starting various programs. The icons in this book fit right in. They're even a little easier to figure out.

TECHNICAL STUFF

Watch out! This signpost warns you that pointless technical information is coming around the bend. Swerve away from this icon to stay safe from awful technical drivel.

TIP

This icon alerts you about juicy information that makes computing easier: a new method for keeping the cat from sleeping on top of your tablet, for example.

REMEMBER

Don't forget to remember these important points (or at least dog-ear the pages so that you can look them up again a few days later).

The computer won't explode while you're performing the delicate operations associated with this icon. Still, wearing gloves and proceeding with caution is a good idea.

Are you moving to Windows 10 from an older Windows version? This icon alerts you to areas where Windows 10 behaves quite differently from its predecessors.

Beyond the Book

Like every Windows For Dummies book, this one comes with a free Cheat Sheet that brings together some of the most commonly needed information for people struggling with Windows. It describes how Microsoft changed Windows 10 one year after its release, and offers keyboard shortcuts as well as tips on using Windows 10 on a touchscreen. To get the Cheat Sheet, head for www.dummies.com and, using the Search box, search for **Windows 10 For Dummies Cheat Sheet**.

Where to Go from Here

Now you're ready for action. Give the pages a quick flip and scan a section or two that you know you'll need later. Please remember, this is *your* book — your weapon against the computer nerds who've inflicted this whole complicated computer concept on you. Please circle any paragraphs you find useful, highlight key concepts, add your own sticky notes, and doodle in the margins next to the complicated stuff.

The more you mark up your book, the easier it will be for you to find all the good stuff again.

1

Windows 10 Stuff Everybody Thinks You Already Know

IN THIS PART . . .

Understand the changes in Windows 10.

Navigate and customize the Start menu.

Store files in the Cloud with OneDrive.

Chapter **1**

What Is Windows 10?

C hances are good that you've heard about *Windows:* the boxes and windows that greet you whenever you turn on your computer. In fact, millions of people worldwide are puzzling over Windows as you read this book. Almost every new computer and laptop sold today comes with Windows preinstalled, ready to toss colorful boxes onto the screen.

This chapter helps you understand why Windows lives inside your computer, and I introduce Microsoft's latest Windows version, *Windows 10.* I explain how Windows 10 differs from previous Windows versions and help you determine whether you should upgrade your computer to Windows 10.

Finally, I explain what's new in Windows 10 and whether you should install this upgrade onto your Windows 7 or 8.1 computer.

What Is Windows, and Why Are You Using It?

Created and sold by a company called Microsoft, Windows isn't like your usual software that lets you calculate income taxes or send angry emails to politicians. No, Windows is an *operating system*, meaning it controls the way you work with your computer. It's been around since 1985, and the latest incarnation is called *Windows 10*, shown in Figure 1-1.

FIGURE 1-1:
Although Windows 10 looks different on different PCs, it usually looks much like this.

The name *Windows* comes from all the little windows it places on your computer screen. Each window shows information, such as a picture, a program, or a baffling technical reprimand. You can place several windows onscreen simultaneously and jump from window to window, visiting different programs. Or, you can enlarge one window to fill the entire screen.

When you turn on your computer, Windows jumps onto the screen and begins supervising any running programs. When everything goes well, you don't really notice Windows; you simply see your programs or your work. When things don't go well, though, Windows often leaves you scratching your head over a perplexing error message.

In addition to controlling your computer and bossing around your programs, Windows comes with a bunch of free programs and *apps* — mini-programs. These programs and apps let you do different things, such as write and print letters, browse the Internet, play music, and send your friends dimly lit photos of your latest meal.

And why are you using Windows? Well, you probably didn't have much choice. Nearly every computer, laptop, or Windows tablet sold after July 2015 comes with Windows 10 preinstalled. A few people escaped Windows by buying Apple computers (those nicer-looking computers that cost a lot more). But chances are good that you, your neighbors, your boss, and millions of other people around the world are using Windows.

TIP

SEPARATING THE ADS FROM THE FEATURES

Microsoft touts Windows as a helpful companion that always keeps your best interests in mind, but that description isn't really true. Windows always keeps *Microsoft's* interests in mind.

For example, Microsoft uses Windows to plug its own products and services. *Microsoft Edge*, the new Windows web browser, opens with links to Microsoft's own websites. The browser's Favorites area, a place for you to add *your* favorite web destinations, comes stocked with *Microsoft* websites.

Windows 10 places a link to OneDrive, its online storage service, in every folder. But Microsoft isn't as quick to mention that you must pay an annual fee when you reach your storage limit.

Ads appear on the Start menu, as well as the Windows *Lock Screen,* the screen that appears when you haven't used your PC for a while.

The Maps app uses the Microsoft Bing mapping service, rather than Google Maps or another competitor.

Microsoft also wants you to start buying *apps* rather than traditional programs. Apps are sold only through the bundled Microsoft Store app, and Microsoft takes a cut of each sale.

Simply put, Windows not only controls your computer but also serves as a huge Microsoft advertising vehicle. Treat these built-in advertising flyers as a salesperson's knock on your door.

>> Microsoft wants Windows 10 and its gang of apps to run on *everything:* PCs, laptops, tablets, video game consoles, phones, and even yet-to-be-invented gadgets. That's why Windows 10 includes many large buttons for easier poking with fingers on touchscreens. Windows 10 can also run *apps,* small programs usually found on smartphones and tablets, in windows on a desktop PC.

>> To confuse everybody, Microsoft never released a Windows 9. Microsoft skipped a version number when moving from Windows 8.1 to Windows 10.

NEW

>> The desktop's traditional Start menu, missing from Windows 8 and 8.1, returns in Windows 10. Microsoft has tinkered with the popular menu since Windows 10's initial release, making it a little easier to understand. (I explain how to customize the new Start menu to your liking in Chapter 2.)

What's New in Windows 10?

Microsoft views Windows 10 as a one-size-fits-all computing solution that runs on laptops and desktop PCs (shown earlier in Figure 1-1) as well as tablets, shown in Figure 1-2.

FIGURE 1-2: Windows 10 behaves almost identically on laptops and desktop PCs (shown earlier) and tablets (above).

Windows 10 can even run on your TV through Microsoft's Xbox One game console. Windows 10 behaves almost identically on every device, and it brings a bonus: Apps known as *universal apps* will run on a Windows 10 tablet, PC, laptop, and Xbox One.

NEW

Besides aiming to run on everything but clock radios, Windows 10 brings these changes to your computer:

>> **Start button and menu:** Removed from Windows 8 and half-heartedly tacked back onto Windows 8.1, the Start button and Start menu triumphantly return to the desktop in Windows 10. The revamped Start menu sports a column of icons, as well as fingertip-sized tiles for launching apps. (Tile haters find instructions for removing them in Chapter 2.)

>> **Apps on the desktop:** *Apps,* which are small programs from the world of phones and tablets, consumed the full screen in Windows 8 and 8.1. Windows 10 lets you choose whether to run apps full screen or within desktop windows.

>> **Cortana:** The digital assistant in Windows 10, Cortana, helps you manage your computing by fetching lost files, stocking your calendar with appointments, grabbing up-to-date traffic information about your commute, and extracting informational tidbits from the Internet. Controlled through either your voice or keyboard, Cortana works from the Search box adjacent to the Start button.

>> **OneDrive:** Microsoft's online file storage service comes built into the Windows 10 desktop. OneDrive lets you choose which files and folders should live *only* on the cloud (Microsoft's Internet-connected computers) and which should live on both the cloud *and* your computer. That lets you adjust the settings depending on your computer's amount of available storage space.

>> **More Apps:** The Microsoft Store offers more than 700,000 apps. That's nowhere near the number of apps found for the iPhone, iPad, or Android phones and tablets, but you can find plenty of big names like Facebook and Netflix, with more on the way.

>> **Multiple desktops:** Windows 10 lets you create extra desktops, and you can switch between them with a click or tap. You can set up one desktop for work and another for gaming, for example. (Or, you can completely ignore the feature.)

>> **Windows Hello:** This welcome security update allows you to sign into your computer without typing in a password. With the right fingerprint reader or camera, your computer can recognize either your face, fingerprint, or iris and automatically let you in. You can even access supported websites without having to type in your username and password.

>> **Windows Ink:** This big update lets you write on your tablet's screen with a special pen, letting you add handwritten notes and drawings to apps like Maps, the Microsoft Edge browser, and Office.

>> **Windows Timeline:** This new feature lets you see what apps, programs, and websites you accessed on previous days, letting you quickly revisit past work.

>> **Windows 10 is now a service:** Perhaps most important, Microsoft treats Windows 10 as a constantly evolving *service* rather than a finished product. Microsoft keeps tinkering with Windows 10, adding, changing, or removing apps and features for as long as you own the device. (There's no way to stop Microsoft from changing Windows 10; you're expected to stomach these changes which take place automatically in the background.)

Unlike Windows 8 and 8.1, Windows 10 no longer feels like two operating systems crammed into one computer. It feels like a single operating system that brings out the best in both tablets and desktop PCs.

TIP

For its first year of release, Windows 10 was a free upgrade for people owning fully patched Windows 7, 8, or 8.1 computers. The upgrade is no longer free, but it still keeps your files, apps, and programs in place. Owners of older PCs can also upgrade to Windows 10, but the upgrade will wipe out all your files and programs. You'll need to reinstall everything from a backup. (If your old computer is a slow crawler, it will *still* be a slow crawler after upgrading to Windows 10. You're probably better off buying a new PC with Windows 10 preinstalled.)

TECHNICAL STUFF

Windows no longer comes in a Windows RT version. If you bought a Windows RT tablet, such as the Surface RT or Surface 2, you can't upgrade it to Windows 10.

Should I Bother Upgrading to Windows 10?

If you're happy with your current version of Windows, don't bother upgrading to Windows 10. Most people stick with the Windows version that came preinstalled on their computers. That way they avoid the chore of figuring out a new version. Windows 10 comes with a steep learning curve because it's quite different from earlier Windows versions.

Also, many of the biggest changes in Windows 10 work best with *touchscreens* — those fingertip-controlled screens found on expensive cellphones, tablets, and some of the latest laptops and desktop monitors. Most desktop PC owners don't need that feature.

Instead of upgrading, stick with the masses and stay with your current Windows version. When you're ready to buy a new computer, Windows 10 will be installed and waiting for you.

But if you're running Windows 8 or Windows 8.1, and you're unhappy with it, you may enjoy upgrading to Windows 10. The update smooths over many of the rough edges of those Windows versions, especially on desktop PCs and tablets that convert into PCs.

After Windows 7, Microsoft ended its support for *Windows XP mode,* a popular way to run a Windows XP desktop within Windows 7. If you rely on Windows XP mode in Windows 7, stick with Windows 7. The same holds true for *Windows Media Center,* a popular way to record TV shows and watch DVDs. If you rely on either of those two programs, don't upgrade to Windows 10.

HISTORY FOR WINDOWS 7 UPGRADERS

Windows 7 diehards missed a lot of hubbub by skipping Windows 8 and 8.1. Those two poorly received Windows versions affected Windows 10 quite a bit, so here's a wee bit of history so you'll understand Windows 10 a little better.

For years, Microsoft had watched helplessly as hordes of people bought iPhones, iPads, and *apps* — small and simple programs for lightweight touchscreen tasks. To compete, Microsoft designed Windows 8 for touchscreen tablets and unleashed it in 2012. Like the competition, Windows 8 opened to a screen full of touchable colorful tiles, each representing an app.

Even the desktop was relegated to an app, a tiny tile on the screen. But when opened, the Desktop app lacked its Start button and menu. Microsoft expected people to return to the tile-filled opening screen to launch their desktop programs.

Most desktop owners hated Windows 8. And because very few people bought Windows 8 tablets, Windows 8 bombed in the marketplace. Windows 8.1 made a few amends, but not enough.

With Windows 10, Microsoft aims to placate desktop lovers by bringing back a more traditional Start button and Start menu. To please tablet owners, the Start menu can fill the screen on command, making it easier to control with fingertips.

Best of all, Windows 10 is smart enough to change shape depending on what device it's installed on. On a tablet, Windows 10 presents the tile-filled, full-screen Start menu, which subtly changes its spacing to accommodate finger taps. On desktop PCs, Windows 10 shows the traditional desktop, Start menu, and Start button. And the menus remain small, which works well for the pinpoint clicks of a mouse.

With Windows 10, Microsoft hopes Windows will finally serve the needs of both desktop traditionalists *and* tablet owners.

What's So Different About Windows 10?

Today, computing falls into two camps: creating and consuming. People turn to their desktop PC for *creating* things. They write papers, send email, prepare tax returns, update blogs, edit videos, or, quite often, tap whichever keys their boss requires that day.

But when *consuming*, people often walk away from their desktop PCs. They pull out their smartphone or tablet to read email, watch videos, listen to music, and browse the web.

That split creates a problem. Desktop PCs, phones, and tablets all work differently; each offers different screen sizes, programs, and commands. What works well with fingers doesn't always work well with a mouse and keyboard. Sharing files among gadgets can be a nightmare.

Windows 10 aims to fix those problems by creating one operating system that works well on *everything*, letting both consumers and creators work on a single device. To do that, Windows 10 includes two different modes:

>> **Tablet mode:** For on-the-go information grabbers with touchscreen tablets, the Windows 10 Start menu fills the entire screen with large, colorful tiles that constantly update to show the latest stock prices, weather, email, Facebook updates, and other tidbits. Shown earlier in Figure 1-2, that information appears before you touch a button. And *touch* is a keyword: The full-screen Start menu works best with a touchscreen monitor or tablet.

>> **Desktop mode:** When it's time for work, the traditional Windows desktop brings all its power — as well as its more powerful and detailed menus.

Some people like the convenience of having both types of computers built into one: a touchscreen laptop, for example, or a tablet with a docking station that lets you plug in a mouse and keyboard. Others find the two experiences to be oddly disjointed.

>> If you can stomach the initial confusion, Windows 10 may offer you the best of both worlds: You can stay on the full-screen Start menu for quick, on-the-go browsing. And when work beckons, you can head for the desktop, where your traditional Windows programs await.

>> If you're sitting at a desktop PC, Windows 10 should automatically open to the desktop. Windows 10 tablets usually open to a full-screen Start menu.

- ≫ If Windows 10 doesn't open to the mode you prefer, click the Action Center icon (shown in the margin) found on the taskbar at the bottom of the screen; when the Action Center pane appears, click the Tablet mode toggle button. Your Start menu should quickly return to its proper size.

TECHNICAL STUFF

- ≫ Microsoft's game console, the Xbox One, runs in Tablet mode. The Xbox One's game controller serves as your finger, letting you move from tile to tile by pressing the controller's arrow keys.

- ≫ I explain the new Windows 10 Start menu in Chapter 2; the Windows desktop awaits your attention in Chapter 3.

Why Does Windows 10 Keep Changing?

Microsoft calls Windows 10 a *service* rather than an operating system. Like any other service, it's subject to changes. Every month or two, Microsoft changes Windows 10 slightly. Some of Microsoft's changes occur more quickly: Your apps, for example, can update weekly. Some update daily.

Other changes arrive every six months, packed into large groups. You may have heard about the Anniversary Update in mid-2016, and the Creator's Update in 2017. Another big update arrived in early 2018, bringing even more changes. (This edition of the book is up-to-date with all those changes.)

You may not notice these changes. Indeed, most of them just fix hundreds of annoying bugs, making Windows 10 run and install more smoothly.

Microsoft sends these updates automatically to your computer through Windows Update; you don't need to jump through hoops to find and install them.

Your apps update themselves automatically through the Microsoft Store. That's why the Music app automatically changed its name to the Groove Music app, for example. The Photos app suddenly added a way to search your photos by folder and to create slideshows.

So, when something suddenly changes with Windows 10, don't think it's your fault. Microsoft constantly changes Windows 10, and Windows will keep changing for years to come.

Can My Current PC Still Run Windows 10?

If you want to upgrade to Windows 10, your computer probably won't complain. Windows 10 should run without problem on any PC currently running Windows 7, 8, or 8.1.

If your PC runs Windows Vista or Windows XP, it may still run Windows 10, but not very well. I don't recommend it.

TECHNICAL
STUFF

If you have a technogeek in your family, have him or her translate Table 1-1, which shows the Windows 10 hardware requirements you can find written in the fine-print for new computers.

TABLE 1-1

The Windows 10 Hardware Requirements

Architecture	x86 (32-bit)	x86 (64-bit)
Processor	1 GHz or faster	
Memory (RAM)	At least 1GB	At least 2GB
Graphics Card	DirectX 9 graphics device with Windows Display Driver Model (WDDM) driver	
HDD free space	At least 16GB	At least 20GB
Firmware	Unified Extensible Firmware Interface (UEFI) 2.3.1 with secure boot enabled	

In common language, Table 1-1 simply says that nearly any computer sold in the past five years can be upgraded to Windows 10 with little problem.

Windows 10 runs nearly any program that runs on Windows Vista, Windows 7, Windows 8, and Windows 8.1. It even runs some Windows XP programs as well. Some older programs, however, won't work, including older games and most security-based programs, such as antivirus, firewall, and security suites. You'll need to contact the program's manufacturer for an upgraded version.

TIP

Don't know what version of Windows runs on your current PC? If clicking the Start button brings a Start menu, right-click the menu's Computer entry, and choose Properties. The screen that appears lists your Windows version.

If there's no Start button, you're running Windows 8. And if clicking your Start button fills the screen with a bunch of colorful tiles, you're running Windows 8.1.

Finally, if *right-clicking* your Start menu brings a large pop-up menu, you're running Windows 10. Choose the menu's System entry, and the About window appears. Your version of Windows 10 is listed in the Windows Specifications section.

The Different Flavors of Windows 10

NEW

Microsoft offers several different versions of Windows 10, but you'll probably want only one: the aptly titled "Home" version.

Small businesses will choose Windows 10 Pro, and larger businesses will want Windows 10 Enterprise.

Here are some guidelines for choosing the version you need:

>> If you'll be using your PC at home or in your small business, pick up **Windows Home.**

>> If you need to connect to a domain through a work network — and you'll know if you're doing it — you want **Windows Pro.**

>> If you don't mind running only apps from the Microsoft Store, with no desktop programs, you might be a candidate for the more secure **Windows 10 S.** (It costs less than other Windows versions, making it more attractive to students.)

>> If you're a computer tech who works for businesses, go ahead and argue with your boss over whether you need **Windows Pro** or **Windows Enterprise.** The boss will make the decision based on whether it's a small company (Windows Pro) or a large company (Windows Enterprise).

For more details about upgrading to Windows 10, visit Microsoft's Windows website at `www.windows.com`.

Chapter **2**

Starting with the Start Menu

The Windows 10 Start menu doesn't look much like the Start menu in your earlier version of Windows. The latest update added a few buttons and features, but the basic mechanics remain the same.

Click the Start button in the screen's bottom-left corner, and the Start menu rises, listing the apps and programs installed on your PC. Click an app or program, and it leaps to the screen, ready for action.

In this chapter, I explain how to figure out this odd, shape-shifting Start menu. On touchscreen tablets, the Start menu fills the entire screen. Its large tiles make them easy to tap with your fingertips. On a desktop computer, however, the Start menu retreats to a corner of the screen, where you can click its tiny buttons and menus with your mouse pointer.

Whether you're using a tablet or desktop PC, this chapter shows how to make the Start menu do its main job: launch your apps and programs.

TIP

If you're using a touchscreen computer, substitute the word *tap* when you read the word *click.* Tapping twice works like *double-clicking.* And when you see the term *right-click,* touch and hold your finger on the glass; lift your finger when the right-click menu appears.

Being Welcomed to the World of Windows

Starting Windows is as easy as turning on your computer — Windows leaps onto the screen automatically with a flourish. But before you can begin working, Windows stops you cold: It displays a locked screen, shown in Figure 2-1, with no entrance key dangling nearby.

9:14

Sunday, May 15

FIGURE 2-1:
To move past this lock screen, press a key on the keyboard or drag up on the screen with your mouse or finger.

Introduced back in Windows 8, the lock screen appears before you can sign in to your computer with your account name and password.

How do you unlock the lock screen? The answer depends on whether you're using a mouse, keyboard, or touchscreen:

>> **Mouse:** On a desktop PC or laptop, click any mouse button.

>> **Keyboard:** Press any key, and the lock screen slides away. Easy!

>> **Touch:** Touch the screen with your finger and then slide your finger *up* the glass. A quick flick of the finger will do.

When you're in the door, Windows wants you to *sign in*, as shown in Figure 2-2, by clicking your name and typing in a password.

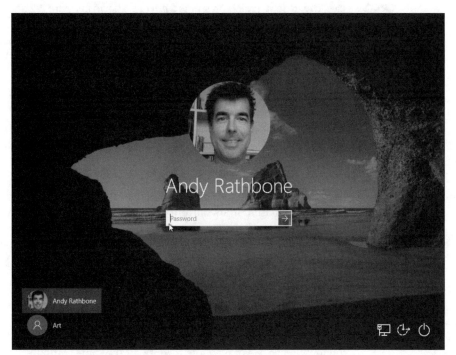

FIGURE 2-2:
Click your user account name and then type your password on the next screen.

I've customized my lock screen and Sign In screen. Yours will look different. When facing the Sign In screen, you have several options:

>> **If you see your name or email address listed, type your password.**
Windows lets you in and displays your Start menu, just as you last left it.

>> **If you don't see your name, but you have an account on the computer, look in the screen's bottom-left corner.** There, Windows displays a list of all the account holders. You may see the computer owner's name.

>> **If you bought a new computer, use the account you created when turning on your computer for the first time.** As part of its setup process, Windows guides you through creating an account on your computer.

>> **No account?** Then find out who owns the computer and beg that person to set up an account for you.

If you need more information about user accounts, including creating new ones and managing old ones, flip ahead to Chapter 14.

Don't *want* to sign in at the Sign In screen? Two of the screen's bottom-corner buttons offer these other options:

>> **The little wheelchair-shaped button,** shown in Figure 2-2 and the margin, customizes Windows for people with physical challenges in hearing, sight, or manual dexterity, all covered in Chapter 12. If you choose this button by mistake, click or touch on a different part of the screen to avoid changing any settings.

>> **The little round button,** shown in Figure 2-2 and the margin, lets you shut down or restart your PC, as well as put it to sleep — a power-saving state that quickly awakes. (If you've accidentally clicked the button and shut down your PC, don't panic. Press the power button on your PC's case, and your PC returns to this screen.)

Even while locked, as shown earlier in Figure 2-1, your computer's screen displays current information in its bottom-left corner. Depending on how your PC is configured, you can see the time and date; your wireless Internet signal strength (the more radio waves in the icon, the better your connection); battery strength (the more colorful the icon, the better); your next scheduled appointment; a count of unread email; and other items.

Understanding user accounts

Windows allows several people to work on the same computer, yet it keeps everybody's work separate. To do that, it needs to know who's currently sitting in front of the keyboard. When you *sign in* — introduce yourself — by clicking your username and typing your password, as shown in Figure 2-2, the Windows Start menu and desktop appear as you just left them, ready for you to make your own personalized mess.

When you're through working or just feel like taking a break, sign out (explained at this chapter's end) so that somebody else can use the computer. Later, when you sign back in, your own files will be waiting for you.

Although you may turn your work area into a mess, it's your own mess. When you return to the computer, your letters will be just as you saved them. Jerry hasn't accidentally deleted your files or folders while playing *Words with Friends.* Tina's Start menu still contains links to her favorite scrapbooking websites. And nobody will be able to read your email.

Until you customize your username picture, you'll be a silhouette, like the account listed in the bottom-left corner of Figure 2-2. To add a photo to your user account, open the Start menu and click your username. (It's the top icon in the column of icons directly over the Start button.) Choose Change Account Settings from the pop-up menu. When the Settings menu's Your Info section appears, click the Camera icon to take a quick shot with your computer's built-in camera. Still wearing your pajamas? Then choose the Browse For One link to choose a photo already stored in your Pictures folder.

Keeping your account private with a password

Because Windows lets many people use the same computer, how do you stop Diane from reading Rob's love letters to Miley Cyrus? How can Grace keep Josh from deleting her *Star Wars* movie trailers? Using a *password* solves some of those problems.

In fact, a password is more important than ever in Windows 10 because some accounts can be tied to a credit card. By typing a secret password when signing in, you enable your computer to recognize *you* and nobody else. If you protect your username with a password, nobody can access your files. And nobody can rack up charges for computer games while you're away from home.

Also, if your computer is ever stolen, a password keeps the thieves from logging in to your account and connecting to any websites with your account.

To set up or change the password on your account, follow these steps:

1. **Click the Start button and then click the Settings icon.**

   When the Start menu appears, click the Settings icon near the menu's bottom-left corner. (It's the little gear directly above the Power icon.) The Settings app appears.

2. **Click the Accounts icon (shown in the margin). When the Accounts pane appears, click the words Sign-in Options along the pane's left edge.**

   Options for signing in to your computer appear on the right.

3. **From the Password section on the app's right side, click the Change button, shown in Figure 2-3. If you don't have a password, you'll see an Add button to click, instead.**

   You may need to type your existing password to gain entrance.

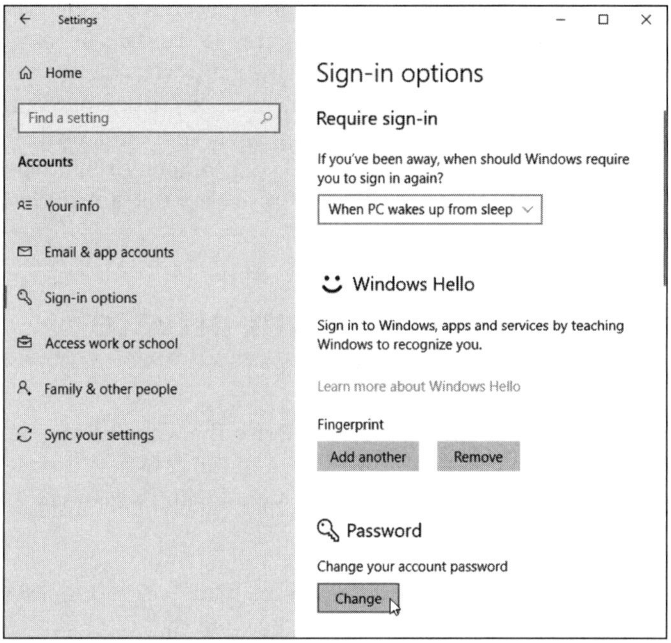

FIGURE 2-3:
Click the
Password
section's Change
button.

4. **Type a password that will be easy to remember.**

TIP

   Choose something like the name of your favorite vegetable, for example, or your dental floss brand. To beef up its security level, capitalize some letters and embed a number or two in the password, like **TurnipsR4Me** or **Floss2BKleen.** (Don't use these exact two examples, though, because they've probably been added to every password cracker's arsenal by now.)

5. **If asked, type that same password into the Retype Password text box so Windows knows you're spelling it correctly.**

6. **In the Password Hint box, type a hint that reminds you — and only you — of your password.**

   Windows won't let you type in your exact password as a hint. You have to be a bit more creative.

7. **Click the Next button and click Finish.**

   Do you suspect you've botched something during this process? Click Cancel to return to Step 3 and either start over or exit.

After you've created the password, Windows begins asking for your password whenever you sign in.

>> Passwords are case-sensitive. The words Caviar and caviar are considered two different passwords.

>> Afraid that you'll forget your password someday? Protect yourself now: Flip ahead to Chapter 14, where I describe how to make a Password Reset Disk, which is a special way of resetting forgotten passwords for local accounts. (You can reset a lost Microsoft account password online at `http://live.com`.)

REMEMBER

>> When you change your Microsoft account password on your PC, you also change it on your Xbox, your Windows tablet, and every other device where you sign in with a Microsoft account. (I cover Microsoft accounts in this chapter's next section.)

>> Windows also allows you to create a picture password in Step 4, where you drag a finger or mouse over a photo in a certain sequence. Then, instead of entering a password, you redraw that sequence on the sign-in picture. (Picture passwords work much better on touchscreen tablets than desktop monitors.)

>> Another option that you may see in Step 4 is to create a PIN. A *PIN* is a four-or-more character code like the ones you punch into Automated Teller Machines (ATMs). The disadvantage of a PIN? There's no password hint. Unlike Microsoft accounts, your PIN only works on the computer where it was created.

TIP

>> Tired of constantly entering your password? Connect a Windows 10 compatible fingerprint reader or camera to your PC. (Some laptops, tablets, and keyboards have them built in.) Your computer quickly lets you in after you either scan your fingertip or gaze into your PC's camera. I describe how to sign in with Windows Hello in Chapter 14.

>> Forgotten your password *already?* When you type a password that doesn't work, Windows automatically displays your hint (if you created one) which should help to remind you of your password. Careful, though — anybody can read your hint, so make sure that it's something that makes sense only to you. As a last resort, insert your Password Reset Disk, a job I cover in Chapter 14.

I explain much more about user accounts in Chapter 14.

Signing up for a Microsoft account

Whether you're signing in to Windows for the first time, trying to access some apps, or just trying to change a setting, you'll eventually see a screen like the one in Figure 2-4.

FIGURE 2-4:
You need a
Microsoft account
to access many
Windows
features.

You can sign in to your computer with either a *Microsoft* account or a *Local* account. Although a Microsoft account makes Windows much easier to work with, each type of account serves different needs:

>> **Local account:** This account works fine for people using traditional Windows programs on the Windows desktop. However, Local account holders can't store files on OneDrive. They can't download apps from the Microsoft Store app, either.

>> **Microsoft account:** Required to access many of Microsoft's services, this consists of simply an email address and a password. Microsoft account holders can store files on the Internet with OneDrive, download apps from the Microsoft Store, and monitor their children's online activities.

You can sign in with a Microsoft account in one of two ways, ranked according to simplicity:

>> **Use an existing Microsoft account.** If you already have an account with Hotmail, MSN, Xbox Live, Outlook.com, or Windows Messenger, you already have a Microsoft account and password. Type in that email address and password at the screen shown in Figure 2-4, and then click the Sign In button.

>> **Sign up for a new Microsoft account.** Click the words Microsoft Account, shown in Figure 2-4. Click the Create One! link, and Microsoft takes you to a website where you can create your own Microsoft account. You can use any email address for a Microsoft account. You simply enter that email address, create a new password to go with it, and wham: You've created a Microsoft account.

If you're signing in to Windows on a newly purchased computer for the first time and don't want a Microsoft account, click the words Skip This Step near a screen's lower-left corner. On the next screen, Windows 10 walks you through creating a Local account, which is limited to your own computer.

But until you sign in with a Microsoft account, the nag screen in Figure 2-4 will haunt you whenever you try to access a Windows feature that requires a Microsoft account. (I explain how to convert a Local account into a Microsoft account in Chapter 14.)

TIP

When you first sign in to your new account, Windows may ask whether you want to find other PCs, devices, and content on your network. If you're using a home or work network, click the Yes button. (That lets you print to network printers, as well as share files with other networked computers.) If you're connecting to a *public* network, perhaps at a hotel, coffee shop, or airport, click the No button.

Figuring Out the Windows 10 Start Menu

In Windows, everything starts with the Start button and its Start menu. Whether you're ready to blow up spaceships, do your taxes, or read the news, you start by clicking the Start button in the screen's bottom-left corner: The Start menu leaps up with a list of your apps and programs.

In theory, you spot the name or tile for your desired app or program and click it; the app launches, and you're off to work. In reality, it's a little more confusing.

On a desktop PC, for example, the Start menu's right edge is filled with groups of tiles, shown in Figure 2-5. Each tile represents an *app* (a small program designed mainly for touchscreens). On the left edge, the menu lists your most recently accessed apps and programs, as well as frequently accessed places on your PC.

The desktop PC's Start menu sports a strip of unlabeled icons along its left edge:

>> **Expand:** A click on this icon in the Start menu's upper-left corner reveals the labels of the mysterious icons I'm describing now.

>> **User Account:** This icon looks like your user account picture. Click it to change your account's settings to lock your PC to prevent access while you leave your desk, or to sign out of your account.

>> **Documents:** A quick click on this icon jumps you to the desktop, opens File Explorer, and lets you browse your Documents folder for files.

>> **Pictures:** Click here, and File Explorer opens your Pictures folder, the repository for photos snapped by your computer.

>> **Settings:** Clicking this little gear icon takes you quickly to the Settings app (formerly known as the PC Settings app) for changing how your PC behaves.

>> **Power:** When you're through working, click this to put your computer to sleep, shut it down, or restart it (handy when it's misbehaving).

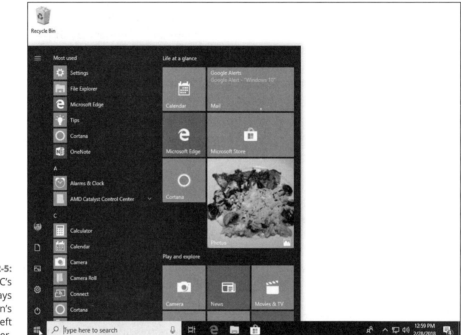

FIGURE 2-5:
A desktop PC's
Start menu stays
in the screen's
bottom-left
corner.

The Start menu changes drastically when switched to Tablet mode, commonly used on tablet PCs. The Start menu's tiles fill the entire screen, shown in Figure 2-6. The menu also hides the left pane shown in Figure 2-5.

>> **Expand:** Just as when in desktop mode, a click on this icon reveals labels for other icons along the screen's left edge.

>> **Pinned Tiles:** The default option, this displays the Start menu's tiles across the entire screen.

>> **All Apps:** Can't find a favorite app? Click this to see an alphabetical list of all your installed apps and programs.

FIGURE 2-6:
A tablet's Start menu fills the entire screen with easy-to-touch buttons.

Despite the Start menu's remodel, it still offers a way to start programs; adjust Windows settings; find help for sticky situations; or, thankfully, shut down Windows and get away from the computer for a while.

The tiles along the Start menu's right edge aren't mere visual baggage. For example, the Calendar tile constantly updates to show the current date and day, as well as your next appointment. The Mail tile cycles through the first words of your latest emails.

Your Start menu will change as you add more programs and apps to your computer. That's why the Start menu on your friend's computer, as well as in this book, is probably arranged differently than your computer's Start menu. And if the tiles don't meet your needs, you can remove them completely, as I describe later in this chapter.

TIP

Try the following tricks to make the Start menu feel a little more like home:

>> To launch a program or app, click or tap its name or tile. The program leaps to the screen.

>> Keyboard fans can fetch the Start menu by pressing the ⊞ key on their keyboard.

>> Were you unable to spot your desired program or app listed on the Start menu? Then scroll down the list of alphabetically sorted apps. (I describe how to scroll down lists in Chapter 4.)

>> On a touchscreen, navigate the Start menu with your finger: Pretend the Start menu is a piece of paper lying on a table. As you move your finger, the Start menu's items move along with it.

 >> If the Start menu fills the entire screen on your desktop, you're in Tablet mode. To turn off Tablet mode, click the Action Center icon in the screen's bottom-right corner (shown in the margin). When the Action Center pane appears, click the Tablet mode tile in the pane's bottom-left corner. The Start menu will retreat to its normal corner.

Toggling between Tablet and Desktop mode

Much of the confusion around Windows 10 centers on one thing: Tablet mode. With Tablet mode turned on, Windows 10 works great on touchscreen tablets. The buttons and menus are bigger, making them easier to control with fingers.

But when a desktop PC runs in Tablet mode, confusion reigns. Desktop owners who face Tablet mode on their screens will see these anomalies:

>> **Start button failure.** Pressing the Start button won't fetch the familiar Start menu. Pressing the Start button won't seem to do anything, in fact. That's because Tablet mode stretches the Start menu across the entire screen, where it looks and behaves differently than the desktop's corner-bound Start menu.

>> **Everything runs fullscreen.** Apps and programs will run, but they consume the entire screen. You never see the traditional desktop, either, because an app or program always runs fullscreen on top of it.

>> **The Restore button doesn't work.** Desktop programs still include their Minimize, Restore, and Close buttons in their upper-right corner. But clicking the Restore button doesn't restore the fullscreen program to a window. The Restore button no longer works because Tablet mode forces both apps and programs to remain fullscreen.

>> **Missing Search box.** Tablet mode hides the Search box, which normally lives next to the Start menu. To bring it to the screen, simply start typing: The Search box magically reappears to accept your incoming words.

>> **Missing app list.** In Tablet mode, the Start menu lacks the alphabetically sorted list of tiles along the left edge.

For many people, the Tablet mode screen just doesn't look right. And unless you know how to turn off Tablet mode, you'll feel like nothing matches what you're expecting — or what you're seeing in this book.

To turn off Tablet mode and return to the regular desktop Start menu, follow these steps:

1. **Click or tap the Action Center icon (shown in the margin) near the taskbar's right end.**

   The Action Center lists *notifications* — bits of information you may need to act on, like newly received emails and news tidbits. When you receive a new notification, a number appears on the Action Center's icon to show how many notifications await your attention.

2. **When the Action Center pane appears along the screen's right edge, click or tap the Tablet mode icon.**

   Your computer will toggle Tablet mode on or off with each press.

Press the Tablet mode icon a few times so you can get the feel for the two types of Start menus in Windows 10. Then you'll know what to do when you're facing the menu you don't want.

Launching a Start menu program or app

Windows stocks your Start menu's right side with *apps,* which are small programs for performing simple tasks. In fact, Windows now refers to *all* Windows programs as apps. To see all the apps and programs installed on your PC, click the Start button in the screen's bottom-left corner. An alphabetical list of every installed program and app appears. (If your computer is in Tablet mode, you also need to tap the All Apps icon shown in the margin.)

Each name or tile on the Start menu is a button for starting an app or a traditional Windows program. Of course, Windows complicates things by offering several ways to launch an app or a program:

>> **Mouse:** Point at the tile and click the left mouse button.

>> **Keyboard:** Press the arrow keys until a box surrounds the desired tile. Then press the Enter key. (Press the Tab key to jump between different sections of the Start menu.)

>> **Touchscreen:** Tap the tile with your finger.

No matter which app you've chosen, it jumps onto the screen, ready to inform you, entertain you, or, if you're lucky, do both.

I explain the Start menu's built-in apps later in this chapter. If you feel like digging in, you can begin downloading and installing your own by clicking the Start menu's Microsoft Store tile. (I explain how to download apps in Chapter 6.)

WHAT'S AN APP?

Short for *application,* apps herald from the world of *smartphones,* which is what people call cellphones that are powerful enough to run small programs. The new-fangled Windows apps differ from traditional Windows programs in several ways:

- Unless preinstalled on your computer, Windows apps come from one place: the Microsoft Store app. The Store app, one of several apps preinstalled on Windows, lets you download more apps. Once downloaded, the apps automatically install themselves on your computer. Lots of apps are free, but others cost money.

- Only Windows apps can run on Windows. Apps found on iPhones, iPads, and Android phones and tablets won't run on your Windows computer. Even if you've already bought a favorite Android or iPhone app, you have to pay again to buy that app's Windows version.

- On the positive side, Windows 10 apps will run on your Windows 10 PC, laptop, and tablet. If they're universal Windows apps, they'll also run on an Xbox One video game console.

- Most apps perform small tasks, usually in a way that works well on touchscreens. Some apps make it easier to visit websites such as Facebook. Others let you play games, listen to Internet radio, track your car's mileage, or find nearby restaurants that are still open.

- Although most apps are fairly simple to use, simplicity brings limitations. Unlike desktop programs, many apps don't let you copy words, photos, files, or web links. There's often no way to share an app's contents with a friend.

In an effort to sound young and hip, Windows now refers to traditional desktop programs as *apps.* Don't be surprised to hear most people still use the term *program* to describe older software designed for the Windows desktop, such as Photoshop or TurboTax.

Finding something on the Start menu

You can scour the Start menu until your eagle eyes spot the program or tile you need, and then you can pounce on it with a quick mouse click or finger tap. But when the thrill of the hunt wanes, Windows offers several shortcuts for finding apps and programs hidden inside a crowded Start menu.

In particular, look for these Start menu sections:

>> **Recently Added:** When you view your list of alphabetically sorted apps, the Start menu automatically stocks the list's top edge with recently installed apps or programs. (This area eventually disappears until you add more apps from the Microsoft Store.)

>> **Most Used:** Your most frequently visited apps and programs appear here. Look here first to find your favorite computing destinations.

>> **Suggested:** In this section, companies pay to list their apps. This is yet another spot for Microsoft to inject ads into your computer. (You can turn the ads off by clicking the Start menu's Settings icon, choosing Personalization, and clicking Start. Finally, click to toggle off the setting called Occasionally Show Suggestions in Start.)

>> **All Apps:** In Desktop mode, the Start menu *always* displays a list of alphabetically sorted apps. Tablet mode viewers must first click the All Apps icon (shown in the margin) to see an alphabetical list of *all* their installed apps and programs.

TIP

Chances are good that you'll spot your desired item on the Start menu without much digging. But when an app or program proves to be particularly elusive, try these tricks:

>> After opening the Start menu, keyboard owners can simply begin typing the name of their desired app or program, like this: **facebook.** As you type, Windows lists all the apps matching what you've typed so far, eventually narrowing down the search to the runaway.

>> Don't spot your desired app listed as a Start menu tile along the right edge? That right column is scrollable with an upward flick of your finger. Or, point your mouse at the column, and flick the mouse's scroll wheel that lives between the mouse's two buttons. No scroll wheel? Then drag down the scroll bar along the right edge of the Start menu's column of tiles. Either way, more tiles — if there are any — will scroll into view.

>> If the tiles you see don't reflect the way you work, it's time to customize the Start menu to meet your needs. Head for this chapter's upcoming "Customizing the Start menu" section for a heads up.

Viewing, closing, or returning to apps

On a desktop PC, it's fairly easy to move from one app to another. Because they're all in windows on your desktop, you just click the app you want: It pops to the forefront, ready for work. (For more details about the desktop, flip ahead to Chapter 3.)

On a tablet, apps and programs hog the entire screen when running, making it more difficult to switch between them.

Whether you're running Windows on a PC, laptop, or tablet, you can bring any missing app to the forefront by following these two quick steps:

1. **Click or tap the Task View button.**

The screen clears, and Windows displays miniature views of your open apps and programs, shown in Figure 2-7.

Beneath the views of currently open apps, Windows also lists programs you've used within the past 30 days. Known as the Timeline, this new feature lets you quickly return to apps you worked on in the past.

NEW

2. **Tap or click any thumbnail to return the app or program to full size.**

FIGURE 2-7:
Click the Task View button to see thumbnail views of each of your currently running apps and programs.

These three tips can help you keep track of your running apps as well as close the ones you no longer want open:

>> Currently running apps and programs also appear as icons on the *taskbar,* the narrow strip along the bottom of the screen. (I cover the taskbar in Chapter 3.)

>> To close an unwanted app shown in thumbnail view, click or tap the X in its upper-right corner (shown in the margin). With a mouse, you can also right-click the app's thumbnail, and choose Close from the pop-up menu.

REVISITING PAST WORK WITH TIMELINE

Timeline, one of the big new features in the latest Windows 10 update, brings several surprises. In the past, a click on the Task View button merely showed your currently open windows, allowing you to return to them with a click.

But the Spring update adds a new twist: Not only can you return to currently open windows, but you can fetch windows you've used within the past 30 days, letting you quickly reopen past projects.

Timeline view, shown earlier in Figure 2-7, lists your currently open windows along the top, just as before. But just beneath them and separated by calendar dates, you now see previously opened windows. To scroll down quickly to windows you'd opened on previous dates, drag the sliding bar along the screen's right edge until you see either your desired window or the date you worked on that window.

Click on a miniature window from the past, and it appears in the present, ready for you to work again.

A Search box in the upper-right corner lets you filter the results. Type the name of a program, a few words from a previously opened website, or a filename, and Windows hides the windows that don't match your search term.

To zero in on *everything* you opened on a certain day, click the words See All Activities next to that particular date; every window you opened that day will appear in miniature, ready to be reopened with a click.

Don't want Windows to remember so much of your work history? Open the Settings app, choose the Privacy section, and open the Activity History section from the left column. There, you can turn off Microsoft's data collection in the Activity History section.

>> After you close an app, the miniature views of the other running apps remain onscreen, letting you either switch to them or close them. Or, to leave the Task View mode, click or tap the desktop.

Getting to know your free apps

The Windows Start menu comes stocked with several free apps, each living on its own square or rectangular tile. Every tile is labeled, helping you know what's what.

The tiles for some apps, known as *live tiles*, change constantly. The Money app tile, for example, constantly updates with the stock market's latest swings, and the Weather tile always tells you what to expect when you venture outdoors.

Here are some of Windows 10's most popular apps, ready to be launched at the click of a mouse or touch of a finger:

>> **Alarms & Clock:** This offers a world clock, timer, and stopwatch, but you'll probably visit for the alarm clock. It lets you set different wakeup times for every day of the week.

>> **Calculator:** With a toggle between standard, scientific, and a variety of converter modes, this app will please grade schoolers, math majors, chefs, and physicists.

>> **Calendar:** This app lets you add your appointments or grab them automatically from calendars you've already created through your online accounts. It works in tandem with the Mail app, and I cover them both in Chapter 10.

>> **Camera:** Covered in Chapter 17, the Camera app lets you snap photos with your computer's built-in camera or webcam.

TIP

>> **Connect:** This lets some computers, tablets, and laptops connect wirelessly to displays and projectors. It only works if both your device and the display support technology called *Miracast*.

>> **Cortana:** This fetches Cortana, your personal search assistant, who responds to your commands, both verbal and typed into the Search box.

>> **Get Help:** Click here to begin your journey through Microsoft's official technical support channels, all covered in Chapter 21.

>> **Groove Music:** Covered in Chapter 16, this app plays music stored on your PC and on OneDrive, Windows 10's built-in online storage service.

>> **Mail:** Covered in Chapter 10, the Mail app lets you send and receive email. If you enter a Windows Live, Yahoo!, or Google account, the Mail app sets itself up automatically and stocks your People list with your contacts.

>> **Maps:** Handy for trip planning, the Maps app brings up a version of Microsoft Bing Maps.

>> **Messaging:** Don't get excited: This only shows SMS messages from your cellular provider about your device's data plan. It can't send texts, unfortunately.

>> **Microsoft Edge:** Microsoft's new browser, Microsoft Edge, arrives in Windows 10, ready to replace Internet Explorer.

>> **Microsoft Solitaire Collection:** This app replaces the card games found in previous Windows versions. (The old versions are available as free, downloadable apps from the Microsoft Store.)

>> **Mixed Reality:** These two apps, the Portal and the Viewer, let people wear funny-looking headsets and pretend they're living in a 3D movie.

>> **Money:** This live tile opens with business headlines. Scroll to the right to see a 30-minute delay of the Dow, NASDAQ, and S&P with the usual charts depicting fear and uncertainty.

>> **Movies & TV:** Microsoft's video storefront lets you rent or buy movies and TV shows, as covered in Chapter 17. The app also lets you watch videos you've taken with your camera or smartphone.

>> **News:** Visit here to read the news of the day, compiled from news services around the world. (Techie alert: You can add RSS feeds from your favorite websites.)

>> **OneDrive:** This term describes the Microsoft Internet cubbyhole where you can store your files. By storing them online in OneDrive, covered in Chapter 5, you can access them from nearly any Internet-connected computer, phone (both Android and Apple), or tablet.

>> **OneNote:** This popular note-taking app receives an entry on the Start menu in Windows 10.

>> **Paint 3D:** This overly complicated app replaces the simple Paint program, which now hides in the Start menu's Windows Accessories section.

>> **People:** Windows 10's People app simply collects your friends' names and contact info.

>> **Phone Companion:** This app helps you link your Android or Apple phone with Windows so they can share information.

>> **Photos:** Covered in Chapter 17, the Photos app displays photos stored in your computer, as well as on OneDrive, your Internet storage space.

>> **Settings:** This takes you to the Windows 10 Settings app, which contains almost all of the settings found in the Control Panel from earlier Windows versions. (I cover the Settings app in Chapter 12.)

>> **Sports:** You can find sports news and scores here, as well as a way to add listings for your favorite sports teams.

>> **Store:** Covered in Chapter 6, the Microsoft Store is the only way to add more apps on your Start menu. The Microsoft Store also carries some programs you can install on your Windows desktop, covered in Chapter 3.

>> **Tips:** Drop by here to see flashcards listing steps for performing simple tasks in Windows 10.

>> **Voice Recorder:** The name says it all. When the app appears, click the Microphone icon to begin recording; click the icon again to stop. The app lists your recordings along its left edge.

>> **Weather:** This weather station forecasts a week's worth of weather in your area, but only if you grant it permission to access your location information. (Unless your computer has a GPS — Global Positioning System — the app narrows down your location by closest major city rather than street address.)

>> **Windows Defender Security Center:** Click this to access the built-in antivirus program. Flip ahead to Chapter 11 for more details.

>> **Xbox:** Coveted mostly by owners of Microsoft's Xbox One video game console, this lets you track high scores (for both you and your gaming buddies), chat with other gamers, view your achievements, and visit the Microsoft Store app to buy more games.

The bundled Windows apps work best when running fullscreen on a tablet, and they're not as powerful as normal desktop programs. But for some odd reason, Microsoft configured the Windows *desktop* to use some of these Start menu apps rather than the programs that you may prefer.

TIP

I explain in Chapter 3 how to choose which apps and programs handle which tasks, but here's a temporary hint: On the desktop, right-click a file and choose Open With. A menu appears, letting you choose which program should handle the job. To stay on the desktop, choose your desktop program from the menu, not the currently assigned Start menu app.

Adding or removing Start menu items

Microsoft dumped a random assortment of items on the Windows 10 Start menu. The resulting jumble of tiles consumes a lot of real estate, includes advertisements, and is certainly not tailored to *your* personal interests or work habits. This section lets you fix that shortcoming.

Removing tiles from the Start menu is easy, so you can begin there. To remove an unwanted or unused tile from the Start menu, right-click it and choose Unpin from Start from the pop-up menu. The unloved tile slides away without fuss.

On a touchscreen, hold down your finger on the unwanted tile. When the Unpin icon appears, tap it to remove the tile.

After removing the unwanted items, spend some time *adding* items to the Start menu, making them as easy to reach as a pencil holder on an office desk.

To add programs or apps to the Start menu, follow these steps:

1. **Click the Start button; on a desktop PC, an alphabetical list of apps appears along the Start menu's left side. (In Tablet mode, click the All Apps icon, shown in the margin.)**

   The Start menu presents an alphabetical list of all your installed apps and programs.

2. **Right-click the item you want to appear on the Start menu; then choose Pin to Start.**

   Each selected item appears as a new Start menu tile. Repeat until you've added all the items you want. Unfortunately, you must right-click and pin each item separately. Windows 10 doesn't let you select and add several items simultaneously.

3. **From the desktop, right-click desired items and choose Pin to Start.**

   The Start menu tiles aren't limited to apps and programs. From the desktop, right-click any folder, file, or other item you want added to the Start menu and then choose Pin to Start from the pop-up menu. Newly attached items appear at the Start menu's bottom-right corner. (On well-stuffed Start menus, you may need to scroll down to see them.)

When you're through, your Start menu will have grown considerably with all your newly added destinations.

TIP

Can't find a newly installed app? Chances are good that it's hiding in the Start menu's All Apps area. Windows places newly downloaded apps in the All Apps area rather than as a tile on the Start menu. If you want it visible as a tile along the Start menu's right edge, you need to pin it there yourself.

After you've stuffed your Start menu with your favorite desktop destinations, head to this chapter's "Customizing the Start menu" section to finish organizing. When you finish, you'll have created a Start menu that meets your needs.

Customizing the Start menu

The Start menu contains mostly tiles — clumps of tiles arranged in rectangles. The clumps of tiles consume a lot of space, but they're not very organized. How can you find your favorite stuff?

Give yourself a fighting chance by organizing your Start menu. The following steps begin with a small dose of organization: purging unwanted tiles and adding tiles for your favorites.

Keep following these steps, and you'll eventually reach organizational nirvana: A Start menu full of neatly labeled *groups* (collections of related tiles) that match *your* interests.

You can organize the tiles any way you want, into any number of groups with any names. For example, you may want to organize the Start menu tiles into four groups: People, Work, Play, and Web. (For a quick peek at what organized and labeled groups look like, page ahead to Figure 2-9.)

But no matter how organized you want to be, follow these steps to begin turning that haphazard Start menu into your *own* piles o' tiles:

1. **Remove tiles you don't need.**

Spot a tile you don't need? Right-click it and choose Unpin from Start from the pop-up menu. Repeat until you've removed all the tiles you don't use. (On a touchscreen, hold your finger down on an unwanted app and then tap the Unpin icon.)

REMEMBER

Choosing Unpin from Start doesn't *uninstall* the app or program; removing the tile merely removes that item's "start" button from the Start menu. In fact, if you accidentally remove the tile for a favorite app or program, you can easily put it back in Step 3.

2. **Move related tiles next to each other.**

   As an example, you might want to keep your people-oriented apps — Mail, People, and Calendar — next to each other. To move an app to a new location, point at its tile with your mouse and then hold down your left mouse button as you drag the tile to the desired spot. As you drag the tile, other tiles automatically move out of the way to make room for the newcomer.

TIP

   On a touchscreen, hold down your finger on the app; when the pop-up menu appears, drag the app to its new position.

   When you've dragged an app's tile to the desired spot, lift your finger or release the mouse button to set the tile into its new place.

TIP

   To conserve screen real estate, shrink a large tile to a small square tile: Right-click the wide tile, choose Resize from the pop-up menu, and choose a smaller size from the second menu. (You can also enlarge an app's tiny tile, turning it into a live tile that shows updated information about the app's contents.)

3. **Add tiles for apps, programs, folders, and files you need.**

   I explain how to add tiles for apps, programs, folders, and files earlier, in this chapter's "Adding or removing Start menu items" section.

   After you've purged any unwanted tiles, rearranged the remaining tiles, and added new tiles for items you need, your Start menu may meet your needs. If so, stop. You're done!

   But if your Start menu still sprawls below the Start menu's bottom edge and you can't find important items, keep reading.

   Still here? Okay. Look closely at the Start menu, and you see several groups of tiles. Windows labels them with names like "Create," "Play," and "Explore." If you're like most people, you probably didn't notice the subtle gap separating the two groups. And that brings you to the next step.

4. **To create a new group, drag and drop any tile away from the two existing groups.**

   Drag and hold a tile away from the existing groups. A horizontal bar appears, as shown in Figure 2-8, creating an empty space below it for your incoming tile. Drop the tile, and the tile forms a *new* group of one lonely tile, located below the two other groups.

5. **To add more tiles to your newly created group, drag and drop additional tiles into the group.**

   Drag and drop new tiles next to your new group's first tile to keep it company. After you drop a tile into a group, you can drag the tile around to a new position within the group.

FIGURE 2-8:
To create a new group, drag and hold a tile between two existing groups. When the bar appears, drop the tile.

Want to create yet another group? Then repeat Steps 4 and 5, dragging and dropping a tile away from the existing groups to create yet another group.

You might find groups of related tiles to be enough organization for you. If so, stop. But if you want to label the groups, go to the next step.

6. **Name the groups.**

Click the existing name above any group of tiles, and a box appears, ready for you to type in a name or replace the existing name. After typing the name, press Enter, and the box disappears, leaving your tile group bearing its new name.

When you've finished naming or renaming the tile groups, you can finally bask in your organizational prowess, as shown in Figure 2-9.

REMEMBER

>> There's no right or wrong way to organize the Start menu. Just as in real life, be as organized or as messy as you want. You can move groups, as well, by dragging and dropping them by their titles.

>> As you install new apps and desktop programs, remember to look for them in the *All Apps* area, not on the Start menu itself. To keep things organized, right-click the newcomers and choose Pin to Start menu. After you place your new apps as tiles on the Start menu, you can drag and drop them into your existing groups or make new groups for the new tiles.

>> Feel free to create a group for your favorite websites, as well, making it easy to get to them straight from the Start menu. (To pin a website to the Start menu, click the More icon (three dots) in the Edge browser and choose Pin this Page to Start from the drop-down menu.)

PERSONALIZING THE START MENU

Windows 10's Settings app offers additional ways to tweak the Start menu. I cover the Settings app in Chapter 12, but this section applies particularly to the Start menu.

To find the Start menu settings, click the Start button, choose the Settings icon, and click the Settings app's Personalization tile. When the Personalization page appears, click Start in the left pane, and the Start menu's options spill out to the right.

The Start menu section offers these options:

- **Show more tiles on Start:** Turn this on to widen the Start menu and see more tiles without needing to scroll down.

- **Show app list in Start menu:** This toggles the alphabetical list of apps from appearing along the Start menu's left edge. Turning it off shrinks the menu yet leaves the All Apps icon; a click on that icon temporarily reveals the alphabetical list of apps.

- **Show recently added apps:** Leave this on, and newly installed apps appear in their own section.

- **Show most used apps:** Leave this on to let the Start menu automatically stock your Start menu's Most Used section.

(continued)

(continued)

- **Show suggestions occasionally in Start:** Turn this off to remove the Start menu's "Suggested" apps. (It's actually an advertisement.)

- **Use Start fullscreen:** This makes the Start menu fill the screen, just as it does in Tablet mode.

- **Show recently opened items in Jump Lists on Start or the taskbar:** Leave this turned on so you can return to favorite destinations, both listed on the Start menu and on the taskbar's jump lists, covered in Chapter 3.

- **Choose which folders appear on Start:** The Start menu's lower-left edge normally offers links to File Explorer and Settings. Click here to stock that section with other destinations, including Documents, Downloads, Music, Pictures, Videos, Network, and Personal Folder, which opens to show links to all your most popular folders.

There's no right or wrong way to set these settings. Stick with the default settings or experiment to see which settings work for you. They're all toggle switches, so you can always return and flip the toggle again if a change doesn't meet your needs.

Exiting from Windows

Ah! The most pleasant thing you'll do with Windows all day could very well be to stop using it. Exiting Windows brings a hurdle to the process, however: You must decide whether to Lock, Sign Out, Shut Down, Restart, or Sleep your computer.

The answer depends on how long you're abandoning your computer. Are you simply stepping away from the computer for a few moments, or are you through working for the day?

I cover both scenarios — a temporary sojourn and leaving your computer for the day — in the next two sections.

But if you don't want to trudge through a manual in order to turn off your PC, here's the quickest way to turn it off:

1. **Click the Start button and then click the Power icon (shown in the margin) near the Start menu's lower-left corner.**

2. **Choose Shut Down from the drop-down menu.**

3. **If the computer protests, saying you'll lose unsaved work, choose Sleep instead.**

The following two sections deal with the finer points of what's become an alarmingly complex chore.

TIP

Power users like this quick shut down trick: Right-click the Start button, choose Shut Down or Sign Out from the pop-up menu, and choose Shut Down from the pop-up menu.

Temporarily leaving your computer

Windows offers three options when you're leaving your computer temporarily, perhaps to reheat some fish in the office microwave and sneak back to your cubicle before anybody notices. To make the right choice among the various "temporary leave" scenarios in Windows, follow these steps:

1. **Click the Start button to fetch the Start menu.**

2. **Click your user account picture from the Start menu's left edge.**

   There, as shown in Figure 2-10, you can choose one of these options:

FIGURE 2-10: Click your account name near the Start menu's lower-left corner to choose from these options.

- **Change account settings:** This option whisks you straight to the Settings app, where you can tweak your account's settings. You can change your photo, for example, or change the password of a Local account.

- **Lock:** Meant to add privacy while you take short trips to the water cooler, this option locks your PC, veiling your screen with the Lock screen picture. When you return, unlock the screen by pressing any key and then typing your password. Windows quickly displays your work, just as you left it.

- **Sign Out:** Choose this option when you're through working at the PC and somebody else wants to have a go at it. Windows saves your work and your settings and then returns to the Lock screen, ready for the next person to log on.

- **Another account:** Below your name, as shown earlier in Figure 2-10, Windows lists names of any other accounts on the computer. If one of those people wants to borrow the computer for a few minutes while you're grabbing some coffee, let him choose his name from the list. When he types in his password, his customized screen appears, ready for him to work. When he signs out and you log back in, all your work reappears, just as you left it.

Each of these options lets you give up your computer for a little while, but leaves it waiting for your return.

If you're finished for the day, though, you're ready for the next section.

Leaving your computer for the day

When you're done computing for the day — or perhaps you just want to shut down the laptop while on the subway or that flight to Rome — Windows offers three ways to handle the situation.

Follow this step to choose from the available options:

 Click the Start button and click the Power icon (shown in the margin).

The Power icon's pop-up menu offers three settings, as shown in Figure 2-11.

Here's the rundown on your options:

>> **Sleep:** The most popular choice, this saves your work in your PC's memory *and* on its hard drive and then lets your PC slumber in a low-power state. Later, when you return to your PC, Windows quickly presents everything — even your unsaved work — as if you'd never left. And if the power goes out, your PC will still wake up with everything saved, but it will take a few more seconds.

FIGURE 2-11:
Choosing Sleep
makes your
computer wake
up more quickly
when turned back
on. Choosing
Shut Down turns
off the power
completely.

>> **Shut Down:** This option turns off your computer completely. It's just like Restart but without turning back on again. And, if you're worried about preserving battery life on a laptop or tablet, it's your best choice.

>> **Restart:** Choose this option as a first cure when something weird happens (a program crashes, for example, or Windows seems dazed and confused). Windows turns off your computer and then starts itself anew, hopefully feeling better. (Patches from Windows Update, as well as newly installed programs, occasionally ask you to restart your PC.)

That should be enough to wade through. But if you have a little more time, here are some other facts to consider:

REMEMBER

You don't *have* to shut down your computer each night. In fact, some experts leave their computers turned on all the time, saying it's better for their computer's health. Other experts say that their computers are healthier if they're turned *off* each day. Still others say the Sleep mode gives them the best of both worlds. However, *everybody* says to turn off your monitor when you're done working. Monitors definitely enjoy cooling down when not in use.

Want your laptop or tablet to wake up in Airplane mode, cut off from Internet access? Then switch to Airplane mode and use Sleep rather than Shut Down. When your laptop or tablet wakes back up on your transatlantic flight, it stays in Airplane mode, disconnected from the Internet. (I cover Airplane mode in Chapter 23.)

TIP

To turn off your computer as quickly as possible, right-click the Start button, choose Shut Down or Sign Out from the pop-up menu, and choose Shut Down from the pop-out menu.

Chapter **3**

The Traditional Desktop

The Tablet mode in Windows 10 works well for couch-top computing. When the Start menu fills the screen with finger-friendly apps, you can easily listen to music, check your email, watch the latest funny cat videos, and track your friends' misadventures on Facebook.

But when Monday morning inevitably rolls around, it's time to switch gears. Working usually requires ditching the simple Windows apps and firing up more full-featured programs. Employers prefer that you work with spreadsheets and word processors rather than play *Words with Friends.*

That's when the second half of Windows, the desktop, comes into play. When you turn off Tablet mode, the Windows 10 desktop appears, ready to work the same way it's worked for the past decade. Optimized for a mouse and keyboard, it's where you arrange your work in windows and make things happen.

The Windows 10 Start menu and its gang of apps bring many changes, but the desktop works much like the familiar workhorse of yesteryear. This chapter shows you how to transform your computer from an entertainment device back into an office.

Finding the Desktop and the Start Menu

The Windows 10 Start menu may look drastically different from its predecessors, but the *desktop*, shown in Figure 3-1, is almost indistinguishable from the one in Windows 7.

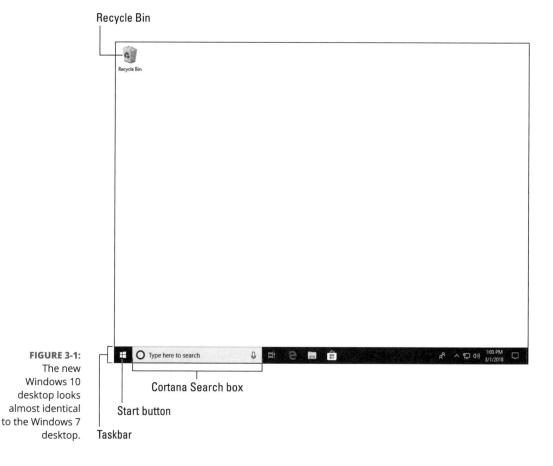

Recycle Bin

Cortana Search box

Start button

Taskbar

The Windows 10 desktop will run nearly all the Windows programs that ran on your old Windows 7, Windows 8, or Windows 8.1 computer. Exceptions are antivirus programs, security suites, high-performance video games, and some utility programs. Those don't usually transfer well from one Windows version to another.

Unlike Windows 8 and Windows 8.1, Windows 10 will run apps within a window on the desktop. If your apps can't run inside a desktop window, turn off Tablet mode, which I describe in the "Toggling between Tablet mode and the desktop" section later in this chapter.

WORKING ON THE DESKTOP WITH A TOUCHSCREEN

TIP

Fingers work well for tapping the Start menu's extra-large tiles. And if you have especially dainty fingertips, your touchscreen's touch controls will still work on the desktop's small buttons and borders. Here's how to control the desktop with your fingers:

- **Select:** To select something on the desktop, tap it with a fingertip; the pad of your finger may be too large. Try your pinky finger if your index finger is too large.

- **Double-click:** To double-click something, tap it twice. Again, your fingertip works best.

- **Right-click:** To right-click an item, press your fingertip gently on it and wait for a small square to appear onscreen. When the square appears, remove your finger, and the pop-up menu stays on the screen. Then you can tap your desired option on the menu.

If your fingertip seems too wide for delicate desktop window maneuvers, buy a Bluetooth mouse and keyboard for your tablet. They turn your tablet into two computers: one that uses lightweight apps for casual computing and the other with a full Windows desktop for doing some *real* work.

One word of caution: When run in Tablet mode, apps and programs always cover the entire screen; they never run inside desktop windows. If you need to view and right-click the desktop *itself*, you must first turn off Tablet mode.

Working with the Desktop

The desktop lets you run several apps and programs simultaneously, each living within its own little *window*. That separation lets you spread several programs across the screen, sharing bits of information among them.

When first installed, Windows starts with the freshly scrubbed, nearly empty desktop shown earlier in Figure 3-1. After you've been working for a while, your desktop will fill up with *icons* — little buttons that load your files with a quick double-click. Many people leave their desktops strewn with icons for easy access.

Other people organize their work: When they finish working on something, they store their files in a *folder*, a task covered in Chapter 4.

But no matter how you use the desktop, it comes with four main parts, labeled earlier in Figure 3-1:

>> **Start button:** To launch a program, click the Start button in the desktop's lower-left corner. When the Start menu appears, click the name or tile for the app or program you want to run.

I cover the Start menu and all its quirks in Chapter 2. (Flip back to that chapter if you want to remove or rearrange the Start menu's app tiles.) For easy access to your favorite programs, place them on your desktop's taskbar (described below).

>> **Cortana Search box:** Also known as *Cortana*, this combination search box and digital assistant lets you search both your computer and the Internet for files and information. I describe Cortana in Chapter 7.

>> **Taskbar:** Resting lazily along the bottom edge of your screen, the taskbar shows icons for the apps and programs you currently have open, as well as icons for launching a few favored programs. (Point at a program's icon on the taskbar to see the program's name or perhaps a thumbnail photo of that program in action.) I describe how to add your favorite programs' icons to the taskbar in this chapter's later "Customizing the taskbar" section.

>> **Recycle Bin:** The desktop's *Recycle Bin,* that wastebasket-shaped icon, stores your recently deleted files and folders for easy retrieval. Whew!

I cover those items later in this chapter and throughout the book, but these tips will help you until you page ahead:

>> PC and laptop owners can start new projects directly from the Windows desktop: Right-click a blank part of the desktop, choose New, and choose the project of your dreams from the pop-up menu, be it loading a favorite program or creating a folder to store new files. (The New menu lists most of your computer's programs, sparing you a journey back to the Start menu.) In Tablet mode, by contrast, you can start projects only from the Start menu.

REMEMBER

>> Are you befuddled about a desktop object's reason for being? Timidly rest the pointer over the mysterious doodad, and Windows pops up a little box explaining what that thing is or does. Right-click the object, and the ever-helpful Windows usually tosses up a menu listing nearly everything you can do with that particular object. This trick works on most icons and buttons found on your desktop and its programs.

WARNING

>> All the icons on your desktop may suddenly disappear. To bring your work back to life, right-click your empty desktop and choose View from the pop-up menu. Then make sure the Show Desktop Icons menu option has a check mark so that everything stays visible. If that doesn't work, try turning off Tablet

mode: Tap the Action Center icon next to the clock in the screen's lower-right corner. Then click or tap the Tablet mode button to toggle it off. (Tablet mode hides everything on the desktop.)

Launching apps with the Start menu

The Start button never strays from your desktop's lower-left corner. A click or tap of the Start button fetches the Start menu, which lists all your installed apps and programs. When the Start menu appears, you click the app or program you'd like to run.

I cover the Start menu in Chapter 2, but here's a quick step-by-step on how to open the Start menu and launch an app or program:

1. **Click the Start button in your screen's lower-left corner.**

The Start menu appears, as shown in Figure 3-2. (If your PC is running in Tablet mode, described later in this chapter, the Start menu fills the screen.)

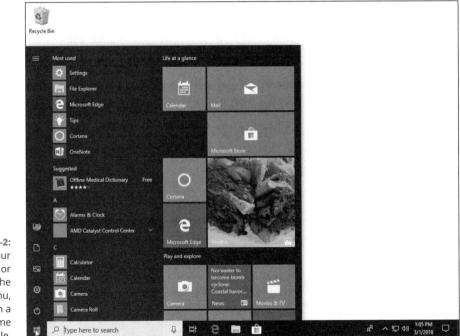

FIGURE 3-2:
If you spot your desired app or program on the Start menu, launch it with a click on its name or tile.

The Start menu automatically lists names of your most recently accessed apps and programs in its upper-left corner. To the right, another column or two displays tiles of popular apps installed on your computer.

2. **If you see your desired app or program listed on the Start menu, click it.**

   Click a name or a tile, and the app or program rises to the top of your desktop, ready for action.

Don't see the name of your desired app or program? The Start menu's left column presents an alphabetical list of all your apps and programs. That leaves you with several choices:

>> If you don't see your desired app's name, scroll down the list of names by clicking in the bar just to the right of the names. (I describe how to scroll with a scroll box in Chapter 4.)

>> To see an alphabetical list of apps when in Tablet mode, click or tap the All Apps icon (shown in the margin) near the screen's upper-left corner.

>> If your app doesn't appear on the list, chances are good that it's not installed on your computer. To download it, visit the Microsoft Store app, which I cover in Chapter 6.

You can also fetch the Start menu by pressing the ⊞ key on your keyboard or tablet.

After you've opened an app or program, you'll eventually want to close it, a task I cover in Chapter 4. (But here's a spoiler: To close an app, move your mouse pointer to the app's upper-right corner and click the little X, shown in the margin.)

I explain more about the Start menu, including how to customize it to meet your needs, in Chapter 2.

Jazzing up the desktop's background

To jazz up your desktop, Windows covers it with a pretty picture known as a *background*. (Many people refer to the background simply as *wallpaper*.)

When you tire of the built-in scenery, feel free to replace it with a picture stored on your computer:

1. **Click the Start button and choose the Settings icon.**

   Located just above the Power button, the Settings icon resembles a gear. Click it, and Windows 10's Settings app appears.

2. **Click the Personalization icon (shown in the margin).**

The Settings app's Personalization section opens to the Background page.

3. **Click any one of the pictures, shown in Figure 3-3, and Windows quickly places it onto your desktop's background.**

Found a keeper? Then you're done; your change takes place immediately. Or, if you're still searching, move to the next step.

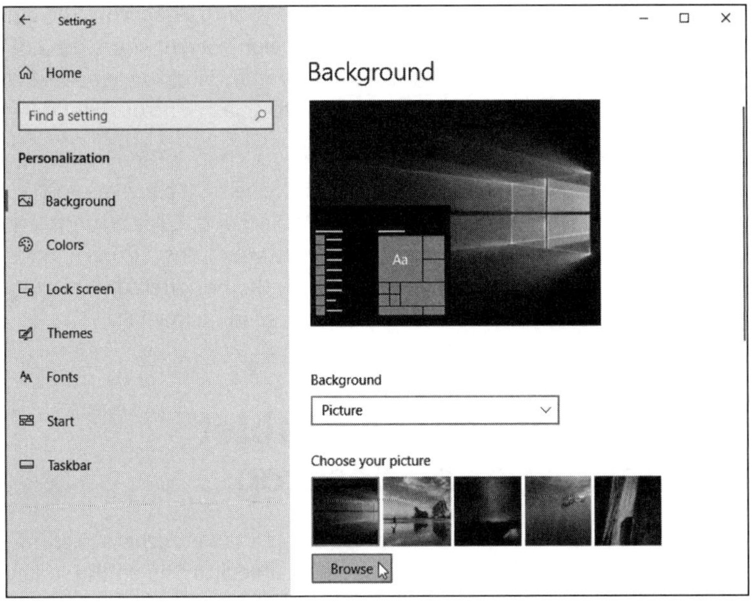

FIGURE 3-3:
Try different backgrounds by clicking them. Click the Browse button to see pictures from different folders.

4. **Click the Browse button to see photos inside your Pictures folder.**

Most people store their digital photos in their Pictures folder. (I explain browsing folders in Chapter 5.)

5. **Click different pictures to see how they look as your desktop's background.**

When you find a background you like, you're done. The change takes place automatically. Exit the program with a click in its upper-right corner, and your chosen photo drapes across your desktop.

Here are some tips on changing your desktop's background:

TIP

» Options listed on the Background page's Choose a Fit drop-down menu let you choose whether the image should be *tiled* repeatedly across the screen, *centered* directly in the middle, or *stretched* to fill the entire screen. The Tile, Fill, and Fit options work best with small photos by repeating or enlarging them to fit the screen's borders.

>> The Microsoft Edge web browser can borrow most pictures found on the Internet for a background. Right-click the website's picture and choose Save Picture As from the pop-up menu. Microsoft sneakily offers to copy the image into your Pictures folder, where you can choose it as a background in Step 4 of the preceding list.

>> If a background photograph makes your desktop icons too difficult to see, splash your desktop with a single color instead: After Step 2 of the preceding list, click Colors from the Personalization window's left pane. When the colored squares appear, click one to splash it across your desktop.

>> To change the entire *look* of Windows, choose Themes from the Personalization window's left edge in Step 2. The right pane lets you customize your computer's look by clicking the Background, Color, Sounds, and Mouse Cursor buttons, and then changing them to your liking. I explain more about themes in Chapter 12. (If you download any themes offered on the Internet, check them with antivirus software, covered in Chapter 11.)

Toggling between Tablet mode and the desktop

Some people work with Windows 10 on a tablet; others prefer a desktop. Still others prefer a tablet that can double as a desktop by adding a keyboard and mouse. Making your tablet work like a desktop PC can introduce a problem, though: Tablets work best with your fingertips, but the desktop is best controlled with a mouse and keyboard.

To please both camps, Windows 10 lets you toggle Tablet mode on and off. Turning on Tablet mode, for example, makes all your apps and programs fill the screen. (The Start menu runs fullscreen as well, hiding the desktop.) Tablet mode also subtly increases the spacing between your menus and icons, making them easier to tap with fingers.

In many cases, Windows 10 notices how you're working and automatically turns Tablet mode on and off when necessary. But if you find Windows 10 working in the wrong mode, follow these steps to toggle between Tablet mode and Desktop mode manually:

1. **Click the Taskbar's Action Center icon.**

The Action Center icon lives near the right edge of the *taskbar,* that strip running along the bottom of every screen.

The Action Center pane appears, shown in Figure 3-4.

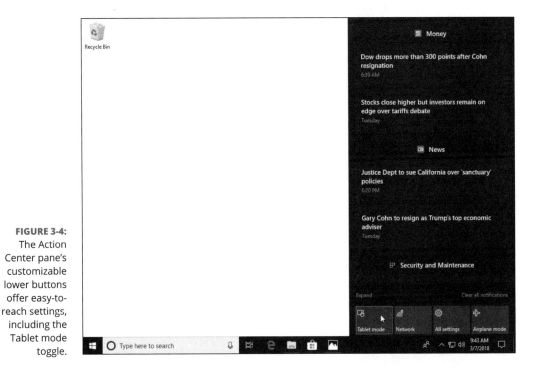

FIGURE 3-4:
The Action Center pane's customizable lower buttons offer easy-to-reach settings, including the Tablet mode toggle.

2. **Click or tap the Tablet mode button along the bottom left of the Action Center pane.**

When the Tablet mode button is highlighted with color, Tablet mode is on; when the button's color disappears, Tablet mode is off and the desktop behaves normally.

TIP

To fetch the Action Center pane quickly on a tablet, slide your finger in from the screen's right edge. The Action Center pane appears, letting you quickly tap the Tablet mode toggle.

Don't see the Tablet mode button? Click the word Expand listed above the four buttons along the bottom of the Action Center. All the available Action Center buttons spring into view, including the previously hidden Tablet mode button.

CHAPTER 3 **The Traditional Desktop** 59

Dumpster diving in the Recycle Bin

 The Recycle Bin, that wastebasket icon in the upper-left corner of your desktop, works much like a *real* recycle bin. Shown in the margin, it lets you retrieve the discarded desktop files you thought you'd never need.

You can dump something from the desktop or File Manager — a file or folder, for example — into the Recycle Bin in either of these ways:

>> Simply right-click the unwanted item and choose Delete from the pop-up menu. Windows asks cautiously if you're *sure* that you want to delete the item. Click Yes, and Windows dumps it into the Recycle Bin, just as if you'd dragged it there. Whoosh!

>> For a quick deletion rush, click the unwanted object and poke your Delete key.

Want something back? Double-click the Recycle Bin icon to see your recently deleted items. Right-click the item you want and choose Restore. The handy little Recycle Bin returns your precious item to the same spot where you deleted it. (You can also resuscitate deleted items by dragging them to your desktop or any other folder; drag 'em back into the Recycle Bin to delete them again.)

TIP

The Recycle Bin can get pretty crowded. If you're searching frantically for a recently deleted file, tell the Recycle Bin to sort everything by the date and time you deleted it: Right-click an empty area inside the Recycle Bin and choose Sort By. Then choose Date Deleted from the pop-up menu.

TIP

To delete something *permanently*, just delete it from inside the Recycle Bin: Click it and press the Delete key. To delete *everything* in the Recycle Bin, right-click the Recycle Bin icon and choose Empty Recycle Bin.

To bypass the Recycle Bin completely when deleting files, hold down Shift while pressing Delete. Poof! The deleted object disappears, ne'er to be seen again — a handy trick when dealing with sensitive items, such as credit-card numbers or bleary-eyed selfies.

>> The Recycle Bin icon changes from an empty wastepaper basket to a full one (as shown in the margin) as soon as it's holding any deleted file or files.

>> The Recycle Bin holds only items deleted from the *desktop*. It doesn't retain information deleted from Start menu apps.

>> Your Recycle Bin keeps your deleted files until the garbage consumes about 5 percent of your computer's available space. Then it purges your oldest deleted files to make room for the new. If you're low on hard drive space, shrink the bin's size by right-clicking the Recycle Bin and choosing Properties.

Decrease the Custom Size number to purge the bin more quickly; increase the number, and the Recycle Bin hangs onto files a little longer.

WARNING

>> The Recycle Bin saves only items deleted from your *own* computer's drives. That means it won't save anything deleted from a CD, memory card, phone, MP3 player, flash drive, or digital camera.

>> Already emptied the Recycle Bin? You might still be able to retrieve the then-trashed-now-treasured item from the Windows File History backup, covered in Chapter 13.

WARNING

If you delete something from somebody else's computer over a network, it can't be retrieved. The Recycle Bin holds only items deleted from your *own* computer, not somebody else's computer. (For some awful reason, the Recycle Bin on the other person's computer doesn't save the item, either.) Be careful, and make sure every computer in your house has a backup system in place.

Bellying Up to the Taskbar

Whenever more than one window sits across your desktop, you face a logistics problem: Programs and windows tend to overlap, making them difficult to spot. To make matters worse, programs such as web browsers and Microsoft Word can contain several windows apiece. How do you keep track of all the windows?

The Windows solution is the *taskbar* — a special area that keeps track of your currently running programs and their windows. Shown in Figure 3-5, the taskbar lives along the bottom of your desktop, constantly updating itself to show an icon for every currently running app or desktop program.

Unlike Windows 8, Windows 10 keeps the taskbar firmly in place, even when run in Tablet mode. The taskbar remains accessible along the screen's bottom edge, even when apps or the Start menu fill the screen. (You can toggle the taskbar's appearance in Tablet mode by right-clicking the taskbar; a pop-up menu offers several settings you can toggle.)

TIP

The taskbar also serves as a place to launch your favorite programs. By keeping your favorite programs' icons in sight and one quick click away, you're spared a detour to the Start menu.

Not sure what a taskbar icon does? Rest your mouse pointer over any of the taskbar icons to see either the program's name or a thumbnail image of the program's contents, as shown in Figure 3-5. In that figure, for example, you can see that the Photos app is displaying three photos.

FIGURE 3-5:
Point at a taskbar
icon to see its
currently running
programs.

From the taskbar, you can perform powerful magic, as described in the following list:

REMEMBER

>> To play with a program listed on the taskbar, click its icon. The window rises to the surface and rests atop any other open windows, ready for action. Clicking the taskbar icon yet again minimizes that same window.

>> Whenever you load an app or program, its icon automatically appears on the taskbar. If one of your open windows ever gets lost on your desktop, click its icon on the taskbar to bring it to the forefront.

>> To close an app or program listed on the taskbar, right-click its icon and choose Close from the pop-up menu. The program quits, just as if you'd chosen its Exit command from within its own window. (The departing program thoughtfully gives you a chance to save your work before it quits and walks off the screen.)

>> Taskbar icons with a thin underline along their bottom edge let you know that their app or program is currently running.

>> Traditionally, the taskbar lives along your desktop's bottom edge, but you can move it to any edge you want, a handy space saver on extra-wide monitors. (**Hint:** Try dragging it to your screen's side. If it doesn't move, right-click the taskbar and click Lock the Taskbar to remove the check mark by that option.)

>> Can't find an open app or window? Click on the taskbar's Task View icon (shown in the margin) to see *all* your open apps and programs, both now and a list of ones you've opened in the recent past. Click the one you want to revisit, and it rises to the top of the screen.

>> When running in Tablet mode, your computer shows the taskbar, but hides the icons for your currently open apps and programs. To show those hidden icons, right-click the taskbar and choose Show App Icons from the pop-up menu.

>> When your PC isn't running in Tablet mode, you can quickly jump to the taskbar page in the Settings app by right-clicking the taskbar and choosing Taskbar Settings.

>> If the taskbar keeps hiding below the screen's bottom edge, point the mouse at the screen's bottom edge until the taskbar surfaces. Then right-click the taskbar and click the Automatically Hide the Taskbar option to remove its check mark.

TIP

You can add your favorite apps and programs directly to the taskbar: From the Start menu, right-click the favored program's name or tile, choose More, and choose Pin to Taskbar from the next pop-up menu. The program's icon then lives on the taskbar for easy access, just as if it were running. Tired of the program hogging space on your taskbar? Right-click it, choose More, and choose Unpin from Taskbar from the pop-up menu.

Shrinking windows to the taskbar and retrieving them

Windows spawn windows. You start with one window to write a letter of praise to your local deli. You open another window to check an address, and then yet another to ogle an online menu. Before you know it, four windows are crowded across the desktop.

To combat the clutter, Windows provides a simple means of window control: You can transform a window from a screen-cluttering square into a tiny button on the taskbar along the bottom of the screen. The solution is the Minimize button.

See the three buttons lurking in just about every window's upper-right corner? Click the *Minimize button* — the button with the little line in it, shown in the margin. Whoosh! The window disappears, represented by its little button on the taskbar at your screen's bottom.

To make a minimized program on the taskbar revert to a regular, onscreen window, just click its icon on the taskbar. Pretty simple, huh?

REMEMBER

>> Can't find the taskbar icon for the window you want to minimize or maximize? If you hover your mouse pointer over the taskbar button, Windows displays a thumbnail photo of that program or the program's name.

>> When you minimize a window, you neither destroy its contents nor close the program. And when you click the window's name on the taskbar, it reopens to the same size you left it, showing its same contents.

Switching to different tasks from the taskbar's Jump Lists

The Windows taskbar doesn't limit you to opening programs and switching between windows. You can jump to other tasks, as well, by right-clicking the taskbar's icons. Right-clicking the File Explorer icon brings up a quick list of your recently visited folders, as shown in Figure 3-6. Click any folder on the list to make a quick return visit.

FIGURE 3-6:
Right-click File Explorer to see a clickable list of recently visited locations.

Called *Jump Lists*, these pop-up menus add a new trick to the taskbar: They let you jump quickly to previously visited locations, letting you work more quickly.

Jump List items work any time. Even if you haven't opened File Explorer, for example, you right-click its taskbar icon and jump to a listed folder.

The Microsoft Edge browser breaks with tradition by not offering Jump Lists to previously visited websites, but Microsoft may add them later.

Clicking the taskbar's sensitive areas

Like a crafty card player, the taskbar comes with a few tips and tricks. For example, here's the lowdown on the icons near the taskbar's right edge, shown in Figure 3-7, known as the *Action Center.* Different items appear in the Action Center depending on your PC and programs, but you'll probably encounter some of these:

FIGURE 3-7:
Click the arrow to
see the taskbar's
hidden icons.

>> **Minimize Windows:** This small strip hidden against the taskbar's far-right edge instantly minimizes all open windows when you click it. Click it again to put the windows back in place. (This strip disappears in Tablet mode because every app and program runs fullscreen.)

>> **Time/Date:** Click the time and date icon to fetch a handy monthly calendar, a clock, and a list of upcoming appointments from the Calendar app. If you want to change the time or date or even add a second time zone, right-click the Time/Date area and choose Adjust Date/Time, a task I cover in Chapter 12.

>> **Location:** Your computer is currently sharing your location with an app, often seen when checking maps or other location-specific apps.

>> **Bluetooth:** Click this to see your options for connecting wirelessly with Bluetooth, commonly used with mice, keyboards, and speakers.

>> **Safely Remove Hardware:** Before unplugging a storage device, be it a tiny flash drive, a portable music player, or a portable hard drive, click here. That tells Windows to prepare the gadget for unplugging.

» Action Center: Click this to fetch the Action Center, a strip along the screen's right edge which keeps you up-to-date on your emails and appointments, as well as your computer's performance.

 » Wired Network: Found mostly on desktop PCs, this icon appears when you're connected to the Internet or other PCs through a wired network. Not connected? A red X appears over the icon.

 » Wireless Network: This appears when your PC is wirelessly connected to the Internet or other network. The more waves you see on the icon, the more powerful your wireless signal. (I explain how to connect to wireless networks in Chapter 9.)

 » Volume: Click or tap this ever-so-handy little speaker icon to adjust your PC's volume, as shown in Figure 3-8. (Or right-click the icon and choose Open Volume Mixer to bring up a mixing panel. Mixers let you adjust separate volume levels for each program, so you can keep your music player's volume louder than your other programs' annoying beeps.)

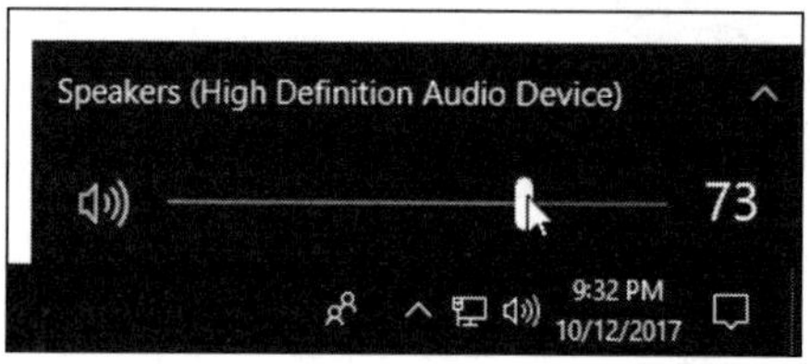

FIGURE 3-8:
Slide the lever
to adjust
the volume.

 » Task Manager: Coveted by computer technicians, this little program can end misbehaving programs, monitor background tasks, monitor performance, and do other stuff of techie dreams.

 » People: This pop-up list contains your most frequently emailed contacts, handy for sending quick emails or seeing when they're trying to contact you.

 » OneDrive: When your computer is synchronizing its files with OneDrive (your Internet storage space), little arrows appear beneath this icon.

 » Power, Outlet: This shows that your laptop or tablet is plugged into an electrical outlet and is charging its battery.

» Power, Battery: Your laptop or tablet is running on batteries only. (Rest your mouse pointer over the icon to see how much power remains.)

» Arrow: Sometimes the taskbar hides things. If you see a tiny upward-pointing arrow at the start of the taskbar's notification area, click it to see a few hidden icons slide up and out. (Check out the later "Customizing the taskbar" section for tips and tricks on whether icons should hide.)

CHATTING WITH CORTANA

NEW

You may notice an odd box on the taskbar, just to the right of the Start button. That's *Cortana*, your new digital assistant bundled with Windows 10. Cortana helps you find information, both on your computer and on the Internet.

For example, type a few words from one of your files into the box, and Cortana should find the file and list its name, ready for you to open it with a click. Cortana should do the same if you type the name of a setting or program.

Cortana also understands your verbal commands, if your computer's microphone is powerful enough. Click the little microphone in the box and say your command. Or, you can adjust the settings so Cortana listens for your command. When you say the words, "Hey Cortana," Cortana responds to your request.

Or at least, she usually does. Cortana takes some time to grow used to your voice, and you need time to grow used to her limited vocabulary. I cover Cortana in Chapter 7.

You can pick and choose which notification icons should always be visible by right-clicking the taskbar and choosing Taskbar Settings. When the Taskbar Settings page appears, click the link called Select Which Icons Appear on the Taskbar. A new window appears, with sliding on/off toggles for all the icons. (Turn on as many as will fit comfortably.)

Opening the Action Center

The taskbar's right edge is often stuffed with icons. Unless you've memorized the chart in this book's previous section, they're pretty mysterious. Well, just click the Action Center icon, and then the Action Center pane appears, as shown in Figure 3-9, and demystifies that area by giving you more details about both your computer and your personal information.

The Action Center lists information about your latest emails, for example, as well as times of upcoming appointments and other notifications. It also provides a list of handy buttons along the bottom. Windows 10 usually displays these four buttons:

>> **Tablet mode:** Click or tap this button to toggle Tablet mode. (When it's colored, you're in Tablet mode, which works well only on touchscreens.)

>> **Network:** This displays information about your current network connections, including the Internet.

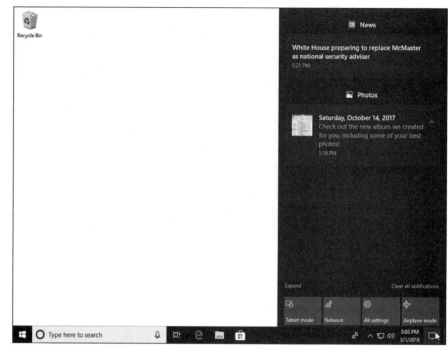

FIGURE 3-9:
Click the Action
Center icon to see
the Action Center
pane, which
displays current
information
about your
computer.

>> **Location:** This lets you toggle your computer's knowledge of your geographic location.

>> **All Settings:** This brings up the Windows 10 Settings app, a huge panel of organized switches, which replaces most of the Control Panel found in older Windows versions. (You can also reach the Settings app by clicking the Start button and clicking the Settings icon.)

Although the Action Center's bottom usually shows only four buttons, click the word Expand over the left-most button to reveal hidden buttons. The available buttons vary according to your particular model of computer or tablet.

Keep these things in mind to reap the most benefits from the Action Center:

>> The Action Center sometimes goes overboard, reminding you about an appointment from yesterday. To remove an item, point at it and then click the X that appears in its upper-right corner.

>> To clear everything listed in the Action Center, click the words Clear All Notifications in its lower-right corner.

>> Tired of seeing notifications from an over-eager app? Right-click the unwanted notification and choose Turn Off Notifications for App from the pop-up menu.

TIP

TIP

>> Tablet owners can quickly fetch the Action Center by sliding their finger inward from the screen's right edge.

>> When the Action Center's icon changes to show a number inside of it, you know how many unclicked notifications await inside.

>> To customize the Action Center's bottom buttons, click the All Settings button in the pane's bottom edge. When the Windows Settings window appears, click the System section and click that section's Notifications & Actions link. When the Notifications & Actions window appears, you see your four current buttons listed along the top of a grid of buttons. Drag the buttons to place your four favorites on the top row, and they subsequently replace the Action Center's buttons.

>> While you're at the Settings page, check out the toggles that control which apps may send you notifications. You can turn off notifications for apps you don't particularly care about.

Customizing the taskbar

Windows offers a whirlwind of options for the lowly taskbar, letting you play with it in more ways than a strand of spaghetti and a fork.

And that's especially important if you don't care for the new Start menu: By stocking the taskbar with icons for oft-used programs, you can avoid unnecessary trips to the Start menu.

First, the taskbar's left edge comes preloaded with icons for four apps: Microsoft Edge (the new Windows 10 web browser), File Explorer (your file browser), the Microsoft Store app (for downloading apps and programs), and the Mail app. Like all your taskbar icons, they're movable, so feel free to drag them to any order you want.

If you spot a favored program's icon or tile on the Start menu, right-click the icon, choose More from the pop-up menu, and choose Pin to Taskbar from the next pop-up menu.

For even more customization, right-click a blank part of the taskbar and choose Taskbar Settings. The Taskbar page appears in the Settings app, as shown in Figure 3-10.

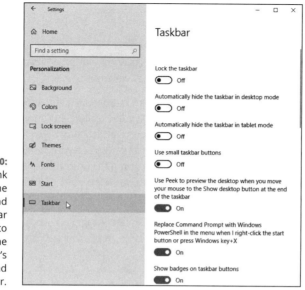

FIGURE 3-10:
Right-click a blank
portion of the
taskbar and
choose Taskbar
Settings to
customize the
taskbar's
appearance and
behavior.

Table 3-1 explains the most-used taskbar settings, as well as my recommendations for them.

TABLE 3-1 ## Most-Used Taskbar Settings

Setting	My Recommendations
Lock the Taskbar	Turning this on locks the taskbar in place, keeping you from changing its appearance. Once you've set up the taskbar to suit your needs, lock it to protect it from inadvertent settings changes.
Automatically Hide the Taskbar	Handy mostly for small screens, this option makes the taskbar automatically hide itself when you're not near it. (Point your cursor at the screen's bottom edge to bring it back into view.) I leave this option toggled Off to keep the taskbar always in view. An adjacent toggle also lets you hide the taskbar in Tablet mode, handy for some tablets.
Use Small Taskbar Buttons	Another helper for the small screens found on some laptops and tablets, this setting shrinks the taskbar to half-height, letting you pack in a few extra tiny icons.
Use Peek	When you activate this feature, pointing at the taskbar's far-right edge makes the windows transparent, letting you peek at your underlying desktop. (Clicking that area minimizes all open windows.)
Show Badges on Taskbar Buttons	Leave this on to see little reminders on your taskbar app's buttons. The Mail app's taskbar icon, for example, will continuously display your number of unread emails.
Taskbar Location On Screen	Your taskbar can live on any edge of your desktop, not just the bottom. Choose any of the four edges here.

Setting	My Recommendations
Combine Taskbar Buttons	When you open lots of windows and programs, Windows accommodates the crowd by grouping similar windows under one button: All open Microsoft Word documents stack atop one Microsoft Word button, for example. To protect the taskbar from overcrowding, select the option called Always, Hide Labels. (Without this turned on, each icon lists its name in text, consuming way too much space.)
Notification Area	This section's two links let you choose which icons should appear in the Notification area. You can turn off the notification for Battery level, for example, if you're working on a desktop PC.
Multiple Displays	Head here if you hook up a second monitor to your PC. You can then choose whether the taskbar should extend to the second monitor. (Choose Off if you watch videos or presentations on the second screen, for example; choose On if you simply want to extend your desktop across both displays.)

Feel free to experiment with the taskbar until it looks right for you. Your changes take place immediately. Don't like the change? Click the toggle switch again to reverse your decision.

After you set up the taskbar just the way you want it, turn the Lock the Taskbar toggle to On, described in Table 3-1.

Setting Up Multiple Desktops

TECHNICAL STUFF

Some people connect two or more monitors to their computer so that they can double their desktop real estate. These computing enthusiasts can then view a spreadsheet on one monitor, for example, while viewing the other to write a report about the spreadsheet. (I describe how to set up two monitors in Chapter 12.)

To accommodate those on a budget, Windows 10 introduces a way to run several desktops on a *single* monitor. Called *virtual* desktops, the desktops can be swapped into view, letting you shift your work from one desktop to another. That can be handy for people with small monitors who want to toggle among several sets of adjacent windows, for example. Instead of juggling windows, they can just switch between desktops.

To create virtual desktops and work between them, follow these steps:

1. **Click the taskbar's Task View button and then click the words New Desktop.**

   A click or tap on the Task View button, shown in the margin, and the screen clears, showing thumbnails of all your open windows. In the upper-right corner, shown in Figure 3-11, you see the words New Desktop.

FIGURE 3-11:
Click the taskbar's
Task View button,
and the words
New Desktop
appear above the
taskbar.

Click the words New Desktop, and a tiny desktop thumbnail immediately appears along the screen's top edge, shown in Figure 3-12.

2. **Click the thumbnail of the new desktop, and your new desktop fills the screen.**

   The thumbnail expands into a new desktop. The new desktop is a replica of your original desktop but without any open programs or windows.

That's it. You've created a second virtual desktop and moved to it. Windows keeps your other desktop tucked away until you want to switch back to it with a return click on the Task View button.

Some people love virtual desktops. Other people find the whole concept needless and confusing. But whether you love or hate virtual desktops, these tips will come in handy:

» To switch between desktops, click the Task View button. When your miniature virtual desktop windows appear along the screen's top edge, as shown in Figure 3-12, click the one you want.

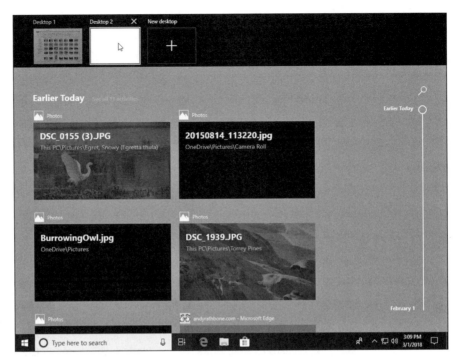

FIGURE 3-12:
When the
thumbnail of the
second desktop
appears, switch
to it with a click.

» To see a virtual desktop's currently open windows, click the Task View button. When the miniature desktops appear along the screen's top edge, hover your mouse pointer over a miniature desktop; the screen changes to show thumbnails of *that* desktop's open windows. To revisit a window on any desktop, just click the window's thumbnail.

» To close an unwanted desktop, click the Task View button, and then click the X (shown in the margin) in that desktop's thumbnail. (Hover your mouse pointer over the desktop, and the X appears.) Any open windows on that desktop will be dumped onto your original, "real" desktop. That's important: You won't lose any unsaved work by accidentally closing a virtual desktop.

» To create even more virtual desktops, click the Task View button. From the screen that appears, click the plus sign (shown in the margin) near the screen's upper-right corner.

» Keyboard lovers can add a desktop by holding the Windows key and then pressing Ctrl+D. Your current desktop immediately disappears, replaced by a new, empty desktop. (Pressing ⊞+Tab opens the Task View mode, letting you see all your open windows, as well as any virtual desktops.)

>> To move an open window from one virtual desktop to another, click the Task View button to see the thumbnails of your open virtual desktops. Then drag the desired window down to the desired desktop thumbnail along the screen's bottom edge. (Right-clicking a desired window fetches a pop-up menu that lists all your virtual desktop options.)

NEW

>> Keen-eyed observers will notice a sliding bar along the screen's right edge in Figures 3-11 and 3-12. Slide the bar up or down to revisit apps and websites you've opened in the last 30 days. Known as Timeline, the feature debuted in Spring 2018, and I cover it in Chapter 2.

Making Programs Easier to Find

Whenever you install a new program on your computer, the program usually asks way too many obtuse questions. But perk up your ears when you see this question: "Would you like a shortcut icon placed on your desktop or taskbar?"

Say yes, please, as that will save you from dashing out to the Start menu to find the program's icon or tile.

But if your favorite programs don't yet have icons on the desktop or taskbar, put them there by following these steps:

1. **Head to the Start menu and scroll down the list of apps in the menu's left column.**

   As you scroll up or down, an alphabetical list of icons for all your apps and programs scrolls up or down, as well. (When in Tablet mode, click the All Apps icon, shown in the margin, to see all your apps.)

2. **Right-click the name of any program or app you want to appear on the taskbar, choose More from the pop-up menu, and choose Pin to Taskbar from the second pop-up menu.**

   If you're using a touchscreen, hold down your finger on the desired app icon for a second or two. Then lift your finger, tap the word More, and tap the Pin to Taskbar option on the pop-up menu.

Now, instead of heading to the Start menu, you can launch your oft-used apps with a click on their taskbar icon.

TIP

After you've stocked your taskbar with icons, pretend they're numbered, from left to right, but don't number the Task View icon. Pressing ⊞+1 from the desktop opens the first program; ⊞+2 opens the second program; and so on. You've created automatic shortcuts!

Chapter **4**

Basic Desktop Window Mechanics

The Windows 10 Start menu boasts bright colors, big letters, and large buttons. It's easy to see what you're poking at with a finger or mouse.

The Windows desktop, by contrast, includes miniscule, monochrome buttons, tiny lettering, unlabeled buttons, and windows with pencil-thin borders. The windows come with way too many parts, many with confusing names that programs expect you to remember. To give you a hand, this chapter provides a lesson in windows anatomy and navigation.

You eventually need to know this stuff because windows tend to cover each other up on the desktop; you need to manually push and prod them into view.

I've dissected each part of a window so you know what happens when you click or touch each portion. By all means, use this book's margins to scribble notes as you move from the fairly simple Start menu to the powerful yet complicated Windows desktop.

Dissecting a Typical Desktop Window

Figure 4-1 places a typical window on the slab, with all its parts labeled. You might recognize the window as your Documents folder, that storage tank for most of your work.

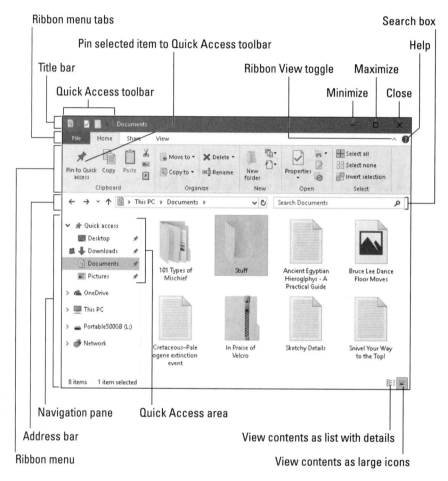

FIGURE 4-1:
Here's how the
ever-precise
computer nerds
address the
different parts of
a window.

Just as boxers grimace differently depending on where they've been punched, windows behave differently depending on where they've been clicked. The next few sections describe the main parts of the Documents window in Figure 4-1, how to click them, and how Windows jerks in response.

>> Windows veterans remember their My Documents folder, that stash for almost all of their files. Windows 10 calls it simply the Documents folder. (No matter what it's called, you're still supposed to stash your files inside it.)

- A thick, control-filled panel called the Ribbon lives atop every folder. Some people like the Ribbon's larger buttons and menus; others preferred the older menu system. Don't like the Ribbon? Gaze at the folder's top-right corner and click the tiny arrow next to the question mark, and the Ribbon disappears. (Repeat to put it back.)

TECHNICAL STUFF

- Windows no longer shows libraries in the Navigation Pane. Most people won't miss them. If you do, put them back: Right-click a blank place inside the Navigation Pane and choose Show Libraries from the pop-up menu.

TECHNICAL STUFF

- After the Spring 2018 update, Windows 10 no longer shows Homegroups in the Navigation Pane, either. There's no way to put them back. I cover alternative networking and file sharing solutions in Chapter 15.

- Windows is full of little oddly shaped buttons, borders, and boxes. You don't need to remember all their names, although that would give you a leg up on figuring out the scholarly Windows Help menus. When you spot an odd portion of a window, just return to this chapter, look up its name in Figure 4-1, and read its explanation.

- You can deal with most things in Windows by clicking, double-clicking, or right-clicking. Hint: When in doubt, always right-click.

TIP

- Navigating desktop windows on a touchscreen computer? For some touching tips, drop by the sidebar in Chapter 3 on touching desktop programs on a Windows tablet.

- After you click a few windows a few times, you realize how easy it is to boss them around. The hard part is finding the right controls for the *first* time, like figuring out the dashboard on that rental car.

Tugging on a window's title bar

Found atop nearly every window (see examples in Figure 4-2), the title bar usually lists the program name and, if applicable, the file or folder it's currently displaying. For example, Figure 4-2 shows the title bars from the Windows File Explorer program (top) and the Settings app (bottom).

Although mild-mannered, the mundane title bar holds hidden powers, described in the following tips:

- To find the window you're currently working on, look at the title bar along the window's top edge. One title bar will usually be darker than the other. See how the File Explorer title bar (Figure 4-2, top) is darker than the Settings app's title bar (Figure 4-2, bottom)? That color distinguishes that window from windows you *aren't* working on. By glancing at all the title bars on the desktop, you can tell which window is awake and accepting anything you type.

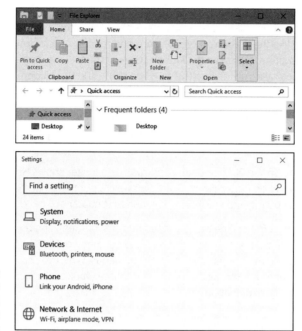

FIGURE 4-2:
A title bar from
File Explorer (top)
and the Settings
app (bottom).

>> Microsoft isn't consistent with its title bars. Almost all programs have them, but some apps don't show title bars at all, much less show them in different colors.

>> Title bars make convenient handles for moving windows around your desktop. Point at a blank part of the title bar, hold down the mouse button, and move the mouse around: The window follows along as you move your mouse. Found the right location? Let go of the mouse button, and the window sets up camp in its new spot.

>> Don't see a title bar across a window's top edge? Microsoft still put it there, but sneakily made it invisible. To reposition that window, aim at the window's top, where the title bar *should* be, and drag the window to its new place on your desktop.

>> Double-click a blank portion of the title bar, and the window leaps to fill the entire desktop. Double-click it again, and the window retreats to its original size.

>> See the cluster of little icons in the top-left corner of the File Explorer window? Those icons form the Quick Access toolbar, which is part of what Microsoft calls a *Ribbon interface.* The icons offer one-click access to common tasks such as creating a new folder.

DRAGGING, DROPPING, AND RUNNING

Although the phrase *drag and drop* sounds as if it's straight out of a Mafia guidebook, it's really a nonviolent mouse trick used throughout Windows. Dragging and dropping is a way of moving something — say, an icon on your desktop — from one place to another.

To *drag,* put the mouse pointer over the icon and *hold down* the left or right mouse button. (I prefer the right mouse button.) As you move the mouse across your desk, the pointer drags the icon across the screen. Place the pointer/icon where you want it and release the mouse button. The icon *drops,* unharmed.

Holding down the *right* mouse button while dragging and dropping makes Windows toss up a helpful little menu, asking whether you want to *copy* or *move* the icon.

Helpful Tip Department: Did you start dragging something and realize midstream that you're dragging the wrong item? Don't let go of the mouse button — instead, press Esc to cancel the action. Whew! (If you've dragged with your right mouse button and already let go of the button, you can take another exit: Choose Cancel from the pop-up menu.)

» In Windows 10, both programs and apps place three buttons on the right end of every title bar. From left to right, they let you Minimize, Restore (or Maximize), or Close a window, topics all covered in the "Maneuvering Windows Around the Desktop" section, later in this chapter.

» Don't see those three buttons at the top of the title bar? In another odd move, Microsoft sometimes makes them invisible. They'll appear if you point the mouse where the buttons should be, which is the window's upper-right corner.

Navigating folders with a window's Address bar

Directly beneath every open folder's title bar or Ribbon lives the *Address bar,* shown near the top of the folder in Figure 4-3. Web surfers will experience déjà vu: The Windows Address bar is lifted straight from the top edge of web browsers like Internet Explorer and glued atop every open folder.

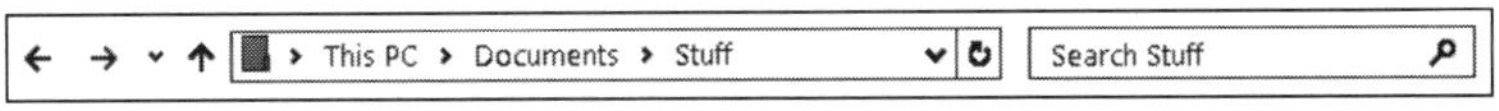

FIGURE 4-3:
An Address bar.

| ← → ∨ ↑ | ▣ › This PC › Documents › Stuff | ∨ | ↻ | Search Stuff | 🔎 |

The Address bar's four main parts, described from left to right in the following list, perform four different duties:

>> **Backward and Forward buttons:** These two arrows track your path as you forage through your PC's folders. The Backward button backtracks to the folder you just visited. The Forward button brings you back.

>> **Down Arrow button:** Click this extraordinarily tiny arrow to see a drop-down list of folders you've visited previously. You can click any listed folder for a quick revisit.

>> **Up Arrow button:** Click the Up Arrow button to move up one folder from your current folder. For example, if you've been sorting files in your Documents folder's "Stuff" folder, click the Up arrow to return to your Documents folder.

>> **Address:** Just as a web browser's Address bar lists a website's address, the Windows Address bar displays your current folder's address — its location inside your PC. For example, the Address bar shown in Figure 4-3 shows three words: This PC, Documents, and Stuff. Those words tell you that you're looking inside the Stuff folder inside the Documents folder on This PC. (That's *your* PC, as opposed to somebody else's PC.) Yes, addresses are complicated enough to warrant an entire chapter: Chapter 5.

>> **Search box:** Every Windows folder sports a Search box. Instead of searching the Internet, though, it rummages through your current folder's contents. For example, if you type the word **carrot** into a folder's Search box, Windows digs through that folder's contents and retrieves every file or folder mentioning *carrot.* (For more tips on finding things, flip ahead to Chapter 7.)

TIP

In the Address bar, notice the little arrows between the words *This PC, Documents,* and *Stuff.* The arrows offer quick trips to other folders. Click any arrow — the one to the right of the word *Documents,* for example. A little menu drops down from the arrow, letting you jump to any other folder inside your Documents folder.

Finding commands on the Ribbon

The Windows desktop has more menu items than an Asian restaurant. To keep everybody's minds on computer commands instead of seaweed salad, Windows places menus inside a tab-filled *Ribbon* that lives atop every folder. (See Figure 4-4.)

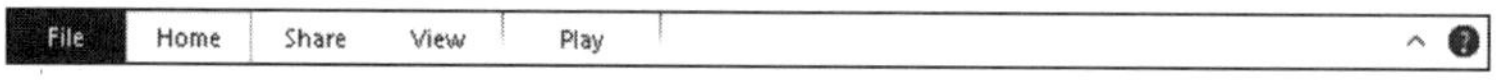

FIGURE 4-4:
The Ribbon's
tabs.

| File | Home | Share | View | | Play | | ∧ ❶ |

The Ribbon's tabs each offer different options. To reveal the secret options, click any tab — Share, for example. The Ribbon quickly changes, as shown in Figure 4-5, presenting all your options related to *sharing* a file.

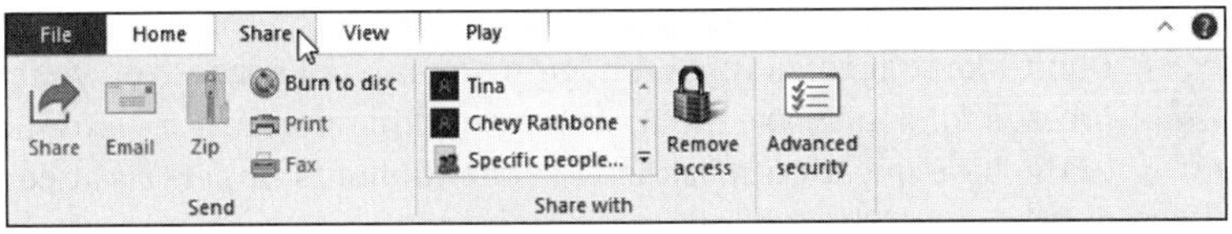

FIGURE 4-5:
Click any Ribbon tab to see its associated commands.

Just as restaurants sometimes run out of specials, a window sometimes isn't capable of offering all its menu items. Any unavailable options are *grayed out*, like the Print option in Figure 4-5. (Because you can't print music files, that option is grayed out.)

TIP

If you accidentally click the wrong tab on the Ribbon, causing the wrong commands to leap onto the screen, simply click the tab you *really* wanted. A forgiving soul, Windows displays your newly chosen tab's contents instead.

You needn't know much about the Ribbon because Windows automatically places the correct buttons atop each program. Open your Music folder, for example, and the Ribbon quickly spouts a new Play tab for listening sessions.

If a button's meaning isn't immediately obvious, hover your mouse pointer over it; a little message explains the button's *raison d'être.* My own translations for the most common tabs and buttons are in the following list:

» **File:** Found along every Ribbon's left edge, this tab offers little in rewards: It gives you options for opening new windows and returning to popular locations.

» **Home:** Found on every folder's Ribbon, the Home tab usually brings pay dirt, so every folder opens showing this tab's options. The Home tab offers tools to select, cut, copy, paste, move, delete, or rename a folder's items.

» **Share:** As the name implies, this tab offers ways to let you share a folder's contents with other people, whether by burning the contents to a CD, emailing them, using the new Nearby Share feature, or sharing them on a network. (I cover both Nearby Share and network sharing in Chapter 15.)

» **View:** Click here to change how files appear in the window. In your Pictures folder, for example, choose Extra Large Icons to see larger thumbnails of your photos. Choose Details to see specific information about a file: its size, for example, its creation date, and other trivia.

» **Manage:** Found only on special folders, this general-purpose tab shows customized ways to handle your folder's items. Atop a folder full of pictures, for example, the Manage tab offers a Slide Show button, as well as buttons to rotate skewed photos or turn them into desktop backgrounds.

REMEMBER

Don't like that thick Ribbon hogging an inch of space atop your window? If you're pressed for space, axe the Ribbon by clicking the tiny upward-pointing arrow next to the blue question mark icon in the Ribbon's upper-right corner. Click it again to bring back the Ribbon.

Quick shortcuts with the Navigation Pane

Look at most "real" desktops, and you'll see the most-used items sitting within arm's reach: the coffee cup, the stapler, and perhaps a few crumbs from the coffee room snacks. Similarly, Windows gathers your PC's most frequently used items and places them in the Navigation Pane, shown in Figure 4-6.

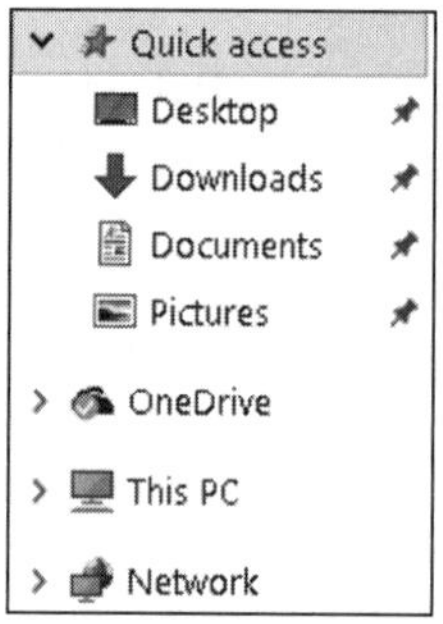

FIGURE 4-6:
The Navigation Pane offers shortcuts to places you visit most frequently.

NEW

Found along the left edge of every folder, the Navigation Pane contains several main sections: Quick Access, OneDrive, and This PC. (On PCs connected through a network, you'll see an entry for Network, as well.) Click any of those sections — Quick Access, for example — and the window's right side quickly shows you the contents of what you've clicked.

Here's a more detailed description of each part of the Navigation Pane:

» **Quick Access:** Formerly called *Favorites,* these locations serve as clickable shortcuts to your most frequently accessed locations in Windows.

• **Desktop:** Your Windows desktop, believe it or not, is actually a folder that's always spread open across your screen. Clicking Desktop quickly shows you the contents of your desktop.

- **Downloads:** Click this shortcut to find the files you've downloaded while browsing the Internet. Ah, that's where they ended up!

- **Documents:** A perennial favorite, this folder stores most of your work: spreadsheets, reports, letters, and other things you've created.

- **Pictures:** Another popular destination, this takes you to photos you've shot yourself or saved from the Internet.

>> **OneDrive:** This free online storage space was handed to you by Microsoft when you created a Microsoft account. (Without a Microsoft account, it's simply another folder on your PC.) Because OneDrive is password-protected and online, it's tempting to fill it with favorite files for access from any PC, phone, or other Internet-connected device. But when your stored files exceed your storage limit, Microsoft asks for your credit card to pay for the extra space. I cover OneDrive at the end of Chapter 5.

>> **This PC:** This section lets you browse through your PC's folders and hard drives. (Many of these commonly used storage areas live in the Navigation Pane's Quick Access area, as well.) The This PC section holds these areas:

NEW

- **3D Objects:** Embraced mostly by procrastinators and game designers, this folder contains pictures that become movable 3D objects when opened in the new Paint 3D program. Chances are, you'll never set foot in this virtual weirdness.

- **Desktop:** Click this to see the files and folders stored on your desktop. (Or, you can just close the folder and see your desktop in person.)

- **Documents:** This opens the Documents folder, a convenient repository for letters, forms, and reports.

- **Downloads:** Downloaded a file from a website? Then look in here to be reintroduced.

- **Music:** Yep, this shortcut jumps straight to your Music folder, where a double-click on a song starts it playing through your PC's speakers.

- **Pictures:** This shortcut opens your Pictures folder, the living quarters for all your digital photos.

- **Videos:** Click here to visit your Videos folder, where a double-click on a video opens it for immediate viewing.

TECHNICAL STUFF

- **Local Disk (C:):** A holdover for old techies, this entry lets you crawl through any folder on your PC. Unless you know specifically what item you're seeking, though, you probably won't find it. Stick with the other destinations, instead.

- **Disc Drives:** If your PC includes extra disc drives, icons for those appear here. Insert a flash drive into your USB port, and its icon appears here, as well.

» **Network:** Once you create a network from the PCs in your home, their names appear here. I cover networks in Chapter 15.

Here are a few tips for making the most of your Navigation Pane:

» To avoid treks back to the Start menu, add your own favorite places to the Navigation Pane's Quick Access area: Right-click a favorite folder and choose Pin to Quick Access from the pop-up menu. (Similarly, right-click any unwanted listing in the Quick Access area and remove it by choosing Unpin from Quick Access.)

» If you've connected to a network at home or work, the pane's This PC section may include those other computers' music, video, and photos (which are sometimes referred to as *media*). Click those computers' icons to access those goodies as if they were stored on your own computer.

TECHNICAL STUFF

» Windows 7 owners may notice that Windows 10 doesn't show libraries in the Navigation Pane. Libraries still exist, but they're hidden in the background. To bring them back into view, click a blank portion of the Navigation Pane and choose Show Libraries from the pop-up menu. (You must also manually add the Public folders to each library in order to return them to the glory days of Windows 7.)

Moving inside a window with its scroll bar

The scroll bar, which resembles a cutaway of an elevator shaft (see Figure 4-7), rests along the edge of all overstuffed windows. You can even find a scroll bar along the side of an extra-long Start menu.

Inside the shaft, a little elevator (technically, the *scroll box*) rides along as you move through the window's contents. In fact, by glancing at the box's position in the scroll bar, you can tell whether you're viewing items in the window's beginning, middle, or end.

By clicking in various places on the scroll bar, you can quickly view different parts of things. Here's the dirt:

» Click inside the scroll bar in the direction you want to view. On a *vertical* scroll bar, for example, click above the scroll box to move your view up one page. Similarly, click below the scroll box to move your view down a page.

Scroll boxes

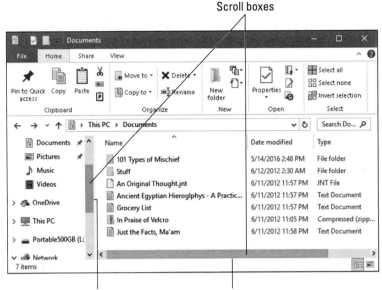

FIGURE 4-7:
Horizontal and
vertical scroll bars.

Vertical scroll bar   Horizontal scroll bar

NEW

>> The Start menu's extreme right edge contains a difficult-to-see scroll bar, but it pops into view when the mouse pointer is nearby. Many apps also hide their scroll bars until you point at where they should be. Welcome to Microsoft's new secret club of invisible items!

>> Don't see a scroll bar or a box in the bar, even when you point your mouse at the screen's edge? Then you're already seeing all that the window has to offer; there's nothing to scroll.

>> To move around in a hurry, drag the scroll box inside the scroll bar. As you drag, you see the window's contents race past. When you see the spot you want, let go of the mouse button to stay at that viewing position.

>> Are you using a mouse that has a little wheel embedded in the poor critter's back? Spin the wheel, and the elevator moves quickly inside the scroll bar, shifting your view accordingly. It's a handy way to explore a tile-packed Start menu, long documents, and file-filled folders.

Boring borders

A *border* is that thin edge surrounding a window, including desktop windows containing apps. Compared with a scroll bar, it's really tiny.

To change a window's size, drag the border in or out. (When the mouse pointer turns into a two-headed arrow, you're in the right place to start dragging.) Some windows, oddly enough, don't have borders. Stuck in limbo, their size can't be changed — even if they're an awkward size.

Except for tugging on them with the mouse, you won't be using borders much.

Maneuvering Windows Around the Desktop

A terrible dealer at the poker table, Windows tosses windows around your desktop in a seemingly random way. Programs cover each other or sometimes dangle off the desktop. The following sections show you how to gather all your windows into a neat pile, placing your favorite window on the top of the stack. If you prefer, lay them all down like a poker hand. As an added bonus, you can change their size, making them open to any size you want, automatically.

Moving a window to the top of the pile

Windows says the window atop the pile that's getting all the attention is called the *active* window. Being the active window means that it receives any keystrokes you or your cat happen to type.

You can move a window to the top of the pile so that it's active in any of several ways:

>> Move the mouse pointer until it hovers over any portion of your desired window; then click the mouse button. Windows immediately brings the window to the top of the pile.

>> On the taskbar along the desktop's bottom, click the icon for the window you want. Chapter 3 explains what the taskbar can do in more detail.

TIP

>> Hold down the Alt key while tapping and releasing the Tab key. With each tap of the Tab key, a small window pops up, displaying a thumbnail of each open window on your desktop. (You also see thumbnails of open Start menu apps.) When your press of the Tab key highlights your favorite window, let go of the Alt key, and your window leaps to the forefront.

>> A click of the Task View button (shown in the margin) also places miniature views of each window on the screen, even if they're on different virtual desktops. Click the desired miniature window, and it rises to the top, ready for action. I cover the Task View button and virtual desktops in Chapter 3.

TIP

Is your desktop too cluttered for you to work comfortably in your current window? Then hold down your mouse pointer on the window's title bar and give it a few quick shakes; Windows drops the other windows down to the taskbar, leaving your main window resting alone on an empty desktop.

Moving a window from here to there

Sometimes you want to move a window to a different place on the desktop. Perhaps part of the window hangs off the edge, and you want it centered. Or maybe you want one window closer to another.

In either case, you can move a window by dragging and dropping its *title bar*, that thick bar along its top. (If you're not sure how dragging and dropping works, see the sidebar "Dragging, dropping, and running," earlier in this chapter.) When you *drop* the window in place, the window not only remains where you've dragged and dropped it, but it also stays on top of the pile — until you click another window, that is, which brings *that* window to the pile's top.

Making a window fill the whole desktop

Sooner or later, you'll grow tired of all this multiwindow mumbo jumbo. Why can't you just make one window fill the screen? Well, you can.

To make any desktop window grow as large as possible, double-click its *title bar*, that bar along the window's topmost edge. The window leaps up to fill the entire desktop, covering up all the other windows.

To reduce the pumped-up window back to its former size, double-click its title bar once again. The window quickly shrinks to its former size, and you can see things that it covered.

>> If you're morally opposed to double-clicking a window's title bar to expand it, you can click the Maximize button. Shown in the margin, it's the middle of the three buttons in the upper-right corner of every window.

>> When a window is maximized to fill the desktop, the Maximize button turns into a Restore button, shown in the margin. Click the Restore button, and the window returns to its smaller size.

>> Need a brute force method? Then drag a window's top edge until it butts against the top edge of your desktop. The shadow of the window's borders will expand to fill the desktop; let go of the mouse button, and the window's borders fill the desktop. (Yes, simply double-clicking the title bar is faster, but this method impresses any onlookers from neighboring cubicles.)

TIP

Too busy to reach for the mouse? Maximize the current window by holding down the ⊞ key and pressing the up-arrow key. (Hold down the ⊞ key and press the down-arrow key to return to normal size.)

Closing a window

When you're through working in a window, close it: Click the little X in its upper-right corner. Zap! You're back to an empty desktop.

If you try to close your window before finishing your work, be it a game of Solitaire or a report for the boss, Windows cautiously asks whether you'd like to save your work. Take it up on its offer by clicking Yes and, if necessary, typing in a filename so that you can find your work later.

Making a window bigger or smaller

Like big lazy dogs, windows tend to flop on top of one another. To space your windows more evenly, you can resize them by *dragging and dropping* their edges inward or outward. It works like this:

1. **Point at any corner with the mouse arrow. When the arrow turns into a two-headed arrow, you can hold down the mouse button and drag the corner in or out to change the window's size.**

2. **When you're happy with the window's new size, release the mouse button.**

   The window settles down into its new position.

Placing two windows side by side

The longer you use Windows, the more likely you are to want to see two windows side by side. For example, you may want to copy things from one window into another or compare two versions of the same file. By spending a few hours with the mouse, you can drag and drop the windows' corners until they're in perfect juxtaposition.

If you're impatient, Windows lets you speed up this handy side-by-side placement several ways:

NEW

NEW

>> For the quickest solution, drag a window's title bar against one side of your desktop; when your mouse pointer touches the desktop's edge, let go of the mouse button. Repeat these same steps with the second window, dragging it to the opposite side of the desktop.

>> If you drag a window to fill one edge of the screen, Windows immediately shows thumbnails of your minimized windows. Click the thumbnail of the window you'd like to see fill the screen's other half.

>> To place four windows onscreen simultaneously, drag the title bar of each window to a different corner of the screen. Each window resizes itself to grab its own quarter of the screen.

>> Right-click on a blank part of the taskbar (even the clock will do) and choose Show Windows Side by Side. The windows align next to each other, like pillars. To align them in horizontal rows, choose Show Windows Stacked. (If you have more than three open windows, Show Windows Stacked tiles them across your desktop, which is handy for seeing just a bit of each one.)

>> If you have more than two windows open, click the Minimize button (the leftmost icon in every window's top-right corner) to minimize the windows you don't want tiled. Then use the Show Windows Side by Side from the preceding bullet to align the two remaining windows.

TIP

>> To make the current window fill the desktop's right half, hold the 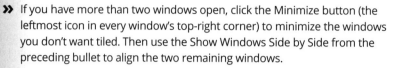 key and press the right-arrow key. To fill the desktop's left half, hold the key and press the left-arrow key.

Making windows open to the same darn size

Sometimes a window opens to a small square; other times, it opens to fill the entire desktop. But windows rarely open to the exact size you want. Until you dis-cover this trick, that is: When you *manually* adjust the size and placement of a window, Windows memorizes that size and always reopens the window to that same size. Follow these three steps to see how it works:

1. **Open your window.**

   The window opens to its usual unwanted size.

2. **Drag the window's corners until the window is the exact size and in the exact location you want. Let go of the mouse to drop the corner into its new position.**

   Be sure to resize the window *manually* by dragging its corners or edges with the mouse. Simply clicking the Maximize button won't work.

3. **Immediately close the window.**

   Windows memorizes the size and placement of a window at the time it was last closed. When you open that window again, it should open to the same size you last left it. But the changes you made apply only to the program you made them in. For example, changes made to the Internet Explorer window will be remembered only for *Internet Explorer,* not for other programs you open.

Most windows follow these sizing rules, but a few renegades may misbehave, unfortunately.

IN THIS CHAPTER

» Managing files with the desktop's File Explorer

» Navigating drives, folders, and flash drives

» Creating and naming folders

» Selecting and deselecting items

» Copying and moving files and folders

» Writing to CDs and memory cards

» Understanding Windows OneDrive

Chapter **5**

Storage: Internal, External, and in the Cloud

B y leaving their paper-strewn oak desktops and moving to computers, everybody hoped things would be easier. Important papers would no longer slide behind the desk or languish in dusty drawers. Twenty years later, though, we know the truth: Computers come with just as many nooks, crannies, and hiding places as did the desks they replaced . . . maybe even more.

In Windows, File Explorer serves as your computerized filing cabinet. Insert a flash drive or portable hard drive into your computer, and File Explorer appears, ready for you to start rustling through folders.

You're stuck with File Explorer whenever you need to find folders inside your computer, *outside* your computer on plug-in drives and digital cameras, and even in some storage spots on the Internet.

TIP

MANAGING FILES ON A TOUCHSCREEN

Most touchscreen tablets run in Tablet mode by default. While Tablet mode includes big buttons and finger-friendly apps, it hides the desktop, which creates a file management problem. Windows 10 doesn't include a touch-friendly file manager, so you're stuck with the desktop's File Explorer.

Chances are good that your fingers won't enjoy poking the File Explorer's tiny buttons and menus. So, start improving things by turning off Tablet mode: Slide a finger inward from the screen's right edge, and when the Action Center appears, tap the pane's Tablet mode button to turn it off, letting you use the desktop more easily. After turning off Tablet mode, you can once again view the desktop and its folders within movable windows.

If you plan to spend a lot of time on the desktop, invest in an inexpensive Bluetooth (wireless) mouse for clicking the controls. And, to remove the tablet's onscreen keyboard that blocks much of your view of the desktop, consider buying a Bluetooth keyboard, as well.

If you want your tablet to double as a desktop PC, buy a *docking station* instead. A docking station lives on your office desk and lets you permanently attach a monitor, wired mouse, and wired keyboard. Then, when you slide your tablet into a docking station, it's nearly indistinguishable from a desktop PC.

Whether you're using a touchscreen tablet, a laptop, or a desktop PC, files and folders still rule the computing world. And unless you grasp the Windows folder metaphor, you may not find your information very easily.

This chapter explains how to put File Explorer to work. (You may recognize it as *Windows Explorer*, its name from older Windows versions.) This chapter also explains how to use OneDrive, your Internet storage space, to store files away from your computer.

Along the way, you ingest just enough Windows file management skills for you to save and retrieve your work without too much discomfort.

Browsing the File Explorer File Cabinets

To keep your programs and files neatly arranged, Windows cleaned up the squeaky old file cabinet metaphor with whisper-quiet Windows icons. Inside File Explorer, the icons represent your computer's storage areas, allowing you to copy, move, rename, or delete your files before the investigators arrive.

To open File Explorer, shown in Figure 5-1, and begin rummaging around inside your computer, click the Start menu's File Explorer icon. Shown in the margin, it's near the Start menu's lower-left corner.

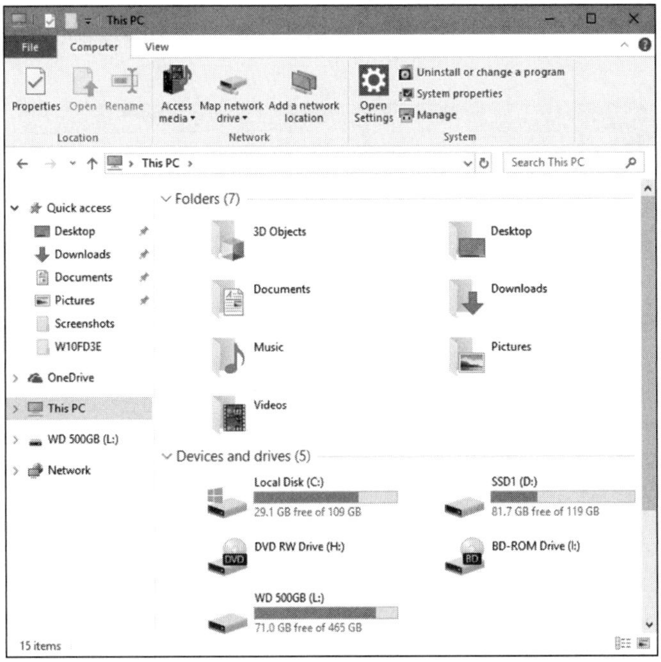

FIGURE 5-1:
The File Explorer window displays popular storage areas and your most recently opened files.

You can also open File Explorer with a click on its icon (shown in the margin) on the *taskbar*, that strip along the screen's bottom edge.

In previous versions of Windows, File Explorer opened to show your computer's largest file cabinets, called *drives* or *disks* in computer lingo. Windows 10 goes one step further.

Instead of dropping you off at the drives and forcing you to dig for your files, the Windows 10 File Explorer tries to be more helpful. It simply lists your most popular folders. For example, it shows Documents, where you store most of your files, and Downloads, the holding tank for everything you download from the Internet. (You also see shortcuts to your Music, Videos, and Pictures folders.)

NEW

Below those main folders, in the Recent Files section, File Explorer may list shortcuts to the items you've opened most recently. If you worked on a spreadsheet yesterday, for example, find it again by opening File Explorer: A link to that spreadsheet lives on the front page, ready to be reopened with a double-click.

Seeing your main storage folders and recently opened files may be all you need to start working. But if you need to see *all* your computer's storage areas, click the words This PC in the pane along the left edge. File Explorer opens to the view you've seen in previous Windows versions, shown in Figure 5-2.

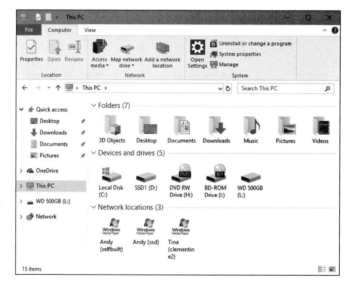

FIGURE 5-2:
Click This PC to see your computer's storage areas, which you can open to find your files.

The File Explorer images shown above will look slightly different from the ones on your PC, but you can still see the same basic sections:

» **Navigation Pane:** The handy Navigation Pane, that strip along every folder's left edge, lists shortcuts to different storage spaces on your PC, on OneDrive, and on any other connected computers. (I cover the Navigation Pane in Chapter 4.)

» **Folders:** When opened, File Explorer lists shortcuts to your main storage folders, as well as your *computing history,* a list of recently accessed folders and files. Unless you're starting a brand-new project, you can probably find your most recent work here.

» **Devices and Drives:** Shown in Figure 5-2, this area lists your PC's storage areas and devices. (The term *devices* usually refers to gadgets plugged into your PC.) Every computer has at least one hard drive. Double-clicking a hard drive icon displays its files and folders, but you can rarely find much useful information when probing that way. No, your most important files live in your Documents, Music, Pictures, and Videos folders, which appear near the top of Figure 5-2.

Notice the hard drive bearing the little Windows icon (shown in the margin)? That means that Windows lives on that drive. If you click View from the top menu and select Tiles, a multicolored line appears next to each drive's icon. The more colored space you see in the line, the more files you've stuffed onto your drive. When the line turns red, your drive is almost full, and you should think about deleting some unwanted files, uninstalling some unused programs, or upgrading to a larger drive.

You may also see some detachable gadgetry attached to your computer. Here are some of the more common items:

- **CD, DVD, and Blu-ray drives:** As shown in Figure 5-2, Windows places a short description next to each drive's icon. For example, *CD-RW* means the drive can write to *CDs* but not DVDs. *DVD-RW* means that it can both read and write to DVDs *and* CDs. A *BD-ROM* drive can read Blu-ray discs, but it can write only to CDs and DVDs. And the ever-so-versatile *BD-RE* and *BD-R* drives can read and write to Blu-ray discs, DVDs, *and* CDs.

  Writing information to a disc is called *burning.* Copying information from a disc is called *ripping.*

- **Flash drives:** The icon for some flash drive brands resembles the actual flash drive. Most flash drives simply show a generic icon like the one in the margin.

  Windows doesn't display icons for your computer's memory card readers until you've inserted a card into them. To see icons for your *empty* card readers, open File Explorer, click the View tab, and select the Hidden Items check box in the View tab's Show/Hide section. Repeat to hide them again.

- **iPads, phones, and MP3 players:** A Windows phone receives a nice icon, but Android phones, iPads, and iPhones usually receive a generic icon of a hard drive or MP3 player. If you own an iPhone or iPad, you need the Apple iTunes software (www.apple.com/itunes) that runs on the Windows desktop. Windows can't copy songs to and from an iPod or iPad by itself. (I cover MP3 players in Chapter 16.)

- **Cameras:** When plugged into your computer's USB port, digital cameras usually appear as camera icons in the File Explorer window. To import your camera's photos, turn on your camera and set it to its View Photos mode rather than its Take Photos mode. Then right-click the camera's icon in File Explorer and choose Import Pictures and Videos from the pop-up menu. After Windows walks you through the process of extracting the images (see Chapter 17), it places the photos in your Pictures folder.

If you plug a digital camcorder, cellphone, or other gadget into your PC, the File Explorer window often sprouts a new icon representing your gadget. If Windows neglects to ask what you'd like to do with your newly plugged-in gadget, right-click the icon to open a list of everything you can do with that item. No icon? Then you need to install a *driver* for your gadget, a precipitous journey detailed in Chapter 13.

NEW

If you prefer that File Explorer opens to the traditional This PC view rather than the new Quick Access view, first open any folder. Then click that folder's File tab and choose Change Folder and Search Options. When the Folder Options window appears, open the drop-down menu along the window's top edge and choose This PC instead of the default Quick Access.

To see the contents of an item listed in File Explorer, perhaps a flash drive or your digital camera, double-click it. To back out of that view, click the left-pointing arrow (shown in the margin) above the Navigation Pane.

TIP

Tip for tablets: When you read the word *click*, substitute *tap*. Similarly, *right-click* means *touch and hold*. And the term *drag and drop* means *slide your finger along the screen as if your finger is the mouse pointer and then lift the finger to drop the item.*

Getting the Lowdown on Folders

This stuff is dreadfully boring, but if you don't read it, you'll be just as lost as your files.

A *folder* is a storage area, just like a real folder in a file cabinet. Windows divides your computer's hard drives into many folders to separate your many projects. For example, you store all your music in your Music folder and your pictures in your Pictures folder. That lets both you and your programs find them easily.

Windows gives you seven main folders for storing your files. For easy access, they live in the This PC section of the Navigation Pane along the left side of every folder. Shown earlier, Figure 5-2 shows your main storage areas: 3D Objects, Desktop, Documents, Downloads, Music, Pictures, and Videos.

Keep these folder facts in mind when shuffling files in Windows:

>> You can ignore folders and dump all your files onto the Windows desktop. But that's like tossing everything into your car's back seat and pawing around to find your sunglasses a month later. Organized stuff is much easier to find.

» If you're eager to create a folder or two (and it's pretty easy), page ahead to this chapter's "Creating a New Folder" section.

» The new Windows 10 web browser, Microsoft Edge, conveniently drops all your downloaded files into your Downloads folder. Until you delete them, every file you've downloaded will be in that folder.

» File Explorer folders use a tree metaphor as they branch out from one main folder (a drive) that contains folders which contain even more folders.

TECHNICAL STUFF

Peering into Your Drives, Folders, and Other Media

Knowing all this folder stuff not only impresses computer store employees but also helps you find the files you want. (See the preceding section for a lowdown on which folder holds what.) Put on your hard hat and get ready to go spelunking among your computer's drives and folders as well as your CDs, DVDs, and smart-phones. The following sections are your guide.

Seeing the files on a drive

Like everything else in Windows, disk drives are represented by buttons, or *icons*. The File Explorer program also shows information stored in other areas, such as phones, digital cameras, networked gadgetry, portable hard drives, flash drives, or scanners. (I explain these icons in the section "Browsing the File Explorer File Cabinets," earlier in this chapter.)

Opening an icon usually lets you access the device's contents and move files back and forth, just as with any other folders in Windows.

When you double-click a hard drive icon in File Explorer, Windows promptly opens the drive to show you the folders packed inside. But how should Windows react when you insert something new into your computer, such as a CD, DVD, or flash drive?

Earlier versions of Windows tried to second-guess you. When you inserted a music CD, for example, Windows automatically began playing the music. Today's newer, politer Windows, by contrast, asks how you prefer it to handle the situation, as shown by the pop-up notification in the lower-right corner of Figure 5-3.

FIGURE 5-3:
Windows asks
how it should
handle newly
inserted items.

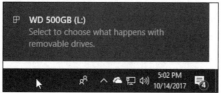

When that message appears, choose it with a click of the mouse. A second message appears, as shown in Figure 5-4, listing every way your PC and its gang of apps and programs can handle that item.

FIGURE 5-4:
Choose how
Windows should
react the next
time you insert
that item.

Choose an option — Open Folder to View Files, for example — and Windows fires up File Explorer to display your newly inserted drive's contents. The next time you plug that drive into your PC, your computer won't bother asking; it will automatically summon File Explorer and display your drive's folders.

But what if you change your mind about how Windows should treat a newly inserted item? Then you need to change how Windows reacts: In File Explorer's This PC section, right-click the inserted item's icon and choose Open AutoPlay. Once again, Windows shows the message from Figure 5-4 and asks you to plot the future course.

TIP

Adjusting the AutoPlay settings comes in particularly handy for USB thumbdrives. If your flash drive carries a few songs, Windows may want to play them, slowing your access to your flash drive's other files. To prevent that, select the AutoPlay option, Open Folder to View Files.

REMEMBER

>> When in doubt as to what you can do with an icon in File Explorer, right-click it. Windows presents a menu of all the things you can do to that object. (You can choose Open, for example, to see the files on a flash drive, making it simpler to copy them to your computer.)

>> If you double-click an icon for a CD, DVD, or Blu-ray drive when no disk is in the drive, Windows stops you, gently suggesting that you insert a disk before proceeding further.

>> Spot an icon under the heading Network Location? That's a little doorway for peering into other computers linked to your computer — if there are any. You find more network stuff in Chapter 15.

TECHNICAL STUFF

WHAT'S ALL THIS PATH STUFF?

A *path* is merely the file's address, similar to your own. When a letter is mailed to your house, for example, it travels to your country, state, city, street, and (with any luck) apartment or house. A computer path does the same thing. It starts with the letter of the disk drive and ends with the file's name. In between, the path lists all the folders the computer must travel through to reach the file.

For example, look at the Downloads folder. For Windows to find a file stored in my Downloads folder, it starts from the computer's C: drive, travels through the Users folder, and then goes through the Andy folder. From there, it goes into the Andy folder's Downloads folder. (Internet Explorer follows that path when saving your downloaded files.)

Take a deep breath and exhale slowly. Now add in the computer's ugly grammar: In a path, the Windows disk drive letter is referred to as C:\. The disk drive letter and colon make up the first part of the path. All the other folders are inside the big C: folder, so they're listed after the C: part. Windows separates these nested folders with something called a *backslash,* or \. The downloaded file's name — *Tax Form 3890,* for example — comes last.

Put it all together, and you get C:\Users\Andy\Downloads\Tax Form 3890. That's my computer's official path to the Tax Form 3890 file in Andy's Downloads folder. Of course, on your computer, you can substitute your own username for *Andy.* (Microsoft account usernames usually start with the first few letters of the linked Microsoft account email address.)

This stuff can be tricky, so here it is again: The letter for the drive comes first, followed by a colon and a backslash. Then come the names of all the folders leading to the file, separated by backslashes. Last comes the name of the file itself.

Windows automatically puts together the path for you when you click folders — thankfully. But whenever you click the Browse button to look for a file, you're navigating through folders and traversing along the path leading to the file.

Seeing what's inside a folder

Because folders are really little storage compartments, Windows uses a picture of a little folder to represent a place for storing files.

To see what's inside a folder, either in File Explorer or on the Windows desktop, just double-click that folder's picture. A new window pops up, showing that folder's contents. Spot another folder inside that folder? Double-click that one to see what's inside. Keep clicking until you find what you want or reach a dead end.

Reached a dead end? If you mistakenly end up in the wrong folder, back your way out as if you're browsing the web. Click the tiny Back arrow (shown in the margin) at the window's top-left corner. That shows you the contents of the folder you just left. If you keep clicking the Back arrow, you end up right where you started.

The Address bar provides another quick way to jump to different places in your PC. As you move from folder to folder, the folder's Address bar — that wide word-filled box at the folder's top — constantly keeps track of your trek.

Notice the little arrows between the folder names. Those little arrows provide quick shortcuts to other folders and windows. If you try clicking any of the arrows, menus appear, listing the places you can jump to from that point. For example, click the arrow after Music, shown in Figure 5-5, and a menu drops down, letting you jump quickly to your other folders.

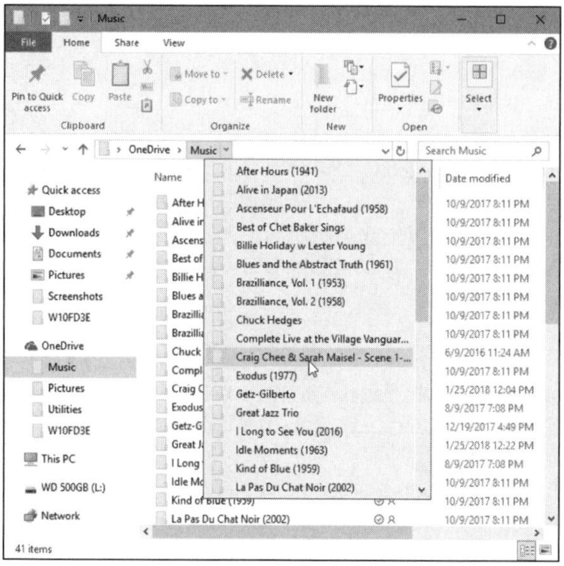

FIGURE 5-5:
Click the little arrow after Music to jump to any place that appears in the Music folder.

Here are some more tips for finding your way in and out of folders:

>> Sometimes a folder contains too many files or folders to fit in the window. To see more files, click that window's scroll bars along a window's bottom or right edges. (I cover scroll bars in your field guide, Chapter 4.)

>> While burrowing deeply into folders, take note of the little arrows in File Explorer's top-left corner, just to the left of the Address bar. Click the little downward-pointing arrow, and a menu drops down, listing the folders you've plowed past on your journey. Click any name to jump quickly to that folder.

>> Click the Up Arrow button, located just to the left of the Address bar, to move your view up one folder. Keep clicking it, and you'll eventually wind up at someplace recognizable: your desktop.

>> Can't find a particular file or folder? Instead of aimlessly rummaging through folders, check out the Start menu's Search box, which I describe in Chapter 7. Also known as *Cortana*, the Search box can automatically find your lost files, folders, email, and nearly anything else hiding in your PC, as well as on the Internet.

>> When faced with a long list of alphabetically sorted files, click anywhere on the list. Then quickly type the first letter or two of the desired file's name. Windows immediately jumps up or down the list to the first name beginning with those letters.

>> Libraries, a sort of super folder introduced in Windows 7, vanished in Windows 8.1: Microsoft dropped them from the Navigation Pane, and they're still missing from Windows 10. If you miss them, add them back by right-clicking a *blank* portion of the Navigation Pane and choosing Show Libraries from the pop-up menu.

Creating a New Folder

To store new information in a file cabinet, you grab a manila folder, scrawl a name across the top, and start stuffing it with information. To store new information in Windows — notes for your autobiography, for example — you create a new folder, think up a name for the new folder, and start stuffing it with files.

To create a new folder quickly, click Home from the folder's toolbar buttons and choose New Folder from the Ribbon: A folder appears, ready for you to type in its name.

If the menus seem to be hiding, though, here's a quick and foolproof method:

1. **Right-click on a blank spot inside your folder (or on the desktop) and choose New.**

   The all-powerful right-click shoots a menu out the side.

2. **Choose Folder.**

   When you choose Folder, shown in Figure 5-6, a new folder quickly appears, waiting for you to type a new name.

3. **Type a new name for the folder.**

   A newly created folder bears the boring name of New Folder. When you begin typing, Windows quickly erases the old name and fills in your new name. Done? Save the new name by either pressing Enter or clicking somewhere away from the name you've just typed.

☀ AMD Catalyst Control Center	
View >	
Sort by >	
Refresh	
Paste	
Paste shortcut	
New >	Folder
🖵 Display settings	🔗 Shortcut
🖵 Personalize	🖼 Bitmap image
	📇 Contact
	📄 Rich Text Document
	📄 Text Document
	🗜 Compressed (zipped) Folder

FIGURE 5-6:
Right-click where you want a new folder to appear, choose New, and select Folder from the menu.

If you mess up the name and want to try again, right–click the folder, choose Rename, and start over.

» Certain symbols are banned from folder (and file) names. The "Using legal folder names and filenames" sidebar spells out the details, but you never have trouble when using plain old letters and numbers for names.

TIP

» Shrewd observers notice that in Figure 5-6 Windows offers to create many more things than just a folder when you click the New button. Right-click inside a folder anytime you want to create a new shortcut or other common item.

» Cautious observers may remark that their right-click menu looks different than the one shown in Figure 5-6. There's nothing wrong; programs and apps often add their own items to the right-click menus, making the menu look different on different PCs.

USING LEGAL FOLDER NAMES
AND FILENAMES

Windows is pretty picky about what you can and can't name a file or folder. If you stick to plain old letters and numbers, you're fine. But don't try to stick any of the following characters in there:

```
: / \ * | < > ? "
```

If you try to use any of those characters, Windows bounces an error message to the screen, and you have to try again. Here are some illegal filenames:

```
1/2 of my Homework
JOB:2
ONE<TWO
He's no "Gentleman"
```

These names are legal:

```
Half of my Term Paper
JOB=2
Two is Bigger than One
A #@$%) Scoundrel
```

Renaming a File or Folder

Sick of a filename or folder name? Then change it. Just right-click the offending icon and choose Rename from the menu that pops up. Windows highlights the file's old name, which disappears as you begin typing the new one. Press Enter or click the desktop when you're through, and you're off.

Or you can click the filename or folder name to select it, wait a second, and click the name again to change it. Some people click the name and press F2; Windows automatically lets you rename the file or folder.

> » When you rename a file, only its name changes. The contents are still the same, the file is still the same size, and the file is still in the same place.

» To rename large groups of files simultaneously, select them all, right-click the first one, and choose Rename. Type in the new name and press Enter, and Windows renames that file. However, it also renames all your other selected files to the new name, adding a number as it goes: cat, cat(2), cat(3), cat(4), and so on. It's a handy way to rename photographs.

» Renaming some folders confuses Windows, especially if those folders contain programs. And please don't rename your main folders: Downloads, Documents, Pictures, Music, or Videos.

» Windows won't let you rename a file or folder if one of your programs currently uses it. Sometimes closing the program fixes the problem. Other times, you need to restart your PC. That releases the program's clutches so you can rename it.

Selecting Bunches of Files or Folders

Although selecting a file, folder, or other object may seem particularly boring, it swings the doors wide open for further tasks: deleting, renaming, moving, copying, and performing other file–juggling tricks discussed in the rest of this chapter.

To select a single item, just click it. To select several files and folders, hold down the Ctrl key when you click the names or icons. Each name or icon stays highlighted when you click the next one.

To gather several files or folders sitting next to each other in a list, click the first one. Then hold down the Shift key as you click the last one. Those two items are highlighted, along with every file and folder sitting between them.

Windows lets you *lasso* desktop files and folders, as well. Point slightly above the first file or folder you want and then, while holding down the mouse button, point at the last file or folder. The mouse creates a colored lasso to surround your files. Let go of the mouse button, and the lasso disappears, leaving all the surrounded files highlighted.

» You can drag and drop armfuls of files in the same way that you drag a single file.

» You can also simultaneously cut or copy and paste these armfuls into new locations using any of the methods described in the "Copying or Moving Files and Folders" section, later in this chapter.

TIP

>> You can delete these armfuls of goods, too, with a press of the Delete key. (They all drop into the Recycle Bin and are available for emergency retrieval.)

>> To quickly select all the files in a folder, choose Select All from the folder's Edit menu. (No menu? Then select them by pressing Ctrl+A.) Here's another nifty trick: To grab all but a few files, press Ctrl+A, and while still holding down Ctrl, click the ones you don't want.

Getting Rid of a File or Folder

Sooner or later, you'll want to delete a file that's no longer important — yesterday's lottery picks, for example, or a particularly embarrassing digital photo. To delete a file or folder, right-click its name or icon. Then choose Delete from the pop-up menu. This surprisingly simple trick works for files, folders, shortcuts, and just about anything else in Windows.

To delete in a hurry, click the offending object and press the Delete key. Dragging and dropping a file or folder to the Recycle Bin does the same thing.

WARNING

The Delete option deletes entire folders, including any files or folders stuffed *inside* those folders. Make sure that you select the correct folder before you choose Delete.

NEW

>> Unlike earlier Windows versions, Windows 10 doesn't toss a box in your face, asking whether you're *sure* you want to delete the file. If you prefer being asked, right-click the Recycle Bin, choose Properties, and place a check mark next to Display Delete Confirmation Dialog.

>> Be extra sure that you know what you're doing when deleting any file that depicts a little gear in its icon. These files are usually sensitive hidden files that belong to apps or programs, and the computer wants you to leave them alone. (Other than that, they're not particularly exciting, despite the action-oriented gears.)

>> Icons with little arrows in their corner (like the one in the margin) are shortcuts, which are push buttons that merely load files. (I cover shortcuts in Chapter 6.) Deleting shortcuts deletes only a button that loads a file or program. The file or program itself remains undamaged and still lives inside your computer.

>> As soon as you find out how to delete files, trot off to Chapter 3, which explains several ways to *un*delete them. (***Hint for the desperate:*** Open the Recycle Bin, right-click your file's name, and choose Restore.)

TECHNICAL STUFF

DON'T BOTHER READING THIS HIDDEN TECHNICAL STUFF

You're not the only one creating files on your computer. Programs often store their own information in a *data file*. They may need to store information about the way your computer is set up, for example. To keep people from confusing those files for trash and deleting them, Windows hides them.

However, if you want to play voyeur, you can view the names of these hidden files and folders:

1. Open any folder and click the View tab from along the top edge.

The Ribbon changes to show different ways you can view that folder's files.

2. Select the checkbox named Hidden Items.

Don't see the Hidden Items checkbox? Make the folder's window a little wider until that option appears in the Ribbon's Show/Hide section.

These steps expose the hidden files alongside the other filenames. Be sure not to delete them, however: The programs that created them will gag, possibly damaging them or Windows itself. To avoid trouble, deselect the Hidden Items checkbox again to drape the veil of secrecy back over those important files.

Copying or Moving Files and Folders

To copy or move files to different folders on your hard drive, it's sometimes easiest to use your mouse to *drag* them there. For example, here's how to move a file to a different folder on your desktop. In this case, I'm moving the Traveler file from the House folder to the Morocco folder.

1. Align the two windows next to each other.

I explain this in Chapter 4. If you skipped that chapter, try this: Click the first window and then hold the ⊞+key and press the right-arrow key. To fill the screen's left half, click the other window, hold the ⊞+key, and press the left-arrow key.

2. Aim the mouse pointer at the file or folder you want to move.

In my example, I point at the Traveler file.

3. **While holding down the right mouse button, move the mouse until it points at the destination folder.**

As you see in Figure 5-7, I'm dragging the Traveler file from the House folder to the Morocco folder.

Moving the mouse drags the file along with it, and Windows explains that you're moving the file, as shown in Figure 5-7. (Be sure to hold down the right mouse button the entire time.)

REMEMBER

Always drag icons while holding down the *right* mouse button. Windows is then gracious enough to give you a menu of options when you position the icon, and you can choose to copy, move, or create a shortcut. If you hold down the *left* mouse button, Windows sometimes doesn't know whether you want to copy or move.

4. **Release the mouse button and choose Copy Here, Move Here, or Create Shortcuts Here from the pop-up menu.**

FIGURE 5-7:
To move a file or folder from one window to another, drag it there while holding down the right mouse button.

When dragging and dropping takes too much work, Windows offers a few other ways to copy or move files. Depending on your screen's current layout, some of the following onscreen tools may work more easily:

» **Right-click menus:** Right-click a file or folder and choose Cut or Copy, depending on whether you want to move or copy it. Then right-click inside your destination folder and choose Paste. It's simple, it always works, and you needn't bother placing any windows side by side.

>> **Ribbon commands:** In File Explorer, click your file or folder, click the Ribbon's Home tab at the top, and then click the Copy To (or Move To) button. A menu drops down, listing some common locations. Don't spot the right spot? Then click Choose Location and click through the drive and folders to reach the destination folder, and Windows transports the file accordingly. Although a bit cumbersome, this method works if you know the exact location of the destination folder.

I explain more about the Ribbon in Chapter 4.

>> **Navigation Pane:** Described in Chapter 4, this panel along File Explorer's left edge lists popular locations: drives, networks, OneDrive, and oft-used folders. That lets you drag and drop items into a folder on the Navigation Pane, sparing you the hassle of opening a destination folder.

WARNING

After you install a program on your computer, don't ever move that program's folder. Programs wedge themselves deeply into Windows. Moving the program may break it, and you'll have to reinstall it. However, feel free to move a program's *shortcut.* (Shortcut icons contain a little arrow in their lower-left corner.)

Seeing More Information about Files and Folders

Whenever you create a file or folder, Windows scrawls a bunch of secret hidden information on it, such as the date you created it, its size, and even more trivial stuff. Sometimes Windows even lets you add your own secret information, including reviews for your music files or thumbnail pictures for any of your folders.

You can safely ignore most of the information. Other times, tweaking that information is the only way to solve a problem.

To see what Windows is calling your files and folders behind your back, right-click the item and choose Properties from the pop-up menu. Choosing Properties on a song, for example, brings up bunches of details, as shown in Figure 5-8. Here's what each tab means:

>> **General:** This first tab (far left in Figure 5-8) shows the file's *type* (an MP3 file of the song "Getting Better"), its *size* (6.42MB), the program that *opens* it (in this case, the Groove Music app), and the file's *location.*

TIP

TECHNICAL STUFF

Want a different program to open your file? Right-click the file, choose Properties, and click the Change button on the General tab, shown in Figure 5-8. A list of your computer's available music players appears, letting you choose your preferred program.

» **Security:** On this tab, you control *permissions,* which are rules determining who can access the file and what they can do with it. System administrators earn high wages mostly for understanding this type of stuff.

» **Details:** True to its name, this tab reveals arcane details about a file. On digital photos, for example, this tab lists EXIF (Exchangeable Image File Format) data: the camera model, f-stop, aperture, focal length, and other items loved by photographers. On songs, this tab displays the song's *ID3 tag* (IDentify MP3), which includes the artist, album title, year, track number, genre, length, and similar information.

» **Previous Versions:** After you set up the Windows File History backup system, this tab lists all the previously saved versions of this file, ready for retrieval with a click. I cover File History in Chapter 13.

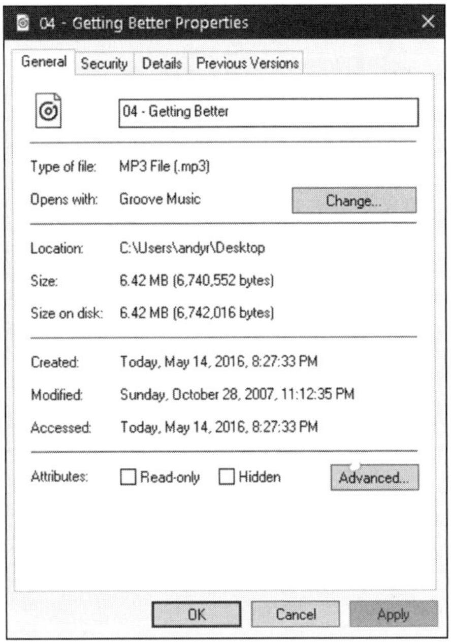

FIGURE 5-8:
A file's Properties dialog box shows which program automatically opens it, the file's size, and other details.

04 - Getting Better Properties	✕

General | Security | Details | Previous Versions

04 - Getting Better

Type of file: MP3 File (.mp3)

Opens with: Groove Music   [Change...]

Location: C:\Users\andyr\Desktop

Size: 6.42 MB (6,740,552 bytes)

Size on disk: 6.42 MB (6,742,016 bytes)

Created: Today, May 14, 2016, 8:27:33 PM

Modified: Sunday, October 28, 2007, 11:12:35 PM

Accessed: Today, May 14, 2016, 8:27:33 PM

Attributes: ☐ Read-only ☐ Hidden [Advanced...]

[OK] [Cancel] [Apply]

Normally, these tidbits of information remain hidden unless you right-click a file or folder and choose Properties. But what if you want to see details about all the files in a folder, perhaps to find pictures taken on a certain day? For that, switch your folder's view to Details by following these steps:

1. **Click the View tab on the Ribbon along the folder's top edge.**

   A menu appears, listing the umpteen ways a folder can display your files.

2. **In the Layout group, select Details, as shown in Figure 5-9.**

   The screen changes to show your files' names, with details about them stretching to the right in orderly columns.

Try all the views to see which view you prefer. (Windows remembers which views you prefer for different folders.)

» If you can't remember what a folder's toolbar buttons do, rest your mouse pointer over a button. Windows displays a helpful box summing up the button's mission.

» Switch among the different views until you find the one that fits what you're trying to accomplish, be it to see a particular photo's creation date or see thumbnails of every photo in a folder.

» Folders usually display files sorted alphabetically. To sort them differently, right-click a blank spot inside the folder and choose Sort By. A pop-up menu lets you choose to sort items by size, name, type, and other details.

TIP

>> When the excitement of the Sort By menu wears off, try clicking the words at the top of each sorted column. Click Size, for example, to reverse the order, placing the largest files at the list's top.

TIP

>> Feel free to add your own columns to Details view: Right-click a column header you don't need, and a drop-down menu appears, letting you choose a different criterion. (I always add a Date Taken column to my photos, so I can sort my photos by the date I snapped them.)

Writing to CDs and DVDs

Most computers today write information to CDs and DVDs by using a flameless approach known as *burning.* To see whether you're stuck with an older drive that can't burn discs, first remove any discs from inside the drive. Then from the desktop, click the taskbar's File Explorer icon and look at the icon for your CD or DVD drive.

Because computers always speak in secret code, here's what you can do with the disc drives in your computer:

>> **DVD-RW:** These drives both read and write to CDs *and* DVDs.

>> **BD-ROM:** These can read and write to CDs and DVDs, plus they can read Blu-ray discs.

>> **BD-RE:** Although these have the same icon as BD-ROM drives, they can read and write to CDs, DVDs, *and* Blu-ray discs.

TECHNICAL STUFF

If your PC has two CD or DVD burners, tell Windows which drive you want to handle your disc-burning chores: Right-click the drive, choose Properties, and click the Recording tab. Then choose your favorite drive in the top box.

Buying the right kind of blank CDs and DVDs for burning

Stores sell two types of CDs: CD-R (short for CD–Recordable) and CD-RW (short for CD–ReWritable). Here's the difference:

>> **CD-R:** Most people buy CD-Rs because they're very cheap and they work fine for storing music or files. You can write to them until they fill up; then you can't write to them anymore. But that's no problem because most people

don't want to erase their CDs and start over. They want to stick their burned disc into the car's stereo or stash it as a backup.

» **CD-RW:** Techies sometimes buy CD-RWs for making temporary backups of data. You can write information to them, just as you can with CD-Rs. But when a CD-RW fills up, you can erase it and start over with a clean slate — something not possible with a CD-R. However, CD-RWs cost more money, so most people stick with the cheaper and faster CD-Rs.

DVDs come in both R and RW formats, just like CDs, so the preceding R and RW rules apply to them, as well. Most DVD burners sold in the past few years can write to any type of blank CD or DVD.

TECHNICAL STUFF

Buying blank DVDs for older drives is chaos: The manufacturers fought over which storage format to use, confusing things for everybody. To buy the right blank DVD, check your computer's receipt to see what formats its DVD burner needs: DVD-R, DVD-RW, DVD+R, or DVD+RW.

» Discs come rated by their speed. For faster disc burning, buy the largest number "x" speed you can find, usually 52x for CDs and 16x for DVDs.

» Blank CDs and DVDs are cheap; borrow one from a neighbor's kid to see whether it works in your drive. If it works fine, buy some of the same type.

» Blank Blu-ray discs cost a lot more than CDs or DVDs. Luckily, Blu-ray drives aren't very picky, and just about any blank Blu-ray disc will work.

» For some odd reason, Compact Discs and Digital Video Discs are spelled as discs, not disks.

» Although Windows can handle simple disc-burning tasks, it's extraordinarily awkward at duplicating discs. Most people give up quickly and buy third-party disc-burning software. I explain how Windows creates music CDs in Chapter 16.

» It's currently illegal to make duplicates of movie DVDs in the United States — even to make a backup copy in case the kids scratch up the new Disney DVD. Windows can't copy DVDs on its own, but some programs on websites from other countries can handle the job.

Copying files to or from a CD or DVD

CDs and DVDs once hailed from the school of simplicity: You simply slid them into your CD player or DVD player, and they played. But as soon as those discs graduated to PCs, the problems started. When you create a CD or DVD, you must tell your PC *what* you're copying and *where* you intend to play it: Music for a CD player? Photo slideshows for a TV's DVD player? Or files to store on your computer?

If you choose the wrong answer, your disc won't work, and you've created yet another coaster.

Here are the Disc Creation rules:

>> **Music:** To create a CD that plays music in your CD player or car stereo, flip ahead to Chapter 16. You need to fire up the age-old Windows Media Player program and burn an *audio CD.*

>> **Photo slideshows:** Windows doesn't include the Windows DVD Maker bundled with Windows Vista and Windows 7. To create photo slideshows on a DVD, you need a third-party program. If one didn't come with your computer, you need to purchase one.

If you just want to copy *files* to a CD or DVD, perhaps to save as a backup or to give to a friend, stick around.

Follow these steps to write files to a new blank CD or DVD. (If you're writing files to a CD or DVD that you've written to before, jump ahead to Step 4.)

1. **Insert the blank disc into your disc burner and push in the tray. Then click or tap the Notification box that appears in the screen's bottom-right corner.**

2. **When the Notification box asks how you'd like to proceed, click the box's Burn Files to a Disc option.**

   Windows displays a Burn a Disc dialog box and asks you to create a title for the disc.

   If the Notification box disappeared before you could click on it, eject your disc, push it back in, and have your hand ready on the mouse. (Alternatively, you can bring back the Notification box by right-clicking the disc drive's icon in File Explorer and choosing the Open Autoplay option.)

3. **Type a name for the disc, describe how you want to use the disc, and click Next.**

   Unfortunately, Windows limits your CD's or DVD's title to 16 characters. Instead of typing **Family Picnic atop Orizaba in 2018**, stick to the facts: **Orizaba 2018**. Or, just click Next to use the default name for the disc: the current date.

Windows can burn the files to the disc two different ways. To help you decide which method will work best for you, the Windows menu offers two options:

- **Like a USB flash drive:** This method lets you read and write files to the disc many times, a handy way to use discs as portable file carriers. Unfortunately, that method isn't compatible with some CD or DVD players connected to home stereos or TVs.

- **With a CD/DVD player:** If you plan to play your disc on a fairly new home stereo disc player that's smart enough to read files stored in several different formats, select this method.

Armed with the disc's name, Windows prepares the disc for incoming files.

4. **Tell Windows which files to write to disc.**

Now that your disc is ready to accept the files, tell Windows what information to send its way. You can do this in any of several ways:

- Drag and drop your files and/or folders into the drive's File Explorer window.

- Right-click the item you want to copy, be it a single file, folder, or selected files and folders. When the pop-up menu appears, choose Send To and select your disc burner from the menu. (The pop-up menu lists the disc's title you chose in Step 3.)

- Drag and drop files and/or folders on top of the burner's icon in File Explorer.

- From your Music, Pictures, or Documents folder, click the Share tab and then click Burn to Disc. This button copies all of that folder's files (or just the files you've selected) to the disc as files.

- Tell your current program to save the information to the disc rather than to your hard drive.

No matter which method you choose, Windows dutifully looks over the information and copies it to the disc you inserted in the first step. A progress window appears, showing the disc burner's progress. When the progress window disappears, Windows has finished burning the disc.

5. **Close your disc-burning session by ejecting the disc.**

When you're through copying files to the disc, push your drive's Eject button (or right-click the drive's icon in File Explorer and choose Eject). Windows closes the session, adding a finishing touch to the disc that lets other PCs read it.

TIP

If you try to copy a large batch of files to a disc — more than will fit — Windows complains immediately. Copy fewer files at a time, perhaps spacing them out over two discs.

DUPLICATING A CD OR DVD

Windows doesn't include any way to duplicate a CD, DVD, or Blu-ray disc. It can't even make a copy of a music CD. (That's why so many people buy CD-burning programs.)

But it can copy all of a CD's or DVD's files to a blank disc by using this two-step process:

1. **Copy the files and folders from the CD or DVD to a folder on your PC.**

2. **Copy those same files and folders back to a blank CD or DVD.**

That gives you a duplicate CD or DVD, which is handy when you need a second copy of an essential backup disc.

You can try this process on a music CD or DVD movie, but it won't work. (I tried.) It works only when you're duplicating a disc containing data files.

Most programs let you save files directly to disc. Choose Save from the File menu and select your CD burner. Put a disc (preferably one that's not already filled) into your disc drive to start the process.

Working with Flash Drives and Memory Cards

Digital camera owners eventually become acquainted with *memory cards* — those little plastic squares that replaced the awkward rolls of film. Windows can read digital photos directly from the camera after you find its cable and plug it into your PC. But Windows can also grab photos straight off the memory card, a method praised by those who've lost their camera's cables.

The secret is a *memory card reader* — a little slot-filled box that stays plugged into your PC. Slide your memory card into the slot, and your PC can read the card's files, just like reading files from any other folder. Some tablets, laptops, and PCs include built-in memory card readers.

Most office supply and electronics stores sell memory card readers that accept most popular memory card formats: Compact Flash, SecureDigital High Capacity (SDHC), Micro-SecureDigital High Capacity (SDHC), Micro-SecureDigital Extended Capacity (SDXC), and a host of other tongue twisters. Some computers even come with built-in memory card readers on the front of their case.

The beauty of card readers is that there's nothing new to figure out: Windows treats your inserted card just like an ordinary folder. Insert your card, and a folder appears on your screen to show your digital camera photos. The same drag-and-drop and cut-and-paste rules covered earlier in this chapter still apply, letting you move the pictures or other files off the card and into your Pictures folder.

Flash drives — also known as *thumbdrives* — work just like memory card readers. Plug the flash drive into one of your PC's USB ports, and the drive appears as an icon (shown in the margin) in File Explorer, ready to be opened with a double-click. Skip back to this chapter's "Copying or Moving Files and Folders" section for step-by-step instructions on transferring the flash drive's contents to your PC.

WARNING

>> First, the warning: Formatting a card or flash drive wipes out all its information. Never format a card or flash drive unless you don't care about the information it currently holds.

>> Now, the procedure: If Windows complains that a newly inserted card isn't formatted, right-click its drive and choose Format. (This problem happens most often with brand-new or damaged cards.)

>> Most smartphones and tablets contain memory card slots, as well. Their cards work the same as the ones found in digital cameras.

OneDrive: Your Cubbyhole in the Clouds

When you're sitting in front of your computer, you naturally store your files inside your computer. It's the easiest place to put them. When you leave your computer, you can bring along important files by stashing them on flash drives, CDs, DVDs, and portable hard drives — if you remember to grab them on the way out.

But how can you access your files from *any* of your computers, even if you've forgotten to bring along the files? How can you grab your home files from work, and vice versa? How can you view an important document or hear some favorite tunes while traveling? How can you grab your PC's files with your smartphone?

Microsoft's answer to those questions is called *OneDrive*. It's your own private file storage space on the Internet, and it's built into Windows 10. With OneDrive, your files are available from any computer with an Internet connection. You can even grab them from phones or tablets from Apple, Android, Blackberry, or Windows: Microsoft offers a free OneDrive app for all of them.

If you change a file stored on OneDrive, that updated file is available on *all* your computers and devices. OneDrive automatically keeps everything in sync. You only need the following things in order to put OneDrive to work:

>> **Microsoft account:** You need a Microsoft account in order to upload, view, or retrieve your files from OneDrive. Chances are good that you created a Microsoft account when you first created your account on your Windows PC. (I describe Microsoft accounts in Chapter 2.)

>> **An Internet connection:** Without an Internet signal, either wireless or wired, your web-stashed files remain floating in the clouds, away from you and your computer. (You can avoid that problem by choosing to keep all of your OneDrive files stored on your computer as well as the Cloud.)

>> **Patience:** Uploading files takes longer than downloading files. Although you can upload small files fairly quickly, larger files such as digital photos or movies take much longer to upload.

For some people, OneDrive offers a safe Internet haven, sometimes called the "cloud," where they can always find their most important files. For others, OneDrive brings another layer of complication, as well as another possible hiding place for that missing file.

The following sections explain how to access OneDrive from within Windows 10, as well as from a web browser on any other PC or device. They also explain how to tweak OneDrive's many settings so it works perfectly on both desktop PCs, laptops, and tiny tablets.

Setting up OneDrive

Windows 10 places a link to OneDrive in every folder's Navigation Pane, where it's easily accessible. There, OneDrive works like any other folder but with one exception: Files and folders you place inside your OneDrive folder are also copied to your OneDrive storage space on the Internet.

That can create a problem: Today's smaller phones, tablets, and laptops don't include much storage space. OneDrive, by contrast, can hold *lots* of files. Some smaller computers, usually small tablets, don't have enough room to keep a copy of *everything* you've packed away on your desktop PC's OneDrive folder.

To meet everybody's needs, OneDrive can work in either of these three ways:

>> **All files:** The simplest option, and the one chosen by most desktop PC owners, this puts all your OneDrive files on both the Internet and your

PC. Then, it keeps them all in sync: Update a file on your PC, and it's updated on the Internet, and vice versa. It's a convenient way to keep your most important files instantly accessible and always backed up.

>> **Some files:** Designed for devices with limited amounts of storage like some tablets and laptops, this lets you pick and choose which folders should live only on OneDrive, and which should also be stored on your computer, too.

>> **Files On Demand:** The best option for people with limited storage space, this lets your PC display names of *all* your OneDrive files and folders. Then, when you open a file or folder, Windows quickly downloads it to your device for you to display its contents. It requires an Internet connection, and it's a little slower, but it lets you access any of your OneDrive files without them all hogging your PC's storage space.

When you first click the OneDrive folder on a new PC, Windows begins the set-up process, described in the steps listed below. If you've already set up OneDrive, but want to change its settings, skip ahead to the next section, "Changing your OneDrive settings."

To set up OneDrive on a new PC, follow these steps:

1. **From the taskbar, click the File Explorer icon and click the OneDrive icon in the folder's left edge.**

   Since this is the first time you've set up OneDrive on the computer, OneDrive displays an opening screen.

2. **If asked, sign in with your Microsoft account and password.**

   Only Local account holders will need to sign in; Microsoft account holders already sign in when they sign into their user account. (I describe how to convert a Local account into a Microsoft account in Chapter 14.)

   Local account holders can sign in with any Microsoft account. They don't need to convert their account to a Microsoft account.

   After you enter a Microsoft account name and password, a window appears, pointing out the location of your OneDrive folder.

3. **If you want to change where to store your OneDrive files, click the Change Location button. Otherwise, click the Next button.**

   If you're using a desktop PC with plenty of storage space, just click the Next button. OneDrive will store all your OneDrive files on your C drive, which normally has plenty of room.

Inexpensive tablets and laptops, by contrast, contain very limited storage space. To add more storage, many tablet owners buy a memory card and slide it into their tablet's memory slot. If you've bought and inserted a memory card into your tiny tablet, click this window's Change Location button and tell OneDrive to save its files on your tablet's memory card instead of the default C drive. (The memory card is usually called the D drive.)

If an advertisement appears, asking you to increase your storage for a monthly fee, click the words Not Now. (You can always change your mind later.)

4. **If asked, choose which folders to sync to your PC.**

   OneDrive lists your existing OneDrive folders, if you have any, as shown in Figure 5-10.

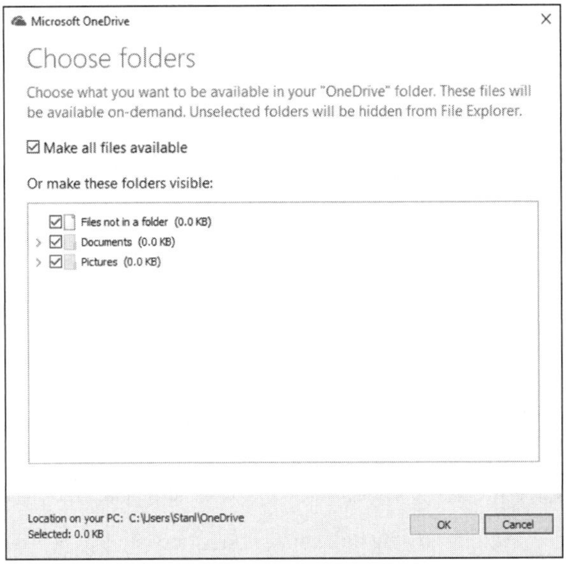

FIGURE 5-10:
Place a check mark next to the folders you want to stay on both your computer *and* OneDrive.

5. **Select the files and folders you'd like to keep synced between your PC and OneDrive, then click the Next button.**

   OneDrive gives you two options, which you can change later:

   ● **Sync All Files and Folders in my OneDrive:** Unless you have a reason not to, select this option to keep all your OneDrive files mirrored on your PC's or tablet's memory card. Most desktop PCs won't have a problem with this option, and it's the most trouble-free way to access OneDrive.

- **Sync Only These Folders:** Select this option on tablets or PCs with very little storage. If you select this option, place a check mark next to the folders you consider to be essential enough to warrant storage both on your PC and OneDrive.

6. **Click Next to save your changes.**

   OneDrive leaves you with an Open my OneDrive Folder button which you can click to see the results of your file syncing decisions.

Feel free to sync different folders on different computers. For example, you can choose to sync only the essentials on your small tablet — perhaps just your photos. On a desktop PC with large storage, you can choose to sync everything.

NEW

In Spring, 2018, Windows 10 began offering a new, third way to set up OneDrive that mixes the two options described above. This new way is called *OneDrive Files On Demand.* I describe its pros and cons in an upcoming section, "Customizing OneDrive for different devices with OneDrive Files On Demand."

Changing your OneDrive settings

Windows usually guesses your correct settings when you first set up OneDrive. To revisit your OneDrive settings and ensure that they're set correctly for your particular computer or other device, follow these steps:

1. **From the taskbar's notification area, right-click the OneDrive icon and choose Settings.**

   You may need to click the little upward-pointing arrow in the notification area to see the OneDrive icon (shown in the margin). I cover the taskbar's notification area — the tiny icon-filled area to the taskbar's far right — in Chapter 3.

   OneDrive's Settings dialog box appears, as shown in Figure 5-11, open to the Account tab.

2. **To change which files should live both on your PC and on OneDrive, click the Choose Folders button.**

   The Sync Your OneDrive Files to This PC window opens, listing all your OneDrive folders, as shown earlier in Figure 5-10.

3. **Make any changes, and click the OK button.**

   This area lets you adjust which of your PC's folders live only on your PC, only on the Internet, or on both.

FIGURE 5-11:
The Microsoft
OneDrive Settings
dialog box lets
you change how
OneDrive
communicates
with your
computer.

The Microsoft OneDrive Settings window opens to the Account tab, shown in Figure 5-11, but these other tabs are also worth exploring:

» **Settings:** A check box here lets you tell OneDrive to start syncing automatically when you log in to Windows. Another check box lets you use OneDrive to fetch any files on your PC, a handy option I describe in the "Accessing Your Desktop PC from the Internet" sidebar later in this chapter. This area also lets you turn on the new Windows 10 OneDrive Files On Demand, a feature I cover in this chapter's next section. (I keep all these checkboxes turned on.)

» **Auto Save:** This tab lets you choose whether all your new work should automatically be saved on your PC or in the cloud on OneDrive. It's a decision required only by people who don't keep all their files synced with OneDrive.

» **Network:** Designed for people without speedy Internet connections, this lets you control how quickly OneDrive should sync. Unless you have good reason, keep this set to Don't Limit.

» **Office:** This tab lets you control how OneDrive interacts with documents created in Office, Microsoft's suite of software that includes Outlook, Word, Excel, and other popular programs.

» **About:** Probably tossed in by the legal department, this offers links to Microsoft's pages of legalese: Terms of Use and its Privacy and Cookies policy. For OneDrive troubleshooting information, click the Get Help with OneDrive link.

When you click the window's OK button, OneDrive begins syncing your files and folders according to your changes.

When rolling out OneDrive, Microsoft gave everybody 15GB of free OneDrive storage space, but Microsoft subsequently reduced the amount to only 5GB. (You can increase that amount by paying a monthly fee.)

The Accounts tab shown in Figure 5-11 also shows your amount of available OneDrive storage space, as well as offers a Get More Storage link in case you're running low on space.

Opening and saving files from OneDrive

When you first sign into Windows 10 with a new Microsoft Account, Windows stocks your OneDrive with two empty folders: Documents and Photos.

To see the two folders, open any folder. Don't have a folder open? Then click the File Explorer icon (shown in the margin) on the taskbar. OneDrive is listed in the folder's Navigation Pane along the left edge. Click the word OneDrive, and OneDrive's contents spill out into the folder's right side. You can see the two empty folders, named Documents and Photos. If you already have a OneDrive account, you see your existing OneDrive folders, instead. You have nothing new to learn with OneDrive; its folders work like any other folder on your computer:

>> To view the contents of a OneDrive folder, double-click it. The folder opens to show its contents.

>> To edit a file stored in a OneDrive folder, double-click it. The file opens in the program that created it.

>> To save something new inside a OneDrive folder, save it to a folder inside OneDrive — its Documents folder, for example. Don't just save it to the Documents folder on your PC.

>> To delete something from OneDrive, right-click it and choose Delete. The item moves to your desktop's Recycle Bin, where it can be retrieved later if necessary.

No matter what changes you make to your files and folders in your computer's OneDrive folder, Windows 10 automatically changes the Internet's copies to match.

Later, when you visit OneDrive through anything with a Web browser — your smartphone, tablet, or even another PC — your up-to-date files will be waiting for you to peruse.

>> By storing a shopping list on OneDrive, you can add needed grocery items while sitting at your PC. Then, when you're at the store, you can view that up-to-date shopping list on your phone. (Microsoft makes OneDrive apps for iPhones and Android phones, as well as phones from Blackberry and Windows.)

>> Want to copy a few favorites to your OneDrive folder? I describe how to copy and move files between folders earlier in this chapter.

>> To share a OneDrive file or folder with friends, right-click it and choose Share a OneDrive link. Windows copies a link to the file to the Clipboard, where you can paste it into an email. When your friends click the emailed link, they'll have access to your OneDrive-stored file or folder.

>> Many people keep a few desert island discs on OneDrive. Whenever you have an Internet connection, the Windows 10 Groove Music app, covered in Chapter 16, automatically lists and plays any music you store on OneDrive. (The old school Media Player program, by contrast, plays only the music stored physically on your PC.)

Customizing OneDrive for different devices with OneDrive Files On Demand

When you first set up OneDrive, it offers only two options: You can copy every folder to your OneDrive online cubbyhole, or just copy a few important folders.

This works well for most devices, but some people need more options. For example, if you choose to sync only a handful of folders, the rest of your folders remain invisible: You won't be able to see them on your PC, even if you need them at a later date.

Windows 10 fixes that complaint. Dubbed "Files On Demand," this feature lets you see the names of every file and folder you've stored on OneDrive. Then, you can quickly open a OneDrive file or folder even if it's not stored locally on your PC. OneDrive simply grabs the file from the Internet and places it onto your computer. (This depends on your having a working Internet connection at the time, of course.)

OneDrive's new Files On Demand feature lets you see all your files on all your devices. Yet, it lets you save space on devices that don't have much storage space. For example, you can sync your entire music collection only on devices with a lot of storage spaces. But your device that lacks storage can still see the music and, if you have an Internet connection, listen to it whenever you like.

You can even see thumbnails of more than 270 different file types — even if they're not stored on your computer.

To turn on OneDrive Files On Demand, follow these steps:

1. **From the taskbar's notification area, right-click the OneDrive icon and choose Settings.**

   You may need to click the little upward-pointing arrow in the notification area to see the OneDrive icon (shown in the margin). I cover the taskbar's notification area — the tiny icon-filled area to the taskbar's far right — in Chapter 3.

   OneDrive's Settings dialog box appears, as shown earlier in Figure 5-11, open to the Account tab.

2. **Click the Settings tab, and in the Files On Demand section, select the Save Space and Download Files as You Use Them check box.**

3. **Click the OK button to close the window.**

Now, even though your OneDrive files aren't saved on your PC, you can see their names, as shown in Figure 5-12.

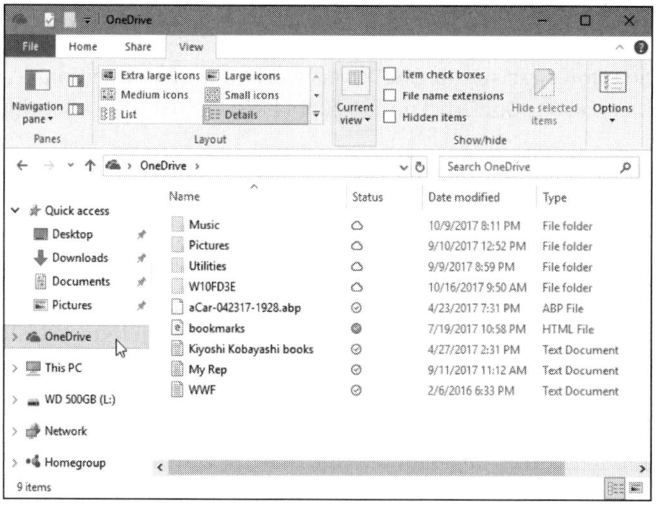

FIGURE 5-12: OneDrive Files On Demand shows the name of every stored file and folder, as well as its status.

The key to understanding OneDrive Files On Demand is to look at the three little icons next to each file's name, shown in Figure 5-12. Here is what each icon means:

» **Online only:** This file is available online only; you need an Internet connection in order to access it.

» **Locally available:** You've opened an online only file, so now it's available on your PC. Any edits you make will also change the copy stored on OneDrive. If you need to free up space and remove it from your PC, right-click it and choose Free Up Space. (A copy will remain on OneDrive, and the file's icon on your PC will change to Online Only.)

» **Always keep on this device:** Files and folders with this icon are always available on your PC, even without an Internet connection.

To change the status of a file or folder, right-click it. There, you can choose between these three settings:

» **View Online:** This downloads your file or folder to your PC and opens it for you to view or edit.

» **Always Keep On This Device:** This also downloads the file or folder to your PC. However, it doesn't open it. It's handy mostly for grabbing folders that you always want to have available, even without an Internet connection.

» **Free Up Space:** This deletes the file from your device, which frees up storage space. It keeps that file stored on OneDrive, though, where you can fetch it again whenever you have an Internet connection.

TIP

These tips will help you discover whether OneDrive Files On Demand is worth turning on, and how to use it on different devices:

» If your device has plenty of storage space, as do most desktop PCs, don't bother with Files On Demand. Simply choose Make All Files Available, described earlier in this chapter's "Setting Up OneDrive" section.

» If your device doesn't have much storage, but you want to see the names of all your OneDrive files and folders, turn on OneDrive Files On Demand. Then, when you have an Internet connection and need a file or folder, just open it, as if it lived on your PC. Windows will quickly download and open it.

» If you store a lot of music or videos on OneDrive, you may want to turn on OneDrive Files On Demand. That way you can see every file and access them when you have an Internet connection, but you needn't store all of them on that device.

By assessing your needs, your device's storage limits, and the availability of your Internet connection, you can customize OneDrive's Files On Demand feature to meet each of your device's needs.

ACCESSING YOUR DESKTOP PC FROM THE INTERNET

OneDrive makes sharing files with all your gadgets pretty easy. But what if the file you need *isn't* stored on OneDrive? What if it's sitting on the desktop of your Windows 10 PC back home?

Here's a solution: You can make *all* your PC's files and folders available from the OneDrive website. Right-click your taskbar's OneDrive icon, choose Settings, and, when the Settings window appears, click the Settings tab. Then, select the check box labeled Let Me Use OneDrive to Fetch Any of My Files on This PC.

Selecting that check box lets you access *your entire PC* from the OneDrive website. That's right: You can drop by the OneDrive website to grab *any* of your PC's files and folders, even if they're not shared on OneDrive. You can even access files and folders stored on networks accessible from that PC.

Since you're accessing files stored on your *own* PC rather than on Microsoft's cloud service, this doesn't affect your OneDrive storage limit.

Naturally, Microsoft took some security precautions with such a bold move. Before letting you access a new PC for the first time, OneDrive asks you to type in a code.

In the background, Microsoft sends a text message to the cellphone or email associated with your Microsoft account. When you receive the message, you type it into the computer you're using to access the PC. When Microsoft receives the matching code, it adds that PC to your list of accessible PCs.

You can access only a Windows 7, 8, or 10 PC that's turned on, running OneDrive, and connected to the Internet. If you're planning on using this handy OneDrive feature, be sure to enter your cellphone number as a verifier when setting up your Microsoft account.

Accessing OneDrive from the Internet

Sometimes you may need to access OneDrive when you're not sitting in front of your computer. Or, you may need to reach a OneDrive file that's not synced on your PC. To help you in either situation, Microsoft offers OneDrive access from any Internet browser.

When you need your files, drop by any computer, visit the OneDrive website at `https://OneDrive.live.com`, and, if asked, sign in with your Microsoft account name and password. The OneDrive website appears, shown in Figure 5-13.

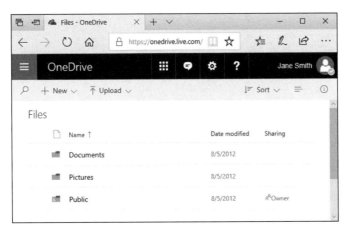

FIGURE 5-13:
You can access your OneDrive files from any computer or device with a web browser.

After you sign in to the OneDrive website, you can add, delete, move, and rename files, as well as create folders and move files between folders. You can even edit some files directly online. (OneDrive even contains a Recycle Bin for retrieving mistakenly deleted files, whether they were deleted online or on your phone, PC, or other device.)

It's much easier to manage your files directly from the folder on your computer. But if you're away from your computer, the OneDrive website provides a handy fallback zone.

The OneDrive website also lets you share files by emailing people links to them, making it a handy way to share folders.

TIP

You can also share OneDrive files with friends directly from your PC: Right-click the file or folder you want to share, and choose Share a OneDrive link. Windows copies a link to the item to your Clipboard, where you can paste it into an e-mail for sharing. When the recipient clicks the link in the email, he's taken online to view the file or folder's contents.

REMEMBER

If you find yourself using OneDrive regularly, take note that Microsoft offers free OneDrive apps for Apple, Android, and Windows smartphones and tablets. OneDrive simplifies file sharing among all your gadgets.

2
Working with Programs, Apps, and Files

IN THIS CHAPTER

» Opening a program, an app, or a document

» Changing which program opens which document

» Installing, uninstalling, and updating apps

» Creating a shortcut

» Cutting, copying, and pasting

Chapter **6**

Playing with Programs, Apps, and Documents

n Windows, *programs* and *apps* are your tools: Load a program or an app, and you can add numbers, arrange words, and shoot spaceships.

Documents, by contrast, are the things you create with apps and programs, such as tax forms, heartfelt apologies, and lists of high scores.

This chapter explains the basics of opening programs and apps from the Start menu in Windows. It explains how to find, download, and install a new app from the Start menu's Store app. It also shows you where to find an app's menus. (Microsoft mysteriously hid most of them.)

As you flip through this chapter's pages, you figure out how to make your *preferred* program open your files. You also create desktop *shortcuts* — buttons that let you quickly load favorite files, folders, and programs.

The chapter ends with the "Absolutely Essential Guide to Cutting, Copying, and Pasting." Put this one trick under your belt, and you'll know how to manipulate words on a word processor, move files between folders, copy files from your camera to your PC, and send files to and from flash drives.

Starting a Program or an App

Windows 10 returns the Start button and menu to their age-old spot in the desktop's bottom-left corner. A click of the Start button brings you the Start menu's latest incarnation, complete with a band of apps clinging to its right side and a string of unlabeled icons along the left. (On touchscreen computers, the Start menu fills the entire screen by default.)

I explain the new Start menu, shown in Figure 6-1, in Chapter 2; head there for tips on how to customize the menu by adding, moving, or removing tiles to ensure you find things more easily.

FIGURE 6-1:
On the Start menu, click the tile for the program you want to open.

If you just want to launch a program or app, follow these steps:

1. Open the Start menu.

Summon the Start menu by clicking or tapping the Start button in the screen's bottom-left corner. If your hands are already on the keyboard, just press the Windows key (⊞).

The Start menu appears, as shown in Figure 6-1, bringing a list of your apps and programs. In fact, the Start menu automatically updates itself to keep the names of your most recently used programs or apps visible.

If the Start menu fills the entire screen, your computer is running in Tablet mode. To switch to the traditional, corner-sized Start screen, click the Action Center icon (shown in the margin). When the Action Center pane appears, click the Tablet mode toggle in the pane's lower edge.

2. **If you spot the tile for your program or app, choose it with a mouse click or, on a touchscreen, a tap of a finger.**

   Don't see a tile for your sought-after program on the Start menu's list? Move to the next step.

3. **Scroll down the screen's right side to see more tiles.**

   Hidden along the Start menu's far right edge is a scroll bar, similar to scroll bars you see in stocked folders. Sometimes you can't see the scroll bar until your mouse pointer rests directly over it. When you see the scroll bar, drag its scroll box down the screen; then you can see any Start menu tiles that were hiding from view. No scroll bar? Then you're already seeing all that the Start menu has to offer.

TIP

   On touchscreens, you can view the tiles hidden below the screen's edge by sliding your finger up the screen over the tiles.

   Still don't see your program or app listed? Head for Step 4.

4. **View *all* your apps.**

   To keep its list of apps and programs manageable, the Start menu's tile-filled section doesn't list every program or app on your computer.

   To reveal them *all,* look at the list of apps along the Start menu's left side. Your most used apps appear along the top; below that appear newly installed apps. And below those, you see all your apps listed alphabetically by name.

   When running in Tablet mode, your computer doesn't show its alphabetized list of apps. To see them, tap the All Apps icon, shown in the margin. All your installed apps and programs suddenly appear, sorted alphabetically.

If you *still* can't find your program on the admittedly crowded Start menu, follow these tips for other ways to open an app or a program:

» Click inside the Cortana Search box next to the Start menu. As you type the first letter, the Search box grows taller to present a list of names beginning with that letter. Type a second or third letter, and the list of matches shrinks accordingly. When you spot the app or program you want, open it with a click (or a tap on a touchscreen). As you type letters, the ever-helpful Cortana also finds matching filenames on your PC, as well as matches from the Internet.

» Open the File Explorer icon (shown in the margin) from the Start menu's left edge. When File Explorer appears, choose Documents, Music, Pictures, or

Videos from the Navigation Pane along the window's left edge, and double-click the file you want to open. The correct program automatically opens with that file in tow. (If the wrong program opens it, head to this chapter's "Choosing Which Program Should Open Which File" section.)

» Double-click a shortcut to the program. Shortcuts, which often sit on your desktop, are handy, disposable buttons for launching files and folders. (I explain more about shortcuts in this chapter's "Taking the Lazy Way with a Desktop Shortcut" section.)

» While you're on the desktop, you may spot the program's icon on the taskbar — a handy strip of icons lazily lounging along your desktop's bottom edge. If so, click the taskbar icon, and the program leaps into action. (I cover the desktop's taskbar, including how to customize its row of icons, in Chapter 3.)

» Right-click on the Windows desktop, choose New, and select the type of document you want to create. Windows loads the correct program for the job. (On a tablet, this trick works only when you turn off Tablet mode, described earlier in this section.)

Windows offers other ways to open a program, but the preceding methods usually get the job done. (I cover the Start menu more extensively in Chapter 2, and the desktop is the star of Chapter 3.)

Opening a Document

Like Tupperware, the Windows desktop is a big fan of standardization. Almost all Windows programs load their documents — often called *files* — the same way:

1. **Click the word File on the program's *menu bar,* that row of staid words along the program's top.**

   If your program hides its menu bar, pressing the Alt key often reveals it.

   Still no menu bar? Then your program might have a *Ribbon,* a thick strip of multicolored icons along the window's top. If you spot the Ribbon, click the tab or button in its leftmost corner to let the File menu tumble down.

2. **When the File menu drops down, choose Open.**

   Windows gives you a sense of déjà vu with the Open window, shown in Figure 6-2. It looks (and works) just like your Documents folder, which I cover in Chapter 5.

   There's one big difference, however: This time, your folder displays only files that your particular program knows how to open — it filters out all the others.

3. **Point at your desired document (shown in Figure 6-2), click the mouse button, and click the Open button.**

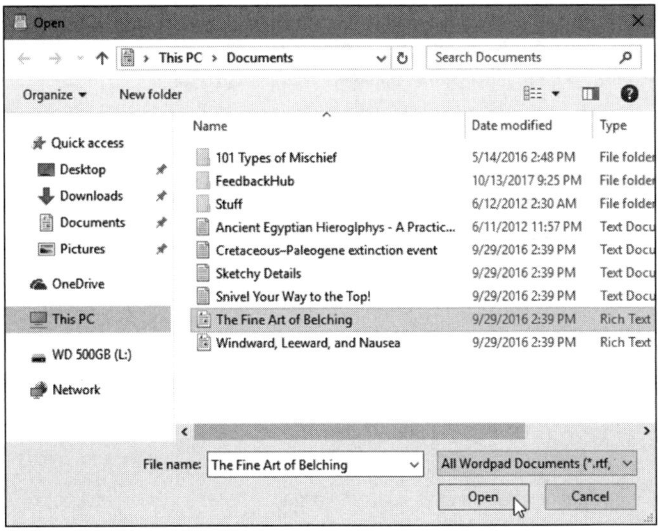

FIGURE 6-2:
Double-click the
filename you
want to open.

TIP

On a touchscreen, tap the document to open it. The program opens the file and displays it on the screen.

Opening a file works this way in most Windows programs, whether written by Microsoft, its corporate partners, or the teenager down the street.

TIP

» To speed things up, double-click a desired file's name; that opens it immediately, automatically closing the Open window.

» Humans store things in the garage, but computers store their files in neatly labeled compartments called folders. (Double-click a folder to see what's stored inside. If you spot your file, open it with a double-click.) If browsing folders gives you trouble, the folders section in Chapter 5 offers a refresher.

» If your file isn't listed by name, start browsing by clicking the buttons or words shown along the left side of Figure 6-2. Click the OneDrive or the This PC folder, for example, to search other folders and their files stored inside.

» Whenever you open a file and change it, even by accident, Windows usually assumes that you've changed the file for the better. If you try to close the file, Windows cautiously asks whether you want to save your changes. If you updated the file with masterful wit, click Yes. If you made a mess or opened the wrong file, click No or Cancel.

WHEN PROGRAMMERS FIGHT OVER FILE TYPES

When not fighting over fast food, programmers fight over *formats* — ways to pack information into a file. To tiptoe around the format wars, most programs let you open files stored in several different types of formats.

For example, look at the drop-down list box in the bottom-right corner of Figure 6-2. It currently lists all WordPad Documents, the format used by the WordPad text editor built into Windows. To see files stored in *other* formats, click in that box and choose a different format. The Open box quickly updates its list to show files from that new format, instead.

And how can you see a list of *all* your folder's files in that menu, regardless of their format? Select All Documents from the drop-down list box. That switches the view to show all of that particular folder's files. Your program probably can't open them all, though, and it will choke while trying.

For example, WordPad may include some digital photos in its All Documents view. But if you try to open a photo, WordPad dutifully displays the photo as obscure coding symbols. (If you ever mistakenly open a photo in a program and *don't* see the photo, don't try to save what you've opened. If the program is like WordPad, saving the file will ruin the photo. Simply turn tail and exit immediately with a click on the Cancel button.)

>> Confused about any icons or commands along the Open window's top or left side? Rest your mouse pointer over the icons, and a little box announces their occupations.

Saving a Document

Saving means to send the work you've just created to a hard drive, flash drive, or disc for safekeeping. Unless you specifically save your work, your computer thinks that you've just been fiddling around for the past four hours. You must specifically tell the computer to save your work before it will safely store it.

Thanks to Microsoft snapping leather whips, a Save command appears in nearly every Windows program no matter what programmer wrote it. Here are a few ways to save a file:

>> Click File on the top menu and choose Save. (Pressing the Alt key, followed by the F key and the S key, does the same thing.)

 >> Click the Save icon (shown in the margin).

>> Hold down Ctrl and press the S key. (*S* stands for *Save.*)

If you're saving something for the first time, Windows asks you to think up a name for your document. Type something descriptive using only letters, numbers, and spaces between the words. (If you try to use one of the illegal characters I describe in Chapter 5, the Windows Police step in, politely requesting that you use a different name.)

REMEMBER

>> You can save files to any folder, CD, DVD, or even a flash drive. But files are much easier to find down the road when they stay in one of your four main folders: Documents, Music, Pictures, or Videos. (Those folders are listed on the left edge of every folder, making it easy to place files inside them.)

>> Choose descriptive filenames for your work. Windows gives you 255 characters to work with. A file named *January 2018 Fidget Spinner Sales* is easier to relocate than one named *Stuff.*

>> If you want to access your current file from other devices, perhaps your phone, tablet, or another PC, save it to the Documents folder on OneDrive: Choose OneDrive from the Save window's left edge and then choose the OneDrive Documents folder. Then click the Save button.

>> Most programs can save files directly to a CD or DVD. Choose Save from the File menu and choose your preferred drive from the right pane's This PC section. Put a disc (preferably one that's not already filled) into your disc-writing drive to start the process.

>> A few newer programs spare you the chore of clicking the Save button: They save your work automatically as you type. Microsoft's OneNote note-taking program and many Start menu apps save your work automatically, so they lack a Save button.

REMEMBER

>> If you're working on something important (and most things are important), click the program's Save command every few minutes. Or use the Ctrl+S keyboard shortcut. (While holding down the Ctrl key, press the S key.) Programs make you choose a name and location for a file when you *first* save it; subsequent saves are much speedier.

Choosing Which Program Should Open Which File

Most of the time, Windows automatically knows which program should open which file. Open a file, and Windows tells the correct program to jump in and let you view its contents.

But sometimes Windows doesn't choose your preferred program, and that holds especially true for Windows 10. For example, the new app–loving Windows tells the Start menu's Groove Music app to play your music. You may prefer that the desktop's Windows Media Player handle the music–playing chores instead.

When the wrong program opens your file, here's how to make the *right* program open it instead:

1. **Right-click your problematic file and choose Open With from the pop-up menu.**

As shown in Figure 6-3, Windows lists a few capable programs, including ones you've used to open that file in the past.

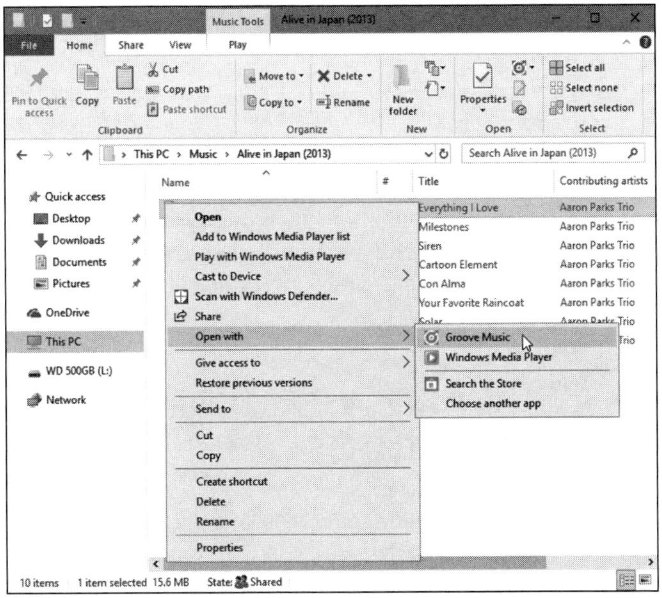

FIGURE 6-3:
Windows lists
some programs
that opened
that type of file
in the past.

2. **Click the Choose Another App option.**

The window that appears, as shown in Figure 6-4, lists more programs, and the currently assigned program appears at the list's top. If you spot your favorite program, double-click to tell it to open your file. (Make sure the Always Use This App to Open Files check box is selected so you don't need to repeat these steps.) Then click OK. You're done!

Don't see the program you want or need to open the file? Move to Step 3.

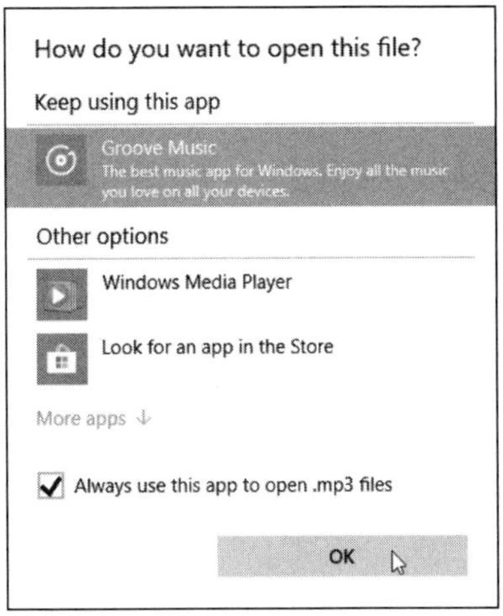

FIGURE 6-4:
Choose the
program you
want and select
the check box at
the bottom.

3. **Click the words Look for An App in the Store and click the OK button.**

   The Store app appears, leaving you at a virtual shelf stocked with apps capable of opening the file.

If you install a new program or an app to open a particular file, the newcomer usually assigns itself the rights to open that type of file in the future. If it doesn't, head back to Step 1. This time, however, your newly installed program or app will appear on the list. Choose it, and you've *finally* finished.

THE AWKWARD WORLD OF FILE ASSOCIATIONS

Every Windows program slaps a secret code known as a *file extension* onto the name of every file it creates. The file extension works like a cattle brand: When you double-click the file, Windows eyeballs the extension and automatically summons the proper program to open the file. Notepad, for example, tacks on the three-letter extension .txt to every file it creates. So, Windows associates the .txt extension with the Notepad program.

Windows normally doesn't display these extensions, isolating users from such inner mechanisms for safety reasons. If somebody accidentally changes or removes an extension, Windows won't know how to open that file.

If you're curious about what an extension looks like, sneak a peek by following these steps:

1. **Click the View tab from atop any folder.**

   The menu quickly changes across the folder's top, showing different ways to view that folder's contents.

2. **Select the File Name Extensions check box.**

   The files inside the folder immediately change to show their extensions — a handy thing to know in technical emergencies.

Now that you've peeked, hide the extensions again by repeating the steps but deselect the File Name Extensions check box.

Warning: Don't change a file's extension unless you know exactly what you're doing. Windows will forget what program to use for opening the file, leaving you holding an empty bag.

>> In a bit of revisionist history, Windows 10 uses the term *app* when referring to both traditional desktop programs and Start menu apps. Be mindful of the Windows terminology when on the desktop. If Windows says an action will affect your apps, it will also affect your desktop programs.

>> Windows lets you choose your default programs from the Start menu, as well. From the Start menu, click the Settings icon, shown in the margin. When the Setting app appears, click the Apps icon. From the Apps window, choose Default Apps from the left pane. Click any app's name, and a list appears for you to hand the reins to a different program.

>> Sometimes you'll want to alternate between different apps or programs when working on the same file. To do so, right-click the file, choose Open With, and select the program you need at that time.

>> Occasionally, you can't make your favorite program open a particular file because it simply doesn't know how. For example, Windows 10 can't play DVD movies. Your only solution is to install a DVD playing program or app from the Microsoft Store.

>> If somebody says something about "file associations," feel free to browse the technical sidebar "The awkward world of file associations," which explains that awful subject.

Navigating the Microsoft Store

Apps, which are mini-programs specialized for single tasks, come from the world of *smartphones* (computerized cellphones). And, like the apps from smartphones, apps come only from an App store. In Windows, they come from the Microsoft Store app, available with a click on the taskbar's Microsoft Store icon (shown in the margin). (Earlier versions of Windows 10 called the store the *Windows Store*.)

Apps differ from traditional desktop programs in several ways:

>> Windows 10 now allows apps to run within desktop windows rather than consuming the entire screen as they did in earlier Windows versions. When running in Tablet mode, though, apps return to their full-screen antics.

>> Apps are tied to your Microsoft account. That means you need a Microsoft account to download a free or paid app from the Store app.

>> When you download an app from the Microsoft Store app, you can usually run it on up to ten PCs or devices — as long as you're signed in to those PCs or devices with your Windows account. (Some apps may raise or lower that number.)

>> Newly installed apps consume just one Start menu tile. Newly installed programs, by contrast, often sprinkle several tiles onto your Start menu.

Apps and programs can be created and sold both by large companies and basement–dwelling hobbyists working in their spare time. It's hard to tell before-hand which one will give you the most support should things go wrong.

Although desktop programs and Start menu apps look and behave differently, Microsoft unfortunately refers to both as *apps.* You might run across this termi-nology quirk when dealing with older programs, as well as newer programs cre-ated by companies not hip to Microsoft's new lingo.

Adding new apps from the Store app

When you're tired of the apps bundled with Windows or you need a new app to fill a special need, follow these steps to bring one into your computer.

TIP

If you own a scanner, practice downloading an app by downloading Microsoft's "Windows Scan" app. Described at the end of Chapter 8, the simple app may be all you need to create quick scans.

1. **Click the Start button and open the Store app from the Start menu.**

   The Store app jumps to the screen, as shown in Figure 6-5. You can also click the Store app (shown in the margin) from the taskbar that always runs along the bottom of your screen.

   Although the Store changes its layout frequently, it usually opens to show its Spotlight category along the top edge, where Microsoft highlights a few chosen apps. Beneath that, you may find links to popular apps. The Store usually offers a Picks For You section which suggests apps you may be interested in, based on your past downloads.

   To see more, point near the Store app's top edge to see the top few apps in each category: Apps, Games, Devices, Movies & TV, and Books. (You can also buy or rent movies and computer gadgets from the Store app.)

   On December 31, 2017, Microsoft discontinued its Groove Music Pass stream-ing service. You can no longer purchase music from the Store app. Instead, Microsoft encourages you to download the Spotify music streaming app.

2. **To narrow your search, choose a category by clicking its name.**

   The Store lists its offerings based on your chosen category.

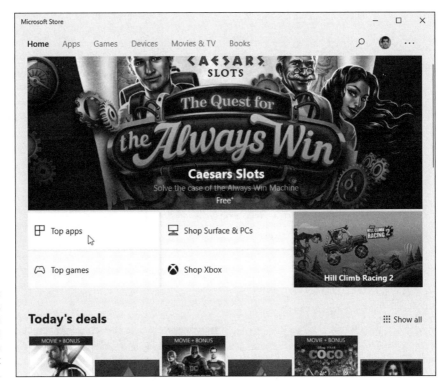

FIGURE 6-5:
The Store app lets you download free, trial, or paid apps to launch from your Start menu.

TIP

Save some time by clicking the "Top Apps" button, if you spot one. (The mouse points to it in Figure 6-5.) If you spot an interesting free app, click it. When the Install button appears, click the button to install the app and get the hang of the process. (Similarly, to buy a paid app, click the button that lists its price.)

Didn't find the right app? Head to the next step.

3. **Search for a particular app by typing a keyword into the Search box in the upper-right corner and pressing Enter.**

   The Search box lives in the store's upper-right corner. Shown in Figure 6-6, the Search box narrows down the apps by a keyword.

REMEMBER

Like the Store app, almost all searchable apps include a built-in Search box, which appears in their upper-right corner.

When you press Enter, the Store app lists all matching apps, games, artists, albums, movies, and TV shows.

4. **Sort the listed apps.**

   The Departments button, found in the Store's upper-left corner, lets you fine-tune your app search with a drop-down menu. Click Apps from the drop-down menu, for example, to further sort your search by categories: apps, games, movies, and other categories.

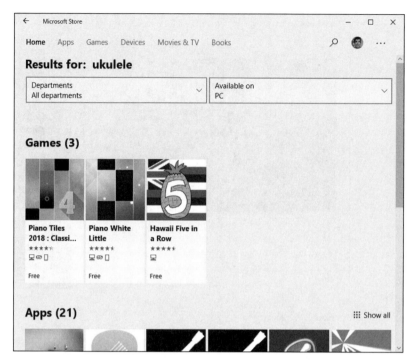

FIGURE 6-6:
Type a keyword
in the Search box
and press Enter
to see relevant
apps.

5. **Click any app to read a more detailed description.**

   A page opens to show more detailed information, including its price tag, pictures, reviews left by previous customers, and more technical information.

6. **Click the Free or Price button.**

   When you find a free app that you can't live without, click the Free button. To buy a paid app, click the button bearing its price tag. The price will be charged to the credit card linked to your Microsoft account. If you haven't yet entered a card, Microsoft walks you through the process.

   The Store may ask you to choose which drive to use for installing your app. Most people choose their C: drive; owners of small tablets may prefer to choose their memory card, instead, which is usually the D: drive. (Tiny tablets traditionally come with tiny C: drives.)

   No matter what you download from the Microsoft Store, the new item appears on your Start menu's alphabetical All Apps list as quickly as your Internet connection speed allows.

To copy an app from the All Apps list to a front-page Start menu tile, right-click the app's name and choose Pin to Start. I explain how to customize your Start menu further in Chapter 2.

Uninstalling apps

Downloaded a dud app? To uninstall any app from the Start menu, right-click its tile. When the pop-up menu appears, click Uninstall.

Uninstalling an app removes that app only from *your* account's Start menu. Your action won't affect other account holders who may have installed the app.

UPDATING YOUR APPS

TIP

Programmers constantly tweak their apps, smoothing over rough spots, adding new features, and plugging security holes. Whenever you connect with the Internet, Windows examines your installed apps. If any are out of date, Windows automatically downloads any waiting updates and applies the updates.

If you're using a cellular connection, don't worry: Apps don't update when you're using a metered Internet connection like those found on cellphones. Windows resumes updating the apps as soon as you connect to a Wi-Fi or wired Internet connection.

Don't want automatic updates for some reason? You can turn off automatic updating by following these steps:

1. **From the Store app, click the icon with three dots next to your account icon and choose Settings from the drop-down menu.**

   Your account icon is your user account photo, located in the Store app's upper-right corner next to the Search box.

2. **When the Settings screen appears, click to make sure the Update Apps Automatically slider is set to Off.**

   Your changes take place immediately. To make sure your apps update automatically, by contrast, set the slider to On.

When the Update Apps Automatically toggle is on, *all* your apps update. You can't keep individual apps from updating, unfortunately. That's why I recommend that you keep your apps set to update automatically. If you try to stop one from updating, you could miss out on security patches as well as improvements to all your other apps.

Taking the Lazy Way with a Desktop Shortcut

As you work, you'll constantly find yourself traveling between the desktop and the Start menu. When you grow tired of meandering through the woods to find a program, folder, disc drive, document, or even a website, create a desktop *shortcut* — an icon that takes you directly to the object of your desires.

Because a shortcut is a mere icon that launches something else, shortcuts are safe, convenient, and disposable. And they're easy to tell apart from the original because they have a little arrow lodged in their bottom-left corner, as you can see on the folder shortcut shown in the margin.

To skip the Start menu, follow these instructions to create desktop shortcuts to your oft-used items:

>> **Folders or Documents:** From the desktop's File Explorer, right-click a favorite folder or document, choose Send To, and select the Desktop (Create Shortcut) option. The shortcut appears on your desktop.

>> **Websites:** On Internet Explorer, see the little icon in front of the website's address in Internet Explorer's Address bar? Drag and drop that little icon to your desktop for quick access later. (Unfortunately, Windows 10's new Microsoft Edge browser doesn't let you create desktop shortcuts.)

>> **Control Panel:** The desktop's Control Panel contains eight sections, each with links beneath it. Every icon and link in the Control Panel can be dragged onto your desktop to create a shortcut. (An easy way to access the Control Panel from the desktop is to right-click in the screen's bottom-left corner and choose Control Panel from the pop-up menu.) The new Settings app doesn't offer this feature.

>> **Storage areas:** Open File Explorer with a click of its icon on the desktop's taskbar. From the Navigation Pane along File Explorer's left side, drag and drop any storage area you want to the desktop. Windows immediately places a shortcut to that drive on your desktop. (This works for your main OneDrive folder, This PC, flash drives, disc drives, and even network locations.)

Here are some more tips for desktop shortcuts:

>> For quick CD or DVD burning, put a shortcut to your disc drive on your desktop. Burning files to disc becomes as simple as dragging and dropping them onto the disc drive's new shortcut. (Insert a blank disc into the disc drive's tray, confirm the settings, and begin burning your disc.)

>> Want to send a desktop shortcut to the Start menu? Right-click the desktop shortcut and choose Pin to Start; the item appears as a tile on the Start menu, as well as in the Start menu's All Apps list.

WARNING

>> Feel free to move shortcuts from place to place, but *don't* move the items they launch. If you do, the shortcut won't be able to find the item, causing Windows to panic and search (usually in vain) for the relocated goods.

>> Want to see what program a shortcut will launch? Right-click the shortcut and click Open File Location (if available). The shortcut quickly takes you to its leader.

Absolutely Essential Guide to Cutting, Copying, and Pasting

Windows took a tip from the kindergartners and made *cut* and *paste* an integral part of computing life. You can electronically *cut* or *copy* just about anything and then *paste* it just about anyplace else with little fuss and even less mess.

For example, you can copy a photo and paste it onto your party invitation fliers. You can move files by cutting them from one folder and pasting them into another. You can cut and paste your digital camera's photos into a folder inside your Pictures folder. And you can easily cut and paste paragraphs to different locations within a word processor.

The beauty of the Windows desktop is that, with all those windows onscreen at the same time, you can easily grab bits and pieces from any of them and paste all the parts into a brand-new window.

TIP

Don't overlook copying and pasting for the small stuff. Copying a name and an address is much faster and more accurate than typing them into your letter by hand. Or, when somebody emails you a web address, copy and paste it directly into your browser's Address bar. It's easy to copy most items displayed on websites, too (much to the dismay of many professional photographers).

The quick 'n' dirty guide to cut 'n' paste

REMEMBER

In compliance with the Don't Bore Me with Details Department, here's a quick guide to the three basic steps used for cutting, copying, and pasting:

1. **Select the item to cut or copy: a few words, a file, a web address, or any other item.**

2. **Right-click your selection and choose Cut or Copy from the menu, depending on your needs.**

   Use *Cut* when you want to *move* something. Use *Copy* when you want to *duplicate* something, leaving the original intact.

   Keyboard shortcut: Hold down Ctrl and press X to cut or C to copy.

3. **Right-click the item's destination and choose Paste.**

   You can right-click inside a document, folder, and some other places.

   Keyboard shortcut: Hold down Ctrl and press V to paste.

The next three sections explain each of these three steps in more detail.

Selecting things to cut or copy

Before you can shuttle pieces of information to new places, you have to tell Windows exactly what you want to grab. The easiest way to tell it is to *select* the information with a mouse. In most cases, selecting involves one swift trick with the mouse, which then highlights whatever you've selected.

» **To select text in a document, website, or spreadsheet:** Put the mouse arrow or cursor at the beginning of the information you want and hold down the mouse button. Then move the mouse to the end of the information and release the button. That's it! That action selects all the stuff lying between where you clicked and released, as shown in Figure 6-7.

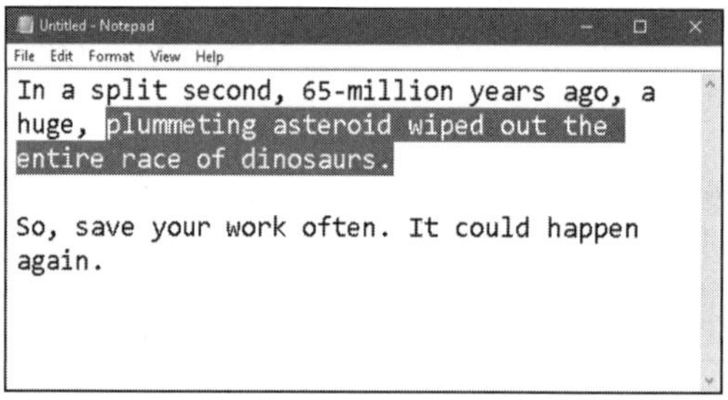

FIGURE 6-7:
Windows highlights the selected text, changing its color for easy visibility.

```
Untitled - Notepad                    –  □  ×
File  Edit  Format  View  Help
In a split second, 65-million years ago, a
huge, plummeting asteroid wiped out the
entire race of dinosaurs.

So, save your work often. It could happen
again.
```

TIP

On a touchscreen, double-tap one word to select it. To extend your selection, touch the highlighted word again, keeping your finger pressed on the glass. Slide your finger along the glass until you've reached the area where the highlighting should stop. Done? Remove your finger to select that portion of text.

Be careful after you highlight a bunch of text. If you accidentally press the K key, for example, the program replaces your highlighted text with the letter *k*. To reverse that calamity, choose Undo from the program's Edit menu (or press Ctrl+Z, which is the keyboard shortcut for Undo).

>> **To select any files or folders:** Simply click a file or folder to select it. To select *several* items, try these tricks:

- **If all the files are in a row:** Click the first item in the bunch, hold down the Shift key, and then select the last item. Windows highlights the first and last items as well as everything in between.

  - **If the files *aren't* in a row:** Hold down the Ctrl key while clicking each file or folder you want to select.

Now that you've selected the item, the next section explains how to cut or copy it.

>> After you've selected something, cut it or copy it *immediately*. If you absent-mindedly click the mouse someplace else, your highlighted text or file reverts to its boring self, and you're forced to start over.

>> To delete any selected item, be it a file, paragraph, or picture, press the Delete key. Alternatively, right-click the item and choose Delete from the pop-up menu.

Cutting or copying your selected goods

After you select some information (which I describe in the preceding section, in case you just arrived), you're ready to start playing with it. You can cut it or copy it. (Or just press Delete to delete it.)

This bears repeating. After selecting something, right-click it. (On a touchscreen, touch it and hold down your finger to fetch the pop-up menu.) When the menu appears, choose Cut or Copy, depending on your needs, as shown in Figure 6-8. Then right-click your destination and choose Paste.

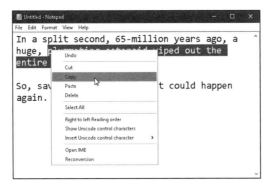

FIGURE 6-8: To copy information into another window, right-click your selection and choose Copy.

TIP

SELECTING INDIVIDUAL LETTERS, WORDS, PARAGRAPHS, AND MORE

When dealing with words in Windows, these shortcuts help you quickly select information:

- To select an individual *letter or character,* click in front of the character. Then while holding down the Shift key, press the right-arrow key. Keep holding down these two keys to keep selecting text in a line.

- To select a single *word,* point at it with the mouse and double-click. The word changes color, meaning it's highlighted. (In most word processors, you can hold down the button on its second click, and then by moving the mouse around you can quickly highlight additional text word by word.)

- To select a single *line* of text, simply click next to it in the left margin. To highlight additional text line by line, keep holding down the mouse button and move the mouse up or down. You can also keep selecting additional lines by holding down the Shift key and pressing the left-arrow key or the right-arrow key.

- To select a *paragraph,* just double-click next to it in the left margin. To highlight additional text paragraph by paragraph, keep holding down the mouse button on the second click and move the mouse.

- To select an entire *document,* hold down Ctrl and press A. (Or choose Select All from the program's Edit menu.)

The Cut and Copy options differ drastically. How do you know which one to choose?

TIP

» **Choose Cut to *move* information.** Cutting wipes the selected information off the screen, but you haven't lost anything: Windows stores the cut information in a hidden Windows storage tank called the *Clipboard,* waiting for you to paste it.

Feel free to cut and paste entire files to different folders. When you cut a file from a folder, the icon dims until you paste it. (Making the icon disappear would be too scary.) Changed your mind in mid-cut? Press Esc to cancel the cut, and the icon reverts to normal.

» **Choose Copy to make a copy of the information.** Compared with cutting, *copying* information is quite anticlimactic. Whereas cutting removes the item from view, copying the selected item leaves it in the window, seemingly untouched. Copied information also goes to the Clipboard until you paste it.

To save a picture of your entire screen, press ⊞+PrtScr. (Some keyboards call that key *Print Screen* or *PrintScr*.) Windows quickly saves the image in a file called Screenshot inside your Pictures folder. Do it again, and the screenshot is named Screenshot (2). (You get the idea.)

Pasting information to another place

After you cut or copy information to the Windows Clipboard, it's checked in and ready for travel. You can *paste* that information nearly anyplace else.

Pasting is relatively straightforward:

1. **Open the destination window and move the mouse pointer or cursor to the spot where you want the stuff to appear.**

2. **Right-click the mouse and choose Paste from the pop-up menu.**

Presto! The item you just cut or copied immediately leaps into its new spot.

Or, if you want to paste a file onto the desktop, right-click on the desktop and choose Paste. The cut or copied file appears where you've right-clicked.

TIP

>> The Paste command inserts a *copy* of the information that's sitting on the Clipboard. The information stays on the Clipboard, so you can keep pasting the same thing into other places if you want.

>> To paste on a touchscreen, hold down your finger where you'd like to paste the information. When the menu pops up, tap Paste.

>> Some programs, including File Explorer, have toolbars along their tops, offering one-click access to the versatile Cut, Copy, and Paste buttons, as shown in Figure 6-9. (Hint: Look on File Explorer's Home tab.)

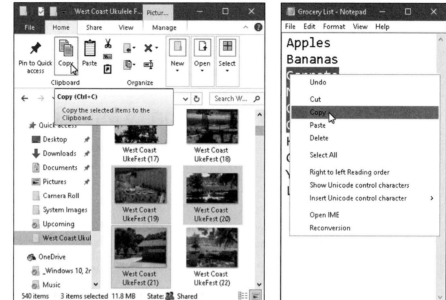

FIGURE 6-9:
The Cut, Copy,
and Paste
commands on
the Ribbon (left)
and traditional
menu (right).

UNDOING WHAT YOU'VE JUST DONE

TIP

Windows offers a way for you to undo your last action, which quickly pours the spilled milk back into the carton:

Hold down the Ctrl key and press the Z key. The last mistake you made is reversed, sparing you from further shame. (Pressing a program's Undo button, if you can find one, does the same thing.)

And, should you mistakenly undo something that really should have stayed in place, press Ctrl+Y. That undoes your last undo, putting it back in place.

IN THIS CHAPTER

» **Finding currently running apps and programs**

» **Finding lost desktop windows and files**

» **Finding lost programs, emails, songs, photos, and documents**

» **Finding other computers on a network**

Chapter **7**

Finding the Lost

S ooner or later, Windows gives you that head-scratching feeling. "Golly," you say as you drum nervous fingers, "that stuff was *right there* a second ago. Where did it go?"

When Windows starts playing hide-and-seek, this chapter tells you where to search and how to make it stop playing foolish games.

Finding Currently Running Apps and Programs

Apps usually hog the entire screen on Windows 10 tablets. Switch to another app, and *it* fills the screen, covering up the previous app. Sure, your current app is easy to read, but at a cost: Your other running apps remain constantly hidden beneath an invisibility cloak.

The Windows desktop, by contrast, lets you run apps and programs in separate windows. But even then, those windows tend to overlap, hiding the ones beneath.

How do you find and return to an app or program you just used? How do you jump between them, perhaps glancing at a report while creating a spreadsheet?

Windows offers a quick solution to the problem: It can clear the screen, shrink all your running apps and programs into miniature windows, and show you the lineup, as displayed in Figure 7-1. Click the app or program you want, and it returns to active duty at its normal size.

FIGURE 7-1:
Click the Task
View button to
see all your
currently running
apps and
programs.

To see the list of your recently used apps and programs (and to close unwanted ones, if desired), employ any of these tricks:

>> **Mouse:** Click the taskbar's Task View button, just to the right of the taskbar's search box, to see your open apps appear. To switch to an app, click it. To close an app, right-click its thumbnail and choose Close. (You can also click the X in the thumbnail's upper-right corner.)

>> **Keyboard:** Press ⊞+Tab to see the list of your most recently used apps, as shown in Figure 7-1. Press the Left or Right arrows to select different miniature windows. When you've selected your desired window, press Enter, and the app fills the screen.

TIP

>> **Touchscreen:** Slide your finger gently inward from the screen's left edge, and your open apps and programs align themselves as miniatures, as shown earlier in Figure 7-1. Tap any app on the strip to make it fill the screen. To close an unwanted app, tap the X in its upper-right corner. (A tap on the Task View icon also brings the thumbnails into view.)

The Windows 10 Task View button shows your currently running apps *and* desktop programs, making it easy to return to work.

Clicking the Task View button also lets you create a *virtual desktop*, an odd Windows 10 concept that I cover in Chapter 3.

Finding Lost Windows on the Desktop

The Windows desktop works much like a spike memo holder. Every time you open a new window or program, you toss another piece of information onto the spike. The window on top is easy to spot, but how do you reach the windows lying beneath it?

If you can see any part of a buried window's edge or corner, a well-placed click fetches it, bringing it to the top.

When your window is completely buried, look at the desktop's *taskbar* — that strip along your screen's bottom edge. Spot your missing window's icon on the taskbar? Click it to dredge the window back to the top. (See Chapter 3 for details about the taskbar.)

Still can't get at that missing window? Hold down the Alt key and press Tab. Shown in Figure 7-2, Windows shows thumbnails of all your open windows, programs, and apps in a strip across the screen's center. While holding down the Alt key, repeatedly press Tab, and Windows highlights a different app or window with each press of the Tab key. When your window is highlighted, let go of the Alt key, and that window appears atop your desktop.

TIP

If you're convinced a window is open but you still can't find it, spread all your open windows across the desktop by right-clicking a blank spot on the taskbar along the desktop's bottom and choosing Show Windows Side By Side from the pop-up menu. It's a last resort, but perhaps you'll spot your missing window in the lineup.

FIGURE 7-2:
Hold down the Alt
key and press Tab
repeatedly to
cycle through
your open
windows.

Locating a Missing App, Program, Setting, or File

The preceding two sections explain how to find *currently running* apps and programs. But what about things that you haven't looked at for a while?

That's the job of the Cortana Search box, which lives next to the Start button. To help you find wandering files, hidden settings, and informational tidbits, Cortana searches through *everything*, both on your PC and the Internet.

To search for missing things, follow these steps:

1. Click or tap in the Cortana Search box and type what you'd like to find.

The Search box accepts typing as soon as you click or tap inside it. (Don't see a Search box? Then your computer is in Tablet mode; tap the Cortana icon, shown in the margin, to bring Cortana's Search box to the screen.)

As you begin typing, Windows immediately begins searching for matches. (You can also verbally tell your computer what to search for, as described in this chapter's "Searching with Cortana" section.)

For example, here's what happens when searching for pianist Aaron Parks: As you begin typing letters, Windows begins listing files with matching names, shown in Figure 7-3. After just typing **Aaron** on my computer, for example, Windows found several matches and organized them in the Search pane in these categories:

- **Best Match:** Cortana's Search box lists the best match at the top, in this case, a link that searches the Internet for the term "aaron."

- **Search suggestions:** Here, Cortana offers Internet links to other potential matches, including Aaron Brothers art store.

- **Music:** Since Aaron Parks' Alive in Japan album is stored on my computer, Cortana lists that album's songs.

- **Store:** You may see this category if an item in the Microsoft Store appears to match your search.

- **Icons:** Click any of these icons along the top of the pane, labelled in Figure 7-3, to route your search to specific areas: matching apps, documents, and the Internet.

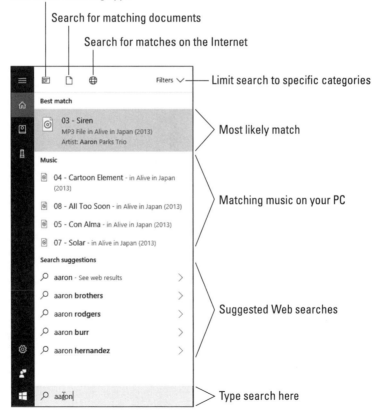

As you begin typing, the Search box concentrates on speed, so it searches only for matching filenames stored on your computer and OneDrive, as well as doing a quick Internet search.

If you spot your missing item, jump ahead to Step 3.

If you finish typing your complete search term but *don't* see your sought-after item on the Search list, move on to Step 2. You need to define your search more thoroughly.

2. **Limit your search to a specific category.**

When launched, the Search box searches only for matching filenames. If it doesn't find a match, route your search to one of the icons along the top of the Search pane: Apps, Documents, or Web.

TIP

Hover your mouse pointer over an icon, and its name appears in a pop-up menu.

To route your search to a specific area, click the word Filters, in the Search pane's upper-right corner. A drop-down menu appears, letting you limit your search to a specific category. Choose Music, for example, and Cortana lists only matching music files, as shown in Figure 7-4.

FIGURE 7-4:
Narrow your search further by limiting it to certain areas.

No matter which category you choose, Windows immediately shows any available matches. Changed your mind about a search category? Click a different icon to route your search there, instead.

3. **Choose a matching item to open it, bringing it to the screen.**

Click a song, for example, and it begins playing. Click a setting, and the Control Panel or Settings app appears, open to your setting's contents. Click a document, and it opens in your word processor.

These tips can help you wring the most out of the Search feature:

>> In its emphasis on speed, the Cortana Search pane lists only files with names that match your search term. While this strategy sometimes helps you find quick matches, it won't find your shopping list if you search for **oranges**. When you don't spot a sure match, finish typing your search term and then click one of the icons along the top of the pane to route your search to the appropriate spot.

>> Don't press the Enter key after typing in your Search. If you do that, Windows calls up the first match, which may not be what you want. Wait to see what matches turn up and then click the desired match.

>> The Cortana Search box scours every file in your Documents, Music, Pictures, and Videos folders. That feature makes storing your files in those folders more important than ever.

>> The Cortana Search box also scours every file you store on your OneDrive space, even if those files aren't also stored on your PC.

>> Windows doesn't search for files stored in removable devices, such as flash drives, CDs, DVDs, or portable hard drives.

>> If you're searching for a common word and Cortana finds too many files, limit your search by typing a short phrase from your sought-after file: **Shortly after the cat nibbled the bamboo**, for example. The more words you type, the better your chances of pinpointing a particular file.

>> The Search box ignores capital letters. It considers **Bee** and **bee** to be the same insect.

Searching with Cortana

Windows 10 includes a friendly personal digital assistant named *Cortana*. Cortana tries to simplify your life by finding not only missing files but also helpful bits of information about you and your surroundings. It finds local weather updates, for example, traffic information about the drive home, and even a list of popular nearby restaurants. A forward thinker, Cortana can even remind you when your favorite band visits your town.

You've already met Cortana: It's the brains behind the Search box next to the Start menu. As Microsoft keeps updating Windows 10, Cortana pitches in with additional tasks. In Chapter 9, for example, I explain how Cortana teams up with the new Microsoft Edge browser to help with your Internet searches.

Cortana can tell you the age of your favorite actor, for example. When she doesn't understand a question well enough to give a confident answer, she fetches your browser and routes the search to the Internet, letting you sort through the results.

Before Cortana works well, though, you need to give it a few tweaks. This section explains how to set up and fine-tune Cortana to make it as helpful as possible. (Don't like robotic assistants? Unfortunately, Microsoft doesn't let you turn off Cortana.)

Setting up Cortana for the first time

In order to serve you better, your servants must know a lot about you, including your habits, interests, and appointments. When your computer plays the role of digital assistant, it must know just as much of your personal information in order to be helpful.

To introduce yourself to Cortana and let her know your habits, follow these steps:

1. **Click in the Search box, and the Cortana pane appears.**

   Cortana speaks to you through the Cortana pane, shown in Figure 7-5. These icons along the left edge of the pane let you control Cortana's behavior:

   - **Home:** Click this to return to Cortana's main screen, shown in Figure 7-5. Once you set up Cortana, this pane shows information about your day: upcoming appointments, traffic and weather updates, local news, and other helpful tidbits.

   - **Notebook:** This area lets you tweak Cortana's behavior in a variety of ways. Enter your music streaming accounts, for example, so Cortana can access them. You can also choose which of your interests Cortana should track, be that finance, health, and fitness; TV shows and movies; or sports, travel, and others. Some are simply on/off toggle switches; others let you enter things like your favorite stocks or sports teams. You can also tell Cortana to remind you about things at certain times.

   - **Devices:** Cortana comes built in on devices like portable speakers. If you have one in the house, this icon lets you control its behavior.

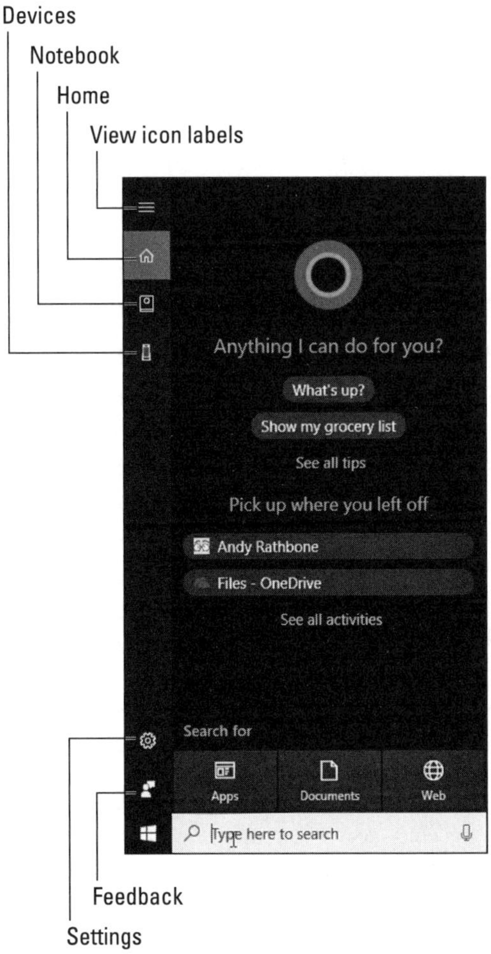

Devices
Notebook
Home
View icon labels

FIGURE 7-5:
Click the icons
along Cortana's
left edge to
change the
program's
settings.

Feedback

Settings

- **Settings:** You won't find a Turn Off Cortana button here, but you can click toggle switches that limit the amount of personal information Cortana may access.

- **Feedback:** Wish Cortana did something a little differently? Here's your chance to tell Microsoft about it.

2. **Choose whether to sign in with a Microsoft account, if asked.**

   Cortana works with a Local account, but not very well. She won't remember things about you, leading to less accurate results. If you sign in with a Microsoft account, Cortana will learn about you, as well as be able to send results to anywhere you've logged in with your Microsoft account, be it another PC, tablet, or phone.

3. **Choose whether to grant Cortana access to your physical location, contacts, appointments, messages, speech patterns, and web browsing history. Then click the Next button.**

   You can say no, of course, but what good is a butler who doesn't know that your coat belongs in the closet?

   Not signing in with a Microsoft account and denying Cortana access to your personal information makes Cortana revert to a fairly standard Search box, as described in the previous section.

4. **Fine-tune Cortana by visiting the Settings and Notebook areas.**

   Drop by the Settings area first. There, you can set up Cortana to understand the nuances of your voice as picked up by your computer's microphone. You can also manage how much of your information Cortana may access.

   Next, visit the Notebook area and tell Cortana about your interests. That helps Cortana tailor its information to things you want to hear.

Don't know where to start with Cortana? Begin by typing, **What can you do?** into the Search box and pressing the Enter key. Cortana begins explaining it all.

TIP

These tips will help you train Cortana into being the most helpful personal assistant:

>> To bypass the Search box and simply talk to Cortana, click Cortana's Settings icon to turn on the voice-activated search. When the Settings pane appears, choose Check the Microphone to make sure Cortana can hear you. Then turn on the Hey Cortana toggle switch.

>> With Hey Cortana turned on, your PC, tablet, or phone waits anxiously for the term "**Hey Cortana**." When Cortana hears you say those two words, it listens closely for your search term and begins processing your request.

>> To search the Internet for the singer Lady Gaga, for example, say "**Hey Cortana Lady Gaga**." Don't pause after saying "Hey, Cortana," or you'll create confusion. Say the phrase in one fairly quick burst.

WARNING

>> Turning on Hey Cortana will drain the batteries more quickly on your phone or tablet. Try it for a while and track your battery life to see whether the trade-off is worth it.

>> Cortana only works when you have an Internet connection.

REMEMBER

>> Drop by the Notebook area's Manage Skills section. There, you can link Cortana to your subscribed music streaming services and Internet-connected home appliances. You can also enter your interests in News, Flights, Finance, and other areas so Cortana can keep you abreast of any important related news.

RUNNING CORTANA ON YOUR PHONE

Cortana isn't limited to your desktop computer. Microsoft makes Cortana apps for Android, Apple, and Windows phones, as well. This way, Cortana can keep offering you helpful reminders and suggestions while you're on the road.

The latest Android app links Cortana with your Windows PC; you can give Cortana a location- or time-based note on your PC, and your phone will remind you to buy milk when you pull in to the grocery store parking lot.

You can even tell Cortana which phone apps should be able to send their notifications to your PC. That way, you can keep up with your phone's nags even when your phone stays in your pocket. (You can respond to them from your PC, as well.)

Turning off Cortana

Some people accept their new robotic overlords with great relief. For years, Apple product owners have relied on *Siri* to find the best sushi joint when they travel. Android phone owners fetch *Google Now* for tailored news articles and traffic updates for the drive to work. Amazon's *Alexa* checks the weather and helps you choose the right movie.

Other people cringe at a tail-wagging robot trying to butt into their personal life. Cortana no longer includes the simple On/Off switch found in earlier versions of Windows 10. To turn Cortana back into a simple Search box, follow these steps:

1. **Click in the Search box, and when the Search pane appears, click the Settings icon (shown in the margin).**

2. **When the Settings app's Cortana page appears, click Permissions & History.**

3. **Turn off all the toggle switches on the Permissions & History page.**

4. **On that same page, visit these sections and click their Clear buttons, turn off their toggle switches, or click their Disconnect buttons:**

    - Change What Cortana Knows About Me in the Cloud

    - Manage What You Permit Cortana to Do, See, and Use

    - Manage the Information Cortana Can Access from this Device

    - Manage the Information Cortana Can Access from Other Services.

5. **Visit the Settings page every month or two to make sure Microsoft hasn't changed any options.**

   Remember that Microsoft sells Windows 10 as a *constantly changing* service. Microsoft constantly updates both Windows 10 and its bundle of apps to add and remove options. You may need to monitor Cortana's options to make sure they haven't changed.

Finding a Missing File inside a Folder

The Start menu's Search box can be overkill when you're poking around inside a single desktop folder, looking for a missing file. To solve the "sea of files in a folder" problem, Windows includes a Search box in every desktop folder's upper-right corner. That Search box limits your search to files within that *particular* folder.

To find a missing file within a specific folder, click inside that folder's Search box and begin typing a word or short phrase from your missing file. As you type letters and words, Windows begins filtering out files that are missing your sought-after word or phrase. It keeps narrowing down the candidates until the folder displays only a few files, including, I hope, your runaway file.

When a folder's Search box locates too many possible matches, bring in some other helping hands: the headers above each column. For best results, select the Details option in the View tab's Layout group, which lines up your filenames in one column, as shown in Figure 7-6. The first column, Name, lists the name of each file, and the adjacent columns list specific details about each file.

TIP

See the column headers, such as Name, Date Modified, and Type, atop each column? Click any of those headers to sort your files by that term. Here's how to sort by some of the column headers you may see in your Documents folder:

» **Name:** Know the first letter of your file's name? Then click here to sort your files alphabetically. You can then pluck your file from the list. (Click Name again to reverse the sort order.)

» **Date Modified:** When you remember the approximate date you last changed a document, click the Date Modified header. That places your newest files atop the list, making them easy to locate. (Clicking Date Modified again reverses the order, a handy way to weed out old files you may no longer need.)

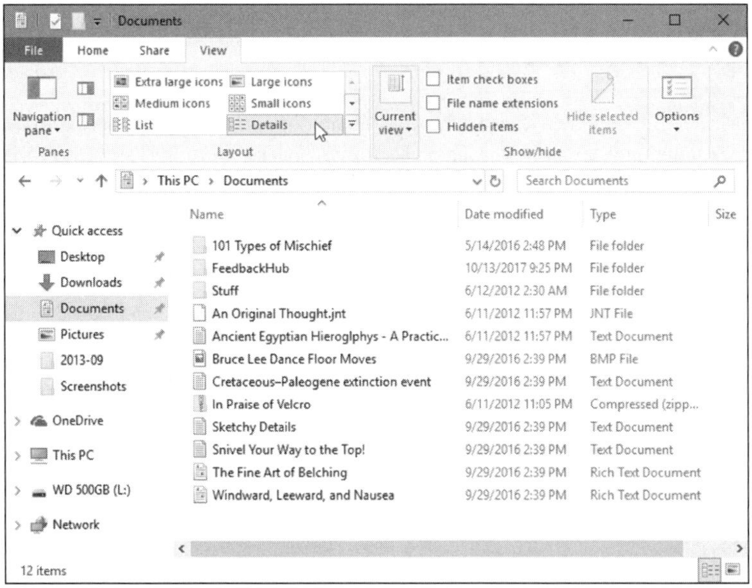

FIGURE 7-6:
Details view lets you sort your files by name, making them easier to find.

>> **Type:** This header sorts files by their contents. All your photos group together, for example, as do all your Word documents. It's a handy way to find a few stray photos swimming in a sea of text files.

>> **Size:** Sorting here places your 45-page thesis on one end and your grocery list on the other.

>> **Authors:** Microsoft Word and some other programs tack your name onto your work. A click on this label sorts the files alphabetically by their creators' names.

>> **Tags:** Windows often lets you assign tags to your documents and photos, a task I describe later in this chapter. Adding the tag "Moldy Cheese" to that pungent photo session lets you retrieve those pictures by either typing the tag or sorting a folder's files by their tags.

TIP

Folders usually display about five columns of details, but you can add more columns. In fact, you can sort files by their word count, song length, photo size, creation date, and dozens of other details. To see a list of available detail columns, right-click an existing label along a column's top. When the drop-down menu appears, select More to see the Choose Details dialog box. Click to put check marks next to the new detail columns you'd like to see and then click OK.

DEEP SORT

TECHNICAL STUFF

A folder's Details view (shown in Figure 7-6) arranges your filenames into a single column, with oodles of detail columns flowing off to the right. You can sort a folder's contents by clicking the word atop any column: Name, Date Modified, Author, and so on. But the sort features in Windows go much deeper, as you'll notice when clicking the little downward-pointing arrow that appears as you hover your mouse pointer over each column's name.

Click the little arrow to the right of the words *Date Modified,* for example, and a calendar drops down. Click a date, and the folder quickly displays files modified on that particular date, filtering out all the rest. Beneath the calendar, check boxes also let you view files created Today, Yesterday, Last Week, Earlier This Month, Earlier This Year, or simply A Long Time Ago. (The available check boxes change depending on the age of the files inside your currently viewed folder.)

Similarly, click the arrow next to the Authors column header, and a drop-down menu lists the authors of every document in the folder. Select the check boxes next to the author names you'd like to see, and Windows immediately filters out files created by other people, leaving only the matches. (This feature works best with Microsoft Office documents.)

These hidden filters can be dangerous, however, because you can easily forget that you've turned them on. If you spot a check mark next to any column header, you've left a filter turned on, and the folder is hiding some of its files. To turn off the filter and see *all* that folder's files, deselect the check box next to the column header and examine the drop-down menu. Click any selected check boxes on that drop-down menu to remove their check marks and remove the filter.

Finding Lost Photos

Windows indexes your email down to the last word, but it can't tell the difference between photos of your cat and photos of your office party. When it comes to photos, the ID work lies in *your* hands, and these tips make the chore as easy as possible:

>> **Store shooting sessions in separate folders.** The Windows photo importing program automatically creates a new folder to store each session, named after the current date. But if you're using some other program to dump photos, be sure to create a new folder for each session. Then name the folder

with a short description of your session: Dog Walk, Kite Surfing, or Truffle Hunt. (Windows indexes the folder names.)

>> **Sort by date.** Have you stumbled onto a massive folder that's a mishmash of digital photos? Try this quick sorting trick: Click the View tab and choose Large Icons to make the photos morph into identifiable thumbnails. Then, from the View tab menu, choose Sort By and select Date Taken. Windows sorts the photos by the date you snapped them, turning chaos into organization.

>> **Rename your photos.** Instead of leaving your Tunisian vacation photos with their boring camera-given names like DSC_2421, DSC_2422, and so on, give them meaningful names: Select all the files in your Tunisia folder by clicking the Home tab on the Ribbon and clicking the Select All button. Then right-click the first picture, choose Rename, and type **Tunisia**. Windows names them as Tunisia, Tunisia (2), Tunisia (3), and so on. (If you messed up, press Ctrl+Z to undo the renaming.)

Following those simple rules helps keep your photo collection from becoming a jumble of files.

REMEMBER

Be *sure* to back up your digital photos to a portable hard drive, CDs, DVDs, or another backup method I describe in Chapter 13. If they're not backed up, you'll lose your family history when your PC's hard drive eventually crashes.

Finding Other Computers on a Network

A *network* is simply a group of connected PCs that can share things, such as your Internet connection, files, or a printer. Most people use a public network every day without knowing it: Every time you check your email, your PC connects to another PC on the Internet to grab your waiting messages.

Much of the time, you needn't care about the other PCs on your private network. But when you want to find a connected PC, perhaps to grab files from the PC in your family room, Windows is happy to help.

To find a PC on your network, open any folder and click Network on the Navigation Pane along the folder's left edge, as shown in Figure 7-7.

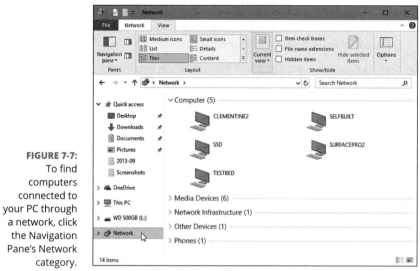

FIGURE 7-7:
To find
computers
connected to
your PC through
a network, click
the Navigation
Pane's Network
category.

Clicking Network lists every PC that's connected to your own PC in a traditional network. To browse files on any of those PCs, just double-click their names.

I walk through the steps of creating your own home network in Chapter 15.

Chapter **8**

Printing and Scanning Your Work

O ccasionally you'll want to take text or an image away from your PC's whirling electrons and place it onto something more permanent: a piece of paper. This chapter tackles that job by explaining all you need to know about printing.

I explain how to print just the relevant portions of a website — without the other pages, the ads, the menus, and the printer-ink-wasting images.

You discover how to print from the Start menu's gang of apps as well as from the desktop's programs.

And should you find yourself near a printer spitting out 17 pages of the wrong thing, flip ahead to this chapter's coverage of the mysterious *print queue.* It's a little-known area that lets you cancel documents *before* they waste all your paper. (I explain how to set up a printer in Chapter 12.)

If you prefer to turn paper into a file on your PC, this chapter closes with a run-down on the Windows Scan app. When combined with a scanner, it transforms maps, receipts, photos, and any other paper items into digital files.

Printing from a Start Menu App

Although Microsoft now tries to pretend that Start menu apps and desktop programs are the same, apps often behave quite differently than traditional desktop programs.

Many of the apps can't print, and those that do allow printing don't offer many ways to tinker with your printer's settings. Nevertheless, when you *must* print something from a Windows app, following these steps ensures the best chance of success:

1. **From the Start menu, load the app containing information you want to print.**

   Cross your fingers in the hopes that your app is one of the few that can print.

2. **Click the app's icon for either Settings, Print, or More to see the drop-down menus, and click the Print option.**

   A click on these three striped lines, known informally as the *hamburger menu*, fetches a drop-down menu. (This drop-down menu sometimes replaces the Charms bar's icons found in Windows 8 and Windows 8.1.)

   Similarly, a click on an icon of three dots (shown in the margin) found in some apps also fetches a drop-down menu. (The three dots menu is sometimes called a *More* or *Expand* menu, because clicking it expands a menu to display more options.)

   Just to confuse things, some apps offer a dedicated Print icon, shown in the margin.

   No matter how you choose an app's Print command, the click reveals the app's Print menu, shown in Figure 8-1. (If the word Print isn't listed on the drop-down menu or is grayed out, that app probably isn't able to print.)

3. **Click the printer to receive your work.**

   Click the Printer box, and a drop-down menu appears, listing any printers available to your computer. Click the name of the printer you want to handle the job.

4. **Make any final adjustments.**

   The Printer window offers a preview of what you're printing, with the total number of pages listed above. To browse the pages you're about to print, click the Forward or Backward arrows above the preview.

   Not enough options? Then click the More Settings link at the bottom of the left pane to see options offered by your particular printer model.

FIGURE 8-1:
Choose your print
options or click
the More Settings
link for additional
options.

5. **Click the Print button.**

   Windows shuffles your work to the printer of your choice, using the settings
   you chose in Step 4.

Although you can print from a few apps, you'll eventually run into limitations:

REMEMBER

» Most apps don't offer many printing options. You can't print a blank monthly
calendar from your Calendar app, for example, but you can print a daily,
weekly, or monthly itinerary.

» The More Settings link, described earlier in Step 4, lets you choose between
Portrait and Landscape mode, as well as choose a printer tray. However, you
usually won't find more detailed adjustments, such as choosing margins or
adding headers and footers.

In short, although you *can* print from a few apps, your results will be quick and
dirty. Desktop programs, described in the rest of this chapter, usually offer much
more control over printing jobs.

Printing Your Masterpiece from the Desktop

Built for power and control, the desktop offers many more options when it comes to printing your work. But that power and control often mean wading through a sea of menus.

When working from the desktop, Windows shuttles your work to the printer in any of a half-dozen ways. Chances are good that you'll be using these methods most often:

>> Choose Print from your program's File menu.

>> Click the program's Print icon, usually a tiny printer.

>> Right-click your unopened document's icon and choose Print.

>> Click the Print button on a program's toolbar.

>> Drag and drop a document's icon onto your printer's icon.

If a dialog box appears, click the OK or Print button, and Windows immediately begins sending your pages to the printer. Take a minute or so to refresh your coffee. If the printer is turned on (and still has paper and ink), Windows handles everything automatically, printing in the background while you do other things.

If the printed pages don't look quite right — perhaps the information doesn't fit on the paper correctly or it looks faded — then you need to fiddle around with the print settings or perhaps change the paper quality, as described in the next sections.

>> To print a bunch of documents quickly, select all their icons. Then right-click the selected icons and choose Print. Windows quickly shuttles all of them to the printer, where they emerge on paper, one after the other.

>> When printing with an inkjet printer, faded colors usually mean you need to replace your printer's color inkjet cartridge. You can buy replacement cartridges both online and at most office supply stores.

>> Still haven't installed a printer? Flip to Chapter 12, where I explain how to plug one into your computer and make Windows notice it.

Adjusting how your work fits on the page

In theory, Windows *always* displays your work as if it were printed on paper. Microsoft's marketing department calls it *What You See Is What You Get,* forever disgraced with the awful acronym WYSIWYG and its awkward pronunciation: "wizzy-wig." If what you see onscreen *isn't* what you want to see on paper, a trip to the program's Page Setup dialog box, shown in Figure 8-2, usually sets things straight.

On desktop programs, the Page Setup dialog box offers many formatting options; on apps, by contrast, it offers a more limited version (shown earlier in Figure 8-1). But they both offer several ways to flow your work across a printed page (and subsequently your screen). Page Setup dialog boxes differ among programs and printer models, but the following list describes the options that you'll find most often and the settings that usually work best:

>> **Paper Size:** This option lets your program know what size of paper currently lives inside your printer. Leave this option set to Letter for printing on standard, 8.5-x-11-inch sheets of paper. Change this setting only if you're using legal-size paper (8.5 x 14), envelopes, or other paper sizes. (The nearby sidebar, "Printing envelopes without fuss," contains more information about printing envelopes.)

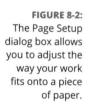

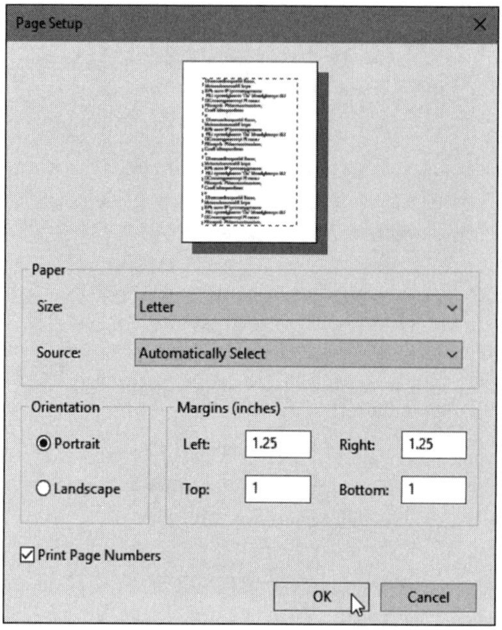

FIGURE 8-2:
The Page Setup
dialog box allows
you to adjust the
way your work
fits onto a piece
of paper.

>> **Source:** Choose Automatically Select or Sheet Feeder unless you're using a fancy printer that accepts paper from more than one printer tray. People who have printers with two or more printer trays can select the tray containing the correct paper size. Some printers offer Manual Paper Feed, making the printer wait until you slide in that single sheet of paper.

>> **Header/Footer:** Type secret codes in these boxes to customize what the printer places along the top and bottom of your pages: page numbers, titles, and dates, for example, as well as their spacing. Unfortunately, different programs use different codes for their header and footer. If you spot a little question mark in the Page Setup dialog box's upper-right corner, click it and then click inside the Header or Footer box for clues to the secret codes.

>> **Orientation:** Leave this option set to Portrait to print normal pages that read vertically like a letter. Choose Landscape only when you want to print sideways, which is a handy way to print wide spreadsheets. (If you choose Landscape, the printer automatically prints the page sideways; you don't need to slide the paper sideways into your printer.)

>> **Margins:** Feel free to reduce the margins to fit everything on a single sheet of paper. Or *enlarge* the margins to turn your six-page term paper into the required seven pages.

TIP

PRINTING ENVELOPES WITHOUT FUSS

Although clicking Envelopes in a program's Page Setup area is fairly easy, printing addresses in the correct spot on the envelope is extraordinarily difficult. Some printer models want you to insert envelopes upside down, but others prefer right side up. Your best bet is to run several tests, placing the envelope into your printer's tray in different ways until you finally stumble on the magic method. (Or you can pull out your printer's manual, if you still have it, and pore over the "proper envelope insertion" pictures.)

After you've figured out the correct method for your particular printer, tape a successfully printed envelope above your printer and add an arrow pointing to the correct way to insert it.

Should you eventually give up on printing envelopes, try using Avery's free downloadable templates from Avery's website (www.avery.com). Compatible with Microsoft Word, the templates place little boxes on your screen that precisely match the size of your particular Avery labels. Type the addresses into the little boxes, insert the label sheet into your printer, and Word prints everything onto the little stickers. You don't even need to lick them.

Or do as I did: Buy a little rubber stamp with your return address. It's much faster than stickers or printers.

>> **Printer:** If you have more than one printer installed on your computer or network, click this button to choose which one to print your work. Click here to change that printer's settings as well, a job discussed in the next section.

When you're finished adjusting settings, click the OK button to save your changes. (Click the Print Preview button, if it's offered, to make sure that everything looks right.)

TIP

To find the Page Setup box in some programs, click the little arrow next to the program's Printer icon and choose Page Setup from the menu that drops down.

Adjusting your printer's settings

When you choose Print from many programs, Windows offers one last chance to spruce up your printed page. The Print dialog box, shown in Figure 8-3, lets you route your work to any printer installed on your computer or network. While there, you can adjust the printer's settings, choose your paper quality, and select the pages (and quantities) you'd like to print.

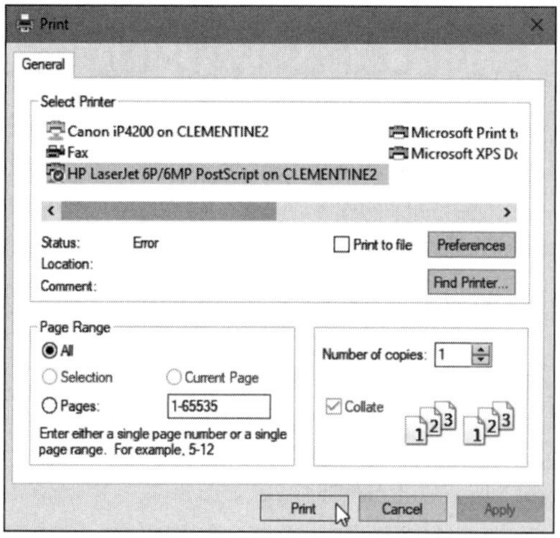

FIGURE 8-3:
The Print dialog box lets you choose your printer and adjust its settings.

You're likely to find these settings waiting in the dialog box:

TIP

>> **Select Printer:** Ignore this option if you have only one printer, because Windows chooses it automatically. If your computer has access to several printers, click the one that should receive the job. If you have a fax modem on your computer or network, click Fax to send your work as a fax through the Windows Fax and Scan program.

The printer called Microsoft XPS Document Writer sends your work to a specially formatted file, usually to be printed or distributed professionally. Chances are good that you'll never use it.

>> **Page Range:** Select All to print your entire document. To print just a few of its pages, select the Pages option and enter the page numbers you want to print. For example, enter **1-4, 6** to leave out page 5 of a 6-page document. If you've highlighted a paragraph, choose Selection to print that particular paragraph — a great way to print the important part of a web page and leave out the rest.

>> **Number of Copies:** Most people leave this set to 1 copy, unless everybody in the boardroom wants their own copy. You can choose Collate only if your printer offers that option. (Most don't, leaving you to sort the pages yourself.)

>> **Preferences:** Click this button to see a dialog box like the one in Figure 8-4, where you can choose options specific to your own printer model. The Printing Preferences dialog box typically lets you select different grades of paper, choose between color and black and white, set the printing quality, and make last-minute corrections to the page layout. (This option varies greatly according to your printer model, so yours may look different.)

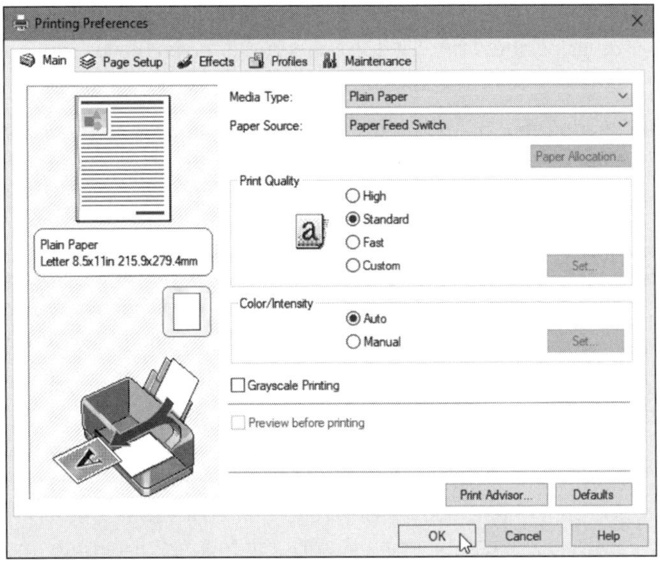

FIGURE 8-4:
The Printing
Preferences
dialog box lets
you change
settings specific
to your printer
model.

Canceling a print job

Just realized you sent the wrong 26-page document to the printer? So you panic and hit the printer's Off button. Unfortunately, many printers automatically pick up where they left off when you turn them back on, leaving you or your co-workers to deal with the mess.

To purge the mistake from your printer's memory, follow these steps:

1. **From the desktop's taskbar, right-click your printer's icon and choose your printer's name from the pop-up menu.**

   To see your printer's icon, you may need to click the little upward-pointing arrow to the left of the taskbar's icons next to the clock.

   When you choose your printer's name, the handy *print queue* window appears, as shown in Figure 8-5.

2. **Right-click your mistaken document and choose Cancel to end the job. If asked to confirm, click the Yes button. Repeat with any other listed unwanted documents.**

Your printer queue can take a minute or two to clear itself. (To speed things up, click the View menu and choose Refresh.) When the print queue is clear, turn your printer back on; it won't keep printing that same darn document.

>> The print queue, also known as the print spooler, lists every document waiting patiently to reach your printer. Feel free to change the printing order by

dragging and dropping documents up or down the list. (You can't move anything in front of the currently printing document, though.)

>> Sharing your printer on the network? Print jobs sent from other PCs sometimes end up in your computer's print queue, so you'll need to cancel the botched ones. (And networked folks who share their printer may need to delete your botched print jobs, as well.)

>> If your printer runs out of paper during a job and stubbornly halts, add more paper. Then to start things flowing again, open the print queue, right-click your document, and choose Restart. (Some printers have an Online button that you push to begin printing again.)

TIP

>> You can send items to the printer even when you're working in the coffee shop with your laptop. Later, when you connect the laptop to your printer, the print queue notices and begins sending your files. (Beware: When they're in the print queue, documents are formatted for your specific printer model. If you subsequently connect your laptop to a *different* printer model, the print queue's waiting documents won't print correctly.)

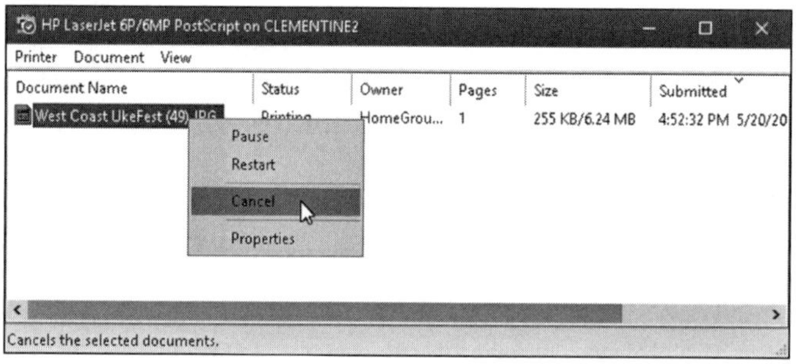

FIGURE 8-5:
Use the print queue to cancel a print job.

Printing a web page

Although information-stuffed web pages look awfully tempting, *printing* those web pages is rarely satisfying because they look so awful on paper. When sent to the printer, web pages often run off the page's right side, consume zillions of additional pages, or appear much too small to read.

To make matters worse, all those colorful advertisements can suck your printer's color cartridges dry fairly quickly. Only four things make for successfully printed web pages, and I rank them in order of probable success rate:

>> **Use the web page's built-in Print option.** Some websites, but not all, offer a tiny menu option called Print This Page, Text Version, Printer-Friendly Version,

or something similar. That option tells the website to strip out its garbage and reformat the page so that it fits neatly onto a sheet of paper. This option is the most reliable way to print a web page.

>> **Choose Print Preview from your browser's File or Print menu.** After 15 years, some web page designers noticed that people want to print their pages, so they tweaked the settings, making their pages *automatically* reformat themselves when printed. If you're lucky, a clean look in the Print Preview window confirms that you've stumbled onto one of those printer-friendly sites.

>> **Copy the portion you want and paste it into a word processor.** Try selecting the desired text from the web page, copying it, and pasting it into a word processor. Delete any unwanted remnants, adjust the margins, and print the portion you want. I explain how to select, copy, and paste in Chapter 6.

>> **Copy the entire page and paste it into a word processor.** Although it's lots of work, it's an option. Right-click a blank portion of the web page and choose Select All. Right-click again and choose Copy. Next, open Microsoft Word or another full-featured word processor and paste the web page inside a new document. By hacking away at the unwanted portions, you can sometimes end up with something printable.

TIP

These tips may also come in handy for moving a web page from screen to paper:

>> The Microsoft Edge web browser in Windows 10 is built for speed, not power, but it still prints. To print what you're viewing in Edge, click the browser's Settings and More icon (three dots in the top-right corner), and choose Print from the drop-down menu.

>> For best results in the Edge browser, turn on the Reading View mode by clicking the Reading View icon (shown in the margin). Reading View strips away ads and other detritus, leaving you with a clean page to send to the printer.

>> If Microsoft Edge still doesn't print well, try printing from Internet Explorer, instead. (You can still find Internet Explorer by typing its name into the Start menu's Search box and pressing Enter.)

>> If you spot an Email option but no Print option, email the page to yourself. Depending on your email program, you may have better success printing it as an email message.

>> To print just a few paragraphs of a web page, use the mouse to select the portion you're after. (I cover the act of *selecting* things in Chapter 6.) Choose Print from Internet Explorer's Tools menu (shown in the margin) to open the Print dialog box, shown earlier in Figure 8-3. Then, in the Page Range box, choose the Selection option.

>> If a web page's table or photo insists on vanishing off the paper's right edge, try printing the page in Landscape mode rather than Portrait. See the "Adjusting how your work fits on the page" section, earlier in this chapter, for details on Landscape mode.

Troubleshooting your printer

When you can't print something, start with the basics: Are you *sure* that the printer is turned on, plugged into the wall, full of paper, and connected securely to your computer with a cable?

If so, try plugging the printer into different outlets, turning it on, and seeing whether its power light comes on. If the light stays off, your printer's power supply is probably blown.

TIP

Printers are almost always cheaper to replace than repair. Printer companies make their money on ink cartridges, so they often sell printers at a loss.

If the printer's power light beams brightly, check these things before giving up:

>> Make sure that a sheet of paper hasn't jammed itself inside the printer. (A steady pull usually extricates jammed paper. Sometimes opening and closing the printer's lid starts things moving again.)

TIP

>> Does your inkjet printer still have ink in its cartridges? Does your laser printer have toner? Try printing a test page: From the desktop, right-click the Start button and choose Control Panel. From the Hardware and Sound category, choose Devices and Printers. Right-click your printer's icon, choose Printer Properties, and click the Print Test Page button to see whether the computer and printer can talk to each other.

>> Try updating the printer's *driver,* the little program that helps it talk with Windows. Visit the printer manufacturer's website, download the newest Windows 10 driver for your particular printer model, and run its installation program. (I cover drivers in Chapter 13.)

Finally, here are a couple of tips to help you protect your printer and cartridges:

>> Turn off your printer when you're not using it. Older inkjet printers, especially, should be turned off when they're not in use. The heat tends to dry the cartridges, shortening their life.

WARNING

>> Don't unplug your inkjet printer to turn it off. Always use the On/Off switch. The switch ensures that the cartridges slide back to their home positions, keeping them from drying out or clogging.

Scanning from the Start Menu

Windows 10 dropped the Scan app that came with Windows 8 and 8.1. However, you can download it for free from the Store app. (It's called Windows Scan in the Store app, which I explain in Chapter 6.)

The new app doesn't work with older scanners, unfortunately. But if your scanner is relatively new, the Scan app is a refreshing change from the complicated software bundled with most scanners.

Note: Setting up a new scanner for the first time? Be sure to *unlock* it by sliding a lever or turning a dial on the scanner to the unlock position. That lock protects the scanner during shipping, but you must turn it off before use.

After installing the Windows Scan app from the Windows Store and connecting your scanner, follow these steps to scan something into your computer:

1. From the Start menu, open the Scan app.

If you don't spot the Scan app on the Start menu, click All Apps in the Start menu's lower-left corner. The Start menu lists all of its apps alphabetically. *Note:* If you don't find the Scan app on your computer, you can download it for free from the Store app.

Click the Scan app, shown in the margin, and the Scan app appears on the screen. If it complains that your scanner isn't connected, make sure you've connected the USB cable between your computer's USB port and the scanner and that the scanner is turned on.

If your scanner is plugged in and turned on, the scan app lists your scanner's name, shown in Figure 8-6, and the *file type* used for saving your files. (The PNG file type is widely accepted by most programs.)

If the app doesn't recognize your scanner, your scanner is too old. You're stuck with your scanner's bundled software — if it works — or, unfortunately, buying a new scanner.

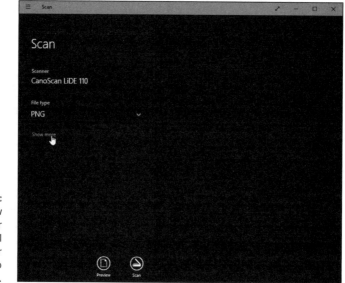

FIGURE 8-6:
Click the Show More link for additional options, or click Preview to test a scan.

2. **(Optional) To change the settings, click the Show More link.**

The app's default settings work fine for most jobs. The Show More link offers these options for specific types of scans:

- **File Type:** PNG works fine for most scans. But to create smaller, lower-resolution scans for emailing, choose JPG from this pull-down menu.

- **Color mode:** Choose Color for color items, such as photos and glossy magazine pages. Choose Grayscale for nearly everything else, and choose Black and White *only* for line drawings or black-and-white clip art.

- **Resolution (DPI):** For most work, the default 300 works fine. Higher resolution scans (larger numbers) bring more detail but consume more space, making them difficult to email. Lower resolution scans show less detail but create smaller file sizes. You may need to experiment to find the settings that meet your needs.

- **Save File To:** The Scan app creates a Scan folder in your PC's Pictures folder, where it stores your newly scanned images. If desired, you can change the Scan folder's name or even create a different folder for each scanning session.

3. **Click the Preview button to make sure your scan appears correct.**

Click the Preview icon, shown in the margin, and the Scan app makes a first pass, letting you preview a scan made with your chosen settings.

If the preview doesn't look right, make sure you've made the right choice for your job in Color Mode, described in the preceding step. If the preview shows a blank white page, make sure you've *unlocked* the scanner as described in the scanner's bundled instruction sheets.

If you're scanning a smaller item that doesn't fill the entire scanner bed, look for the circle markers in each corner of the preview scan. Drag each circle inward to surround the area you want to copy.

4. **Click the Scan button. When the scan finishes, click the View button to see your scan.**

The Scan app scans your image with the settings you've chosen in the previous steps and then saves your image in your Pictures folder's Scan folder.

The Scan app works well for fast, easy scans. But because it relies on the simple, built-in Windows software, your scanner's built-in control buttons won't work.

If you want your scanner's buttons to work or you need finer control over your scans, skip the Scan app, head for the desktop, and install your scanner's bundled software. (On some scanner models, Windows Update installs the scanner's bundled software automatically as soon as you plug in the scanner.)

TIP

For quick-and-dirty scans, just take a picture of the document with the camera built into your phone or tablet. That won't work well for photos, but it's an easy way to keep track of receipts and invoices.

If you need more features than the Scan app offers, check out the desktop's Windows Fax and Scan program. It's more complicated and requires special equipment for faxing, but it offers more features than the Scan app.

3
Getting Things Done on the Internet

IN THIS CHAPTER

» **Finding out about Internet service providers**

» **Connecting to the Internet wirelessly**

» **Navigating the web with Microsoft Edge**

» **Finding the hidden Internet Explorer**

» **Finding information on the Internet**

» **Understanding plug-ins**

» **Saving information from the Internet**

» **Troubleshooting problems**

Chapter **9**

Cruising the Web

ven when being installed, Windows starts reaching for the Internet, hungry for any hint of a connection. After connecting, Windows kindly downloads updates to make your PC run more smoothly. Other motives are less pure: Windows also checks in with Microsoft to make sure that you're not installing a pirated copy.

Windows 10 is so web-dependent that it comes with a savvy new browser named *Microsoft Edge*. Fast and sleek, Microsoft Edge helps you move in and out of today's Internet-dependent world.

In fact, Microsoft Edge is a *universal app,* meaning it looks and behaves the same whether it runs on a tablet, PC, or an Xbox game console. Microsoft even offers free Edge browser apps for iPhones and Android phones, as well.

This chapter explains how to find and fire up Microsoft Edge, connect with the Internet, visit websites, and find what you're seeking online.

For ways to keep out the bad stuff, be sure to visit Chapter 11. It's a primer on safe computing that explains how to avoid the web's bad neighborhoods, which harbor viruses, spyware, hijackers, and other Internet parasites.

What's an ISP, and Why Do I Need One?

Everybody needs three things to connect with the Internet and visit websites: a computer, web browser software, and an Internet Service Provider (ISP).

You already have the computer, be it a tablet, laptop, or desktop PC. And the new Windows 10 browser, Microsoft Edge, handles the software side.

That means most people need to find only an ISP. Most coffee shops, airports, and hotels let you connect wirelessly, and often for free. At home, though, you must pay an ISP for the privilege of surfing the web. When your computer connects to your ISP's computers, Windows automatically finds the Internet, and you're ready to surf the web.

Choosing an ISP is fairly easy because you're often stuck with whichever ISPs serve your particular geographic area. Ask your friends and neighbors how they connect and whether they recommend their ISP. Call several ISPs serving your area for a rate quote and then compare rates. Most bill on a monthly basis, so if you're not happy, you can always switch.

>> Although ISPs charge for Internet access, you don't always have to pay. More and more public businesses share their Internet access for free, usually through a wireless connection. If your phone, laptop, or tablet includes wireless support, and most do, you can browse the Internet whenever you're within range of a free wireless signal. (I cover wireless in the next section.)

>> Although a handful of ISPs charge for each minute you're connected, most charge from $30 to $100 a month for unlimited service. (Some also offer faster connection speeds for more money.) Make sure that you know your rate before hopping aboard or else you may be unpleasantly surprised at the month's end.

>> ISPs let you connect to the Internet in a variety of ways. The slowest ISPs require a dialup modem and an ordinary phone line; they're still a lifeline for some rural areas. (Satellite access also works well in rural areas.) Faster and the most popular are broadband connections: special DSL or ISDN lines provided by some phone companies, and the even faster cable modems supplied by your cable television company. You're only limited by what's offered in your geographic area.

WHERE'S INTERNET EXPLORER?

After 20 years of service, Internet Explorer finally hit its retirement plan with Windows 10. Built in 1995, Internet Explorer carried plenty of baggage. For example, it needed specialized coding to display websites created with older technology. All that old code slowed down Internet Explorer's performance when viewing modern websites. That old code also made Internet Explorer more vulnerable to viruses and other exploits.

So, Microsoft started anew with Microsoft Edge, its faster, but less-powerful browser. If you prefer Internet Explorer, the old-timer is still around: Click inside the Cortana Search box by the Start button, type **Internet Explorer**, and press Enter to revisit the faithful Windows browser of yesteryear.

TIP

>> You need to pay an ISP for only *one* Internet connection. You can share that single connection with any other computers, cellphones, smart TVs, refrigerators, thermostats, lightbulbs, personal assistants like Amazon's Alexa, and other Internet-aware gadgetry in your home, office, or kitchen. (I explain how to share an Internet connection by creating your own wired or wireless network in Chapter 15.)

Connecting Wirelessly to the Internet

Windows *constantly* searches for a working Internet connection, whether your computer plugs into a cable or scans the airwaves for a Wi-Fi (wireless) connection. If your computer finds a Wi-Fi connection that you've previously connected with, you're set: Windows quickly connects to it, passes the news along to Microsoft Edge, and you're ready to visit the web.

When you're traveling, however, the wireless networks around are often new, forcing you to find and authorize these new connections.

To connect to a nearby wireless network for the first time (whether it's one in your own home or in a public place), follow these steps:

1. **Click the taskbar's Wi-Fi icon (shown in the margin) near the clock.**

   Windows lists all the nearby wireless networks, shown in Figure 9-1.

   The networks are ranked by signal strength, with the strongest and fastest network listed at the top.

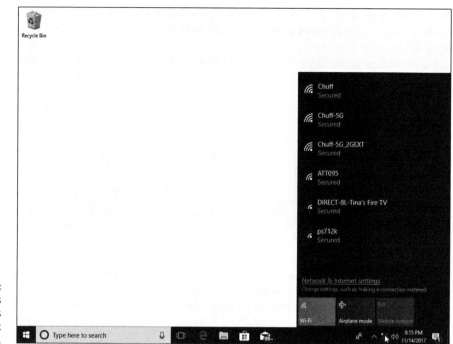

FIGURE 9-1:
Windows lists
every wireless
network
within range.

2. **Choose to connect to the desired network by clicking its name and clicking the Connect button that appears.**

If you're connecting to an *unsecured network* — a network that doesn't require a password — you're finished. Windows warns you about connecting to an unsecured network, but a click or tap of the Connect button lets you connect anyway. (Don't do anything involving money on an unsecured connection.)

But for a more secure connection, skip the unsecured networks. Instead, ask your hotel staff, coffee shop barista, or airport staff for the password to the secure network. Then head to the next step.

TIP

If you select the adjacent Connect Automatically check box before clicking the Connect button, Windows automatically connects to that network the next time you're within range, sparing you from connecting manually each time.

3. **Enter a password if needed.**

If you try to connect to a *security-enabled* wireless connection, Windows asks you to enter a *network security key* — technospeak for *password.* If you're at home, here's where you type in the same password you entered into your router when setting up your wireless network.

If you're connecting to somebody *else's* password-protected wireless network, ask the network's owner for the password. You may need to pull out your credit card at the front counter in some hotels and coffee shops — they may charge for access.

TIP

Microsoft account owners reap a benefit here: Your Microsoft account remembers your Wi-Fi passwords. When you log onto a Wi-Fi network on a desktop PC, you can automatically log onto it later with your Windows tablet without having to retype the password.

4. **Choose whether you want to share your files with other people on the network.**

   If you're connecting on your own home or office network, choose "Yes, turn on sharing and connect to devices." That lets you share files with others and connect to shared devices, such as printers.

   If you're connecting in a public area, by contrast, always choose "No, don't turn on sharing or connect to devices." That helps keep out snoops.

TIP

If you're still having problems connecting, try the following tips:

>> When Windows says that it can't connect to your wireless network, it offers to bring up the Network Troubleshooter. The Network Troubleshooter mulls over the problem and then usually says something about the signal being weak. It's really telling you this: "Move closer to the wireless transmitter."

>> At some hotels, your browser will open to a Terms of Services agreement. There, you must agree to the hotel's terms before being allowed to browse further.

>> If you're in a hotel room, moving your computer closer to a window may help you find a stronger wireless signal. (It might even pick up a wider variety of available wireless networks.) If you don't mind moving outside your room, then wander down to the lobby or hotel coffee shop to find a better connection.

>> If you can't connect to the secured network you want, try connecting to one of the unsecured networks. Unsecured networks work fine for casual browsing on the Internet.

Browsing the Web with Microsoft Edge

Built for speedy browsing of modern websites, Microsoft Edge loads quickly and displays web pages as quickly as your connection allows. Part of its speed and clean look comes from its limitations, though. The browser hides its menus in order to showcase every website's content. That makes navigation challenging.

To open Microsoft Edge, click its icon (shown in the margin) on the taskbar along the bottom of your screen. The browser opens, as shown in Figure 9-2, filling the screen with either your last-viewed site or a launch screen that shows the top news, weather, and links to popular sites.

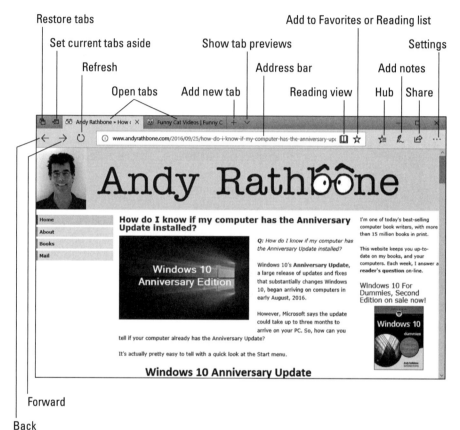

The browser hides most of its menus behind cryptic icons, so I've called them all out in Figure 9-2 and neatly labeled them here:

» **View set-aside tabs:** A click here lets you revisit tabs you've set aside by clicking the adjacent icon, described in the following bulleted paragraph.

» **Set aside current tabs:** Click here to whisk away all of your open tabs and start anew. Edge hides all of your open tabs, ready for a new round of work. (To return quickly to those open tabs, click the adjacent icon described in the preceding bulleted paragraph.)

>> **Back:** This back-arrow icon in the top-left corner lets you revisit the page you just visited.

>> **Forward:** A click on this icon lets you return to the page you just left.

>> **Refresh:** Handy when viewing sites with breaking news, this icon reloads the currently viewed page, gathering the latest material available.

>> **Tabs:** Your currently open sites appear as tabs along the window's top edge, letting you revisit them with a click. (Or you can close them by clicking the X in their tab's right corner.)

>> **Address bar:** Click the name of the currently displayed site, which usually appears along the site's top edge, and the Address bar appears, letting you type in the address of a website you'd like to visit. Don't know where to go? Type in a few descriptive words, and the browser searches for and displays possible matches. Click any match to visit the site.

>> **Open New Tab:** Clicking the plus sign icon, which lives just to the right of your currently open tab or tabs, fetches a blank window with an Address bar along the top. There, you can type in either the address of a coveted website or a few search terms for the browser to fetch.

>> **Show tab previews:** When you've opened too many tabs to remember them all, click this handy icon to see thumbnail previews of every open tab. That quickly lets you revisit a site with a click on its thumbnail.

>> **Reading view:** This changes the current website's layout to resemble a page of a book. How? It ditches a lot of the ads and formatting, leaving only text and pertinent photos. (It's a handy way to print a website, too.)

>> **Add to Favorites or Reading list:** Click the star icon to place your currently viewed page onto your list of *Favorites,* a collection of frequently visited sites. Clicking this offers an option to save a copy of the site to your Reading List for reading later.

>> **Hub:** Despite its nondescriptive name, this icon lets you revisit websites you've marked as Favorites or placed on your Reading List. It also lets you view a history of your visited websites, find downloaded files, or read books purchased from the Microsoft Store app.

>> **Add notes:** Coveted mostly by owners of a tablet and stylus, click the Add notes icon to mark up a web page and save it as a graphic. It's handy for highlighting passages and scrawling a "Read this!" note before sending a website to an interested friend. (Because the marked-up page is sent as a graphic, none of the links will work.)

>> **Share:** Click here to send your currently viewed page to another program, like your Mail app for emailing the link to a friend.

>> **Settings and more:** Clicking this icon with three dots fetches a drop-down list with options for opening a new window, changing the current website's text size, sharing a site with friends, searching for a word on the current page, printing the page, pinning the page to the Start menu, and viewing other settings.

When you're on the go and looking for quick information, Microsoft Edge's speedy browser and its simple menus might be all you need.

TIP

If you've clicked or tapped the wrong button but haven't yet lifted your finger, stop! Command buttons don't take effect until you *release* your finger or mouse button. Keep holding down your finger or mouse button but slide the pointer or finger away from the wrong button. Move safely away from the button and *then* lift your finger.

Moving from one web page to another

Web pages come with specific addresses, just like homes do. *Any* web browser lets you move among those addresses. You can use Microsoft Edge, Internet Explorer, or even a competing browser such as Firefox (www.getfirefox.com) or Chrome (www.google.com/chrome).

No matter which browser you use, they all let you move from one page to another in any of three ways:

>> By pointing and clicking a button or link that automatically whisks you away to another page

>> By typing a complicated string of code words (the web address) into the Address bar of the web browser and pressing Enter

>> By clicking the navigation buttons on the browser's toolbar, which is usually at the top of the screen

Clicking links

The first way to navigate the web is by far the easiest. Look for *links* — highlighted words or pictures on a page — and click them.

For example, see how the mouse pointer turned into a hand (shown in the margin) as it pointed at the word *Books* in Figure 9-3? That hand means the thing you're pointing at (be it a word, button, or picture) is clickable. In this instance, I can click the word *Books* to see a web page with more information about that subject. The mouse pointer morphs into a hand whenever it's over a link. Click any linked word to see pages dealing with that link's particular subject.

FIGURE 9-3:
When the mouse
pointer becomes
a hand, click the
word or picture
to go to a web
page with more
information
about that item.

Typing web addresses in the Address bar

The second method of web surfing is more difficult. If a friend gives you a napkin with a cool website's address written on it, you need to type the website's address into your browser's *Address bar* — the text-filled bar across the top. You'll do fine as long as you don't misspell anything.

See the address for my website along the top of Figure 9-3? I typed **andyrathbone. com** into the Address bar. When I pressed Enter, Microsoft Edge scooted me to my website. (You don't need to type the *http://www* part, thank goodness.)

Using Microsoft Edge's icons

Finally, you can maneuver through the Internet by clicking various buttons on Microsoft Edge's stripped-down menus, as described in the previous section and Figure 9-2. Click the browser's Back arrow button, for example, to return to a page you just visited.

TIP

Hover your mouse pointer over a confusing button in any program, and a pop-up usually appears, explaining its purpose in life.

Making Microsoft Edge open to your favorite site

When you open the desktop's web browser, it needs to show you *something* right away. Well, that something can be any website you want. In computer terms, that's called your *home page,* and you can tell Microsoft Edge to use any site you want.

Naturally, Microsoft wants Microsoft Edge to open to a *Microsoft* website, so you need to jump through these many hoops to make it open to your own favorite site:

1. **Visit your favorite website.**

    Choose any web page you like. If you choose Google News (http://news. google.com), for example, Microsoft Edge always opens with the latest headlines. Take note of the web page's name in the Address bar, along the top of Edge; that address must be entered into another box in Step 3. (I describe how to copy and paste things in Windows in Chapter 6.)

2. **Click the Settings icon in Microsoft Edge and choose Settings from the drop-down menu.**

    The Settings pane appears, listing your options.

3. **Click the Settings pane's Open Microsoft Edge With section; when the drop-down menu appears, choose A Specific Page or Pages.**

    The drop-down menu spills down to offer these options:

    - **New Tab Page:** Designed for people who hate distractions, this option opens Edge with an empty box where you can type in a search term or web page address.

    - **Previous Pages:** This option reminds Edge owners of their last web visit by displaying tabs open to the pages they last viewed.

    - **A Specific Page or Pages:** Choose this to select your favorite site as the opening screen for Edge; an empty box appears beneath it.

4. **Click inside the empty box, and type in the address of the favorite site you visited in Step 1 (see Figure 9-4). Then click the adjacent Save icon to save your change.**

    To open several home pages, each in their own tab, click the Add New Page button below the first web address you enter. A new box appears for you to type in another web address. Repeat until you've stocked Microsoft Edge with all the tabs you'd like to see preloaded whenever you launch Microsoft Edge.

Your changes take place as soon as you click the Save icon. To close the Settings pane, just click on the screen away from the Settings pane. The Settings pane closes, leaving you back at your website.

After Microsoft Edge opens with your chosen home page or pages, you can still browse the Internet, searching for topics by typing them into the Address bar or by simply pointing and clicking different links.

FIGURE 9-4:
Type in the
address of your
favorite website,
and Microsoft
Edge opens to
that site.

TIP

Just as your browser's home page is the site you see when your browser opens, a website's home page is its "cover," like the cover of a magazine. Whenever you navigate to a website, you usually start at the site's home page and begin browsing from there.

Revisiting favorite places

Sooner or later, you'll stumble across a web page that's indescribably delicious. To make sure that you can find it again later, add it to your list of favorite pages. To add the currently viewed page to your Favorites list, follow these steps:

1. **Click the Favorites icon (the little star) near Microsoft Edge's top-right edge. Then choose either Favorites or Reading List from the drop-down menu.**

The menu offers two places to stash your coveted web page:

- **Favorites:** Click Favorites to add the site to your list of favorite sites for quick revisiting. Links added here always take you to the current version of the web page.

- **Reading List:** Choose this option for longer, information-packed web pages that you'd like to read later. Unlike with the Favorites option, web pages added here are saved to Microsoft Edge's *Reading List,* a storage space where you can read them later at your leisure. Since the entire web page is saved, you can read it later without a working Internet connection.

2. **Click the Add button.**

   Whether you choose Favorites or Reading List, a box appears, listing the site's name. (Feel free to edit the name to make it more descriptive.)

   Click the Add button, and the name is added to whichever area you chose: your Favorites list or Reading List.

To return to a favorite page or something you've added to the Reading List, click Microsoft Edge's Hub icon (shown in the margin). When the menu drops down, click either the Favorites icon (the little star icon) from the menu's top or click the adjacent Reading List icon. Your list of added sites appears, letting you return to one with a click on its name.

TIP

To remove a disappointing item from your list of Favorites or Reading List, click the Hub button. When the Hub menu appears, click the appropriate icon to see your Favorites or Reading List. Finally, right-click the name of your unwanted item and choose Delete from the pop-up menu.

Finding things on the Internet

When searching for a book in a library, you usually head straight for the computerized index. The same holds true for the Internet because you need an index to ferret out that piece of information you're after.

MICROSOFT EDGE'S SECRET HISTORY OF YOUR WEB VISITS

Microsoft Edge keeps a record of every website you visit. Although Microsoft Edge's History list provides a handy record of your computing activities, it's a spy's dream.

To keep tabs on what Microsoft Edge is recording, click your Hub button and click the History icon — it looks like a clock — from the drop-down menu's top. Microsoft Edge lists every website you've visited in the past few weeks, sorted by date. (Your latest visits appear at the list's top.) By presenting the sites in the order you viewed them, Microsoft Edge makes it easy to jump back to that site you found interesting this morning, last week, or even several months ago.

To delete a single entry from the history, right-click it and choose Delete from the pop-up menu. That same menu also lets you delete *every* visit to that same site, saving you from having to find and delete each one.

To delete the entire list, click the words Clear All History at the list's top.

To help you out, Microsoft Edge lets you consult a *search engine,* a service that contains a vast index of Internet sites. To search for something, head for the Address bar — that space where you normally type in the address of the website you want to visit.

Instead, though, type your search term — **exotic orchids,** for example — directly into the Address bar and press Enter.

Microsoft Edge fires your search off to Bing, Microsoft's own search engine, and spits out names of websites dealing in exotic orchids. Click a website's name to drop by.

Don't like Bing handling your search needs? You can change that search engine to Google (www.google.com) or any other search engine you like.

Follow these steps to customize Microsoft Edge's searches to your liking:

1. **Visit the website of your favorite search engine with Edge. Then click Microsoft Edge's Settings icon (shown in the margin) in Microsoft Edge's top-right corner and choose Settings from the drop-down menu.**

    The Settings pane appears.

2. **Click the View Advanced Settings button, click the Change Search Engine button, and choose or add your desired search engine.**

    Your change takes place immediately. To close the Settings pane, click anywhere on the main page.

Microsoft Edge then replaces Bing with your newly selected search provider. Changing the search engine in Microsoft Edge won't change the search engine in Internet Explorer; the two browsers work independently.

However, Cortana won't work as effectively, as Microsoft's assistant is designed to work with Bing's results rather than those from another browser.

Finding More Information with Cortana

Clicking a website's links lets you jump easily to other places online. But what if you want to know more about something that *doesn't* have a clickable link? For example, what if you spot an address for a paleo-diet-friendly donut shop and want to see it on a map? What if you see a term you don't understand, and you simply want more information about it?

That's where Ask Cortana comes in. Cortana, the Windows 10 personal assistant, works inside Microsoft Edge to help you find extra information about things you find online.

Here's how it works:

1. **When visiting a web page in Microsoft Edge, highlight the terms you want to explore.**

   Double-click a word or term, for example, to highlight it. Or, point at the beginning of a phrase, hold down the mouse button, and — while holding down the mouse button — point at the end of a phrase. Release the mouse button, and you've highlighted the entire phrase.

   I provide more detail on how to select items in Chapter 6.

2. **Right-click the highlighted information and choose Ask Cortana from the pop-up menu.**

   Cortana appears on the screen's right edge. The little robot searches the Internet for pertinent information for a few seconds and then displays it, as shown in Figure 9-5.

Cortana may display information from Wikipedia, as well as information and images found by Bing, Microsoft's search engine.

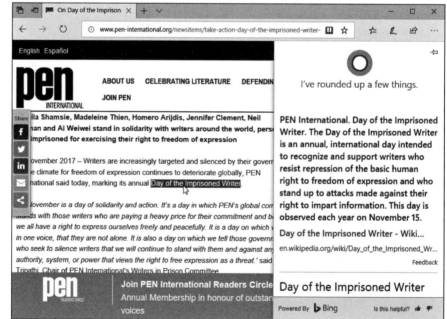

FIGURE 9-5:
Cortana teams up with Microsoft Edge to find information about terms found online.

If Cortana didn't find enough detailed information, scroll down to the bottom of Cortana's information pane. There, you find a link to search for the term on Bing, which gives you more control over your search.

Saving Information from the Internet

The Internet places a full-service library inside your house, with no long checkout lines. And just as every library comes with a copy machine, Microsoft Edge provides several ways for you to save interesting tidbits of information for your personal use.

This section explains how to copy something from the Internet onto your computer, whether it's an entire web page, a single picture, a sound or movie, or a program.

TIP

I explain how to print a web page (or a snippet of information it contains) in Chapter 8.

Saving a web page

Hankering for a handy Fahrenheit/Centigrade conversion chart? Need that Sushi Identification Chart for dinner? Want to save the itinerary for next month's trip to Norway? When you find a web page with indispensable information, sometimes you can't resist saving a copy onto your computer for further viewing, perusal, or even printing at a later date.

Microsoft Edge lets you save web pages by adding them to your Reading List, described earlier in this chapter's "Revisiting favorite places" section.

Saving text

To save just a little of a web page's text, select the text you want to grab, right-click it, and choose Copy. (I explain how to select, copy, and paste text in Chapter 6.) Open your word processor and paste the text into a new document and save it in your Documents folder with a descriptive name.

Saving a picture

As you browse through web pages and spot a picture that's too good to pass up, save it to your computer: Right-click the picture and choose Save Picture As, as shown in Figure 9-6.

The Save As window appears, letting you enter a new filename for the picture, if desired. Click Save to place your pilfered picture in your Pictures folder.

The crowded pop-up menu shown in Figure 9-6 offers other handy options, letting you choose to share (email) the picture or copy it to the Windows clipboard for pasting into another program. (To find out more information about the picture, choose Ask Cortana About This Picture.)

TIP

Remember the little picture by your name on the Windows Start menu? Feel free to use any picture from the Internet. Right-click the new picture and save it to your Pictures folder. Then use the Settings app (see Chapter 2) to transform that picture into your new user account picture.

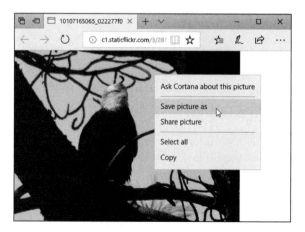

FIGURE 9-6:
Right-click the coveted picture and choose Save Picture As from the pop-up menu.

Downloading a program, song, or other type of file

Microsoft Edge makes it a little easier to download files from the Internet. Best yet, it's easier than ever to *find* the files after you download them.

To download something from a website, click the link to the item or click an adjacent Download button (if one is available). Microsoft Edge downloads the item and automatically places it into your Downloads folder for easy retrieval. The file usually arrives within a few seconds.

WARNING

When choosing the Download button, take some extra time to make sure you're clicking the right button. Many sites deliberately try to confuse you into downloading something else, either spyware, a virus, or something else that gives the website a payback.

You can find your downloaded item in either of two ways:

>> **Downloads folder:** Downloaded items flow into your Downloads folder. To find them, open File Explorer (shown in the margin) from the taskbar. When File Explorer opens, click the Downloads folder listed in the program's left pane. The Downloads folder appears, showing all of your downloaded items.

>> **Microsoft Edge's download queue:** Click the Hub icon (shown in the margin) in Microsoft Edge. When the Hub menu appears, click the Downloads icon from the left pane. Microsoft Edge lists all of your downloaded files for one-click access. You can also click the menu's Open Folder link to head straight for the Downloads folder mentioned in the preceding bullet.

Many downloaded files come packaged in a tidy folder with a zipper on it, known as a *Zip file*. Windows treats them like normal folders, so you can just double-click them to see inside them. (The files are actually compressed inside that folder to save download time, if you care about the engineering involved.) To extract copies of the zipped files, right-click the zipped file and choose Extract All.

Chapter **10**

Being Social: Mail, People, and Calendar

Thanks to the Internet's never-fading memory, your friends and acquaintances never disappear. Old college chums, business pals, and even those elementary school bullies are all waiting for you online. Toss in a few strangers you may have swapped messages with on websites, and the Internet has created a huge social network.

Windows helps you stay in touch with friends you enjoy and avoid those you don't. To manage your online social life, Windows includes a suite of intertwined social apps: Mail, Calendar, and People. You can pretty much guess which app handles what job.

Microsoft has improved the apps since the initial release of Windows 10, and they work together quite well, vastly simplifying the chore of tracking your contacts and appointments. This chapter describes the Windows suite of apps and how to set them up.

Adding Your Accounts to Windows

For years, you've heard people say, "Never tell *anybody* your user account name and password." Now, it seems Windows wants you to break that rule.

When you first open your People, Mail, or Calendar apps, Windows may ask you to enter your account names and passwords from your email services, as well as services such as Google or Apple's iCloud.

It's not as scary as you think, though. Microsoft and the other networks have agreed to share your information *only if you approve it.* And should you approve it, Windows connects to your accounts and imports information about your contacts, email, and calendar.

And, frankly, approving the information swap is a huge timesaver. When you link those accounts to Windows, your computer automatically signs in to each service, imports your friends' contact information, and stocks your apps.

To fill in Windows about your life online, follow these steps:

1. **Click the Start button. When the Start menu appears, open the Mail app.**

   Click the Mail tile, found along the Start menu's right edge, and the app opens.

2. **Enter your accounts into the Mail app.**

   When you first open the Mail app, it prompts you to add your email account or accounts, as shown in Figure 10-1. If you signed up with a Microsoft account that also serves as a Microsoft email address — one ending in Live, Hotmail, or Outlook, for example — that email address should already be listed and set up. You're done!

   To add other accounts, click the Add Account button. Mail then lists the accounts you can add: Outlook.com (which includes mail accounts held at Outlook.com, Live.com, Hotmail, and MSN), Exchange (used mostly by businesses or people using the Office 365 online programs), Google, iCloud (for Apple), Other Account (which means accounts from your Internet Service Provider that use POP or IMAP for access), or Advanced Setup, which lets you set up Exchange ActiveSync or web-based email.

   To add a Google account, for example, click the word Google. Windows takes you to a secure area on Google's website, where you can authorize the transaction by entering your Gmail email address and password and then clicking Accept or Connect.

   To add new email accounts from inside the Mail app, click the Settings icon (it looks like a gear) and choose Accounts from the Settings pane.

   Repeat these steps for any of your other listed accounts, authorizing each of them, if required, to share information with your Windows account.

After you've entered your accounts, Windows automatically fetches your email through your Mail app, fills the People app with your friends' contact information, and adds any appointments in your Calendar app.

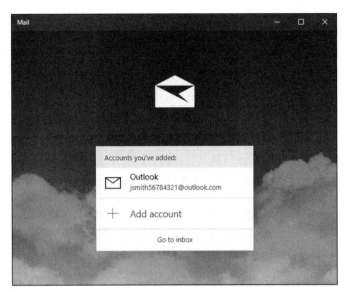

FIGURE 10-1:
The Mail app lets
you enter email
accounts from
services such as
Google, Hotmail,
Outlook, Yahoo!,
and others.

Although it might seem frightening to give Windows your coveted usernames and passwords, it enriches Windows in many ways:

>> Instead of typing in your contacts by hand, they're waiting for you automatically, whether they're from your Google, Hotmail, Outlook, Apple, or Windows Live account.

>> Windows apps work well with apps and programs from other companies. Your friends' birthdays from your Google calendar, for example, show up on the Calendar app without your having to enter them.

REMEMBER

>> Don't like these new-fangled Windows apps? Then ignore them. You can always spend your time on the Windows desktop instead. There you can visit Facebook and your other accounts from your web browser the same way you've always done.

>> If you're already accustomed to firing up your browser and reading your mail on Google, Yahoo, or any other online watering hole, you don't have to use the Mail app. You can still send and receive your mail the old-fashioned way.

Understanding the Mail App

Unlike Windows 7, Windows 10 includes a built-in app for sending and receiving email. Considered a *live* app, the Mail app automatically updates its Start menu's tile. A glance at the Start menu's Mail tile quickly shows you the senders' names and subjects of your latest emails.

NEW

Microsoft constantly tweaks Windows 10 and its apps. It updates Windows 10 twice a year, and it updates the Mail app more often than that. Don't be surprised to see the Mail app change subtly as Microsoft adds new features and drops old ones. The following sections explain how to make sense of the Mail app's menus, as well as how to compose, send, and read emails. (If you haven't already imported your email accounts, skip back to this chapter's first section.)

Switching among the Mail app's views, menus, and accounts

To load the Windows Mail app, open the Start menu (by clicking the Start button in the screen's bottom-left corner) and then click the Mail app tile (shown in the margin).

The Mail app appears, shown in Figure 10-2, displaying emails received from your primary email account — the first account you entered when setting up the app. (Chances are, it's your Microsoft account, which I describe in Chapter 2.) Figure 10-2, for example, shows the currently viewed Microsoft Live account at the pane's top. To see your mail from a different account, click that account's name along the left pane.

NEW

The Mail app separates your mail into two categories: *Focused* and *Other*. Mail from people in your contact list usually lands in the Focused category. Mass-mailed newsletters, by contrast, usually appear in the Other slot. You need to visit both to see all of your e-mail. (To place all of your email back into one category — your Inbox — visit the Mail app's Settings area, choose Focused Inbox, and turn off the toggle switch named Sort Messages into Focused and Other.)

Beneath the name of your currently viewed email account, the Mail app lists its folders:

>> **Inbox:** Shown when you first load the Mail app, the Inbox folder lists your waiting email, with your newest email at the top. The Mail app automatically checks for new email every few minutes, but if you tire of waiting, click the Sync button (shown in the margin) atop that account's list of received emails. That action immediately grabs any waiting mail.

>> **Drafts:** If you write a message but don't send it for some reason, it waits here, ready for your further attention.

>> **Sent Items:** Click here to see the messages you've *sent* rather than received from others.

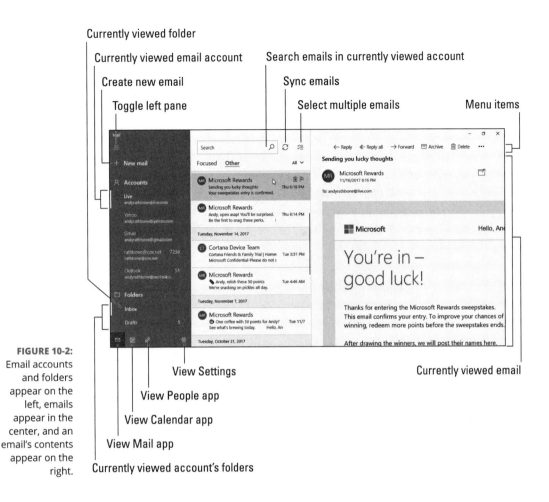

Currently viewed folder

Currently viewed email account

Create new email

Toggle left pane

Search emails in currently viewed account

Sync emails

Select multiple emails

Menu items

View Settings

View People app

View Calendar app

View Mail app

Currently viewed account's folders

Currently viewed email

FIGURE 10-2:
Email accounts and folders appear on the left, emails appear in the center, and an email's contents appear on the right.

>> **More:** If you don't see all of your account's folders, click More to find them. A pop-out menu appears, listing them all. (In particular, peek in here to find your Trash folder, where you can retrieve accidentally deleted emails.)

The icons along the bottom of the left pane let you switch among the Calendar app, the Mail app, the People app (your contacts), and the Mail app's settings.

Click the Settings icon, for example, and a pane appears along the right, offering all the things you can tweak inside the Mail app. The Feedback app, found in several Microsoft apps, lets you play armchair critic, advising Microsoft on how to improve its apps.

TIP

The Mail app, like most apps, changes its width depending on the size of your display and the size of the Mail window itself. If the Mail app lacks the width to display everything, the left pane shrinks to a small strip showing icons instead of words, as shown in Figure 10-3. Click the Expand icon in the app's top-left corner, and the tiny left strip expands, showing you the same left pane shown in Figure 10-2, earlier.

TWEAKING THE MAIL APP'S SETTINGS

Click the little gear icon in the Mail app's bottom-left corner, and the Settings pane slides into view along the app's right edge. There, the Mail app lets you adjust its behavior. Here are some of the most useful switches:

- **Manage Accounts:** Head here to tweak the settings of your currently entered email accounts, as well as to add new accounts. Once an email account's settings finally work, though, you rarely need to change them.

- **Personalization:** Interior decorators can visit here to change the Mail app's colors and background.

- **Signature:** Here's where you can change your *signature* — the words appearing beneath every email you send. You can use a different signature on each of your email accounts.

- **Automatic Replies:** Head here to create an "I'm sunning myself in Mazatlán for the next week" reply. The Mail app then automatically sends that reply to any email you receive while vacationing.

- **Signature:** Microsoft automatically slips the words "Sent from Mail from Windows 10" to every email you send. Head here to either turn it off or change the wording.

- **Trust Center:** This oddly named and mysterious entry lets you control whether Microsoft can send you information based on your email's content. Presumably, this authorizes Microsoft's robots to send you pertinent ads, as well as for Cortana to read your mail. (When the Trust Center pane appears, click the Learn More link to read Microsoft's online privacy page.)

- **Feedback:** A holdover from when Microsoft let people test Windows 10 before its release, this option lets you send Microsoft comments about the app's performance. Presumably, somebody at Microsoft is still listening.

- **About:** Handy mostly when troubleshooting, this area reveals the app's version number.

You may never need to set foot in the Settings area, but when things go wrong, this is usually the first troubleshooting destination.

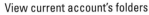

View current account's folders

Switch email accounts

Start new email

Expand left pane   Display formatting options

Insert table, picture, or link

Check spelling, zoom, or search

Discard draft   Send email

Adjust Settings

View People app

View Calendar app

View Mail app

Currently viewed mail

Composing and sending an email

When you're ready to send an email, follow these steps to compose your letter and drop it in the electronic mailbox, sending it through virtual space to the recipient's computer:

1. **From the Start menu, open the Mail app's tile (shown in the margin) and click the New Mail icon (it's a plus sign icon) in the app's top-left corner.**

   A new and blank email appears, awaiting your words.

   If you've added more than one email account to the Mail app, first choose your return address by clicking your desired account name from the Accounts section along the Mail app's right pane. *Then* click the New Mail icon in the program's top-left corner.

   TECHNICAL STUFF

2. **Type your friend's email address into the To box.**

   As you begin typing, the Mail app scans your contacts for both names and email addresses, listing potential matches below the To box. Spot a match on the list? Click it, and the Mail app automatically fills in the rest of the email address.

To add another person to the list, begin typing their name in the To box, as well. Want to send an e-mail regularly to the same group of people? Unfortunately, the Mail app makes you retype everybody's name. It doesn't let you save groups for future mailings. (Microsoft says it's been working on that feature for more than a year.)

3. **Click in the Subject line and type a subject.**

   Click in the line labeled Subject and type your subject. In Figure 10-3, for example, I've added the subject "Garage door opener feature request." Although technically optional, the Subject line helps your friends sort their mail.

4. **Type your message into the large box beneath the Subject line.**

   Type as many words as you want. As you type, the Mail app automatically corrects any noticed misspellings.

5. **If you want, add any formatting, tables, files, or photos to your email.**

   The menu directly above your composed email offers three tabs, each with different options:

   - **Format:** This option lets you change your email's formatting by selecting portions of your email and then clicking the bold, italics, underline, or font color icons along the window's top edge, as shown earlier in Figure 10-3. To change the font size, click the tiny downward-pointing arrow next to the underlined *A* icon. A menu drops down, letting you change the font and font size, as well as clear the formatting from any selected item.

   - **Insert:** Click here to attach files, as I describe in this chapter's later section, "Sending and receiving files through email." This tab also lets you insert tables, pictures, and hyperlinks.

   - **Options:** Click here after composing your email to give it a final spellcheck.

   Most ISPs don't send attached files totaling more than 25MB. That lets you send a song or two, a few digital photos, and most documents. It's not enough room to send any but the smallest videos.

6. **Check your spelling, if desired.**

   The Mail app does a pretty good job of correcting your spelling as you type. But to proofread more closely before sending your mail, click the Options button along the Mail app's top edge. Then choose Spelling from the drop-down menu.

   The Mail app jumps to each error it finds. When it finds a problem, it highlights the word and places a drop-down menu where you can choose from potential replacements.

TIP

If the spellchecker constantly flags a correctly spelled word as being misspelled, choose Ignore All from the drop-down menu. That keeps the program from bugging you about a word it doesn't understand.

7. **Click the Send button along the top-right corner.**

Whoosh! The Mail app whisks your message through the Internet to your friend's mailbox. Depending on the speed of your Internet connection, mail can arrive anywhere from a few seconds to a few hours later, with a few minutes being the average.

Don't want to send the message? Then delete it with a click of the Discard button in the top–right corner.

Reading a received email

When your computer is connected to the Internet, Windows 10 heralds the arrival of a newly received email in several ways. An announcement appears in the Action Center, the pane that periodically appears along the screen's right edge. Also, the Mail app's Start menu tile automatically updates itself to show the sender and subject of your latest unread emails.

To see more information than that — or to respond to the message — follow these steps:

1. **Click the Start menu's Mail tile.**

   Mail opens to show the messages in your Inbox, as shown earlier in Figure 10-3. Each subject is listed, one by one, with the newest one at the top.

   To find a particular email quickly, click the Magnifying Glass icon at the top of your email column. A search box appears alongside the icon where you can type the sender's name or a keyword into the search box. Press the Enter key to see all the matching emails.

TIP

2. **Click the subject of any message you want to read.**

   The Mail app spills that message's contents into the pane along the window's right side.

3. **From here, the Mail app leaves you with several options, each accessed from the buttons along the email's top edge:**

   - **Nothing:** Undecided? Don't do anything, and the message simply sets up camp in your Inbox folder.

   - **Reply:** Click the Reply button, and a new window appears, ready for you to type in your response. The window is just like the one that appears when you first compose a message but with a handy difference: This window is already addressed with the recipient's name and the subject. Also, the original message usually appears at the bottom of your reply for reference.

- **Reply All:** Some people address emails to several people simultaneously. If you see several other people listed on an email's To line, you can reply to *all* of them by clicking Reply All.

- **Forward:** Received something that a friend simply must see? Click Forward to kick a copy of the email to your friend's Inbox.

- **Delete:** Click the Delete button to toss the message into your Trash or Deleted Items folder. (Different email accounts use different words for that folder.)

- **Set Flag:** Clicking the Set Flag icon places a little flag icon next to an email, reminding you to deal with it at a later date.

- **Actions:** Clicking this fetches a drop-down menu that lists any menu items above that didn't fit on your particular screen. The menu's Move option, for example, lets you move an item out of your Inbox and into a different folder. (Save and Print options appear on the Actions drop-down menu, as well.)

Some email accounts also feature an Archive button, which removes the mail from your Inbox and stashes it in a folder named Archive. That keeps the email out of sight, but ready for retrieval later, if desired.

The Mail app works well for basic email needs, but it has its limitations. If you're struggling to find a missing feature, it's probably not included. If you need more, Microsoft encourages you to purchase its Microsoft Office suite of programs or to pay a subscription fee to join its Office 365 mail service.

If you don't want to pay extra, you may be able to open your web browser and manage your email online, such as at Outlook (www.outlook.com), **Google** (www.google.com/gmail), or your ISP's own website.

WARNING

If you ever receive an unexpected email from a bank or any other money related website, don't click any of the email's web links. A criminal industry called *phishing* sends emails that try to trick you into entering your name and password on a phony website. That gives your coveted information to the evil folk, who promptly steal your money. I write more about phishing in Chapter 11.

TIP

Don't want your Mail app's Start menu tile to display your emails' sender and subject? Then right-click its Start menu tile, click More from the pop-up menu, and choose Turn Live Tile Off.

Sending and receiving files through email

Like a gift card slipped into the envelope of a thank-you note, an *attachment* is a file that piggybacks onto an email message. You can send or receive any type of file as an attachment.

The following sections describe how to both send and receive a file through the Mail app.

Saving a received attachment

When an attachment arrives in an email, you'll recognize it: A paperclip icon rests next to the email's subject. And when you open the email, you see a photo thumbnail or a message saying, "Download Message and Pictures."

Saving the attached file or files takes just a few steps:

1. **Download the attached file.**

   The Mail app doesn't download the files until you specifically give it the command. Instead, the Mail app shows generic thumbnails — placeholders for attached folders — along the email's top edge.

   You can save the file either of two ways:

   - Click the attached file's thumbnail icon. When the thumbnail shows a miniature of the attached file, right-click it and choose Save.

   - Right-click the attached file and choose Download from the pop-up menu. When the download completes, the generic thumbnails fill in with images or icons representing the newly downloaded files.

2. **Choose a storage area to receive the saved file.**

   File Explorer's Save As window appears, shown in Figure 10-4, ready for you to save the file in your Documents folder. To save it someplace else, choose any folder listed along the Save As window's left edge. Or, click the words This PC, also on the window's left edge, and begin browsing to the folder that should receive the file.

TIP

   Saving the file inside one of your four main folders — Documents, Pictures, Videos, or Music — is the easiest way to ensure you'll be able to find it later. (I describe files and folders in Chapter 5.) When you choose a folder, you see a list of existing folders where you can stash your new file.

   To create a new folder inside your currently viewed folder, click the New Folder button from the menu along the folder's top and, when the new folder appears, type in a name for the folder.

![Save As dialog window]

3. **Click the Save button in the Save As window's bottom-right corner.**

   The Mail app saves the file in the folder of your choosing.

After you've saved the file, the attachment still remains inside the email. That's because saving attachments always saves a *copy* of the sent file. If you accidentally delete or botch an edit on your saved file, you can always return to the original email and save the attached file yet again.

Windows Defender, the built-in virus checker in Windows, automatically scans your incoming email for evil file attachments. I explain more about Windows Defender in Chapter 11. Still, if you feel suspicious about the attachment, or it arrives unexpectedly, don't download it. (Just delete the entire email.)

Sending a file as an attachment

Sending a file through the Mail app works much like saving an attached file, although in reverse: Instead of grabbing a file from an email and saving it into a folder, you're grabbing a file from a folder and saving it in an email.

To send a file as an attachment in the Mail app, follow these steps:

1. **Open the Mail app and create a new email.**

   I describe creating a new email in this chapter's earlier "Composing and sending an email" section.

2. **Click the Insert tab from the Mail app's top menu and then choose Files from the drop-down menu.**

   When you choose Files from the drop-down menu, File Explorer's Open window appears, showing the contents of your Documents folder.

   If the Documents folder contains the file you'd like to send, jump to Step 4. To send something from a different folder, move to Step 3.

3. **Navigate to the storage area and file you want to send.**

   Click the words This PC along the Open window's left edge, and a menu appears listing all of your storage areas. Most files are stored in your Documents, Pictures, Music, and Videos folders.

   Click a folder's name to open it and see the files lurking inside. Not the correct folder? Click the Up Arrow icon (shown in the margin) to move back out of the folder and try again.

4. **Click the file you want to send and click the Open button.**

   Click a file to select it. To select several files, hold down the Ctrl key while selecting them. Selected too many files? Deselect unwanted files by clicking their names yet again. When you click the Attach button, the Mail app adds the file or files to your email.

5. **Click the Send button.**

   The Mail app whisks off your mail and its attachment to the recipient.

REMEMBER When you send an attached file, you're only sending a copy. Your original stays safely on your computer. Also, most ISPs limit attachment size to 25MB or less. That's enough to send a few photos, but rarely enough for videos. (Share those on YouTube or Facebook.)

Managing Your Contacts in the People App

When you enter your email addresses into the Mail app, Windows grabs all of your online contacts it can find. That means you've probably already stocked the People app with your online friends. The app serves mostly as a simple address book that lists your contacts and their contact information.

Unfortunately, the People app works only with online accounts. It's one of many ways Microsoft subtly nudges you to sign up for a Microsoft account that uses one of Microsoft's email services, either Live or Outlook.

To launch the People app, click the Start menu's People tile. The People app appears, presenting all of your online friends in an alphabetical list, as shown in Figure 10-5.

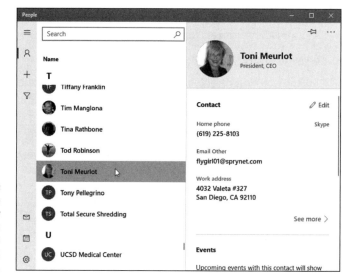

FIGURE 10-5:
The People app automatically stocks itself with contacts from your email accounts.

The People app contains two main panes: Your list of contacts, and the details about the contact you've currently clicked on. Here's what you'll see:

» **Contacts:** The app presents an alphabetical list of your friends. When you click a contact's name, their details spill across the adjacent pane to the right, which offers three options:

- **Profile:** The default view for the second pane, Profile lists your selected friend's photo and contact information.

- **Events:** Click Events to send the People app racing to the Calendar app, where it prepares a dossier of your scheduled meetings. That person's appointments then appear as clickable links to provide quick access.

- **Conversations:** Click this to see a list of clickable emails involving that person.

» **Pushpin:** When you spot a popular contact, click the pushpin icon atop the pane and choose Pin to Start to place their smiling face on a Start menu tile for easy access. Or, choose Pin to Taskbar to place their face on your taskbar along the screen's bottom edge, where's it's *always* visible.

» **Edit:** To edit a contact's details — change a phone number, perhaps — click the Edit link that's next to the pencil icon. (Clicking this also lets you add a photo to a faceless contact.)

>> **See More:** A catch-all area for items that don't fit elsewhere, this area lets you merge duplicate contacts into one.

The People app handles much of its upkeep automatically, updating itself with any changes you make to your iCloud or Google contacts. That means that updates you make to contacts on your iPhone or Android phone automatically appear in the People app and vice versa.

Occasionally, though, you need to add or edit some People entries manually. The following sections explain the occasional pruning needed to keep up with your constantly evolving contacts list.

Adding contacts

TIP

Although the People app loves to add contacts automatically, you can easily add people the old-fashioned way, typing them in by hand. However, the app forces you to choose which of your online accounts should accept the new entry.

To add somebody to the People app, which makes that person available in your Mail and Calendar apps, follow these steps:

1. **Click the People tile on the Start menu.**

The People app appears onscreen.

2. **Click the Add Contact icon (shown in the margin).**

3. **If asked, choose which account to use for saving new contacts.**

The People app asks you to decide which account should receive the new contact.

The answer hinges mainly on which cellphone you own. Choose your Google account if you use an Android phone, so your newly added contact appears in your Gmail contacts. From there, it also appears in your Android phone's contacts list. Similarly, iPhone owners should choose iCloud.

Choose the Outlook account if you own a Windows phone or you run the Outlook app on your iPhone or Android smartphone.

The People app remembers your choice and doesn't ask you again.

4. **Fill out the New Contact form.**

Shown in Figure 10-6, most of the choices are self-explanatory fields such as Name, Phone, Email, Address, and Other. (The Other field lets you add details such as a job title, website, significant other, or notes.)

To add a photo, click the Add Photo button; the Photo app appears, letting you choose from a previously shot photo.

5. **Click the Save button along the window's bottom edge.**

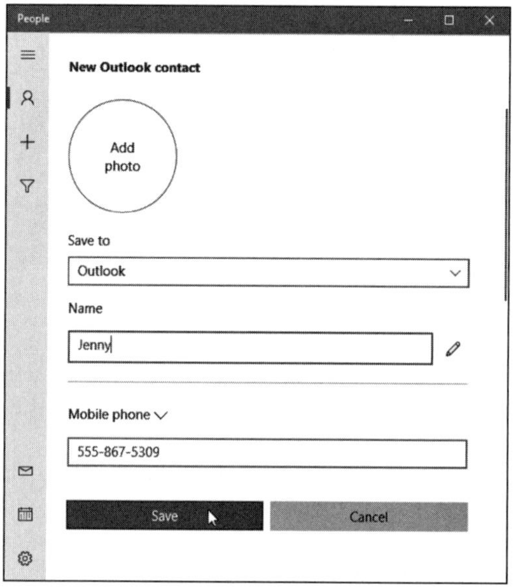

New Outlook contact

Add photo

Save to

Outlook

Name

Jenny

Mobile phone

555-867-5309

Save   Cancel

FIGURE 10-6:
Fill in contact information and then click the Save icon.

The People app dutifully saves your new contact. If you spot a mistake, however, you may need to go back and edit the information, described in the next section.

Deleting or editing contacts

Has somebody fallen from your social graces? Or perhaps someone just changed a phone number? Either way, it's easy to delete or edit a contact manually by following these steps:

1. **Click the People tile on the Start menu.**

    The People app appears, as shown earlier in Figure 10-5.

2. **To delete a contact, right-click his name and choose Delete from the pop-up menu.**

    The person disappears from both the People app and the email account that currently held that contact.

3. **To edit a contact, right-click his name and choose Edit from the pop-up menu.**

    The person's contact information appears, shown earlier in Figure 10-6, for you to edit.

4. **Click the Save button along the window's bottom edge.**

    The People app updates your contacts list, both in the app itself and in the online account where that contact is stored. Edit a Gmail contact in the People app, for example, and Gmail also reflects the changes.

Managing Appointments in Calendar

After you enter your online accounts such as Gmail, Outlook, Live.com, and others, as described in this chapter's first section, you've already stocked the Calendar app with your existing appointments.

 To see your appointments, click the Start menu's Calendar tile, shown in the margin. Or, if you're working in the Mail app, click the Calendar icon from the Mail app's bottom-left corner.

When first opened, the Calendar app asks you to add your email accounts. If you've already entered your accounts into the Mail app, they already show up here.

The Calendar opens to show any appointments associated with your linked email accounts, like Google, iCloud, or Outlook.com. To see more or fewer days displayed, click the Day, Week, Month, or Year button along the top. If you click Week, for example, the Calendar app appears, as shown in Figure 10-7.

Unless you keep all your appointments online, you'll need to edit some entries, add new ones, or delete those you can no longer attend. This section explains how to keep your appointments up-to-date.

TIP No matter which view the Calendar app displays, you can flip through the appointments by clicking the little arrows near the listed month in the screen's top-left corner. Click the right arrow to move forward in time; click the left arrow to move backward.

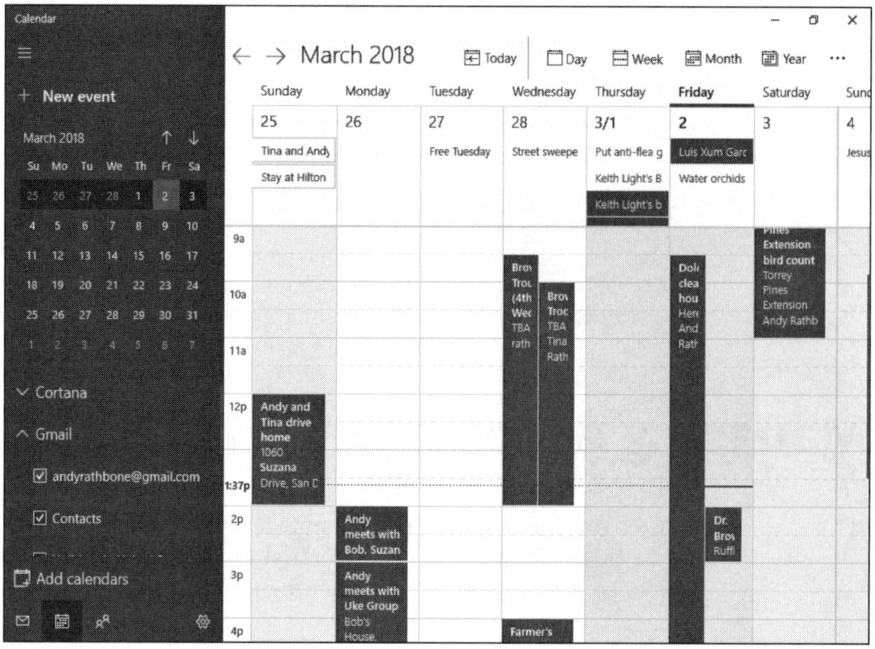

FIGURE 10-7:
The Calendar app displays appointments you add manually or from your online calendars.

To add an appointment to your Calendar app, follow these steps:

1. **Click the Calendar tile on the Start menu.**

   The Calendar app appears, as shown in Figure 10-7.

   If you're in the Mail app, you can also click the Calendar app's icon in the Mail app's lower-left corner (shown in the margin.)

2. **Click the New Event link from the Calendar app's top-left corner.**

   A blank event template appears, ready for you to fill in the time and place, as well as to invite people.

3. **Fill out the Details form.**

   Shown in Figure 10-8, most of the choices are self-explanatory fields.

   The biggest challenge comes with the Details field's drop-down menu, which only appears if you've entered more than one email account into your Mail app. Which email *account* should receive the new calendar appointment?

   Again, the answer depends on your phone. Choose Gmail to send appointments to Gmail's calendar, where they appear on your Android phone. Choose iCloud for your iPhone.

Or, you can choose Outlook: You can then download and install the Outlook app, available on both Android and iPhones. The Outlook app can sync the Windows 10 Calendar app's appointments with your phone.

4. **Click the Save & Close button.**

The Calendar app adds your new appointment to its own calendar, as well as to whichever account you chose in Step 3.

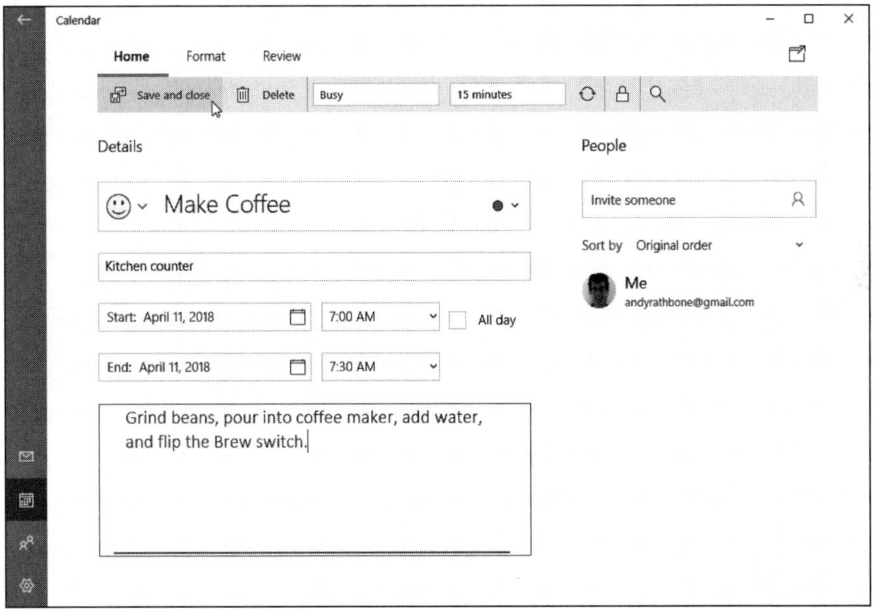

FIGURE 10-8:
Add your appointment's date, start time, duration, and other details.

To edit or delete an appointment, open it from the Calendar app. Click the Delete button (shown in the margin) from the top menu. To edit it, open it from the Calendar app, make your changes, and save your changes by clicking the Save & Close button.

Chapter **11**

Safe Computing

L ike driving a car, working with Windows is reasonably safe as long as you avoid bad neighborhoods, obey traffic signals, and don't steer with your feet while looking out the sunroof.

But in the world of Windows and the Internet, there's no easy way to recognize a bad neighborhood, find a traffic signal, or know what's dangerous. Something that appears to be fun, innocent, or important — a friend's email, a downloaded program, or a message from a bank — may be a virus that infects your computer.

This chapter helps you recognize the bad streets in virtual neighborhoods and explains the steps you can take to protect yourself from harm and minimize any damage. Along the way, it introduces you to the new Windows Defender Security Center and its collection of tools that help identify and avert threats.

Understanding Those Annoying Permission Messages

After more than 20 years of development, Windows is still pretty naive. Sometimes when you run a program or try to change a setting on your PC, Windows can't tell whether *you're* doing the work or a *virus* is trying to move in behind your back.

The Windows solution? When Windows notices anybody (or anything) trying to change something that can potentially harm Windows or your PC, it darkens the screen and flashes a security message asking for permission, like the one shown in Figure 11-1.

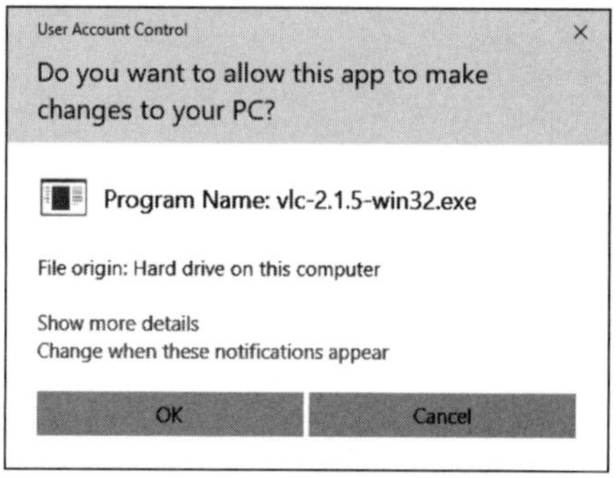

FIGURE 11-1:
Click Don't Install,
Cancel, or
No if a message
like this appears
unexpectedly.

If one of these User Account Control security messages appears out of the blue, Windows may be warning you about a bit of nastiness trying to sneak in. So click Cancel, No, or Don't Install to deny it permission. But if *you're* trying to install a trusted program onto your PC and Windows puts up its boxing gloves, click OK, Yes, or Install instead. Windows drops its guard and lets you in.

If you don't hold an Administrator account, however, you can't simply approve the deed. You must track down an Administrator account holder (usually the PC's owner) and ask her to type her password.

Yes, a rather dimwitted security robot guards the front door to Windows, but it's also an extra challenge for the people who write the viruses.

Staying Safe with the New Windows Defender Security Center

Last year, Microsoft updated Windows 10 with the new Windows Defender Security Center. No longer simply an antivirus program, the Windows Defender Security Center is a handy place to access the seven biggest security features in Windows 10. Hopefully, though, you won't need to visit any of them: The security features all work automatically and come preset to keep you safe. In fact, if an inadvertent settings change leaves you unsafe, the program quickly notifies you and shows you which toggle switch needs to be flipped to the safer position.

To launch the program, click the Start button, and, when the Start menu appears, choose Windows Defender Security Center. The program appears, shown in Figure 11-2.

FIGURE 11-2:
The new Windows Defender Security Center helps keep your computer safe.

The program offers these categories:

>> **Virus & Threat Protection:** Covered in this chapter's next section, this area lets you access settings for Windows Defender Antivirus. The program runs automatically, constantly scanning your PC for threats. But you may want to visit here to run a quick, unscheduled scan if you suspect foul play.

>> **Account Protection:** Visit here to check on the security of your user account. You can also set up a fingerprint reader: a swipe of your fingertip lets you into your PC without having to type in a password.

>> **Firewall & Network Protection:** Hidden in here are settings for the Windows built-in firewall, which helps stop hackers from breaking into your computer through the Internet. It's turned on automatically, so you'll probably never need to visit here.

>> **App & Browser Control:** Leave these switches set to "Warn." That tells Windows Defender to warn you if you try to download an unsafe app or file, or if the Edge browser visits an unsafe website. I cover this subject in the "Avoiding Phishing Scams" section later in this chapter.

>> **Device Security:** This lets you check on the security measures built directly into your PC's hardware, including its memory chips and central processing unit (CPU).

>> **Device Performance & Health:** If Windows doesn't seem to be running correctly, visit this section. It lets you know whether your PC is running low on storage room and notifies you of any problems with *drivers:* pieces of software that let your PC talk with devices like mice, keyboards, and other computer parts. This section also alerts you to trouble with any of your apps or programs. (I devote Chapter 18 to troubleshooting Windows 10.)

>> **Family Options:** This leads you online to set up ways to control and monitor how your children use their PCs and other Windows 10 devices. (I cover this subject in the "Setting Up Controls for Children" section later in this chapter.)

If you've installed third-party antivirus or firewall apps, the Windows Defender Security Center provides updates on those, as well.

When everything's running smoothly, the security center's icons bear a green check mark. The check mark turns into an exclamation point when something's amiss, alerting you that you should visit that category and take the recommended action.

Avoiding and removing viruses

When it comes to viruses, *everything* is suspect. Viruses travel not only through email messages, websites, programs, files, networks, and flash drives, but also in screen savers, themes, toolbars, and other Windows add-ons.

To combat the problem, Windows 10 includes the free Windows Defender Antivirus, part of a suite of programs known as the Windows Defender Security Center.

Windows Defender Antivirus scans everything that enters your computer, whether through downloads, email, networks, messaging programs, flash drives, or discs. Unless you tell it not to, the program casts a watchful eye on your OneDrive files, as well.

When Windows Defender Antivirus notices something evil trying to enter your computer, it lets you know with a message in your screen's lower-right corner, as shown in Figure 11-3. Then the antivirus program quickly quarantines the virus before it has a chance to infect your computer.

Windows Defender Antivirus automatically updates itself to recognize new viruses, and it constantly scans your PC for threats in the background. But if your PC acts strangely, tell Windows Defender Antivirus to scan your PC immediately by following these steps:

FIGURE 11-3:
Windows
Defender detects
and removes an
intruder.

1. **Click the taskbar's Windows Defender Security Center icon (shown in the margin) near the clock.**

   The Security Center program appears, shown earlier in Figure 11-2. Don't spot the program's icon on the taskbar? Then click the little upward-pointing arrow near the taskbar's right edge; a pop-up menu appears, showing the Windows Defender Security Center icon.

   You can also launch Windows Defender Security Center from the Settings app's Update & Security section. (I cover the newly updated Settings app in Chapter 12.)

2. **Click the Security Center's Virus & Threat Protection icon from the left column.**

   The Virus and Threat protection window appears.

3. **Click the program's Scan Now button.**

   Windows Defender Antivirus immediately performs a quick scan of your PC.

   To perform a full scan, which takes longer but scans more files, click the Run a New Advanced Scan link beneath the Scan Now button. When the Advanced Scan window appears, click the Full Scan option, then click the Scan Now button.

IS WINDOWS DEFENDER ANTIVIRUS GOOD ENOUGH?

Like several Windows versions before it, Windows 10 includes the Windows Defender Antivirus program. Windows Defender Antivirus runs quickly, updates automatically, and catches the most common malware before it invades your computer.

But is it *better* than third-party antivirus programs, including the ones that charge recurring subscription fees? The answer depends on several things.

For example, most third-party antivirus programs will catch more viruses than Windows Defender Antivirus. However, doing that extra work can slow down your PC. Some powerful security suites throw up false alarms, as well, leaving you the work of sorting out the problem. Many seem complicated and cumbersome.

Windows Defender Antivirus works best for people who can spot a potential virus as it arrives in the mail and avoid clicking on suspicious email attachments. People who feel more comfortable with a larger safety net will prefer a paid program. There's no right or wrong answer.

Instead, your answer depends on your personal comfort level. If you find a reasonably priced third-party antivirus program that doesn't slow down your computer too much, then stick with it. But if you feel confident in your ability to weed out most potential attackers before you click on them, Windows Defender Antivirus might be all you need.

TIP

To run a quick scan from the desktop, right-click the Windows Defender Security Center icon on your taskbar and choose Run Quick Scan from the pop-up menu.

Even with Windows Defender Security Center watching your back, follow these rules to reduce your risk of infection:

REMEMBER

>> Open only attachments that you're expecting. If you receive something unexpected from a friend, don't open it. Instead, email or phone that person to ask whether he or she really sent you something. Your friend's computer might be infected and trying to infect your computer, as well.

>> Be wary of items arriving in email that ask for a click. For example, if you receive a message saying somebody wants to be a Facebook friend, don't click it. Instead, visit Facebook from your browser and look to see whether the person is listed on your "waiting to be friended" list. The more emailed links you can avoid, the safer you'll be.

>> If you receive an important-looking email from a financial institution that asks you to click a link and type in your name and password, don't do it. Instead,

visit your financial institution's website through your web browser and log in there. Chances are good that there's nothing wrong with your account, and that email was only trying to steal your username and password. (This type of scam is often called phishing, and I describe it further in the next section.)

>> Updates for Windows Defender Antivirus arrive automatically through Windows Update. Windows 10 keeps Windows Update running constantly, so you don't need to worry about keeping Windows Defender updated.

WARNING

>> If you prefer running a third-party antivirus programs, you're welcome to do so. It will turn off Windows Defender Antivirus automatically as part of its install process. But don't install *two* third-party antivirus programs, because they often quarrel.

Avoiding Phishing Scams

Eventually you'll receive an email from your bank, eBay, PayPal, or a similar website announcing a problem with your account. Invariably, the email offers a handy link to click, saying that you must enter your username and password to set things in order.

WARNING

Don't do it, no matter how realistic the email and website may appear. You're seeing an ugly industry called *phishing:* Fraudsters send millions of these messages worldwide, hoping to convince a few frightened souls into typing their precious account name and password.

How do you tell the real emails from the fake ones? It's easy, actually, because all these emails are fake. Finance-related sites may send you legitimate history statements, receipts, or confirmation notices, but they will never, ever email you an unexpected link for you to click and enter your password.

TIP

If you're suspicious, visit the company's *real* website by typing the web address by hand into your web browser's Address bar. Chances are good that the real site won't list anything as being wrong with your account.

Both Internet Explorer and the new Microsoft Edge browser use Windows Defender SmartScreen Filter technology that compares a website's address with a list of known phishing sites. If it finds a match, the SmartScreen filter keeps you from entering, as shown in Figure 11-4. Should you ever spot that screen, close the web page by clicking the words Back to Safety listed on the warning message.

So, why can't the authorities simply arrest those people responsible? Because Internet thieves are notoriously difficult to track down and prosecute. The reach of the Internet lets them work from any place in the world, hidden beneath a maze of networks.

>> If you've already entered your name and password into a phishing site, take action immediately: Visit the real website and change your password. Then contact the company involved and ask it for help. It may be able to stop the thieves before they wrap their electronic fingers around your account.

>> If you've entered credit card information, call the card's issuer immediately. You can almost always find a toll-free, 24-hour phone number on the back of your credit card.

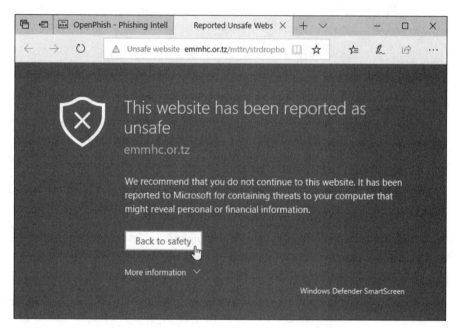

FIGURE 11-4:
Microsoft Edge warns you when you visit a suspected phishing site.

Setting Up Controls for Children

A feature much-welcomed by parents and much-booed by their children, Microsoft's Family Options area offers several ways to monitor how children can access the computer as well as the Internet.

Rather than running as a program on your computer, Microsoft's family controls now work online through a Microsoft website. By tracking your children's activity through their Microsoft account usage, you can monitor their online activity wherever they log in to a Windows 10 PC or Windows 10 smartphone. The online, password-protected records stay online, where you can access them from any PC, tablet, or smartphone.

Microsoft's family controls only work if both you and your children have Microsoft accounts.

To set up Microsoft's family controls, follow these steps:

1. **Add your children and any adults who want to monitor the children as family members when creating their user accounts.**

I describe how to add family members when creating user accounts in Chapter 14. When you add family members to your PC's list of user accounts, each member receives an email inviting them to join your family network; when they accept, their accounts automatically appear on your computer.

2. **Visit Microsoft's family website.**

Click the Start button, click the Settings icon, and choose Accounts. Click Family & Other People from the left pane; on the right pane, click the Manage Family Settings Online link.

Alternatively, you can open any browser and visit the website at https://account.microsoft.com/family/. Log in with your Microsoft Account, and the site opens to show your list of family members who have accepted their invitations. Click the name of a family member, and the website, shown in Figure 11-5, lets you set limits on that child's computer behavior, as well as monitor his activity.

You can also visit the online settings by visiting the Microsoft Defender Security Center, covered earlier in this chapter, choosing Family Options, and choosing the View Family Settings link.

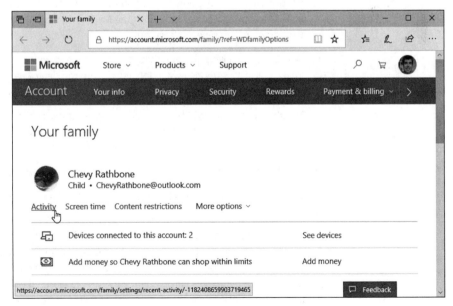

FIGURE 11-5: Microsoft's family website lets you set limits on your children's computer activity.

3. **Turn on the categories you'd like to enforce, and set the limits.**

Microsoft's family area contains a variety of categories that let you monitor or control different areas of behavior. Visit any of the categories described below, and each opens a new page with a toggle control at the top. Turn the toggle to either On or Off, then fine-tune the offered settings. (You can also turn categories Off to temporarily suspend monitoring in those areas.)

Microsoft's family website offers these categories, which apply whenever your child uses his Microsoft account to sign in to any computer, phone, or tablet:

- **Activity:** A haven for time-stressed parents, the Activity area offers a quick rundown of your child's computer activity, along with an option to have the information emailed to you each week.

- **Screen Time:** This area lets you control the hours when your child may access his PC or Xbox game system. Click the On toggle next to either category, and a grid appears for you to choose the exact hours your child is allowed to access the device.

- **Content descriptions:** Visit here to control whether your child needs adult approval for spending money, as well as to block access to inappropriate apps, games, media, and websites.

- **Devices:** This area shows the names of devices your children have logged in to with their Microsoft accounts.

- **Spending:** Want your child to be able to purchase items from the Microsoft Store? Head here and click the button corresponding to the amount. It's withdrawn from the credit card attached to your Microsoft account, and added to your child's account. Click the More Options button, and a drop-down menu reveals these options:

- **Find Child on a Map:** If your child is one of the few with a Windows smartphone, this toggle switch lets you locate the device — and, hopefully, your child — on a map.

- **Remove from Family:** Choose this when your grown child leaves the nest. This removes your child from the Family settings. They still retain their Microsoft account, but you can no longer monitor their activity.

4. **When you're through, close the Microsoft window in your browser.**

Your changes take place immediately. When you're through, just close your web browser.

Although Microsoft's family controls work well, few things in the computer world are foolproof. If you're worried about your children's computer use, cast an occasional eye their way. Also, these controls only monitor your child when he logs in with his Microsoft account and uses either Edge or Internet Explorer. If you spot an unfamiliar account (or a different browser) on the PC, it's time to ask some questions.

4

Customizing and Upgrading Windows 10

IN THIS PART . . .

Customize Windows with the newly upgraded Settings app.

Keep Windows running smoothly.

Share one computer among several people.

Connect computers with a network.

Chapter **12**

Customizing Settings in Windows

Most people hate changing settings in Windows, and for good reason: They're too complicated. How do you know which setting works best? How can you even *find* the right setting? And, if you flip the wrong switch, how do you undo any peripheral damage?

Windows doesn't make this easy, unfortunately, because several things work against you. First, each app includes its own, individual batch of settings. Windows, too, contains another set of master settings known as the Settings app. Finally, Windows 10 occasionally kicks you to that old switch-filled circuit box known as the Control Panel, a remnant from earlier Windows versions.

But no matter which bank of switches you face, they all let you customize the look, feel, behavior, and vibe of Windows and its programs. This chapter explains how to find the settings you need, what to do with them once discovered, and how to undo their handiwork if they simply make things worse.

One word of caution: Some settings can be changed only by the person holding the almighty Administrator account — usually the computer's owner. If Windows refuses to flip a switch, call the PC's owner for help.

Finding the Right Switch

NEW

Microsoft released Windows 10 in July 2015, and the company never stopped updating it. For example, the Settings app alone now sports hundreds of new entries. The Control Panel bundled with earlier Windows versions still lurks in Windows 10, and it holds a few settings yet to be moved to the new Settings app.

To find the right switch to flip, let Windows help you. Follow these steps to find the setting you need:

1. **Click the Start button, click in the adjacent Search box, and type a word describing your desired setting.**

   When you type the first letter, every setting containing that letter appears in a list above the Search box. If you don't know the exact name of your setting, begin typing a keyword: **display, troubleshoot, mouse, user, privacy,** or something that describes your need.

TIP

   Don't see the right setting? Press the Backspace key to delete the letters you've typed and then try again with a different word.

   The Search box, described in Chapter 7, lists other matches for your keyword: files on your computer, apps from Microsoft Store, and even items found on websites. If you see too much clutter, filter the results: Type the word **settings:** into the Search box, followed by a space and your search term. For example, to search for camera settings, type this into the Search box and press Enter:

   ```
   settings: camera
   ```

TIP

   Don't see the Search box? Right-click an empty portion of the taskbar along the screen's bottom edge and choose Cortana from the pop-up menu. Then choose Show Search Box from the second pop-up menu. (Or, if your computer runs in Tablet mode, click the Cortana icon — the little circle near the Start button — to fetch Cortana and the Search box.)

2. **Click your desired setting on the list.**

   Windows takes you directly to that setting.

When searching for a setting, always try the Search box first. Spending a few minutes at the Search pane yields better results than scouring the hundreds of settings haphazardly stuffed into Windows 10.

Looking for the settings inside a particular *app*, rather than inside Windows itself? Look in the app's upper-right corner for an icon containing either three dots in a row or three stacked lines. Click that icon, and a drop-down menu appears, almost always listing an entry for Settings.

Flipping Switches with the Windows Settings App

NEW

Microsoft's Spring 2018 update tossed more settings than ever into the ever-expanding Settings app in Windows 10. Most Windows settings live there now, sparing you a trip to the old Control Panel found in previous Windows versions.

To open the Settings app, click the Start button and click the Settings icon (a little gear) near the bottom of the Start menu's left pane.

The Settings app appears, as shown in Figure 12-1. The Settings app looks nearly identical whether you're viewing Windows 10 on a PC, tablet, laptop, or Windows phone.

FIGURE 12-1:
The Settings app lets you change your computer's behavior.

The Settings app breaks its settings down into an unlucky thirteen categories, each covered in the rest of this chapter.

System

This huge catch-all category collects settings that don't fit neatly anywhere else. For instance, you can find ways to adjust your monitor's *resolution* — the amount of information it can pack onto a screen without making everything too tiny to read. Head to the System category to control all of the notifications that pop up in your screen's lower-right corner, as well.

The rest of this section covers the most important things you'll eventually need to tweak in the System category.

Changing the screen resolution

One of the many change-it-once-and-forget-about-it options in Windows, *screen resolution* determines how much information Windows can cram onto your computer screen. Changing the resolution either shrinks everything to pack more stuff onscreen, or it enlarges everything at the expense of desktop real estate.

To find your most comfortable resolution — or if a program or game mutters something about you having to change your *screen resolution* or *video mode* — follow these steps:

1. **Click the Start button, click the Settings icon, and click the System icon.**

2. **When the System window appears, click the word Display from the left pane.**

The Display settings spill out to the right, as shown in Figure 12-2.

3. **To change the screen resolution, click the Resolution drop-down list and select your desired resolution.**

The drop-down menu lists a variety of resolutions, all sorted by number. The larger the numbers, the higher the resolution, and the more information Windows can pack onto your computer screen. Unfortunately, packing more information onto your screen shrinks the text and images.

Unless you have a good reason not to, choose the resolution with the word *(Recommended)* next to it. That's the highest resolution your computer supports.

Choosing the Windows-recommended setting makes for the clearest text and images.

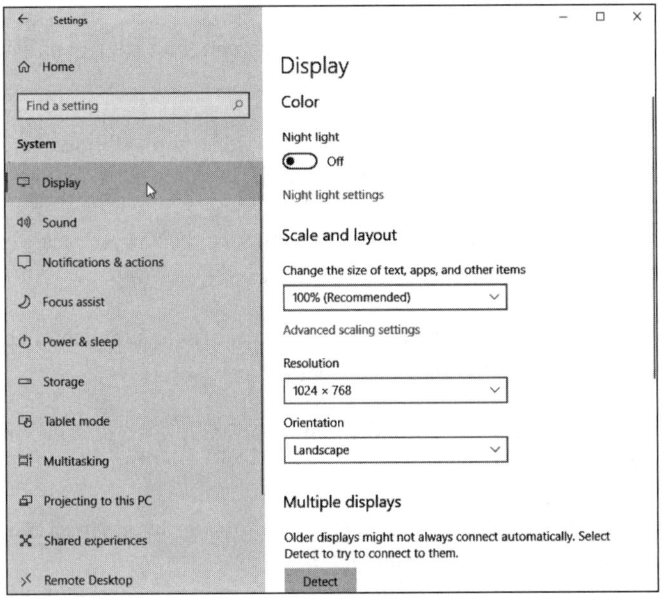

FIGURE 12-2:
The Settings app's
System page
opens to show
the Display
settings.

The settings window shows:

Settings

- ⌂ Home
- Find a setting
- **System**
  - ▭ Display
  - ◁ッ Sound
  - ▢ Notifications & actions
  - ☽ Focus assist
  - ⏻ Power & sleep
  - ▭ Storage
  - ▭ Tablet mode
  - ▭ Multitasking
  - ▭ Projecting to this PC
  - ✕ Shared experiences
  - ✕ Remote Desktop

Display

Color

Night light

⦿ Off

Night light settings

Scale and layout

Change the size of text, apps, and other items

100% (Recommended) ▾

Advanced scaling settings

Resolution

1024 × 768 ▾

Orientation

Landscape ▾

Multiple displays

Older displays might not always connect automatically. Select Detect to try to connect to them.

Detect

4. **View your display changes by clicking the Apply button. Then click the Keep Changes button to authorize the change.**

   When Windows makes drastic changes to your display, it gives you 15 seconds to approve the change by clicking the Keep Changes button. If a technical glitch renders your screen unreadable, you won't be able to see or click the onscreen button. After a few seconds, Windows notices that you didn't approve, and it reverts to your original, viewable display settings.

5. **Click OK when you're done tweaking the display.**

   After you change your video resolution once, you'll probably never return here unless you buy a new monitor or upgrade your computer's video. You might also need to revisit this window if you plug a second computer screen into your PC, which I describe in the following section.

Adding a second monitor or projector

Have you been blessed with an extra computer screen, perhaps a leftover from a deceased PC? Connect it to your PC or tablet, and you've doubled your Windows desktop: Windows stretches your workspace across both computer screens. That lets you view the online encyclopedia in one computer screen while writing your term paper in the other.

Or, if you've connected a projector, you can mirror your laptop's screen with what you see on the projector. You can even connect your computer to a widescreen TV for watching movies.

Laptops and tablets include a built-in screen, and they usually come with a video port for plugging in another monitor.

To perform these video gymnastics on a desktop PC, however, the PC needs *two* video ports, and those ports must match the *connectors* on your second monitor or projector. This poses no problem if they're only a few years old. Most modern Windows PCs, laptops, and tablets include an HDMI port for plugging in a second monitor or projector.

TIP

You may need to buy an adapter or special cable that matches the ports of both your desktop PC and the second display.

After you connect the second monitor or the projector to your computer, follow these steps on your PC:

1. **Click the Start button and click the Settings icon. When the Settings app appears, click the System icon.**

   The Settings app opens to show its Display settings, which depict *two* monitors, side by side, as shown in Figure 12-3.

   If you don't see the portion of Figure 12-3 that shows side-by-side monitors, Windows didn't automatically detect your monitor. Instead, click the Detect button in the right-column's Multiple Displays section. Windows will take another look for your attached second monitor. (You may need to turn the second monitor off, wait 30 seconds, and turn it back on again.)

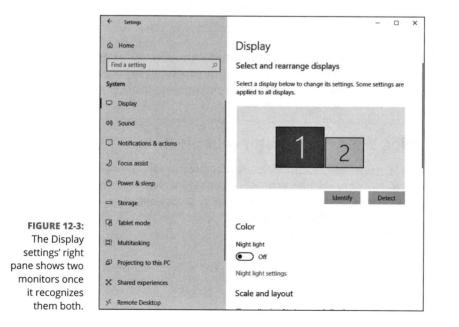

FIGURE 12-3: The Display settings' right pane shows two monitors once it recognizes them both.

2. **Drag and drop the onscreen computer screens to the right or left until they match the physical placement of the *real* computer screens on your desk. Then choose your main display.**

   The window shows your two monitors as little onscreen squares, as shown earlier in Figure 12-3. Not sure which square represents which monitor? Click the Identify button; Windows displays numbers on the onscreen monitors, as well as your real monitors, so you can tell which is which.

   Then, drag and drop the onscreen monitors until they match the placement of your *real* monitors.

3. **Adjust the Orientation setting, if necessary, and the Multiple Displays setting.**

   Windows assumes your monitor is in *landscape* mode, where the monitor's display is wider than it is tall. (Most monitors and all TV sets are set up that way.) If you have a swiveling monitor or tablet that's set up vertically, visit the Orientation menu to tell Windows how you've rotated your monitors.

   The Orientation menu lets you choose between the default Landscape mode, or Portrait mode if you've turned a monitor or tablet sideways, perhaps to better display a full page of reading material.

   Beneath the Orientation menu, the Multiple Displays drop-down list tells Windows how it should display your desktop across the second monitor. It offers these options, each handy for different scenarios:

   - **Duplicate These Displays:** This duplicates your desktop on both screens, which is helpful when you want to project an image of your desktop onto a wall or screen for presentations.

   - **Extend These Displays:** This stretches Windows to fit across both screens, giving you an extra-wide desktop. This works best when you like to view a *lot* of open windows simultaneously.

   - **Show Only on 1:** Choose this before you're ready to show off your presentation; it blanks the screen on the second monitor. When you're ready for action, switch to Duplicate These Displays so your second screen duplicates your first.

   - **Show Only on 2:** Choose this to show only the second display, which is useful when hooking up a PC to a TV for watching movies in a dark room.

   Finally, decide which of the two monitors listed onscreen should reveal the Start menu when you press the Windows key. Click the desired onscreen monitor, then select the Make This My Main Display check box.

4. **Click the Apply button to save your changes.**

   If you move the physical position of either of your two monitors, return to the first step and start over.

Running Windows 10 with two (or more) monitors may need a few other settings tweaks, as well:

» To adjust the screen resolution of your two monitors, follow the directions given in the previous section, "Changing the screen resolution." This time, however, the Advanced Display Settings window shows *both* monitors. Click the monitor you want to change, and the Resolution drop-down list applies to that monitor alone.

» Windows normally extends the taskbar along the bottom of your second monitor, which looks odd when connecting to TVs or during presentations. To turn it off, open the Settings app's Personalization category and choose Taskbar from the left column. Then, in the right column, scroll down to the Multiple Displays section. There, you can click the toggle switched called Show Taskbar on All Displays; that lets you either limit your taskbar to your main display or extend it across the other connected displays, as well.

Cutting back on notifications and ads

What Windows 10 calls "Notifications," other people call "Nags." They're the little informational blurbs that appear for a few seconds in your screen's bottom corner, then hunker down in the Notification pane for later reading.

Some people like to stay instantly up-to-date, glancing at the notifications to see the latest headline, for example, or the subject line of an incoming email. Others find the unexpected messages to be an intrusion. To control them, visit the System category's Notifications & Actions settings by following these steps:

1. **Click the Start button, click the Settings icon, and click the System icon.**

2. **When the System page appears, click Notifications & Actions from the left pane.**

   The Notifications & Actions settings appear along the app's right edge, shown in Figure 12-4. All of the settings apply to the Action Center pane — that information strip that appears when you click the taskbar's Action Center icon (shown in the margin).

3. **Adjust the following settings as needed:**

   • **Show Notifications on the Lock Screen:** This toggle switch allows notifications to appear on the Lock screen, which appears before you log on. Some people like seeing notifications on the Lock Screen; others don't want to broadcast their business to nearby strangers.

   • **Show Reminders and Incoming VoIP calls on the Lock Screen:** Just like the one above, this toggle switch allows reminders and information from Voice Over Internet Protocol calls (like Skype) to appear on the lock screen.

The following appears in the figure screenshot:

Settings

Home

Find a setting

System

Display

Sound

Notifications & actions

Focus assist

Power & sleep

Storage

Tablet mode

Multitasking

Projecting to this PC

Shared experiences

Remote Desktop

Notifications & actions

Quick actions

Press and hold (or select) quick actions, then drag to rearrange them. These quick actions appear in action center.

Tablet mode	Network	All settings	Airplane mode
Location	Focus assist	Bluetooth	VPN
Project	Connect	Night light	Nearby sharing

Add or remove quick actions

Notifications

Show notifications on the lock screen

On

Show reminders and incoming VoIP calls on the lock screen

On

Show me the Windows welcome experience after updates and occasionally when I sign in to highlight what's new and

- **Show Me the Windows Welcome Experience After Updates and Occasionally When I Sign in to Highlight What's New and Suggested:** Toggle off this setting to keep Windows from bugging you about new features.

- **Get Tips, Tricks, and Suggestions as you use Windows:** Tips and tricks are fine, but the "suggestions" are usually advertisements. Turn this off.

- **Get Notifications from Apps and Other Senders:** Toggle this switch to off, and you'll turn off almost *all* notifications. If that's overkill, look further down the list to the Get Notifications from These Senders section. There, you can choose which apps may send notifications by clicking the toggle switch next to their names. That lets you keep a few favorites but silence the others.

- **Suggested:** Found within the alphabetical list of apps, this switch lets Microsoft suggest *anything*, including ads. Turn it off.

By carefully flipping the toggle switches listed above you can remove most of the ads from the Action Center's notification pane.

TIP

To turn off ads from the Start menu, head to the Settings app's Personalization category, and choose Start from the left pane. There, turn off the toggle switch for Show Suggestions Occasionally in Start.

Devices (Adjusting mice, keyboards, scanners, and other gadgets)

In Windows Land, *devices* are physical things such as your mouse, keyboard, printer, memory cards, and scanner. Accordingly, the Devices category contains settings to adjust your mouse's scroll wheel, as well as how your computer reacts when you insert a memory card. In short, it's a hodgepodge of settings that you locate mostly by searching in the Start menu's Search box, as described in this chapter's first section.

But once you find this hidden spot, you can do all of the adjustments covered in the next few sections.

Adding a Bluetooth gadget

Bluetooth technology lets you connect gadgets wirelessly to your computer, removing clutter from your desktop. On a tablet, Bluetooth lets you add a wireless mouse and keyboard, external speaker, and other gadget without hogging one of your coveted USB ports.

Most tablets and laptops come with built-in Bluetooth; you can add it to a desktop PC by plugging a Bluetooth module into a USB port.

Bluetooth can also connect your computer, laptop, or tablet with some cellphones for wireless Internet access — if your wireless provider allows it, of course.

To add a Bluetooth item to a computer, laptop, or tablet, follow these steps:

1. Make sure your Bluetooth device is turned on and ready to pair.

Most Bluetooth devices include a simple On/Off switch. Telling the device to begin pairing is a little more difficult. Sometimes you can simply flip a switch. Other devices make you hold down a button until its little light begins flashing.

When you spot the flashing light, the device is ready to pair with another Bluetooth device including, you hope, your computer.

2. Click the Start button, click the Settings icon, and click the Settings app's Devices icon.

The Settings app opens to show the Devices category, which conveniently opens to Bluetooth and Other Devices shown in Figure 12-5.

3. Click the Add Bluetooth or Other Device button from the right side of the Devices category.

Your computer quickly begins searching for any nearby Bluetooth devices that want to connect, known in Bluetooth parlance as *pair*.

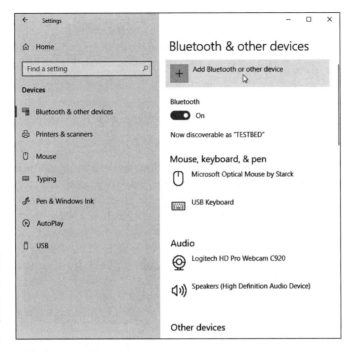

FIGURE 12-5:
To add a
Bluetooth
wireless gadget,
click Add
Bluetooth or
Other Device.

If your device doesn't appear, head back to Step 1 and make sure your Bluetooth gadget is still turned on and ready to pair. (Many impatient gadgets give up and turn off after 30 seconds of waiting for a connection.)

4. **When your device's name appears below the Add Bluetooth or Other Device button, click its name.**

5. **Type in your device's code if necessary and, if asked, click the Pair button.**

Here's where things get sticky. For security reasons, you need to prove that you're sitting in front of your *own* computer and that you're not a stranger trying to break in. Unfortunately, devices employ slightly different tactics when making you prove your innocence.

Sometimes you need to type a secret string of numbers called a *passcode* into both the device and your computer. (The secret code is usually hidden somewhere in your device's manual.) But you need to type quickly before the other gadget stops waiting.

On some gadgets, particularly Bluetooth mice, you hold in a little push button on the mouse's belly at this step.

Cellphones sometimes make you click a Pair button if you see matching passcodes on both your computer and phone.

TIP

When in doubt, type 0000 on your keyboard or press the Enter key. That's often recognized as a universal passcode for frustrated Bluetooth device owners who are trying to connect their gadgets.

Make sure your computer's Bluetooth isn't turned off: The toggle switch beneath the word Bluetooth, shown earlier in Figure 12-5, should be turned On. (Turning it off extends the battery life on tablets and laptops; on desktop PCs, always leave it turned on.)

After a gadget successfully pairs with your computer, its name and icon appear below the Bluetooth toggle switch shown in the right side of Figure 12-5, shown earlier.

 To add a Bluetooth device from the Windows desktop, click the taskbar's Bluetooth icon (shown in the margin), choose Add a Bluetooth Device, and then jump to Step 3 in the preceding list. Don't see the taskbar's Bluetooth icon? Then click the upward-pointing arrow that lives a few icons to the left of the taskbar's clock. The Bluetooth icon appears in the pop-up menu, ready for your click.

Adding a printer or scanner

Quarrelling printer manufacturers couldn't agree on how printers and scanners should be installed. As a result, you install your printer in one of two ways:

>> Some manufacturers say simply to plug in your printer or scanner by pushing its rectangular-shaped connector into a little rectangular-shaped USB port on your PC. Windows automatically notices, recognizes, and embraces your new device. Stock your printer with any needed ink cartridges, toner, or paper, and you're done.

>> Other manufacturers take an uglier approach, saying you must install their bundled software *before* plugging in your device. And if you don't install the software first, the printer or scanner may not work correctly.

Unfortunately, the only way to know how your printer or scanner should be installed is to check the bundled manual. (Sometimes this information appears on a colorful, one-page Quick Installation sheet packed in the printer's box.)

No manual? Most manufacturers now offer them online at their website.

If your printer lacks installation software, install the cartridges, add paper to the tray, and follow these instructions to put it to work:

1. **With Windows up and running, plug your printer into your PC and turn on the printer.**

Windows may send a message saying that your printer is installed successfully, but follow the next step to test it.

2. **Click the Start button, click the Settings icon, and click the Settings app's Devices icon.**

   The Settings app opens to show the Devices category, shown earlier in 12-5.

3. **From the Settings app's left side, choose Printers and Scanners.**

   The Settings app displays any printers and scanners attached to your PC. If you spot your printer listed by its model or brand name, click its icon, choose Manage from the following menu, and click the Print a Test Page link from the Manage Your Device menu. If it prints correctly, you're finished. Congratulations.

   Test page *didn't* work? Check that all the packaging is removed from inside your printer and that it has ink cartridges. If it still doesn't print, your printer is probably defective. Contact the store where you bought it and ask who to contact for assistance.

   The Manage Your Device menu often contains a Properties button, as well. A click on that button lets you access the settings of your printer or scanner, letting you change their behavior.

TIP

   To print your documents to a file that you can email to nearly anybody, choose Microsoft Print To PDF. That saves your printed, formatted file as a PDF file, a format that's accessible with nearly every type of computer, smartphone, or tablet. (If somebody can't read it, tell them to download Adobe Reader from `https://get.adobe.com/reader.`)

That's it. If you're like most people, your printer will work like a charm. If it doesn't, I've stuffed some tips and fix-it tricks in the printing section in Chapter 8.

>> To remove a printer you no longer use, click its name in Step 3 and then choose Remove Device from the pop-up menu. That printer's name no longer appears as an option when you try to print from a program. If Windows asks to uninstall the printer's drivers and software, click Yes — unless you think you may install that printer again sometime.

>> You can change printer options from within many programs. Choose File in a program's menu bar (you may need to press Alt to see the menu bar) and then choose Print Setup or choose Print. The window that appears lets you change things such as paper sizes, fonts, and types of graphics.

TIP

>> When you create a network, which I describe in Chapter 14, you'll be able to share your printer with other PCs on your network. Your printer will be listed as available for all the computers on your network.

>> If your printer's software confuses you, try clicking the Help buttons in its dialog boxes. Many buttons are customized for your particular printer model, and they offer advice not found in Windows.

>> I cover both printers and scanners in Chapter 8.

Phone (Android, iPhone, and Windows)

Technically, a phone is a device. But since it's only connected occasionally to your PC, it receives its own category in the Settings app. There's not much to see here, though, because it does nothing to help you physically connect your phone to your PC. It just provides a way to add Microsoft apps to your phone.

When you open the Settings app, click the Phone category, and click the Add a Phone button on the page's right side, Windows asks you to enter your phone number.

After you enter your phone number, your PC sends your iPhone, Android, or Windows phone a text message to download Microsoft apps from the appropriate store. You can use the OneDrive app on your phone, for example, for a quick way to access your PC's files while on the road.

However, you can do all of this by simply visiting your phone's app store, searching for Microsoft apps, and installing them yourself. (If the app requires a Microsoft account, use the same Microsoft account and password you use when logging on to your PC.)

Network & Internet

The Wi-Fi settings listed in the Network & Internet category are more easily accessed elsewhere. (To find them, click the Wi-Fi icon in the taskbar, as described in Chapter 9.) As a result, this category remains mostly a techie's holdout. Here, geeks can tweak their *VPN* (Virtual Private Network), and old-schoolers can create dial-up Internet connections. Most items listed here simply drop you off in a dusty corner of the age-old Control Panel.

I devote Chapter 15 completely to networking, and the Internet gets its due in Chapter 9.

Personalization (Changing your PC's look and feel)

One of the most popular categories, Settings app's Personalization category lets you change the look, feel, and behavior of Windows in a wide variety of ways. Inside await these six icons:

>> **Background:** Pay dirt for budding interior designers, the Background settings let you choose a particular color or photo (wallpaper) for your desktop. I cover changing wallpaper in the next section.

>> **Colors:** When you're satisfied with your background, choose Colors from the left pane to choose the color of the frames around your Start menu, windows, apps, and taskbar. Click a color from the presented grid, and you're through. (To mix your own favorite color, click the Custom Color button below the color grid.)

>> **Lock Screen:** Normally, Windows chooses from its own bundled photos to place on the *Lock screen* — the image that appears when you first turn on your PC. Here, you can choose your own photo. (While visiting here, tone down the ads by toggling off the setting named, "Get Fun Facts, Tips, and More from Windows and Cortana on Your Lock Screen.")

>> **Themes:** Once you've chosen your favorite background, colors, sounds, and even cursor shape, visit here to save them as a *Theme* — a collection of your embellishment touches that can be easily slipped on or removed. The Get More Themes link takes you to the Microsoft Store, where you can download more themes that change the look of Windows.

>> **Start:** Visit here to control the look and feel of the Start menu itself. (I describe these settings in Chapter 2, which covers the Start menu in detail.)

>> **Taskbar:** Head here to add program shortcuts to your *taskbar,* the strip living along your desktop's bottom edge. I cover this topic in Chapter 3. (To jump quickly to the taskbar's Settings window, right-click the taskbar and choose Properties. The window that appears also lets you change your Start menu's settings.)

In the next few sections, I explain the Personalization tasks that you'll reach for most often and how to handle the settings that appear.

Changing the desktop background

A *background,* also known as wallpaper, is simply the picture covering your desktop. To change it, follow these steps:

1. **Click the Start button, choose the Settings icon, and open the Personalization category.**

   Windows quickly kicks you over to the Settings app's Personalization category, neatly open to the Background setting shown in Figure 12-6.

   TIP

   As a shortcut, you can visit this page by right-clicking the desktop and choosing Personalize from the pop-up menu. The Personalization category opens directly to the Background settings.

2. **Select Picture from the Background drop-down list.**

   The Background menu lets you create a background from a picture, a solid color, or a *slideshow* — a combination of photos that automatically changes at preset intervals.

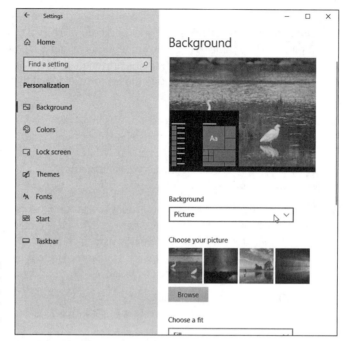

FIGURE 12-6:
The Personaliza-
tion category lets
you control how
Windows looks
on your PC.

3. **Click a new picture for the background.**

If you don't like Microsoft's picture offerings, click the Browse button, listed beneath the available pictures, to search your computer's Pictures folder for potential backgrounds.

TECHNICAL STUFF

Background files can be stored as BMP, GIF, JPG, JPEG, DIB, TIF, or PNG files. That means you can choose a background from nearly any photo or art found on the Internet, shot from a digital camera, or scanned with a scanner.

When you click a new picture, Windows immediately places it across your desktop and shows you a preview atop the Personalization window. If you're pleased, jump to Step 4; otherwise keep browsing the available photos.

4. **Decide whether to fill, fit, stretch, tile, center, or span the picture.**

Although Windows tries to choose the best-looking setting, very few pictures fit perfectly across the desktop. Small pictures, for example, need to be either stretched to fit the space or spread across the screen in rows like tiles on a floor. When tiling and stretching still look odd or distorted, visit the Choose a Fit drop-down menu. There, you can try the Fill or Fit option to keep the perspective. Or try centering the image and leaving blank space around its edges. Choose the Span option only if you've connected your PC to two monitors and want the image to fill both screens.

5. **Click the Save Changes button to save your new background.**

   Windows saves your new background across your screen.

CHOOSING A SCREEN SAVER

In the dinosaur days of computing, computer monitors suffered from *burn-in:* permanent damage when an oft-used program burned its image onto the screen. To prevent burn-in, people installed a screen saver to jump in with a blank screen or moving lines. Today's computer screens no longer suffer from burn-in problems, but some people still use screen savers because they look cool and add a layer of privacy.

Changing your screen saver requires a return to the Control Panel of yesteryear by following these steps:

1. **Click in the Search box next to the Start menu, type** Screen Saver, **and press Enter.**

   The Control Panel's Screen Saver Settings window appears.

2. **Click the downward-pointing arrow in the Screen Saver box and select a screen saver.**

   After choosing a screen saver, click the Preview button for an audition. View as many candidates as you like before making a decision.

   Be sure to click the Settings button because some screen savers offer options, letting you specify the speed of a photo slideshow, for example.

3. **If desired, add security by selecting the On Resume, Display Logon Screen check box.**

   This safeguard keeps both people and cats away from your keyboard while you're fetching coffee. It makes Windows ask for a password after waking up from screen saver mode. (I cover passwords in Chapter 14.)

4. **When you're done setting up your screen saver, click OK.**

   Windows saves your changes.

If you *really* want to extend the life of your display (and save electricity), don't bother with screen savers. Instead, put your computer to sleep before stepping away: Right-click the Start button, click Shut Down or Sign Out, and choose Sleep from the pop-up menu. To wake your PC, tap any key on the keyboard.

TIP

Did you happen to spot an eye-catching picture while web surfing with Microsoft Edge? Right-click that website's picture, choose Save Picture As from the pop-up menu, and save it in your Pictures folder. Then you can follow the preceding steps to place the picture as your desktop's background.

Changing the computer's theme

Themes are simply collections of settings to spruce up your computer's appearance: You can save your favorite screen saver and desktop background as a *theme,* for example. Then, by switching between themes, you can change your computer's clothes more quickly.

To try one of the built-in themes in Windows, follow these steps:

1. Click the Start button, choose the Settings icon, and open the Personalization category.

2. Choose Themes from the Settings app's left side.

The Settings app opens to display themes bundled with Windows 10, as shown in Figure 12-7. Click any theme, and Windows tries it on immediately.

The window offers these themes, with options listed along the window's bottom:

>> **My Themes:** Themes you've personally created appear here. If you have a Microsoft account, you see a Synced Theme, meaning the theme is linked to your Microsoft account. Whenever you log in to any PC with that account, the theme tags along to decorate the current PC's screen.

>> **Windows:** Look here for the bundled themes in Windows, including its original one, called simply Windows.

>> **Windows 10:** Themes created specifically for Windows 10 appear here.

>> **Others:** Themes installed from other places, including the Microsoft Store, appear here.

Instead of choosing from the built-in themes, feel free to make your own by clicking the words Save Theme for saving your currently assigned Desktop Background, Window Color, Sounds, and Screen Saver. Type a name for your theme, and it will appear as a choice in this section.

Apps

Relatively new to Windows 10, this Settings app category lets you uninstall unwanted apps and reset malfunctioning ones. You can also choose *default* apps, for example, the app you want to begin playing music when you open a music file. You can also choose which apps may open automatically as soon as you start Windows. That lets you open the apps faster during the day, but makes Windows load a little more slowly. (I cover apps more completely in Chapter 6.)

Removing an app from your Start menu doesn't take much effort. Right-click the app's tile from the Start menu and choose Unpin from Start from the pop-up menu.

That doesn't physically remove the app, though. The app lives on in the Start menu's alphabetical list and on your computer. To permanently remove an app or program from your PC, follow these steps:

1. **Click the Start button, click the Settings icon from the Start menu, and choose the Apps icon. When the Apps category appears, click Apps & Features from the window's left pane.**

   The Apps & Features window appears, listing your currently installed apps and programs sorted by name.

TIP

To sort the programs by their installation date, click the Sort By box and choose Sort By Install Date from the drop-down menu. You can also view programs installed on certain drives, which comes in handy on small tablets, where you want to store programs on memory cards rather than their main memory. Sorting by Size helps find oversize apps when you're running out of storage space.

2. **Click the unloved program and then click its Uninstall or Move button.**

   Click a listed program, and two buttons appear below it:

   ● **Move:** When you're running out of storage space, choose this option, if available. It lets you move an app or program onto another drive in your PC or onto your tablet's memory card, freeing up space for your files.

   ● **Uninstall:** Click this button — as well as the confirmation button that follows — to completely remove the app or program from your PC.

   Depending on which button you've clicked, shown in Figure 12-8, Windows either boots the program off your PC or moves it to another disk drive or memory card.

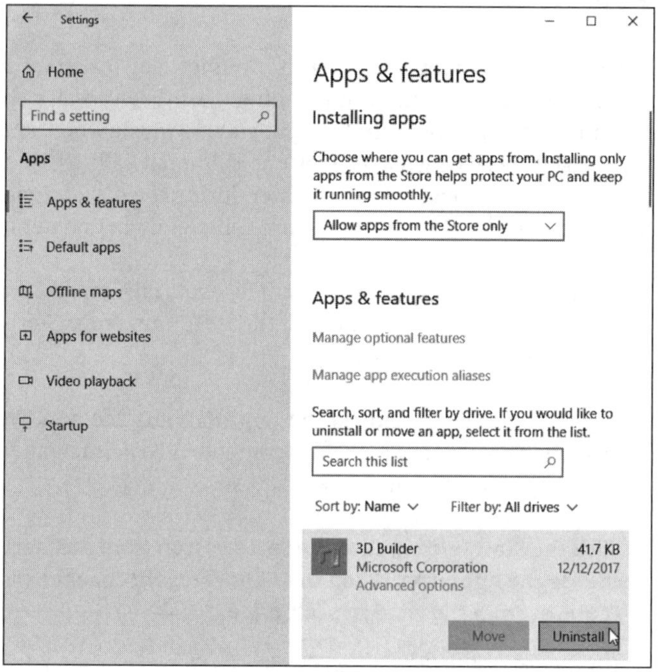

FIGURE 12-8:
Click an unwanted app or program and click the Uninstall button.

After you delete a program, it's gone for good unless you kept its installation CD. Unlike other deleted items, deleted programs don't linger inside your Recycle Bin. Mistakenly deleted apps, however, can almost always be relocated and reinstalled from the Microsoft Store. (The Store also remembers which apps you've purchased, making them easy to reinstall for free.)

WARNING

Always use the Settings app to uninstall unwanted programs. Simply deleting their files or folders doesn't do the trick. In fact, doing so often confuses your computer into sending bothersome error messages.

INSTALLING NEW APPS AND PROGRAMS

Today, most programs install themselves automatically as soon as you choose them from the Microsoft Store, double-click their downloaded installation file, or slide their discs into your PC's drive.

If you're not sure whether a program has installed, go to the Start menu and look for its name. If it appears in the All Apps alphabetical list, the program has installed.

But if a program doesn't automatically leap into your computer, here are some tips that can help:

- You need an Administrator account to install programs. (Most computer owners automatically have an Administrator account.) That keeps the kids, with their Standard or Child accounts, from installing programs and messing up the computer. I explain user accounts in Chapter 14.

- Downloaded a program? Windows saves downloaded files in your Downloads folder. To find the Downloads folder, open any folder and click the word Downloads in the folder's Quick Access area atop its left pane. When the Downloads folder appears, double-click the downloaded program's name to install it.

- Many eager, newly installed programs want to add a desktop shortcut, a Start menu tile, *and* a Quick Launch toolbar shortcut. Say "yes" to all. That way you can start the program from the desktop, avoiding a trip to the Start menu. (Changed your mind? Right-click any unwanted shortcuts and choose either Delete or Unpin to remove them.)

- It never hurts to create a restore point before installing a new program. (I describe creating restore points in Chapter 13.) If your newly installed program goes haywire, use System Restore to return your computer to the peaceful state of mind it enjoyed before you installed the troublemaker.

- When running in the new Windows 10 S mode, you can only install apps from the Microsoft Store. You can't install traditional desktop programs.

Microsoft doesn't let you delete many of the apps bundled with Windows 10, unfortunately. You're simply stuck with them. (But you can still remove them from the Start menu by right-clicking their tiles and choosing Unpin from Start from the pop-up menu.)

TIP

If an app isn't working correctly, look for an Advanced Features link in Step 2. There, you may find buttons for Repair or Reset, which can resuscitate problematic apps.

Accounts

Head to the Accounts category to create or change accounts for people who can use your computer, a chore I cover in Chapter 14, as well as to delete accounts for those no longer welcome. This category also lets you change your password or account picture. If you work on more than one PC, visit the category's Sync Your Settings section to control what settings should link to your Microsoft account. Those settings then appear on any Windows 10 device you log in to with your Microsoft account.

Time & Language

Visited mostly by frequent fliers, this set-it-once-and-forget-it category lets you change your time zone, adjust the time and date formats to match your region, and tweak other settings relating to your language and geographic location.

Laptop and tablet owners will want to drop by here when visiting different time zones. Bilingual computer owners will also appreciate settings allowing characters from different languages.

To visit here, click the Start button, click the Settings icon from the menu, and click the Settings app's Time & Language category. Three entries appear on the left pane:

>> **Date and Time:** These settings are fairly self-explanatory. (Clicking your taskbar's clock and choosing Adjust Date/Time lets you visit here, as well.)

>> **Region & Language:** If you're bilingual or multilingual, visit here when you're working on documents that require characters from different languages.

>> **Speech:** If Windows doesn't recognize your voice well, visit here to fine-tune its speech recognition settings. (You may need to buy and install a better microphone to take advantage of Cortana and other speech-recognition programs.)

Gaming

Another fairly new update, the Gaming category lets you control how you record video games on Windows 10. It also lets you check your PC's connection to Microsoft's Xbox gaming consoles.

Ease of Access

Nearly everybody finds Windows to be particularly challenging, but some people face special physical challenges, as well. To assist them, the Control Panel's Ease of Access category offers a variety of welcome changes.

TIP

If your eyesight isn't what it used to be, you may appreciate the ways to increase the text size on your computer screen.

Follow these steps to modify the settings in Windows:

TIP

1. **Load the Windows Settings app.**

   You can fetch the Settings app any of several ways:

   - **Mouse:** Click the Start button and then click the Settings icon from the Start menu.

   - **Keyboard:** From the desktop, press ⊞ +I.

   - **Touchscreen:** Slide your finger inward from the screen's right edge and tap the All Settings icon.

2. **When the Settings app appears, select the Ease of Access icon.**

   The Ease of Access Center appears, as shown in Figure 12-9.

3. **Change the settings according to your needs.**

   To make your computer easier to control, the Ease of Access window offers three groups of settings: Vision, Hearing, and Interaction. Each offers ways to help you see, hear, or control your PC. To turn a feature on or off, click its toggle button in these categories:

   - **Vision:** Perhaps the most frequently accessed section, this lets you enlarge text in Windows and its apps. You can also change the size of the cursor and mouse pointer. The Magnifier enlarges the area around the mouse pointer when moved, making it easier to track. High Contrast eliminates most onscreen color but helps vision-impaired people view the screen more clearly.

   - **Hearing:** This lets you change your speaker's volume, as well as convert stereo to mono, helpful for people who can only hear out of one ear.

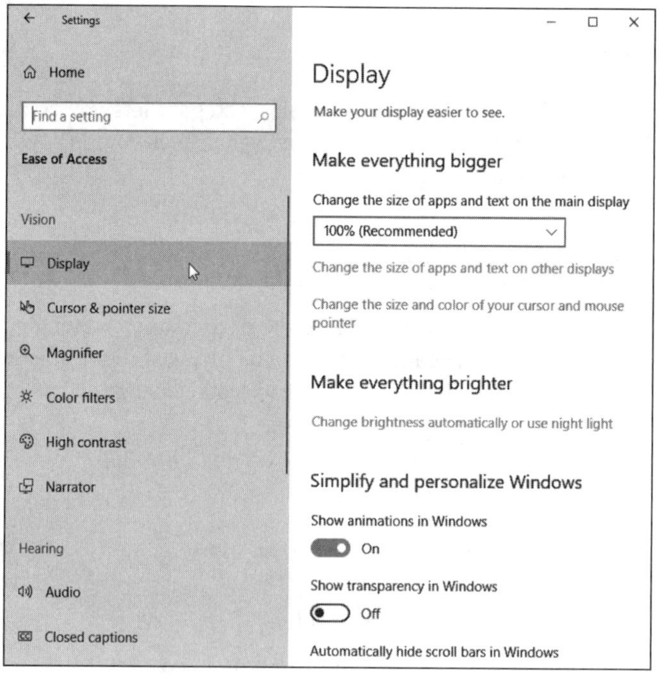

FIGURE 12-9:
The Ease of Access Center provides help for users with physical limitations.

- **Interaction:** Designed for people with physical disabilities, this setting offers speech recognition for commands, improved keyboard access, a way to control the mouse pointer with cursor keys, and even eyeball tracking for people with special equipment.

Choose any option's toggle switch to turn on the feature immediately. If it makes matters worse, choose it again to toggle it off.

Some centers that assist physically challenged people may offer software or assistance for helping you make these changes.

Cortana

Another recently added category, these settings let you control the behavior of Cortana, the digital assistant built into a Search box. Visit here first if Cortana has trouble hearing your voice.

Although there's no way to turn off Cortana completely, you can view (and delete) a history of your interactions with Cortana.

Privacy

There's very little privacy left today when it comes to the Internet. Nonetheless, this category lets you see the controls that Windows offers to limit the amount of information apps and websites can gather about you. For example, you can control which apps can access your location and control your camera, as well as which apps can see your list of contacts in the People app.

Remember, though, that if you deny apps access to your information, they won't be as helpful. The Maps app, for example, needs to know your physical location before it can give you directions.

Update & Security

Drop by the Update & Security category at least once to set up your File History backup, covered in Chapter 18. The category's Recovery settings offer powerful troubleshooting tools, also covered in Chapter 18.

Like an old car or a new friendship, Windows needs occasional maintenance. In fact, a little bit of maintenance can make Windows run so much more smoothly that I devote the majority of Chapter 13 to that subject. There, you discover how to speed up Windows, free up hard drive space, back up your data, and create a safety net called a restore point.

This category's security settings contain a full brigade of soldiers, and I've written field manuals for them in Chapter 11. The backup program in Windows, File History, gets its due in Chapter 13.

THE DESKTOP'S VANISHING CONTROL PANEL

Each update to Windows 10 considerably beefs up the Settings app, but Windows occasionally drops you into a relic of the past: the desktop's Control Panel. You'll probably never need to visit here; if you do find yourself wandering its corridors, it's probably because the Settings app dropped you there to access an uncommon switch.

If you need to visit there out of nostalgia, however, take note that the latest Windows 10 update removed the Control Panel from the Start button's right-click pop-up menu.

To find the Control Panel, type **Control Panel** into the Start menu's Search box and press Enter. The Control Panel will appear, ready for you to wax nostalgic at the look of yesteryear.

Chapter **13**

Keeping Windows from Breaking

I f Windows seems desperately broken, hop ahead to Chapter 18 for the fix; Windows 10 offers more quick fix tricks than ever. But if your computer seems to be running reasonably well, stay right here. This chapter explains how to keep it running that way for the longest time possible.

This chapter is a checklist of sorts, with each section explaining a fairly simple and necessary task to keep Windows running at its best. You discover how to set up and turn on the automatic backup program in Windows called *File History,* for example.

If somebody says your computer has a bad driver, it's not a personal insult. A *driver* is a little program that helps Windows talk to your computer's various parts. This chapter explains how to remove bad drivers by placing an updated driver behind the wheel.

TECHNICAL STUFF

CREATING A RESTORE POINT

Windows is moving away from restore points to its newer Refresh system, covered in Chapter 18. But old-school System Restore fans can still create and use the trusty Windows restore points to return a PC to a time when it was feeling better. Restore points behave a bit like a time capsule, saving your PC's settings at a specific point in time. If those settings become damaged later, returning to an earlier restore point can sometimes solve the problem.

To create a restore point, follow these steps:

1. **Click the Start button, type** System Restore **into the Search box, and click the Create a Restore Point link from the Search results.**

   The System Properties window appears, opened to the System Protection tab, which lists options for System Restore. Look for the Configure and the grayed-out Create buttons near the window's bottom edge.

2. **In the Available Drives window, click your Local Disk C: (System) drive. Then click the Configure button and, when the System Protection for Local Disk (C:) window appears, click the Turn On System Protection button and click OK.**

   That turns on System Protection for your C: drive, which is required before you can use System Restore. When you click OK, the window closes, returning you to the System Properties window. Note how your handiwork now lets you select the Create button.

3. **Click the Create button to fetch the System Protection window, type a name for your new restore point, and then click the window's Create button to save the restore point.**

   Choose a name that describes your computer's condition, such as "Created just before installing new bowling app," so you'll remember it better. Windows creates a restore point with your chosen name, leaving you some open windows to close.

By creating and labelling your own restore points on good days, you'll know which ones to use on bad days. I describe how to resuscitate your computer from a restore point in Chapter 18.

Backing Up Your Computer with File History

Your computer's hard drive will eventually die, unfortunately, and it will take everything down with it: years of digital photos, music, letters, financial records, scanned memorabilia, and anything else you've created or stored on your PC.

That's why you must back up your files on a regular basis. When your hard drive finally walks off the stage, your backup copy lets you keep the show on the road.

Windows 10 includes a free, automatic backup program called *File History*. After you turn it on, File History backs up every file in your main folders every hour. The program is easy to turn on, is simple to figure out, runs automatically, and backs up everything you need.

Before File History can go to work, you need two things:

>> **An external hard drive:** For dependable, automatic backups, you need a portable hard drive, which is a relatively inexpensive hard drive in a little box. A cord connects from the box to one of your computer's USB ports, and when the drive is plugged in, Windows recognizes the drive immediately. Keep the drive plugged in to your computer, and File History gives you completely automatic backups.

TIP

It's hard to keep a portable hard drive constantly plugged in to a laptop or tablet because they're constantly being moved around. A safer but slightly more expensive option is to buy a *wireless* hard drive that stays at home. Windows will find the wireless drive and automatically back up your files when you walk in the front door.

>> **Flip the On Switch:** The File History program comes free in Windows. But the program can't do anything until you tell it to begin running.

Follow these steps to tell your computer to start backing up your work automatically every hour:

1. **Plug your drive or its cable into your USB port. (Alternatively, insert a memory card into your tablet's slot, or turn on your wireless hard drive.)**

   The rectangular-shaped plug on the end of the drive or its cable plugs in to the rectangular-shaped USB port on your computer. (If the plug doesn't fit in the first time, flip it over.)

   If you're backing up to a memory card, check your tablet's manual to see what size and type of memory card it will accept.

   Using a wireless drive? Then install it according to its instructions so that Windows 10 will recognize it. (Unfortunately, I can't give you exact instructions because different brands and models work slightly differently.)

2. **Click the Start button and click the icon for the Settings app.**

The Settings app appears.

3. **Select the Update & Security category and click Backup from the left pane.**

The File History settings area jumps to the screen, shown in Figure 13-1.

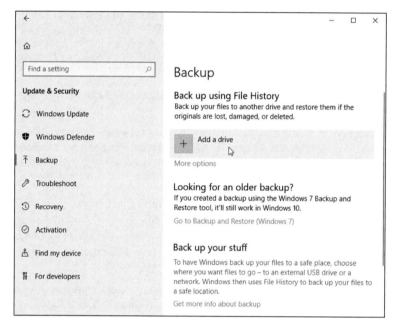

If you've never set up a drive for File History, move to Step 4.

If you've already set up a drive for File History, jump ahead to Step 5.

4. **To select a drive for File History, click Add a Drive, then choose your drive from the drop-down window.**

The Select a Drive window appears, listing all of the available storage spaces. Click the one you want, and click OK. If your drive isn't listed, then Windows isn't recognizing it. Try unplugging it, restarting your computer, and then plugging it back into a different USB port.

Since you've added a drive, the Add a Drive button changes to an On/Off toggle switch.

To choose a networked location, visit the Control Panel's File History settings. Networked drives work well as backup locations for portable PCs, such as tablets and laptops. (I explain how to create a home network in Chapter 15.) If you try to save to a networked drive on another PC, Windows asks you to enter a username and password from an Administrator account on the other PC.

5. Click the On toggle switch.

Click the On toggle switch to start the backup process rolling.

When you turn on File History, Windows immediately starts its backup — even if one isn't scheduled yet. That's because the ever-vigilant Windows wants to make sure that it grabs everything right now, before something goes wrong. After backing up *everything*, Windows backs up only the *changed* files every hour. It keeps the original files, as well, giving you plenty of backups to choose from should you need them.

Although File History does a remarkable job at keeping everything easy to use and automatic, it comes with a few bits of fine print, described here:

>> File History backs up everything in your main folders: Documents, Music, Pictures, Videos, Desktop, Favorites, Downloads, and a few others. To exclude some (perhaps exclude your Videos folder if you already store backup copies of your videos elsewhere), click the More Options link below the On/Off toggle. All of File History's settings appear, letting you add or exclude folders.

>> Windows normally backs up changed files automatically every hour. To change that schedule, click the More Options link below the On/Off toggle. Then choose the backup frequency from the Automatically Back Up My Files menu. (You can choose between every 10 minutes to once a day.)

>> When you turn on File History, it only backs up *your* files and settings. Other people with accounts on your PC will need to turn on File History while logged in to their own accounts, too.

>> File History also provides a handy way to move your files from an old PC to a new PC, a tiresome chore I describe in Chapter 20.

>> I describe how to restore files from the File History backup in Chapter 18. That section is worth looking at now, though: not only does File History work in emergencies, but it also enables you to compare current files with versions you created hours or days before. It lets you revive better versions of files that you've changed for the worse.

>> Windows saves your backup in a folder named FileHistory on your chosen drive. Don't move or delete that folder, or else Windows may not be able to find it again when you choose to restore it.

CREATING A SYSTEM IMAGE BACKUP

TECHNICAL STUFF

Windows 7 introduced a popular way to back up a computer. Instead of backing up *files,* it copies *all* of your hard drive's contents into one file and then stores that file on a second hard drive. System images such as this come in handy for two main reasons:

- **Efficiency:** When your computer's hard drive eventually dies, you can replace the hard drive, restore the system image backup, and have all of your files and programs back. It's a quick way to be up and running again.

- **Completeness:** File History backs up only files in your main folders, and the Windows Store backs up only your apps and settings. A system image backs up those things, as well, but it also backs up your Windows *desktop programs* and their information. For example, File History won't back up your email from the desktop version of Microsoft Office. A system image will, though, because it backs up *everything.*

Windows 10 still offers Windows 7's system image backup method, and it still works fine in Windows 10. You can even store a system image on the same portable drive you use for File History. Make sure your portable drive is large enough to hold all of the information on your computer's C: drive.

To create a system image in Windows 10, click the Start button, scroll down to the Windows System folder, and choose Control Panel from the menu nestled inside. Then, in the Control Panel's System and Security section, choose Backup and Restore (Windows 7). When the Backup and Restore Your Files window appears, click the words Create a System Image from the left pane. Follow the steps to tell Windows 10 to create a system image backup of your computer.

You should do this daily, if possible; if not, do it weekly or monthly. Then, if you ever need to take your computer to a repair shop, take in your portable hard drive and tell the technician you have a "system image backup." The techie can use that backup to rescue all of your computer's files and programs from the date of your last system image backup.

Finding Technical Information about Your Computer

If you ever need to look under the Windows hood, heaven forbid, head for the Settings app by clicking the Start button and choosing the Settings icon shown in the margin. (It's the second icon above the Start button.)

When the Settings app appears, select the System category and choose About from the bottom of the left column. Shown in Figure 13-2, the System window offers an easily digestible technical briefing about your PC's viscera:

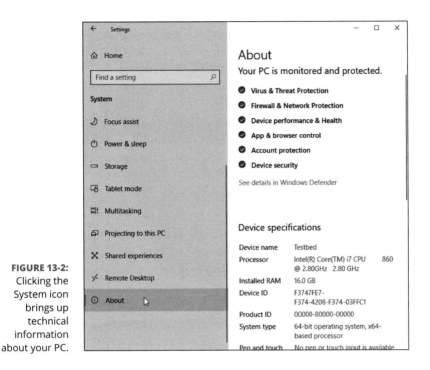

FIGURE 13-2: Clicking the System icon brings up technical information about your PC.

>> **About:** In this section, Windows gives you a report on its own health. A green mark next to a listing means everything's fine. A yellow triangle with an exclamation point inside means there's trouble: Click the See Details in Windows Defender link for the quick fix, which is usually clicking a large button labeled *Turn On.*

>> **Device Specifications:** This area lists your PC's type of *processor* (its brains, so to speak) along with its amount of memory known as RAM. You can upgrade memory fairly easily on a PC or laptop but not on a tablet. If somebody asks you whether your PC is 32-bit or 64-bit, this section lets you know next to the words System Type.

>> **Windows Specifications:** Windows comes in several editions and versions. In this section, Windows lists the edition that's running on your particular computer, as well as the version of that edition. Chances are, you'll see Windows 10 Home or Pro listed here under Edition. The version number usually changes twice a year, because that's how often Microsoft updates Windows 10 with menu changes and new features.

> » **Have a Question:** Clicking this section's Get Help link takes you to
> Microsoft's Virtual Agent, a robot that gives you a mechanical run-around
> when you're looking for help. For better — and human-supplied — answers,
> visit Microsoft's Answer's Forum at https://answers.microsoft.com.

Most of the stuff listed in the Settings app's System window is fairly complicated, so don't mess with it unless you're sure of what you're doing or a technical support person tells you to change a specific setting.

Freeing Up Space on Your Hard Drive

NEW

If Windows begins whining about running out of storage space, you can tell it to fix the problem itself. You just need to turn on *Storage Sense*, a recently introduced Windows 10 feature that tells Windows to take out its own trash.

To turn on Storage Sense, which makes Windows automatically empty its Recycle Bin and delete temporary files left behind by your apps and programs, follow these steps:

1. **Click the Start button and click the Settings icon shown in the margin.**

   The Settings app appears.

2. **Click the System category, and click the word Storage from the System page's left column.**

   The Storage settings appear, as shown in Figure 13-3.

3. **Click the Storage Sense toggle switch to On.**

Windows will automatically begin taking care of its own housekeeping in the future. To fine-tune how Windows manages its storage space, the Settings app's Storage section offers several other options:

> » **Change How We Free Up Space Automatically:** Click this link to delete old
> versions of Windows, which frees up a *lot* of space. You also can toggle
> Storage Sense on and off. And you can tell Storage Sense to delete files in the
> Downloads folder that haven't changed in 30 days, handy if you download a
> lot of stuff from the Internet but never use it. You also can click the Clean Now
> button, which tells Storage Sense to begin work immediately rather than
> waiting until your PC is low on space.

> » **Free Up Space Now:** Meant for people who need extra space immediately,
> this option works like Disk Cleanup in older Windows versions.

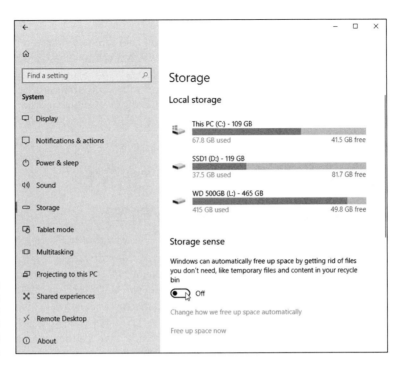

FIGURE 13-3:
The Storage section offers many ways to increase storage space on your PC.

» **Change Where New Content is Stored:** Normally, Windows stores everything on one drive. However, if your drive runs out of room and you've plugged in a portable hard drive, memory card, or second hard drive, visit this section. You can then tell Windows to store new files automatically on that second storage space. This option is handiest for small tablets that have a memory card slot.

» **Manage Storage Spaces:** Meant only for computer gurus, this option lets you set up an array of drives for automatic backups. Don't visit here unless you bring a technically minded friend.

The options above should help you free up enough space to continue working. But if Windows continually complains about not having enough room, you can try these more long-term options:

» **Uninstall unused apps:** If you're no longer using an app, delete it. I explain how to install and uninstall apps in Chapter 12.

» **Copy photos and movies elsewhere:** Photos and videos consume a *lot* of space, and they're often the prime suspect when your computer's storage space runs low. Consider buying a portable hard drive and copying those files there, a task I explain in Chapter 5.

WARNING

If you've upgraded to Windows 10, your old Windows version usually remains on your hard drive in a folder called "Windows.Old." That folder consumes *lots* of space, and several options in the Settings app's Storage section offer to let you delete it. Deleting it, of course, means your computer won't be able to return to that older Windows version, a last-ditch troubleshooting task I cover in Chapter 18.

Setting Up Devices That Don't Work (Fiddling with Drivers)

Windows comes with an arsenal of *drivers* — software that lets Windows communicate with the gadgets you plug in to your PC. Normally, Windows automatically recognizes your new part, and it simply works. Other times, Windows heads to the Internet and fetches some automated instructions before finishing the job.

But occasionally, you'll plug in something that's either too new for Windows to know about or too old for it to remember. Or perhaps something attached to your PC becomes cranky, and you see odd messages grumble about "needing a new driver."

In these cases, it's up to you to track down and install a Windows driver for that part. The best drivers come with an installation program that automatically places the software in the right place, fixing the problem. The worst drivers leave all the grunt work up to you.

If Windows doesn't automatically recognize and install your newly attached piece of hardware — even after you restart your PC — follow these steps to locate and install a new driver:

1. **Visit the part manufacturer's website and download the latest Windows driver.**

You often find the manufacturer's website stamped somewhere on the part's box. If you can't find it, search for the part manufacturer's name on Google (www.google.com) and locate its website.

Look in the website's Support, Downloads, or Customer Service area. There, you usually need to enter your part's name, its model number, and your computer's operating system (Windows 10) before the website coughs up the driver.

No Windows 10 driver listed? Try downloading a Windows 8.1, 8, or 7 driver, instead — they sometimes work just as well.

2. **Run the driver's installation program.**

Sometimes clicking your downloaded file makes its installation program jump into action, installing the driver for you. If so, you're through. If not, head to Step 3.

If the downloaded file has a little zipper on the icon, right-click it and choose Extract All to *unzip* its contents into a new folder that contains the files. (Windows names that new folder after the file you've unzipped, making it easy to locate.)

3. **Right-click the Start button and choose Device Manager from the pop-up menu.**

The Device Manager appears, listing an inventory of every part inside or attached to your computer. A yellow triangle with an embedded exclamation point icon appears next to the troublemaking part.

4. **Click your problematic device listed in the Device Manager window. Then click Action from the Device Manager's menu bar and choose Add Legacy Hardware from the drop-down menu.**

The Add Hardware Wizard guides you through the steps of installing your new hardware and, if necessary, installing your new driver. Beware, though: This last-ditch method of reviving problematic parts can frustrate even experienced techies.

Luckily, you need to install drivers only in either of these two cases:

>> You've just bought and installed a new piece of hardware, and it's not working correctly. The drivers packaged with newly bought computer gadgets are usually old. Visit the manufacturer's website, download the latest driver, and install it. Chances are good that the new driver fixes problems with the first set of drivers.

>> You've plugged in a new gadget that Windows doesn't recognize. Tracking down and installing the latest driver can often fix the problems.

But if you're not having trouble with a piece of hardware, don't bother updating its driver, even if you find a newer one online. Chances are good that newer driver adds support only for newer models of the gadget you own. And that new driver might throw a glitch into something that was already working fine.

Finally, don't bother signing up for a service that claims to keep your computer up-to-date with the latest drivers. They can do more harm than good.

TIP

If your newly installed driver makes things even worse, there's a solution: Head back to Device Manager, double-click the troublesome part's name, and click the Driver tab on the Properties box. Keep your breathing steady. Then click the Roll Back Driver button. Windows ditches the newly installed driver and returns to the previous driver.

IN THIS CHAPTER

» **Understanding user accounts**

» **Adding, deleting, or changing user accounts**

» **Signing in at the Sign In screen**

» **Switching between users**

» **Understanding passwords**

Chapter **14**

Sharing One Computer with Several People

Windows allows several people to share one computer, laptop, or tablet without letting anybody peek into anybody else's files.

The secret? Windows grants each person his or her own *user account*, which neatly isolates that person's files. When a person types in his user account name and password, the computer looks tailor-made just for him: It displays his personalized desktop background, menu choices, programs, and files — and it forbids him from seeing items belonging to other users.

This chapter explains how to set up a separate user account for everybody in your home, including the computer's owner, family members, and roommates.

It also explains how to create accounts for children, which allows you to monitor their computer activity and set limits where you feel necessary.

Understanding User Accounts

Windows wants you to set up a *user account* for everybody who uses your PC. A user account works like a cocktail-party name tag that helps Windows recognize who's sitting at the keyboard. Windows offers two types of user accounts: Administrator and Standard. (It also offers a special Standard account for children.)

To begin playing with the PC, people click their account's name when the Windows Sign In screen first appears, as shown in Figure 14-1.

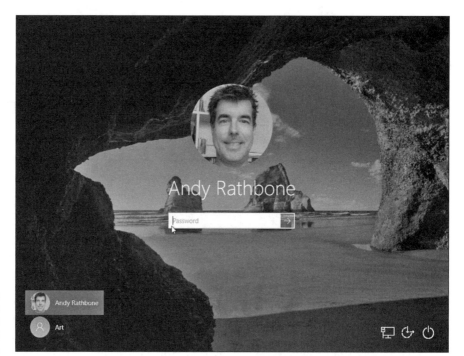

FIGURE 14-1: Windows lets users sign in under their own accounts.

Who cares? Well, Windows gives each type of account permission to do different things on the computer. If the computer were a hotel, the Administrator account would belong to the desk clerk, and each tenant would have a Standard account. Here's how the different accounts translate into computer lingo:

>> **Administrator:** The administrator controls the entire computer, deciding who gets to play with it and what each user may do on it. On a computer running Windows, the owner usually holds the almighty Administrator account. He or she then sets up accounts for each household member and decides what they can and can't do with the PC.

- >> **Standard:** Standard account holders can access most of the computer, but they can't make any big changes to it. They can't run or install new programs, for example, but they can run existing programs.

- >> **Child:** The Child account setting is actually just a Standard account with the Microsoft Family settings automatically turned on. I cover Microsoft Family controls in Chapter 11.

- >> **Guest:** Windows 10 no longer offers guest accounts. Microsoft removed them because most visitors now arrive toting their own smartphones, tablets, or both.

Here are some ways accounts are typically assigned when you're sharing the same computer under one roof:

- >> In a family, the parents usually hold Administrator accounts, and the kids usually have Standard accounts.

- >> In a dorm or shared apartment, the computer's owner holds the Administrator account, and the roommates have Standard accounts, depending on their trustworthiness level (and perhaps how clean they've left the kitchen that week).

To keep others from signing in under your user account, you must protect it with a password. (I describe how to choose a password for your account in this chapter's later "Setting Up Passwords and Security" section.)

TIP

Sometimes somebody will be signed in to her account, but the computer will go to sleep if she hasn't touched the keyboard for a while. When the computer wakes back up, only that person's user account and photo will show up onscreen. Windows 10 lists the other account holders' names in the screen's bottom-left corner, though, letting them sign in with a click on their names.

Changing or Adding User Accounts

Windows 10 offers two slightly different ways to add user accounts. It separates them into the two types of people you're most likely to add to your computer:

- >> **Family members:** By choosing this, you can automatically set up controls on your children's accounts. Any adults you add here will automatically be able to monitor your children's computer usage. All family members must have Microsoft accounts; if they don't already have them, the process helps you create them.

>> **Other members:** This type of account works best for roommates or other long-term guests who will be using your computer but don't need monitoring or the ability to monitor children.

The next two sections describe how to create both types of accounts, as well as how to change existing accounts.

REMEMBER

Only Administrator accounts can add new user accounts to a computer. If you don't have an Administrator account, ask the computer's owner to upgrade your account from Standard to Administrator.

Adding an account for a family member or friend

Adding a family member adds an important distinction to the account. If you add a child, the child's activity will be curtailed according to the limits you set. And if you add an adult, that person will also have the ability to monitor the activity of any added children.

If you want to add an account that's not involved in these family matters, choose the other option, called Adding an Account for Someone Else. There, you can create an account for a roommate or long-term guest.

Administrator account holders can create either type of account by following these steps:

1. **Click the Start button and click the Settings icon.**

2. **When the Settings app appears, click the Accounts icon.**

   The Accounts screen appears, as shown in Figure 14-2, offering ways to change your own account, as well as add accounts for other people.

TIP

3. **Click the words Family & Other People from the left pane.**

   The right pane of the Family & Other People screen, shown in Figure 14-2, lets you create either of two accounts: One for a family member, or one for someone else. If you're creating an account for a family member, move to Step 4. If you're *not* adding a relative, jump ahead to Step 5.

4. **Choose Add a Family Member, and follow the steps to send the person an invitation.**

   A window appears, shown in Figure 14-3, asking if you're adding a child or an adult. Click the appropriate check box, then decide which email address to use for that person. You have several options:

- If you already know the person's email address, type it into the Enter Their Email Address box and click the Next button. (If the email address isn't already a Microsoft account, it will be turned into one.)

- If you don't know the person's email address, click the words, The Person I Want to Add Doesn't Have an Email Address. That takes you to a page where you can sign them up for an email address that also serves as a Microsoft account.

No matter which option you choose, your invited family member, either a child or adult, will receive an email saying they've been invited to have a family account on your computer. Once they accept the offer, they automatically appear as an account on your computer.

At this point, you've finished adding a family member. To add somebody who's not a relative, move to Step 5.

5. **Choose Add Someone Else to This PC.**

Microsoft immediately complicates matters, as shown in the How Will This Person Sign In window in Figure 14-4, by asking for the new account holder's email address.

Microsoft is trying to say that you can choose either of two types of accounts for your new account holder:

- **Microsoft account:** A Microsoft account is required for many Windows 10 features. Described in Chapter 2, a Microsoft account is simply an email address that links to Microsoft, its computers, and its billing department. Only Microsoft account holders can download apps from the Windows Store app, store and retrieve files on an Internet storage space called OneDrive, and access other perks offered by a Microsoft account. To create a Microsoft account, go to Step 6.

- **Local account:** Select this option for people not interested in Microsoft accounts and their privileges. It lets the person use your computer with an account specific to your computer. To create a Local account, jump to Step 7.

TIP

Can't decide which type of account to create? Creating a Local account is always a safe bet. (Local account holders who want or need the advantages of a Microsoft account can upgrade to one at any time.)

6. **Type the email address of the new account holder's Microsoft account into the Email Address text box, click Next, and then click Finish.**

The account will be waiting on the Sign In screen shown back in Figure 14-1.

When the person wants to use the computer, he chooses the account bearing his email address and then types in his Microsoft account password. Windows visits the Internet, and if the email address and password match, the account is ready for action. You've finished.

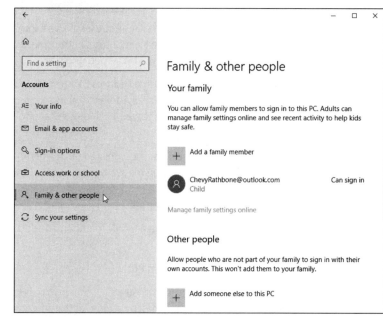

FIGURE 14-2:
Click the words
Family & Other
People to begin
creating a new
user account.

Family & other people

Your family

You can allow family members to sign in to this PC. Adults can manage family settings online and see recent activity to help kids stay safe.

+ Add a family member

ChevyRathbone@outlook.com   Can sign in
Child

Manage family settings online

Other people

Allow people who are not part of your family to sign in with their own accounts. This won't add them to your family.

+ Add someone else to this PC

Accounts

Find a setting

AΞ Your info

✉ Email & app accounts

✎ Sign-in options

▣ Access work or school

A Family & other people

↻ Sync your settings

Add a child or an adult?

Enter the email address of the person you want to add. If they use Windows, Office, Outlook.com, OneDrive, Skype, or Xbox, enter the email address they use to sign in.

◉ Add a child

Kids are safer online when they have their own account

◯ Add an adult

Enter their email address

The person I want to add doesn't have an email address

Next   Cancel

FIGURE 14-3:
Choose whether
you're adding a
child or adult
family member.

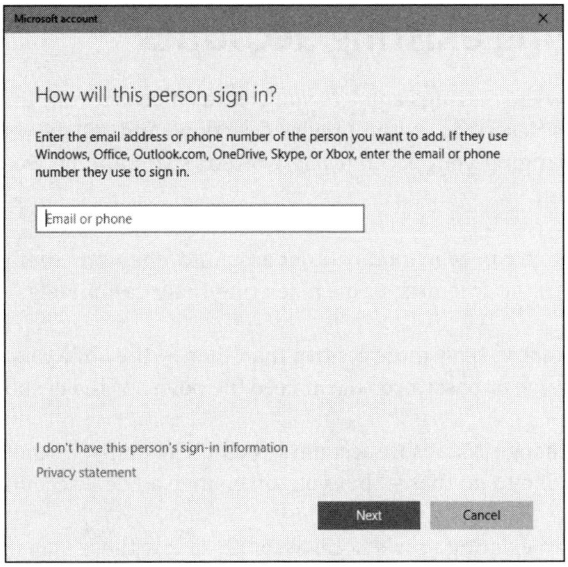

How will this person sign in?

Enter the email address or phone number of the person you want to add. If they use Windows, Office, Outlook.com, OneDrive, Skype, or Xbox, enter the email or phone number they use to sign in.

Email or phone

I don't have this person's sign-in information

Privacy statement

Next   Cancel

FIGURE 14-4:
Enter the email address of the person you want to add.

7. **Click the words I Don't Have This Person's Sign-In Information, shown at the bottom of Figure 14-4.**

   Alarmed that you'd consider choosing a lowly Local account over the wondrous Microsoft account, Microsoft tries to make you create a Microsoft account for the new account.

8. **Click the Add a User Without a Microsoft Account link.**

   This tells Microsoft that yes, you really do want a Local account. (After all, Local account holders can always turn their account into a Microsoft account at any time.)

   A new screen appears, asking for a name for the account (username), the account's password, and a password hint in case you forget the password.

9. **Enter a username, password, and password hint and then click Next.**

   Use the person's first name or nickname for the username. Choose a simple password and hint; the user can change them after he signs in.

   Before you forget, tell the person his new username and password. (Or write them down and keep them in a secure place.) His username will be waiting at the Sign In screen's bottom-left corner for him to begin using the computer.

TIP Windows normally creates Standard accounts for all new users whether or not they've signed in with a Microsoft or Local account. You can upgrade that later to an Administrator account if you want by changing the account, described in the next section.

Changing existing accounts

The Windows 10 Settings app lets you create a new account for a friend or family member, as described in the previous section. And it lets you tweak your own account, changing your account password or switching between a Microsoft or a Local account.

Administrators can even modify other accounts, changing them to either Standard or Administrator accounts, or even deleting them completely.

But if you want to have more control than that — the ability to change an existing account's name or password — you need the power of the desktop's Control Panel.

You can't change Microsoft accounts with these steps — those account holders must go online to do that — but you *can* change a Local account.

To change an existing user's Local account, follow these steps:

TIP

1. **Click the Start button in the screen's bottom-left corner, type** Control Panel **in the Search box, and press the Enter key.**

2. **Click to open the Control Panel's User Accounts category.**

3. **Click the User Accounts link and then click the Manage Another Account link.**

   The Manage Accounts window appears, as shown in Figure 14-5, listing all the accounts on your computer.

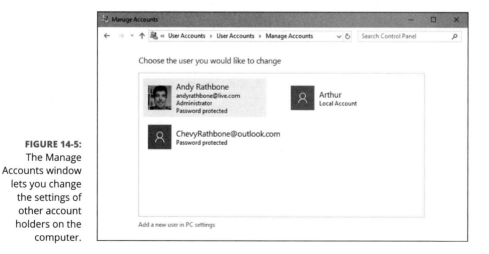

FIGURE 14-5:
The Manage Accounts window lets you change the settings of other account holders on the computer.

4. **Click the account you'd like to change.**

Windows displays a page with the account's photo and lets you tweak the account's settings in any of these ways:

- **Change the Account Name:** Here's your chance to correct a misspelled name on a Local account. Or feel free to jazz up your own Local account name, changing Jane to Crystal Powers.

- **Create a Password:** Every Local account should have a password to keep out other users. Here's your chance to add one.

- **Change the Account Type:** Head here to promote a Standard user of high moral character to an Administrator account or bump a naughty administrator down to Standard.

- **Delete the Account:** Don't choose this option hastily, because deleting somebody's account also deletes all her files. If you *do* choose it, also choose the subsequent option that appears: Keep Files. That option places all of that person's files in a folder on your desktop for safekeeping.

- **Manage Another Account:** Save your current crop of changes and begin tweaking somebody else's account.

WARNING

5. **When you're through, close the window by clicking the X in its top-right corner.**

Any changes made to a user's account take place immediately.

Switching Quickly between Users

Windows enables an entire family, roommates, or employees in a small office to share a single computer or tablet. The computer keeps track of everybody's programs while different people use the computer. Mom can be playing chess and then let Jerry sign in to check his email. When Mom signs back in a few minutes later, her chess match is right where she left it, pondering the sacrifice of her rook.

Known as *Fast User Switching*, switching between users works quickly and easily. When somebody else wants to sign in to his account for a moment, perhaps to check email, follow these steps:

1. **Open the Start menu.**

To open the Start menu, click (or tap) the Start button or press the keyboard's Windows key (⊞).

2. **Click your user account photo from along the screen's left edge.**

A menu drops down, as shown in Figure 14-6.

FIGURE 14-6:
The menu lists
the names of all
user accounts
authorized to use
the computer.

3. **Choose the name of the user account holder who wants to sign in.**

Windows leaves you signed in but immediately fetches the other person's account, letting him type in his password.

When that person finishes with the computer, he can sign out just as you did in Step 2 — by clicking his user account photo in the Start menu's left pane. This time, however, he'll choose Sign Out. Windows closes down his session, letting you sign back in with your own password. And when Windows reappears, so will your work, just as you left it.

TIP

Keep these tips in mind when juggling several people's accounts on a single PC:

>> With all this user switching, you may forget whose account you're actually using. To check, open the Start menu. The current account holder's picture appears in the menu's left pane. (Hover your mouse over the picture to see the name.)

>> To see other accounts currently signed in, open the Start menu and click the current account holder's name. A drop-down menu lists the other user accounts but places the words *Signed In* beneath the name of each account holder who's currently signed in.

WARNING

>> Don't restart the PC while another person is still signed in, or that person will lose any work he hasn't saved. (Windows warns you before restarting the PC, giving you a chance to ask the other person to sign back in and save his work.)

>> If a Standard account owner tries to change an important setting or install software, a window will appear, asking for Administrator permission. If you want to approve the action, just step over to the PC and type your password into the approval window. Windows lets you approve the change, just as if you'd done it while signed in with your own account.

Changing a User Account's Picture

Okay, now the important stuff: changing the boring picture that Windows automatically assigns to your user account. For every newly created user account, Windows chooses a generic silhouette. Feel free to change the picture to something more reflective of the Real You: You can snap a photo with your computer's webcam or choose any photo in your Pictures folder.

To change your user account's picture, head for the Start menu and click your picture along the menu's left edge. When the menu drops down, choose Change Account Settings. Windows presents the screen shown in Figure 14-7.

The Accounts page lets you change your picture two main ways:

>> **Camera:** This option, available only for people with a camera attached to their computers, lets you take a quick selfie for your account photo.

>> **Browse for One:** To assign a picture already on your computer, click the Browse for One button. A new window appears, showing photos in your Pictures folder. Click a desired picture and click the Choose Picture button. Windows quickly slaps that picture atop your Start menu.

TIP

Here are a few more tips for choosing your all-important account photo:

>> After you've chosen an account photo, it attaches to your Microsoft account and anything you sign in to with that account: Your Microsoft phone, for example, Microsoft websites and programs, and any Windows computer you sign in to with your Microsoft account.

WHAT DOES MY MICROSOFT ACCOUNT KNOW ABOUT ME?

TIP

A Microsoft account is simply an email address and a password that lets Microsoft identify you. By logging in with a Microsoft account, you can access many Microsoft services: OneDrive, for example, gives you an online cubbyhole for storing and sharing files across your PC, tablet, and phone, even if it's from Apple or Android. You also need a Microsoft account to download and run many Windows 10 apps.

In short, Windows 10 works much better when you log in with a Microsoft account. I use one; I keep my shopping list on my PC, but thanks to OneDrive, I can read the same list on my Android phone while at the grocery store.

Like just about every company these days, Microsoft collects information about you, which is made easier when you use a Microsoft account. That really shouldn't be a surprise. Google, Facebook, Apple, and every website you visit gathers information about you and your account, as well. Your bank, Internet Service Provider, credit card company, and insurance companies also stockpile information about you.

To combat your erosion of privacy, Microsoft lets you see what information it has stored about you, and it lets you delete portions you aren't comfortable seeing listed.

To do that, visit the Microsoft Privacy Center at https://account.microsoft.com/about and log in with your Microsoft account. There, you can view information about your billing and payments; renew, cancel, or subscribe to Microsoft services like OneDrive and Xbox Live; find your lost devices on a map; clear your Bing search history; and change your marketing preferences. Plus, you can check your kids' computer activity, provided you've set them up with a Microsoft account.

You should also visit the Settings app's new Privacy category, which lets you access similar information.

It's worth taking a look in both places to see what sort of information Microsoft stores, and make sure there aren't any surprises.

>> You can grab any picture off the Internet and save it to your Pictures folder. Then click the Browse for One button mentioned earlier in this section to locate the picture and assign it as your account photo. (Right-click the Internet picture and, depending on your web browser, choose Save Picture As or a similar menu option.)

>> Don't worry about choosing a picture that's too large or too small. Windows automatically shrinks or expands the image to fit the circular space.

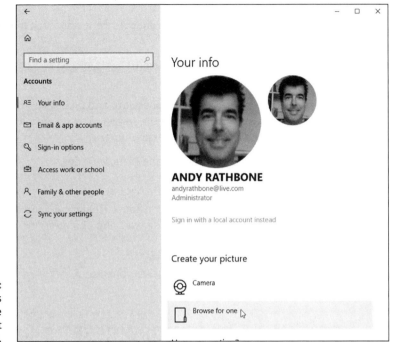

FIGURE 14-7:
Windows lets each user choose an account picture.

Setting Up Passwords and Security

There's not much point to having a user account if you don't have a password. Without one, a snoop from the neighboring cubicle can click your account on the Sign In screen and peek through your files.

Administrators, especially, should have passwords. If they don't, they're automatically letting anybody wreak havoc with the PC: When a permission's screen appears, asking for a protective password, anybody can just press Enter to gain entrance.

Microsoft account holders can change their passwords online by visiting www.live.com. Local account holders can create or change a password by following these steps:

1. **Click the Start button and click the Settings icon from the Start menu.**

2. **When the Settings app appears, click the Accounts icon.**

   The familiar Accounts window appears, shown earlier in Figure 14-2, where you can add other accounts, change your own, and perform other account-related chores.

3. **Choose the Sign-in Options link from the Accounts window's left edge.**

   The Sign-In Options screen appears.

4. **In the Password section on the window's right side, click the Change button.**

   People who haven't created a password should instead click the Create a Password button.

5. **Make up an easy-to-remember password and type it into the New Password text box. Then retype the same characters into the Retype Password text box below it, and click Next.**

   Retyping the password eliminates the chance of typos.

Changing an existing password works slightly differently: The screen shows a Current Password text box where you must first type your existing password. (That keeps pranksters from sneaking over and changing your password during lunch hours.)

You can find out more about passwords in Chapter 2.

TIP

CREATING A PASSWORD RESET DISK

A Password Reset Disk serves as a key, letting you back in to your computer in the event you've forgotten the password to your Local account. (You can't create a Password Reset Disk for a Microsoft account.) To create a Password Reset Disk, follow these simple steps:

1. **Log in to your PC with your Local account, insert a flash drive into a USB port, and wait for Windows 10 to recognize it.**

2. **Click in the Search box by the Start button, type** Password Reset Disk, **and press Enter.**

3. **Click the Create a Password Reset Disk option that appears below the Search box.**

   The Forgotten Password Wizard appears and walks you through the process of creating a Password Reset Disk from a memory card or a USB flash drive.

When you forget your password, you can insert your Password Reset Disk as a key. Windows lets you in to choose a new password, and all will be joyous. Hide your Password Reset Disk in a safe place because it lets *anybody* into your account.

No matter how many times you change your password, your original Password Reset Disk still works, always providing a backup key to get into your account.

Signing in with Windows Hello

Password-protected accounts help keep your account secure, both from strangers on the Internet and from people nearby. But very few people like to stop and type in a password — if they can even remember it.

Windows 10 tries to solve that problem with its Windows Hello technology. Windows Hello lets you skip bothersome passwords and log in securely in less than a second. By attaching either a compatible camera or a fingerprint reader to your computer, you can log in with the swipe of a finger or a glance at the camera.

Some new laptops and PCs include built-in Windows Hello compatible readers and cameras; if yours doesn't, you can buy one that plugs in to your computer's USB port.

To set up Windows Hello, follow these steps:

1. **Click the Start button, click the Settings icon (shown in the margin), and choose Accounts.**

    The Settings app's Accounts page appears.

2. **Click Sign-In Options from the left pane.**

    The screen shows your options for signing in to your account, shown in Figure 14-8. If you don't see an option to set up Windows Hello, make sure your compatible fingerprint reader or camera is plugged in to your computer and fully installed.

3. **Click the Set Up button for either the fingerprint reader or camera, and follow the instructions.**

    Windows walks you through scanning either your fingerprint (any finger will do, as long as you use that finger consistently when you want to sign in to your account), iris, or face. You may need to create a PIN, a four-digit number that adds an additional layer of security for special circumstances.

TIP

Windows Hello may seem more like science fiction than reality, but don't write it off too quickly. You'll appreciate Windows Hello for several reasons:

>> Fingerprint readers are fairly inexpensive and easy to install. You can find several models selling on Amazon for around $30, and they work amazingly well.

>> Many new laptops come with fingerprint readers already installed near the keyboard area. Some tablets, too, include built-in fingerprint readers.

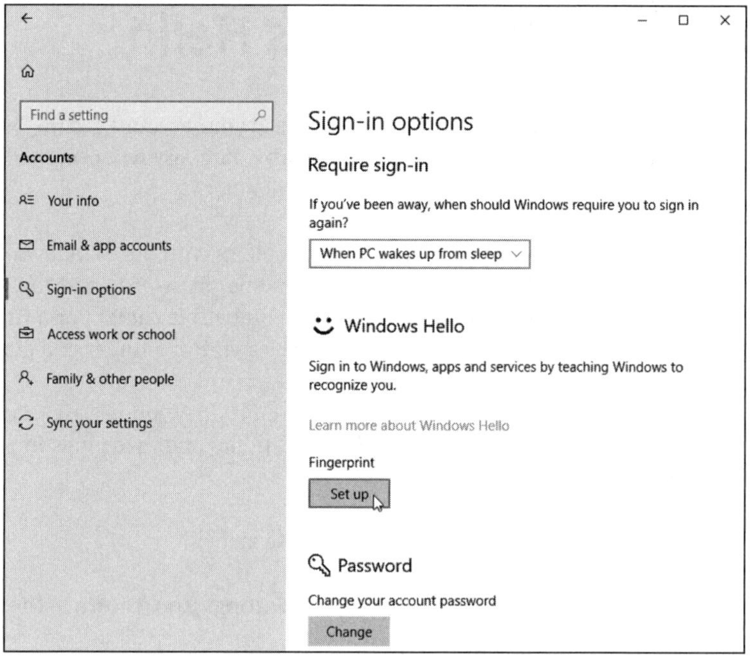

FIGURE 14-8:
Choose an option
from Windows
Hello to sign in
without a
password.

» Windows 10 recognizes most compatible fingerprint readers as soon as they're plugged in to your computer's USB port. You rarely need to install any bundled software.

» Whenever Windows 10 asks you to sign in, just slide your finger across the reader. The screen quickly clears, and you're ready for work. You don't need to remember or type in a complicated password. There's nothing to forget.

» Windows Hello not only lets you sign in to your device, but lets you buy things in the Windows Store, all without typing in a password.

» As the Windows Hello technology grows, Windows Hello may eventually let you enter your favorite password-protected websites, as well.

IN THIS CHAPTER

» **Understanding a network's parts**

» **Choosing between wired and wireless networks**

» **Setting up a small network**

» **Connecting wirelessly to public networks**

» **Sharing files between computers, phones, and other devices**

» **Sharing an Internet connection, files, and printers on a network**

Chapter **15**

Connecting Computers with a Network

B uying yet another PC can bring yet another computing problem: How can two or more PCs share the same Internet connection and printer? And how do you share your files between your two PCs?

The solution involves a *network*. When you connect two or more computers, Windows introduces them to each other, automatically letting them swap information, share an Internet connection, and print through the same printer.

Today, most computers can connect without anybody tripping over cables. Known as *Wi-Fi* or *wireless*, this option lets your computers chatter through the airwaves like radio stations that broadcast and take requests.

This chapter explains how to link a houseful of computers so that they can share things. After you've created a wireless network, you can share your Internet connection with not only your Windows PCs but also smartphones, tablets, and other computerized gadgets. And, if you choose to give the password to your visitors, even they can connect to the Internet.

Be forewarned, however: This chapter contains some pretty advanced stuff. Don't tread here unless you're running an Administrator account and you don't mind doing a little head-scratching as you wade from conceptualization to actualization to, "Hey, it works!"

Understanding a Network's Parts

A *network* is simply two or more computers that have been connected so that they can share things. Although computer networks range from pleasingly simple to agonizingly complex, they all have three things in common:

>> **A router:** This little box works as an electronic traffic cop, controlling the flow of information between each computer, as well as between your network and the Internet. Almost all modern routers support both wired and wireless networks.

>> **A network adapter:** Every computer needs its own *network adapter* — an electronic mouthpiece of sorts. A *wired* network adapter lets you plug in a cable; the cable's other end plugs into your router. A *wireless* network adapter translates your computer's information into radio signals and broadcasts them to the router.

>> **Network cables:** Computers connecting wirelessly don't need cables, of course. But computers without wireless adapters need cables to connect them to the router.

When you plug a modem into the router, the router quickly distributes the Internet signal to every computer on your network. (Some modems come with built-in routers, sparing you from having to connect the two.)

Most home networks resemble a spider, as shown in Figure 15-1, with some computers' cables connecting to the router in the center. Other computers, laptops, tablets, and gadgets connect wirelessly to the same router.

The router divides its attention among networked computers efficiently, letting every computer simultaneously share a single Internet connection.

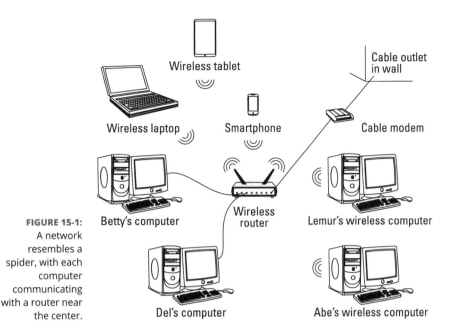

FIGURE 15-1:
A network
resembles a
spider, with each
computer
communicating
with a router near
the center.

Windows lets every computer share a single printer, as well. If two people try to print something simultaneously, Windows stashes one person's files until the printer is free and then sends them automatically when the printer is ready for more work.

TIP

CHOOSING BETWEEN WIRED AND WIRELESS NETWORKS

You can easily string cables between computers, routers, and gadgets that sit on the same desk or live within one room. Beyond that, though, cables quickly become messy. To cut the clutter, most computers today include *wireless (Wi-Fi)* adapters, which let the computers chatter through the air.

But just as radio broadcasts fade as you drive out of the city, wireless signals also fade. The more they fade, the slower the connection becomes. If your wireless signals pass through more than two or three walls, your computers may not be able to communicate. Wireless networks are also more difficult to set up than wired networks.

Although wireless connections are popular, wired connections work more quickly, efficiently, securely, and inexpensively than wireless. But if your spouse wants the cables removed from the hallways, wireless may be your best option. For best results, combine the two: Connect adjacent computers and devices with cables and use wireless for the rest.

REMEMBER

Wireless routers deliver an Internet signal to *all* connected wireless gadgets, not just Windows computers. After you set up your router, it also delivers your Internet signal to iPads and other tablets, Apple computers, smartphones, and even some home theater devices (such as Blu-ray players, game consoles, "smart" televisions, Amazon Echo gadgets, and streaming video gadgets such as a Chromecast, Amazon Fire TV, and Roku boxes).

Setting Up a Small Network

If you're trying to set up a lot of computers — more than ten — you probably need a more advanced book. Networks are fairly easy to set up, but sharing their resources can be scary stuff, especially if the computers contain sensitive material. But if you're just trying to set up a few computers and wireless gadgets in your home or home office, this information may be all you need.

So without further blabbing, here's a low-carb, step-by-step list of how to set up a small and inexpensive network. The following sections show how to buy the three parts of a network, install the parts, and make Windows create a network out of your handiwork.

Buying parts for a network

Visit the computer store across town or online, buy this stuff, and you're well on your way to setting up your network:

>> **Network adapters (optional):** Because most new computers and laptops include both wired *and* wireless adapters, you can probably cross this off your shopping list. But if you need to add an adapter, pick up an inexpensive wired or wireless adapter that plugs into the computer's USB port. (Mobile devices like laptops, tablets, and smartphones *all* include built-in wireless adapters.)

>> **Network cable (optional):** Not using wireless? Then buy *Ethernet* cables, which resemble phone cables but with slightly thicker jacks. Buy a cable for each computer you want to connect. The cables must be long enough to reach from the computer to the router, described next.

>> **Router:** This little box does all the magic. Most routers today include built-in wireless; many also include a broadband modem for Internet access. Wireless routers usually include four jacks to accommodate up to four nearby computers relying on cables.

TIP

Some Internet Service Providers (ISPs) supply you with a wireless router/modem, and they even send a techie to your home to set up your network for you. It never hurts to ask.

Setting up a wireless router

Wireless connections bring a convenience felt by every cellphone owner. But with computers, a wireless connection also brings complication. You're basically setting up a small radio transmitter that broadcasts to tiny radios inside your computers. You need to worry about signal strength, finding the right signal, and even entering passwords to keep outsiders from eavesdropping.

Unfortunately, different brands of wireless routers come with different setup software, so there's no way I can provide step-by-step instructions for setting up your particular router.

However, every router requires you to set up these three things:

>> **Network name (SSID):** Enter a short, easy-to-remember name here to identify your particular wireless network. Later, when connecting to the wireless network with your computer, smartphone, tablet, or other wireless gadget, you'll select this same name to avoid accidentally connecting with your neighbor's wireless network.

>> **Infrastructure:** Of the two choices, choose Infrastructure instead of the rarely used alternative, Ad Hoc.

>> **Security:** To keep out snoops, this option uses a password to encrypt your data as it flies through the air. Most routers offer at least three types of password options: WEP is barely better than no password, WPA is better, and WPA2 is better still. Choose the strongest security option available and create a memorable password with mixed characters, such as **Five&Three=8!**.

Some routers include an installation program to help you change these settings; other routers contain built-in software that you access with your web browser in Windows.

REMEMBER

As you set each of the preceding three settings, write them on a piece of paper: You must enter these same three settings when setting up the wireless connection on each of your computers and other wireless gadgets, a job tackled in the next section. You also need to pass out that information to any houseguests who want to piggyback on your Internet connection while they visit.

Setting up Windows computers to connect to a network

First, a word to the wired crowd: If you've chosen to connect a computer to your router with a cable, plug one end of the cable into your computer's network port. Plug the cable's other end into one of your router's network ports. (The ports are usually numbered; any number will do.) To connect other computers to the same router, connect cables between those computers' network ports and the router's other empty network ports.

If your Internet company didn't do it for you, plug a cable from your broadband modem's LAN or Ethernet port into your router's WAN port. (Those ports are almost always labeled, and if your router and modem live together in one box, you can skip this step.) Turn on your router, and you've finished: You've discovered how easy it is to create a wired network.

Wireless is a different story. After you set up your router to broadcast your network wirelessly, you must tell Windows how to receive it. Chapter 9 offers the full course in connecting to wireless networks, both your own and those you'll find in public, but here's an abbreviated version for connecting to your own network:

1. **Click the Start button and choose the Settings icon from the Start menu.**

2. **When the Settings screen appears, click the Network & Internet icon, then click the Show Available Networks link.**

   The Network & Internet page lists whether you're connected to the Internet and offers a Troubleshoot button for fixing common connection problems.

   Click the Show Available Networks link, and Windows quickly sniffs the airwaves for nearby wireless networks. The taskbar's Wireless Networking icon, shown in Figure 15-2, quickly pops up with a list of all the wireless networks within range of your computer, including, with any luck, your own. (Your network will be the name — the *SSID* — that you chose when setting up your router, described in the previous section.)

3. **Choose the desired wireless network by clicking its name and then clicking the Connect button.**

   The closest wireless network is usually the strongest, so you'll probably spot your own wireless network at the top of the list.

TIP

   If you select the adjacent Connect Automatically check box before clicking the Connect button, Windows automatically connects to that network the next time you're within range, sparing you from following all these steps again.

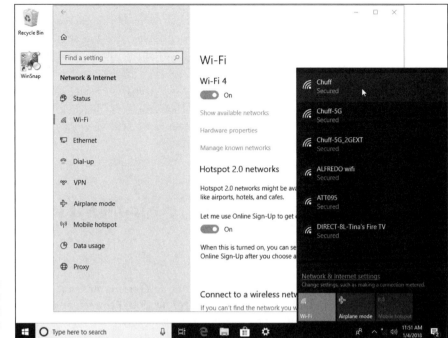

FIGURE 15-2:
Windows places the strongest available network at the list's top.

4. **Enter a password and click Next.**

   Here's where you type in the same password you entered into your router when setting up your wireless network. (To confuse things, Windows 10 refers to your password as a "Network Security Key.")

At this point, Windows 10 treats your newly joined wireless network as a *public* network, the same as one you'd find in a coffee shop or airport. You won't be able to find or access your other networked computers until you make some changes, covered in the next section.

If Windows asks to make your computer discoverable, choose Yes: You're in your own home, and you want your other computers to be able to swap files. But if you're connecting to somebody *else's* network — a public network, for example, click No. You only want your PC to be discoverable when on your *own* network.

TIP

If you're still having problems connecting, try the following tips:

>> Head back to Step 2 and click the Troubleshoot button. Windows 10 performs some basic diagnostics and resets your networking equipment. If the trouble-shooter can't fix the problem, it offers clues as to the connection-robbing culprit.

>> Cordless phones and microwave ovens can interfere with wireless networks, oddly enough. If you're having trouble with signal strength, try to keep your cordless phone out of the same room as your wireless computer, and don't heat up that sandwich when web browsing.

 >> From the Windows desktop, the taskbar's wireless network icon (shown in the margin) provides a one-click way to see available wireless networks. If your desktop's taskbar contains a wireless network icon, click it and jump to Step 3 in the preceding steps.

Sharing Files with Your Networked Computers

Creating a network between your computers makes it easier for them to share resources, such as an Internet connection, printers, and even your files. But how can you share some files while keeping others private?

Microsoft's solution used to be called a *Homegroup*. It was an automatic way of flipping networking switches so that Windows PCs could see each other, as well as share their files, folders, and printers.

Once the Spring 2018 update arrives, Windows 10 no longer lets you create Home-groups. That means you need to flip your computer's networking switches manually.

The rest of this section explains which switches to flip so Windows 10 can still share files with other computers and devices on your network.

Setting your home network to private

In Windows 7, 8, 8.1, and previous versions of Windows 10, Homegroup provided a fairly easy way to share your files. With a few clicks, it automatically let other people on your network share your Music, Pictures, and Videos folders. And, it conveniently left out the folder most people *don't* want to share: Documents.

Now, with Homegroup support dropped, Windows 10 doesn't share *any* files or folders: It treats your home network as a *public* network. Public networks work fine in coffee shops and airports, where you don't want anybody to know about your connected computer, much less access its private files.

SWITCHING FROM PUBLIC TO PRIVATE

When you first open File Manager's Network area, Windows displays some banners that can be confusing. Here's the right way to click all of the pop-up messages and banners so that Windows will quickly switch your network from Public to Private and turn on File Sharing.

If you're not sure you clicked everything correctly, following the steps in the next three sections will make sure all of the switches are flipped in the right direction. If you'd like to, try clicking through the pop-up messages and banners.

1. **Open File Manager and click Network in the left pane.**

2. **When the Network Discovery Is Turned Off message appears, click OK.**

3. **Click the yellow banner atop File Manager that says, Network Discovery and File Sharing Are Turned Off. Click Here to Change.**

4. **When the pop-up menu appears below the banner, choose Turn On Network Discovery and File Sharing.**

5. **When the Network Discovery and File Sharing window appears, choose the top of the two options, No, Make the Network that I am Connected to a Private Network.**

This does two things: It lets your PC see other PCs on your network, and it lets them see you. When anybody on your network clicks your computer's name, they can see everything in your user account: all of your files and folders. If your network still isn't working correctly, then follow the rest of the steps in this section to complete the setup process.

However, you want a *private* network at home. To switch your network to private, follow these steps:

1. **Click the Start button, click the Settings icon from the Start button, and choose the Settings app's Network & Internet category.**

   The Settings app opens to show your computer's Network & Internet settings, shown in Figure 15-3.

2. **Click the Change Connection Properties link.**

   The Network Profile page comes up for your network.

3. **In the Network Profile section, choose Private instead of Public.**

   Choosing the Private network, shown in Figure 15-4, loosens the security, allowing your network computers to see each other, as well as share files and folders that you've designated as *shared*.

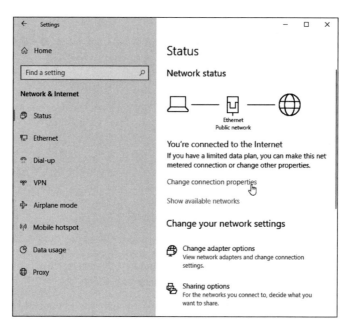

FIGURE 15-3:
Click the Change
Connection
Properties link.

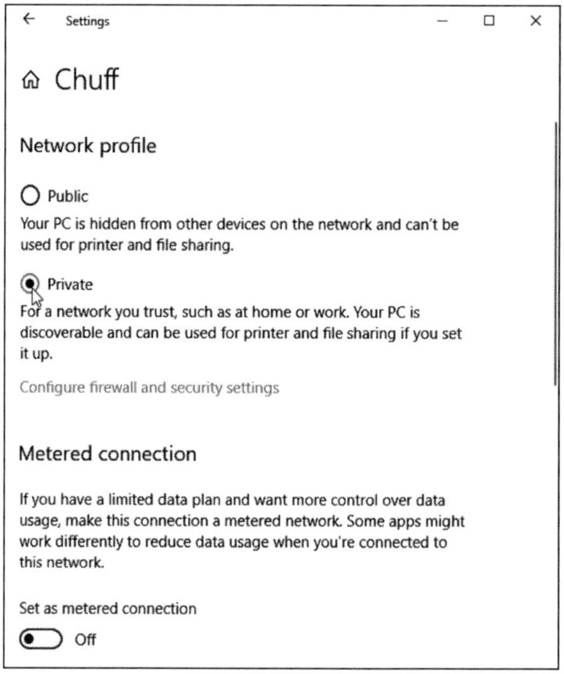

FIGURE 15-4:
Click the Private
option for your
home network.

REMEMBER

If you're connecting to a public network away from your home, the setting should be Public, which tightens the security, keeping your computer from being discovered and preventing access to its files.

4. Return to the previous page by clicking the back arrow in the window's upper-left corner.

The Network & Internet settings page appears, shown earlier in Figure 15-3.

5. Choose Sharing Options.

If you don't see the Sharing Options link, click the Status link from the window's left pane. Then, when you click the Sharing Options link, the Change Sharing Options for Different Network Profiles window appears.

6. From the File and Printer Sharing section, click the Turn on File and Printer Sharing button.

While you're on that page, make sure that Turn On Network Discovery is selected, and that there's a check mark in the box called Turn On Automatic Setup of Network Connected Devices.

Windows takes the necessary background steps that begin sharing your printer and allow you to start choosing which files and folders to share.

Most people only need to follow these steps once, when first setting up their *home* network. Windows automatically treats every newly encountered network as Public, adding the tighter security controls that go along with it.

After you've set up your network as private, several things happen:

» Your networked computers will show up in File Manager's Network area, located on the bottom of File Manager's left pane. (Your other computers should now be able to see your computer, as well.)

» You can see any files shared by other PCs on your network.

» Although Windows 10 doesn't let you create or join Homegroups, it lets you view files and folders shared through Homegroups on earlier Windows versions.

» You can begin sharing files and folders on your Windows 10 computer, a task I describe in the next section.

Sharing files and folders on your private network

Once you've made your network private, as described in the previous section, other computers on your network can finally see your computer. But they can't access its files or folders.

Before they can do that, you must manually share your files and folders by following these steps:

1. **Open File Explorer by clicking its icon on the taskbar and navigate to the folders you want to share.**

   When File Explorer appears, click the This PC link in its left pane; your most popular folders appear along File Explorer's right side.

2. **Select the folder or folders you want to share.**

   While holding down the Ctrl key, click the folders you want to share. Good candidates are your Music, Videos, and Pictures folders.

   I explain how to navigate File Explorer and select items in Chapter 5.

3. **Right-click your selected folder and, when the pop-up menu appears, shown in Figure 15-5, choose Give Access To. Then, in the following pop-up menus, choose the people who should have access to the folders.**

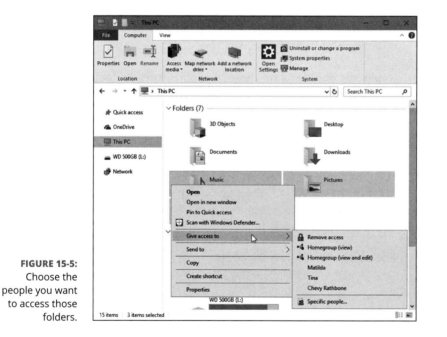

FIGURE 15-5:
Choose the people you want to access those folders.

The Give Access To menu offers several options:

- **Remove Access:** Choose this to stop sharing previously shared items.

- **Homegroup (View):** If a homegroup is currently set up on your network, perhaps by earlier Windows versions running on the network, choose this option. That lets other people in the homegroup view your folders and their contents, but not delete or change them. (If they want to change the files, they can copy them to their own PC and change them there.)

- **Homegroup (View and Edit):** Another option for networks with Homegroups, this option lets others delete or change the files that you're sharing. It's handy mostly when you're collaborating on projects with people you trust.

- **Names:** If there's no existing homegroup on your network, choose the names of other account holders on your PC who should have access to the files or folders.

- **Specific People:** Choose this, and the Choose People to Share With window appears. Click the downward pointing arrow in the box, shown in Figure 15-6, and choose who should be able to access the shared items. Choose Everyone to give access to everybody on your private network. Click the adjacent Add button, and then click the Share button to complete the process.

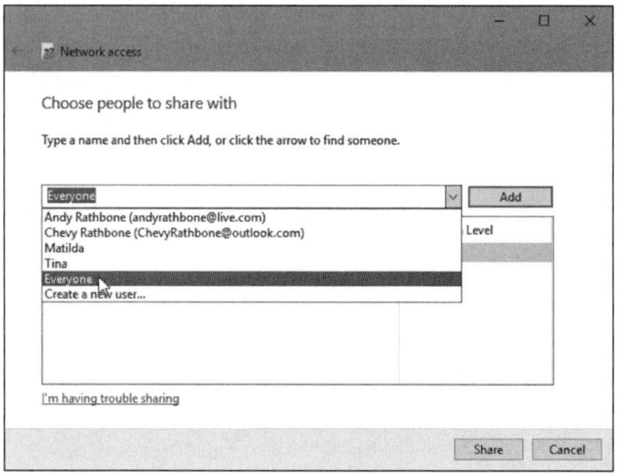

FIGURE 15-6:
Choose the people who should have access to your shared items.

When you're through sharing items, the next section explains how to access items shared on the network.

Accessing what others have shared

To see the shared folders of other people on both your PC and home network, click the File Explorer icon (shown in the margin), found on the taskbar that runs along the bottom of every screen.

When File Explorer appears, click Network, found in the Navigation Pane along File Explorer's left edge. The right side of the window, shown in Figure 15-7, promptly lists the names and icons of every computer owner on your network who has chosen to share files.

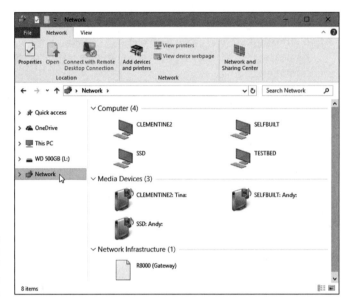

FIGURE 15-7:
Click Network to see other accessible PCs on your network.

To browse the files shared on another networked computer, double-click that computer's name from the Network window. The window promptly displays that computer's shared folders, as shown in Figure 15-8, ready to be browsed as if they were your own.

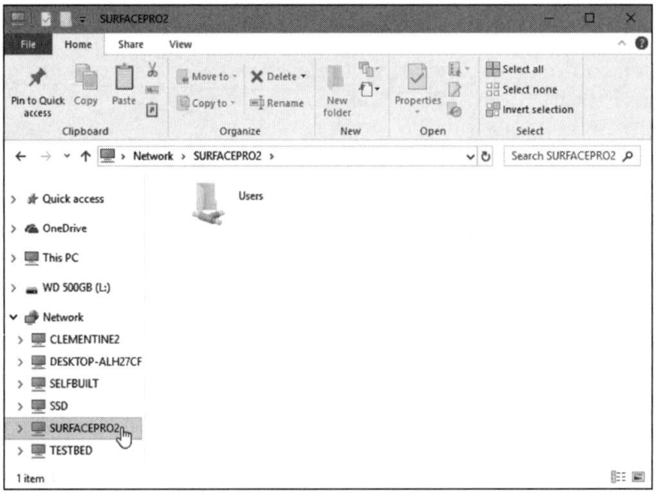

FIGURE 15-8:
Click a computer's name to see its available files.

You can do more than browse those files, as described here:

>> **Opening:** To open a file on a shared folder, double-click its icon, just as you would any other file. The appropriate program opens it. If you see an error message, the sharing person created the file using a program you don't own. Your solution? Buy or download the program from the Internet or ask the person to save the file in a format that one of your programs can open.

>> **Copying:** To copy a file from another networked PC, drag it into your own folder: Point at the file you want and, while holding down the mouse button, point at your own folder within File Explorer. Let go of the mouse button, and Windows copies the item into your folder. Alternatively, right-click the file's icon and choose Copy from the pop-up menu; then right-click inside the destination folder and choose Paste from the pop-up menu.

Sharing a printer on the network

If you've created a network, covered earlier in this chapter, Windows makes sharing a printer extraordinarily easy. After you plug a USB printer — the kind with the connector shown in the margin — into one of your networked Windows PCs, you're set: Windows automatically recognizes the newly plugged-in printer as soon as it's turned on.

Plus, your Windows PC quickly spreads the news to all the PCs in your network. Within minutes, that printer's name and icon appear on all those PCs and in all their programs' print menus.

If you don't see your printer listed, make sure you've followed the steps in this chapter's earlier section, Setting your home network to private.

Here's how to see that shared printer on your other networked Windows PCs:

>> **Windows 10:** Click the Start button and click Settings. When the Settings app appears, click the Devices icon (shown in the margin). When the Devices page appears, click Printers & Scanners along the left edge to see any printer or scanner that's available to your computer.

>> **Windows 8 or 8.1:** Right-click in the screen's bottom-left corner and choose Control Panel from the pop-up menu. From the Control Panel's Hardware and Sound category, click View Devices and Printers. The networked printer appears in the Printers section.

>> **Windows 7:** Click the Start button and choose Devices and Printers. The networked printer appears in the Printers and Faxes section.

Sharing with Nearby Sharing

NEW

Creating a network makes it easier to share files with other PCs in your home. It's the best way to share an Internet connection, as well as printers.

But a network isn't the only way to share files:

>> You can attach files to email and send them to people with the Mail app or any other email program, as I cover in Chapter 10.

>> You can share your OneDrive files and folders with anybody on the Internet, as I explain in Chapter 5.

Plus, you can share files between nearby computers with the new *Nearby Sharing* feature, introduced to Windows 10 in the spring of 2018. Nearby Sharing works with Bluetooth, which comes built-in to nearly every portable computer and device. (If your PC doesn't have Bluetooth, you can add it by buying a Bluetooth adapter and plugging it into one of your PC's USB ports.)

TIP

Nearby Sharing isn't the fastest way to send a file, so don't use it for sending large videos.

The next two sections explain how to turn on Nearby Sharing, as well as how to use it for sharing files with nearby devices.

Turning on Nearby Sharing

Before you can share files with Nearby Sharing, you must first turn on the feature by following these steps:

1. **Click the Start button, choose the Settings icon, and choose the System category.**

The Settings app opens to show its System settings.

2. **Choose Shared Experiences from the left pane.**

The Shared Experiences settings appear, shown in Figure 15-9.

3. **Click the Nearby Sharing toggle to On.**

Windows turns on Nearby Sharing.

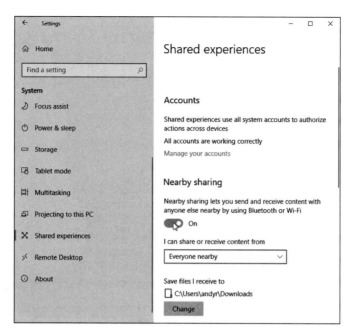

FIGURE 15-9:
Click the Nearby
Sharing toggle
to On.

4. **Choose who can send or receive shared items.**

   Just below the Nearby Sharing toggle, a drop-down menu lets you fine-tune two options:

   - **Everyone nearby:** The most popular option, this allows anybody with the latest version of Windows 10 to both receive and send items through Nearby Sharing. It's a handy way to send somebody a file during a meeting in a boardroom or coffeeshop.

   - **My Devices only:** Choose this only if you want to restrict the Nearby Sharing to your own PCs.

5. **Choose the folder where the incoming files should appear.**

   Unless you have a good reason, leave this folder set to Downloads. That folder is easily accessible whenever you open File Manager.

Once you've turned on Nearby Sharing, you don't need to revisit this setting unless you want to turn it off.

TIP

To turn Nearby Sharing on or off quickly, open the Action Center pane with a click on the Action Center icon on the far-right edge of your taskbar along the bottom of your desktop. When the Action Center pane appears, you can toggle the feature on or off by clicking the Nearby Sharing button. (Don't see it? Click Expand above the four buttons along the Action Center's bottom edge to see all of the available buttons.)

Sharing files with Nearby Sharing

Once you and your friend have turned on Nearby Sharing, a new Share button appears in the Microsoft Edge browser, File Explorer, Photos, and other any apps that support the new feature.

To share a file or folder, follow these steps:

1. **Find the file you want to share.**

   File Explorer offers the easiest way to share things with Nearby Share, but a few other apps also support the new feature.

2. **Select the item or items you want to share, then click the app's Share button.**

   Click the Share menu option in File Explorer, for example, and then click the Share button (shown in the margin) that appears on the ribbon menu.

3. **When the Share window appears, choose how you wish to share the file.**

   The Share window in File Explorer, shown in Figure 15-10, offers three ways to share your items:

FIGURE 15-10:
Click the name
of the computer
which should
receive the file.

- **Email:** Frequently contacted people appear as a row atop the window. Click a person's name and choose their preferred email address to email them the files. This works best for fairly small files, not videos or a large number of photos.

- **Computers:** This unlabeled area lists any nearby computers with Nearby Sharing turned on. Click a computer's name to start sending copies of the files to that computer.

- **Apps:** Choose an app listed from this group to send the file to that app on your own PC.

4. **Have the other person approve the transfer.**

When you choose a computer's name in the previous step, a message pops up on the receiving computer. That lets the owner accept the transfer and, just as important, decline unwanted or unexpected file transfers.

Once the recipient approves the transfer by clicking the Save button, the incoming files appear in their Downloads folder.

5

Music, Photos, and Movies

IN THIS PART . . .

Show your photos to friends.

Copy photos from your camera to your PC.

Watch digital movies on your computer or tablet.

Organize a digital photo album from your digital camera or phone.

Chapter **16**

Playing and Copying Music

B uilt for minimalists, the Windows 10 Groove Music app sticks to the essentials. With a few clicks, it plays music stored on both your computer and OneDrive, your storage space on the Internet.

For some, that's plenty. But the Groove Music app lacks more robust features. Stuck in a world of digital files, the Groove Music app can't copy music CDs onto your computer. It can't create CDs from your music files. It can't even *play* a music CD you've slipped into your PC's disc drive. And since Microsoft discontinued its Groove Music Pass service in January 2018, the app no longer lets you purchase music or listen to Internet radio stations. (Instead, it urges you to subscribe to the Spotify paid streaming music service.)

In short, Groove Music is now a bare-bones player for music you already own. That's fine for Windows tablets and many new laptops; they lack disc drives, so their owners naturally embrace digital music.

On a desktop PC, however, you probably want to stick with the program from yesteryear, Windows Media Player. Windows Media Player works much like it did in earlier Windows versions with one big exception: It can no longer play DVDs.

This chapter explains how and when to jump between the Groove Music app and Windows Media Player. It also explains when you might want to jump ship with the standard Windows options and download a more full-featured app to meet your music needs.

Playing Music with the Groove Music app

In keeping with the music of today's youth, the Windows Groove Music app recognizes music files only if they're stored on either your PC, OneDrive, or, when told, a flash drive you've placed into your computer's USB port. The Groove Music app turns up its nose at playing those old-fashioned CDs or DVDs, so don't even try.

But if you simply want to play music, the Groove Music app handles the job fairly simply and easily. When first opened, as shown in Figure 16-1, the program shows the music stored both on your own PC and in your OneDrive account's Music folder.

To launch the Groove Music app and begin listening to music, follow these steps:

1. **Click the Start menu's Groove Music tile.**

   Fetch the Start menu with a click of the Start button in the screen's lower-left corner. When the Start menu appears, click the Groove Music app's tile, shown in the margin.

   If you don't spot the Groove Music app's tile, choose Groove Music from the Start menu's list of alphabetically sorted apps.

   Don't see the Start menu's alphabetically sorted list of apps? Then your computer is running in Tablet mode. Reveal the apps list by clicking the Start menu's All Apps icon (shown in the margin).

   When launched, the Groove Music app fills the screen, as shown in Figure 16-1, with automatically showing tiles representing your albums, artists, or songs. (When opened for the first time, you may need to click through some welcome screens.)

2. **View your music by album, song, or artist.**

   The Navigation pane along the left edge of the Groove Music app offers these options for viewing your music:

   - **Search:** Type an artist's name, song, or album title into this box, and the app shows you the matches stored on your PC or OneDrive.

   - **My Music:** Click My Music from the Navigation pane, and the app displays your music. Click the Songs, Artists, or Albums links beneath the words My Music, to see your music grouped by song, artist, or album.

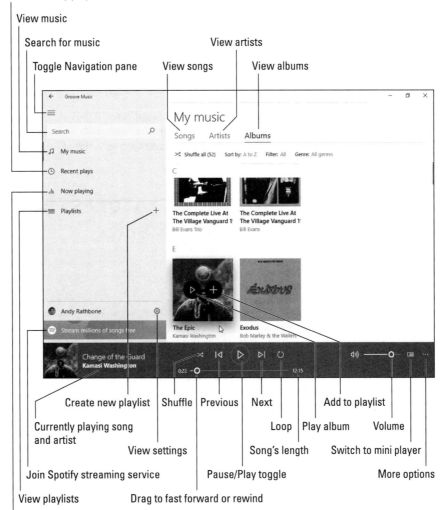

View recently played music

View music

Search for music

Toggle Navigation pane

View songs

View artists

View albums

Create new playlist
Shuffle
Previous
Next
Add to playlist

Currently playing song and artist
Loop
Play album
Volume

View settings
Song's length
Switch to mini player

Join Spotify streaming service
Pause/Play toggle
More options

View playlists
Drag to fast forward or rewind

View currently playing music

FIGURE 16-1:
The Groove Music
app plays music
stored on your
PC, as well as on
OneDrive.

- **Recent Plays:** Recently played music appears here, making it easy to hear a replay.

- **Now Playing:** Choose this to see your currently played song, as well as a list of songs that are queued to play next.

- **Playlists:** Playlists *you* create appear here, ready to be played again with a click of their names. Or, create your own playlist by clicking the adjacent plus sign icon.

Microsoft discontinued its streaming music service on January 1, 2018, so the app no longer offers the Groove Music Pass service or its Your Groove playlist feature.

3. **Tell the app what music to play.**

From the app's right side, click the Songs, Artists, or Albums tabs to view your music sorted by those categories.

Hover your mouse over any tile, and a Play icon appears. Click it to start playing everything contained in the tile, be it a single album or an artist's entire work.

An adjacent Plus sign icon lets you quickly add that item to the current playlist or a new playlist. By hovering over items and clicking the Plus sign, you can quickly create a playlist that will keep you listening to music for hours.

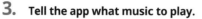

SQUEEZING MORE FEATURES FROM THE GROOVE MUSIC APP

The Groove Music app doesn't do much more than play your music. But you can stretch it to its minimalist limits with these tips:

- **Create playlists:** Hover your mouse pointer over any tile, and a plus sign icon appears either next to a song or atop a list of songs. Click the plus sign icon, and a pop-up list of playlists appears. Click the desired playlist, and the Groove Music app copies that song or songs to the list. If you haven't created any playlists yet, the words New Playlist appear in a box; change those words to a term that describes your list of songs, and you've created your first playlist. Microsoft account owners receive a perk: Playlists created on your PC also appear on your Windows tablet or Xbox One.

- **OneDrive access:** The Groove Music app can play songs stored exclusively in OneDrive's music folder. But you can't access them without an Internet connection. To download a favorite album from OneDrive onto your computer for playing later, right-click the album cover in Groove Music, and click Download from the pop-up menu.

- **Pin to Start menu:** While you're at the pop-up menu button described in the previous tip, you can also choose Pin to Start to add an album, artist, or playlist to the Start menu as an easy-to-reach tile.

- **Buying music:** The app no longer lets you buy music or listen to online radio stations. Instead, it asks you to subscribe to the Spotify streaming service, which isn't owned by Microsoft and requires downloading the Spotify app.

- **Try another app:** If you like the simplicity of apps but want a little more power, look for VideoLAN's VLC app, or try some of the other alternatives available in the Microsoft Store.

4. **Adjust the music while it plays.**

   The App bar, shown along the bottom of Figure 16-1, offers you several icons to control your music: Shuffle, Loop, Previous (to move to the previous song), Pause/Play, and Next (to move to the next song).

To adjust the volume, click the little speaker on the App bar in the screen's bottom corner. Or, from the desktop, click the little speaker icon next to the clock on the taskbar, that strip along the desktop's bottom edge.

TIP

Most touchscreen tablets include a volume rocker switch along one of their edges.

The Groove Music app keeps playing music even if you begin working with other apps or switch to the desktop. To pause or move between tracks, hover your mouse pointer over the Groove Music app's icon on the taskbar; a pop-up menu appears, with controls for playing, pausing, or skipping tracks.

Handing Music-Playing Chores Back to Windows Media Player

Microsoft hopes that the Groove Music app will meet all of your musical needs. Accordingly, Windows tries to shoehorn you into using the Groove Music app. Open a music file from your desktop's Music folder, for example, and the Start menu's Groove Music app butts in to play the file.

With its large and simple controls, the Groove Music app works fine on touch-screen tablets. However, when you switch to the desktop, you may prefer a more full-featured music program. Luckily, Windows 10 still includes Windows Media Player, a Windows desktop staple for a decade.

Follow the steps in this section to hand your music-playing chores back to Windows Media Player and to make the program easier to find.

1. **Click the Start button, and the Start menu appears.**

   The Start menu presents an alphabetical list of *all* your installed apps and programs.

   Don't see the Start menu's alphabetically sorted list of apps? Then your computer is running in Tablet mode, which requires you to click the Start menu's All Apps icon (shown in the margin).

2. **Scroll down the Start menu's list of alphabetically sorted apps, right-click the Windows Media Player tile (shown in the margin), and choose Pin to Start from the pop-up menu.**

That places Windows Media Player's icon as a tile on your Start menu for easy access. (The same right-click menu lets you choose More and select Pin to Taskbar; that places a second link to Windows Media Player on your taskbar, the strip that runs along the bottom of the screen.)

TIP

If you're using a touchscreen, hold down your finger on the Start menu's Windows Media Player entry for a moment and then lift your finger. When the pop-up menu appears, choose Pin to Taskbar.

3. **Click the Start menu's Settings icon to fetch the Settings app.**

The Settings icon, shown in the margin, brings the Settings app to the screen.

4. **When the Settings app appears, click the Apps icon and then click Default Apps from the left pane.**

The right pane lists the apps and programs currently assigned to handle your email, music, videos, and other items.

5. **In the right pane's Music Player section, click the Groove Music app. When the pop-up menu appears, click Windows Media Player, as shown in Figure 16-2.**

This step tells Windows Media Player to play your music instead of the Start menu's Groove Music app.

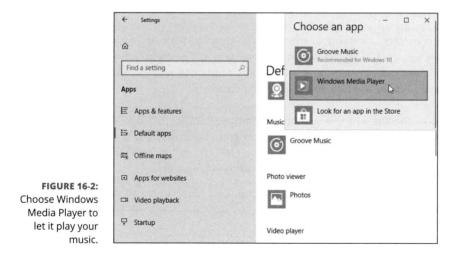

FIGURE 16-2:
Choose Windows Media Player to let it play your music.

After you follow these steps, Windows Media Player jumps into action whenever you double-click a music file on the desktop. You can also launch Windows Media Player directly by clicking its icon (shown in the margin) on your taskbar.

REMEMBER

These steps don't permanently disable or uninstall the Start menu's Groove Music app — it still works fine. To open the Groove Music app, just click its tile from the Start menu. When the Groove Music app appears, it still displays and plays all of your music.

However, when you click a song from the desktop's File Explorer program, Windows Media Player pops up and begins playing your song.

Follow these same steps to choose which other programs should open your favorite files. You're not limited to the choices Microsoft set up with Windows 10.

TIP

RUNNING WINDOWS MEDIA PLAYER FOR THE FIRST TIME

The first time you open the desktop's Windows Media Player, an opening screen asks how to deal with the player's settings for privacy, storage, and the music store. The screen offers two options:

- **Recommended Settings:** Designed for the impatient, this option loads Windows Media Player with Microsoft's chosen settings in place. Windows Media Player sets itself up as the default player for most of your music and video, but *not* your MP3 files. (The Groove Music app still holds title to MP3 files, which are the most common digital music format.) Windows Media Player sweeps the Internet to update your songs' title information, and it tells Microsoft what you're listening to and watching. Choose Recommended Settings if you're in a hurry; you can always customize the settings some other time.

- **Custom Settings:** Aimed at the fine-tuners and the privacy-conscious folks, this choice lets you micromanage Windows Media Player's behavior. A series of screens lets you choose the types of music and video that the player can play, and you can control how much of your listening habits should be sent to Microsoft. Choose this option only if you have time to wade through several minutes of boring option screens.

If you later want to customize any Windows Media Player settings — either those chosen for you in Recommended Settings setup or the ones you've chosen in Custom setup — click Windows Media Player's Organize button in the top-left corner and choose Options.

Stocking the Windows Media Player Library

You can load Windows Media Player by double-clicking its icon in the Start menu or taskbar, that strip along the desktop's bottom edge. No icon in the Start menu or taskbar? The previous section explains how to put it there.

When you run Windows Media Player, the program automatically sorts through your computer's stash of digital music, pictures, and videos, automatically cataloging everything it finds.

But if you've noticed that some of your PC's media is missing from the Windows Media Player Library, you can tell the player where to find those items by following these steps:

Note: Unlike the Groove Music app, Windows Media Player can play OneDrive files only if they are synced to your PC. It can't play music files that are available on OneDrive only through the Internet.

1. **Click Windows Media Player's Organize button (in the program's upper-left corner) and choose Manage Libraries from the drop-down menu to reveal a pop-out menu.**

   The pop-out menu lists the four types of media that Windows Media Player can handle: Music, Videos, Pictures, and Recorded TV.

2. **From the pop-out menu, choose the name of the type of files you're missing.**

   A window appears, as shown in Figure 16-3, listing your monitored folders. For example, the player normally monitors the contents of your Music folder, so anything you add to your Music folder automatically appears in the Media Player Library, as well.

   But if you're storing items elsewhere — perhaps on a portable hard drive, flash drive, network location, or your Public folder — here's your chance to give the player directions to that other media stash.

3. **Click the Add button, select the folder or drive containing your files, click the Include Folder button, and click OK.**

   Clicking the Add button brings the Include Folder in Music window to the screen. Navigate to the folder you'd like to add — the folder on your portable hard drive, for example — and click the Include Folder button. Windows Media Player immediately begins monitoring that folder, adding the folder's music to its library.

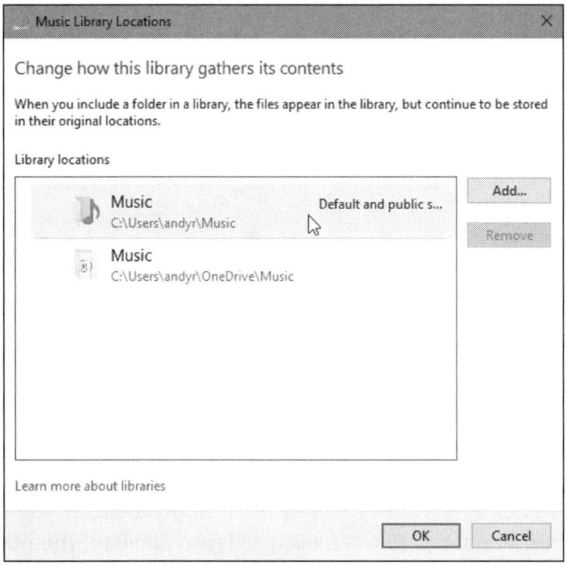

FIGURE 16-3:
Click the Add
button and
browse to a new
folder you want
Windows Media
Player to monitor.

To add music from even more folders or drives — perhaps a folder on another networked PC or a flash drive — repeat these steps until you've added all the places Windows Media Player should search for media.

To stop the player from monitoring a folder, follow these steps, but in Step 3, click the folder you no longer want monitored and then click the Remove button shown in Figure 16-3.

When you run Windows Media Player, the program shows the media it has collected (shown in Figure 16-4), and it continues to stock its library in the following ways:

>> **Monitoring your folders:** Windows Media Player constantly monitors your Music, Pictures, and Videos folders, as well as any other locations you've added. Windows Media Player automatically updates its library whenever you add or remove files from your folders. (You can change what folders Windows Media Player monitors by following the three preceding steps.)

>> **Adding played items:** Anytime you play a music file on your PC or from the Internet, Windows Media Player adds the song or its Internet location to its library so that you can find it to play again later. Unless specifically told to, Windows Media Player *doesn't* add recently played items residing on other people's PCs, USB flash drives, or memory cards. (It can't play any music from OneDrive unless you've chosen to keep that music in sync with your PC, which I cover in Chapter 5.)

>> **Ripped music from CD:** When you insert a music CD into your CD drive, Windows may offer to *rip* it. That's computereze for copying the CD's music to your PC, a task described in the "Ripping (Copying) CDs to Your PC" section, later in this chapter. Any ripped music automatically appears in your Windows Media Player Library. (Windows Media Player won't copy DVD movies to your library, unfortunately, nor does it play the discs.)

>> **Downloaded music from online stores:** When you buy a song and place it in your Music folder, Windows Media Player automatically stocks its library with your latest purchase.

TIP

Feel free to repeat the steps in this section to search for files whenever you want. Windows Media Player ignores the files it has already cataloged and adds any new ones.

TECHNICAL
STUFF

Windows Media Player doesn't offer an advanced editor for changing a song's *tags*, which are described in the nearby sidebar. Instead, the player edits them for you automatically from an online database.

TECHNICAL
STUFF

WHAT ARE A SONG'S TAGS?

Inside every music file lives a small form called a *tag* that contains the song's title, artist, album, and other related information. When deciding how to sort, display, and categorize your music, Windows Media Player reads those tags — *not* the songs' filenames. Nearly every digital music player, including the iPod, also relies on tags.

Tags are so important, in fact, that Windows Media Player visits the Internet, grabs song information, and automatically fills in the tags when it adds files to its library.

Many people don't bother filling out their songs' tags, but other people update them meticulously. If your tags are already filled out the way you prefer, stop Windows Media Player from messing with them: Click the Organize button, choose Options, click the Library tab, and deselect the check box next to Retrieve Additional Information from the Internet. If your tags are a mess, leave that check box selected so that the player will clean up the tags for you.

If Windows Media Player makes a mistake, fix the tags yourself: Right-click the song (or, in the case of an album, the selected songs) and choose Find Album Info. When a window appears listing the player's guess as to the song or album, choose the Edit link. In the new window that appears, you can fill in the album, artist, genre, tracks, title, contributing artist, and composer. Click Done when you're through tidying up the information.

FIGURE 16-4:
Click an item from the left to see its contents on the right.

Browsing Windows Media Player's Libraries

The Windows Media Player Library is where the behind-the-scenes action takes place. There, you organize files, create playlists, burn or copy CDs, and choose what to play.

When first loaded, Windows Media Player displays your Music folder's contents, appropriately enough. But Windows Media Player actually holds several libraries, designed to showcase not only your music but also photographs, video, and recorded TV shows.

All your playable items appear in the Navigation Pane along the window's left edge, shown in Figure 16-5, where they can be accessed with a click. The pane's top half shows your own media collection, appropriately listed with your name at the top.

The bottom half, called Other Libraries, lets you browse the collections of other people with accounts on your PC. You can also access the music shared by other people on your network. (I explain how to create and manage networks in Chapter 15.)

FIGURE 16-5:
Click the type of
media you're
interested in
browsing from
the Navigation
Pane along
the left.

Windows Media Player organizes your media into these categories:

>> **Playlists:** Do you enjoy playing albums or songs in a certain order? Click the
Save List button atop your list of songs to save it as a playlist that shows up in
this category. (I cover playlists in this chapter's later "Creating, Saving, and
Editing Playlists" section.)

>> **Music:** All your digital music appears here. Windows Media Player recognizes
most major music formats, including MP3, WMA, WAV, and even 3GP files
used by some cellphones. (It recognizes non-copy-protected AAC files, sold by
iTunes. And Windows 10 also includes support for the lossless FLAC, a format
that compresses the music without losing any sound quality.)

>> **Videos:** Look here for videos you've saved from a camcorder or digital camera
or for videos you've downloaded from the Internet. Windows Media Player
recognizes AVI, MPG, WMV, ASF, DivX, some MOV files, and a few other
formats. Windows 10 also adds support for MKV files, a relatively new video
format for high-definition videos.

>> **Pictures:** Windows Media Player can display photos individually or in a simple
slideshow, but your Pictures folder and Photos app, both covered in
Chapter 17, handle photos better. (Windows Media Player can't correct
upside-down photos, for example, a feat done easily from within your Pictures
folder of the Photos app.)

>> **Other Libraries:** Here you can find media appearing on other PCs in your
home *network* — a private way of connecting PCs that I describe in Chapter 15.

TIP

YES, WINDOWS SPIES ON YOU

Just like your bank, credit card company, and grocery store club card, Windows 10's Groove Music app and Windows Media Player both spy on you. Microsoft's 5,000-word online Privacy Statement boils down to this: Both players tell Microsoft every song, file, or movie that you play. Some people find that creepy, but if Microsoft doesn't know what you're playing, Windows can't retrieve that artist's profile information and artwork from the Internet.

If you don't care that Microsoft hums along to your music, don't bother reading any further. If you *do* care, choose your surveillance level in Windows Media Player: Click the Organize button in Windows Media Player's top-left corner, choose Options, and click the Privacy tab. Here's the rundown on the Privacy tab options that cause the biggest ruckus:

- **Display Media Information from the Internet:** If this option is selected, Windows Media Player tells Microsoft what CD you're playing and retrieves doodads to display on your screen: CD covers, song titles, artist names, and similar information.

- **Update Music Files by Retrieving Media Info from the Internet:** Microsoft examines your files, and if it recognizes any, it fills in the songs' tags with the correct information. (For more information on tags, see the "What are a song's tags?" sidebar.)

- **Send Unique Player ID to Content Providers:** Known in the biz as *data mining,* this option lets other corporations track how you use Windows Media Player when playing copy-protected music.

- **Cookies:** Like many other programs and websites, Windows Media Player tracks your activity with little files called *cookies.* Cookies aren't necessarily bad, because they help the player keep track of your preferences.

- **Customer Experience Improvement:** When enabled, this feature gives Microsoft your "player usage data," a generic term that could mean anything. I turn mine off.

- **History:** Windows Media Player lists the names of your recently played files for your convenience — and for the possible guffaws of your co-workers or family. To keep people from seeing the titles of music and videos you've recently played, remove *all* the check marks from this section and click the two buttons called Clear History and Clear Caches.

For more information about your privacy settings, visit Microsoft's privacy center online at http://www.microsoft.com/privacy.

After you click a category, Windows Media Player's Navigation Pane lets you view the files in several different ways. Click Artist in the Navigation Pane's Music category, for example, and the pane shows the music arranged alphabetically by artists' first names.

Similarly, clicking Genre in the Music category separates songs and albums by different types of music, shown earlier in Figure 16-5. Instead of just showing a name to click — blues, for example — the player arranges your music into piles of covers, just as if you'd sorted your albums or CDs on your living room floor.

TIP

To play anything in Windows Media Player, right-click it and choose Play. Or to play all your music from one artist or genre, right-click the pile and choose Play All.

Playing Music Files in a Playlist

Windows Media Player plays several types of digital music files, but they all have one thing in common: When you tell Windows Media Player to play a song or an album, Windows Media Player immediately places that item on your *Now Playing list* — a list of items queued up for playing one after the other.

You can start playing music through Windows Media Player in a number of ways, even if Windows Media Player isn't currently running:

» Click the File Explorer icon (shown in the margin) on your taskbar, right-click an album or a music-filled folder, and choose Play with Windows Media Player. The player jumps to the screen and begins playing your choice.

» While you're still viewing your own Music folder, right-click items and choose Add to Windows Media Player List. Your computer queues them up in Windows Media Player, ready to be played after you've heard your currently playing music.

» Place a music CD in your computer's CD drive tray and push the tray into your computer. Click the Select to Choose What Happens with Audio CDs pop-up message. When the second pop-up menu appears, choose Play Audio CD, and Windows will automatically play future audio CDs as soon as you insert them.

» Double-click a song file, whether it's sitting on your desktop or in any folder. Windows Media Player begins playing it immediately.

To play songs listed within Windows Media Player's own library, right-click the song's name and choose Play. Windows Media Player begins playing it immediately, and the song appears in the Now Playing list.

Here are other ways to play songs within Windows Media Player:

>> To play an entire album in Windows Media Player's library, right-click the album from the library's Album category and choose Play.

>> Want to hear several files or albums, one after the other? Right-click the first one and choose Play. Right-click the next one and choose Add to Now Playing List. Repeat until you're done. Windows Media Player queues them all up in the Now Playing list.

>> To return to a recently played item, right-click Windows Media Player's icon in the taskbar. When the list of recently played items appears, click your item's name.

>> No decent music in your music folder? Then start copying your favorite CDs to your computer — a process called *ripping*, which I explain in the "Ripping (Copying) CDs to Your Computer" section, later in this chapter.

Controlling Your Now Playing Items

You can play music directly from the Windows Media Player Library: Just right-click a file, album, artist, or genre and then choose Play. Windows Media Player begins playing the music, but the program stays put, often filling the screen.

 To summon a smaller, more manageable player, click the Library/Player toggle button shown in the margin and summon the Now Playing window shown in Figure 16-6. (The Library/Player toggle button lives in the library's bottom-right corner.) Don't see the controls? Hover your mouse pointer over the Media Player window, and the controls appear along the window's bottom edge.

The minimalist Now Playing window shows what's currently playing, be it a video or artwork from your currently playing song. Onscreen controls let you adjust the volume, skip between listed songs or videos, or pause the action.

Windows Media Player offers the same basic controls when playing any type of file, be it a song, video, CD, or photo slideshow. Figure 16-6 shows Windows Media Player open to its Now Playing window as it plays an album. The labels in the figure explain each button's function. Or rest your mouse pointer over an especially mysterious button, and Windows Media Player displays a pop-up explanation.

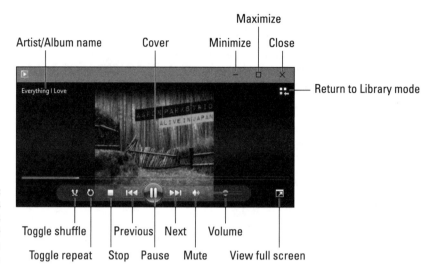

Maximize

Artist/Album name   Cover   Minimize   Close

Return to Library mode

FIGURE 16-6:
The window's
bottom buttons
work much like
the buttons on a
CD player.

Toggle shuffle   Previous   Next   Volume

Toggle repeat   Stop   Pause   Mute   View full screen

The buttons along the bottom work like those found on any CD player, letting you play, stop, rewind, fast-forward, and mute the current song or movie. For even more controls, right-click anywhere in the Now Playing window. A menu appears, offering to perform these common tasks:

» **Show List:** Shows the playlist along the right side, which is handy for jumping directly to different songs.

» **Full Screen:** Enlarges the window to fill the screen.

» **Shuffle:** Plays songs randomly.

» **Repeat:** Loops the same song.

» **Visualizations:** Choose between showing the album cover, wavy lines, groovy spirals, dancing waves, or other freaky eye games.

» **Enhancements:** Opens an equalizer, balance adjuster, playback speed, volume balancer, and other sound options.

» **Lyrics, Captions, or Subtitles:** Display these items, if they're available, which come in handy when practicing for Karaoke night.

» **Always Show Now Playing on Top:** Keeps the window above your other windows on the desktop.

» **More Options:** Brings up the Options page, where you can tweak Windows Media Player's habits when ripping CDs, stocking your Windows Media Player Library, and other tasks.

» **Help with Playback:** Fetches the Help program to deal with head-scratchers.

The Now Playing controls disappear from the screen when you haven't moved the mouse for a while. To bring them back, move your mouse pointer over the Now Playing window.

To return to the Windows Media Player Library, click the Library/Player toggle icon in the window's upper-right corner.

When you minimize Windows Media Player to the desktop's taskbar, hover your mouse pointer over the player's icon: A control pops up, letting you pause or jump between songs.

Playing CDs

As long as you insert the CD in the CD drive correctly (usually label-side up), playing a music CD is one of Windows Media Player's easiest tasks. Start by pushing the drive's Eject button, a rarely labelled button that lives next to or on the disc drive on the front of your computer.

When the drive tray emerges, drop the CD (label-side up) into your CD drive and push the tray back into the drive. Windows Media Player jumps to the screen to play it, usually identifying the CD and its artist immediately. In many cases, it even tosses a picture of the cover art on the screen.

The controls along the bottom, shown earlier in Figure 16-6, let you jump from track to track, adjust the volume, and fine-tune your listening experience.

If for some odd reason Windows Media Player doesn't start playing your CD, look at the Library item in Windows Media Player's Navigation Pane along the left side of the window. You should spot either the CD's name or the words *Unknown Album*. When you spot the listing, click it and then click the Play button to start listening.

Press F7 to mute Windows Media Player's sound and pick up that phone call. Pressing Ctrl+P toggles the pause/play mode.

Want to copy that CD to your PC? That's called *ripping,* and I cover ripping in the "Ripping (Copying) CDs to Your PC" section, later in this chapter.

Playing DVDs

And now for a bit of bad news: Windows Media Player can't play DVDs. That news comes as a bit of a shock, considering that the Media Player in Windows 7 *could* play DVDs. What gives?

According to Microsoft, DVDs are old-school technology that's no longer needed. Today's ultrathin laptops and tablets don't even have DVD drives. Most people watch movies by streaming them to their computers over the Internet, Microsoft says. Or, they watch their DVDs on TV.

TECHNICAL STUFF

Also, Microsoft no longer wanted to pay licensing fees to the companies owning the patents required for playing DVDs.

But although Windows Media Player can no longer play DVDs, Windows can still play DVDs if you buy some DVD playing software. Microsoft and other companies sell DVD playing software through the Microsoft Store app. (I cover the store and its apps in Chapter 6.)

Playing Videos and TV Shows

Many digital cameras and smartphones can capture short videos as well as photos, so don't be surprised if you find several videos in the Video library of Windows Media Player.

Playing videos works much like playing a digital song. Click Videos in the Navigation Pane along Windows Media Player's left side. Double-click the video you want to see and start enjoying the action, as shown in Figure 16-7.

FIGURE 16-7:
Move the mouse over the video to make the controls appear along the bottom.

PLAYING INTERNET RADIO STATIONS

Windows Media Player doesn't offer an easy way to play Internet radio stations. However, Windows offers you several ways to listen to music over the Internet:

- Head to Google (www.google.com) and search for *Internet radio station* to see what turns up. When you find a station broadcasting in MP3 or Windows Media Audio (WMA) format, click the website's Tune In or Listen Now button to load Windows Media Player and start listening.

- I like the stations at SomaFM (www.somafm.com). It offers more than two dozen stations in a variety of genres, all playable through Windows Media Player.

- Install a music streaming app, such as TuneIn Radio or Spotify, which lets you tune in to thousands of stations from around the world. Both are available through the Microsoft Store app.

Windows Media Player lets you watch videos in several sizes. Make it fill the screen by holding down Alt and pressing Enter, for example. (Repeat those key-strokes to return to the original size.)

» To make the video adjust itself automatically to the size of your Windows Media Player window, right-click the video as it plays, choose Video from the pop-up menu, and select Fit Video to Player on Resize.

» You can also toggle full-screen mode by clicking the Full Screen toggle in the video's bottom-right corner, shown in Figure 16-7.

» When choosing video to watch on the Internet, your connection speed determines its quality. Broadband connections can usually handle high-definition videos, but slower connections and slower computers often have problems. You can't damage your computer by choosing the wrong quality of video; the video just skips and pauses while playing.

Creating, Saving, and Editing Playlists

A *playlist* is simply a list of songs (and/or videos) that play in a certain order. So what? Well, the beauty of a playlist comes with what you can *do* with it. Save a playlist of your favorite songs, for example, and they're always available for play-back with a single click.

You can create specially themed playlists to liven up long–distance drives, parties, special dinners, workouts, and other events.

To create a playlist, follow these steps:

TIP

1. **Open Windows Media Player and find the playlist pane.**

   Don't see a playlist hugging Windows Media Player's right edge? Click the Play tab near the top-right corner. Or when the player is in Now Playing mode, right-click a blank part of the Windows Media Player window and choose Show List from the pop-up menu: The list of currently playing items appears along Media Center's right edge.

2. **Right-click the album or songs you want, choose Add To, and select Play List.**

   Alternatively, you can drag and drop albums and songs onto the Playlist pane along Windows Media Player's right edge, as shown in Figure 16-8. Either way, Windows Media Player begins playing your playlist as soon as you add the first song. Your song choices appear in the right pane in the order you've selected them.

FIGURE 16-8:
Drag and drop albums and songs onto the Playlist pane.

3. **Fine-tune your playlist to change the order or remove songs.**

   Added something by mistake? Right-click that item from the playlist and choose Remove from List. Feel free to rearrange your playlist by dragging and dropping items farther up or down the list.

Check the line at the bottom of the playlist to see how many items you've added to the playlist as well as your playlist's duration in minutes.

4. **When you're happy with your playlist, click the Save List button at the list's top, type a name in the highlighted box, and press Enter.**

   Windows Media Player lists your new playlist in the library's Playlists section, ready to be heard when you double-click it.

After you save a playlist, you can burn it to a CD with one click, as described in the next tip.

TIP

Make your own Desert Island Disc or Greatest Hits playlists and then burn them to a CD to play in your car or on your home stereo. After you create a playlist of less than 80 minutes, insert a blank CD into your CD burner and click the Burn tab. Take up the player's offer to import your current playlist and then click the Start Burn button.

TIP

To edit a previously created playlist, double-click the playlist's name in the Library's Playlists area. Rearrange, add, or delete items in the playlist and then click the Save List button.

Ripping (Copying) CDs to Your PC

In a process known as *ripping*, Windows Media Player can copy your CDs to your PC as MP3 files, the industry standard for digital music. But until you tell the player that you want MP3 files, it creates *WMA* files — a format that won't play on iPads, most smartphones, nor many other music players.

TIP

To make Windows Media Player create songs with the more versatile MP3 format instead of WMA, click the Organize button in the top-left corner, choose Options, and click the Rip Music tab. Choose MP3 instead of WMA from the Format drop-down menu and nudge the audio quality over a tad from 128 to 256 or even 320 for better sound. (For even better sound, choose FLAC instead of WMA or MP3; however, the files will consume more space.)

To copy CDs to your PC's hard drive, follow these instructions:

1. **Open Windows Media Player, insert a music CD, and click the Rip CD button.**

   You may need to push a button on the front or side of your computer's disc drive to make the tray eject.

Windows Media Player connects to the Internet; identifies your CD; and fills in the album's name, artist, and song titles. Then the program begins copying the CD's songs to your PC and listing their titles in the Windows Media Player Library. You're through.

If Windows Media Player can't find the songs' titles automatically, however, move ahead to Step 2.

2. **Right-click the first track and choose Find Album Info, if necessary.**

    If Windows Media Player comes up empty-handed, right-click the first track and choose Find Album Info.

    If you're connected to the Internet, type the album's name into the Search box and then click Search. If the Search box finds your album, click its name, choose Next, and click Finish.

    If you're not connected to the Internet, or if the Search box comes up empty, right-click the first song, click Edit, and manually fill in the song title. Repeat for the other titles, as well as the album, artist, genre, and year tags.

Here are some tips for ripping CDs to your computer:

>> Normally Windows Media Player copies every song on the CD. To leave Tiny Tim off your ukulele music compilation, however, remove the check mark from the box next to Tiny Tim's name. If Windows Media Player has already copied the song to your PC, feel free to delete it from within Windows Media Player. Click the Library button, right-click the song sung by the offending yodeler, and choose Delete.

>> Windows Media Player automatically places your ripped CDs into your Music folder. You can also find your newly ripped music there as well as in the Windows Media Player Library.

Burning (Creating) Music CDs

To create a music CD with your favorite songs, create a playlist containing the CD's songs, listed in the order you want to play them; then burn the playlist to a CD. I explain how to do that in the "Creating, Saving, and Editing Playlists" section, earlier in this chapter.

But what if you want to duplicate a CD, perhaps to create a disposable copy of your favorite CD to play in your car? No sense scratching up your original. You'll want to make copies of your kids' CDs, too, before they create pizzas out of them.

Unfortunately, neither Windows Media Player nor Windows 10 offers a Duplicate CD option. Instead, you must jump through the following five hoops to create a new CD with the same songs in the same fidelity as the original CD:

1. **Rip (copy) the music to your hard drive.**

Before ripping your CD, change your burning quality to the highest quality: Click Organize, choose Options, click the Rip Music tab, and change the Format box to a lossless format like WAV, ALAC, or FLAC. Click OK.

2. **Insert a blank CD into your writable CD drive.**

3. **In Windows Media Player's Navigation Pane, click the Music category and choose Album to see your saved CDs.**

4. **Right-click the newly ripped album in your library, choose Add To, and choose Burn List.**

If your Burn List already had some listed music, click the Clear List button to clear it; then add your CD's music to the Burn List.

5. **Click the Start Burn button.**

Now, for the fine print. Unless you change the quality to a lossless format when copying the CD to your PC, Windows Media Player compresses your songs as it saves them on your hard drive, throwing out some audio quality in the process. Burning them back to CD won't replace that lost quality. If you want the most accurate duplicates Windows Media Player can handle, change the Ripping Format to WAV (Lossless).

TIP

THE WRONG PLAYER KEEPS OPENING MY FILES!

You'd never hear Microsoft say it, but Windows Media Player isn't the only Windows program for playing songs or viewing movies. Many people use iTunes for managing their songs and movies because it conveniently drops items into their iPads and iPhones for on-the-road enjoyment.

But when your computer includes more than one media player, the players start bickering over which one handles your media-playing chores.

Windows settles these arguments with its Defaults area in the Settings area. To choose the player that should open each format, head for this chapter's earlier section, "Handing Music-Playing Chores Back to Windows Media Player." That section explains how to choose which player should handle which types of media files.

REMEMBER If you do change the format to WAV (Lossless) in order to duplicate a CD, remember to change it back to MP3 afterward, or else your hard drive will run out of room when you begin ripping a lot of CDs.

A simpler solution might be to buy CD-burning software from your local office supply or computer store. Unlike Windows Media Player, most CD-burning programs have a Duplicate CD button for one-click convenience.

IN THIS CHAPTER

» Copying your photos and videos from your camera or phone into your computer

» Taking photos with your computer's camera

» Viewing photos in your Pictures folder

» Saving digital photos to a CD

Chapter **17**

Fiddling with Photos (And Videos)

For years, Windows graciously offered to import your photos as soon as you plugged in your camera. When Windows 10 arrived, though, that feature fell by the wayside. Now, with a few years of updates under its belt, Windows 10 welcomes your camera once again and offers five ways to process your photos.

This chapter walks you through copying your digital photos from your phone or camera into your computer. From there, you can show them off to friends and family, email them to distant relatives, and save them in places where you can easily relocate them.

One final note: After you've begun creating a digital family album on your computer, please take steps to back it up properly by turning on File History, the automatic backup feature in Windows that I describe in Chapter 13. (This chapter explains how to copy your photos to a CD or DVD, as well.) Computers come and go, but your family memories can't be replaced.

Dumping a Camera's Photos into Your Computer

Most digital cameras come with software that grabs your camera's photos and places them into your computer. That software can be complicated and unwieldy, though. Thankfully, Windows can easily fetch photos from nearly any make and model of digital camera, as well as most phones. In keeping with Windows 10's theme of moving away from the desktop, Windows now lets the Photos app handle the job of importing and organizing your photos.

These steps work for most digital cameras and Android phones; iPhone owners must go through iTunes to copy their photos to their computer.

To import photos from your camera or phone into your computer, follow these steps:

1. **Plug the phone or camera's cable into your computer.**

Many cameras come with two cables: one that plugs into your TV set for viewing, and another that plugs into your computer. You need to find the one that plugs into your computer for transferring photos. (With phones, your USB charging cable usually handles the job.)

Plug the transfer cable's small end into your camera or phone, and plug the larger end (shown in the margin) into your computer's *USB port,* a rectangular-looking hole about ½-inch long and ¼-inch high. USB ports live on the back of the older computers, along the front of newer computers, and along the sides of laptops and tablets.

TIP

If the USB plug doesn't want to fit into the port, turn over the plug and try again.

If you plug in an Android phone, be sure to tell it to connect in "Camera Mode" mode rather than "Media Device" mode. That lets Windows recognize your phone as a camera rather than a complicated phone.

If Windows doesn't recognize your digital camera, make sure that the camera is set to *display mode* — the mode where you can see your photos on the camera's display. If you still have problems, unplug the cable from your computer, wait a few seconds, and then plug it back in.

2. **Turn on your phone or camera (if it's not already turned on), wait for Windows to recognize it, and click the pop-up window that says Select to Choose What Happens with This Device.**

If the pop-up window disappears before you can click it, turn your camera off, wait a few seconds, and turn it back on. The pop-up will reappear.

3. **When the second pop-up appears, choose Import Photos and Videos (Photos).**

The second pop-up, named after your camera model, offers a plethora of options as shown in Figure 17-1. Depending on the model of your camera or phone, you may see these:

FIGURE 17-1:
When Windows
recognizes your
camera, it offers
to copy its photos
to your computer.

- **Import Photos and Videos (Photos):** Choose this and the Photos app appears, ready to import your photos and movies. Move to Step 4.

- **Import Photos and Videos (OneDrive):** This copies your camera's photos and videos to OneDrive, your storage space on the Internet. I cover OneDrive in Chapter 5. *Tip:* If you install the OneDrive app on your phone, your phone can automatically upload every snapped photo to OneDrive, which automatically copies them to your PC's OneDrive folder, too. That's a simple way to not only back up your photos but to view them on your PC.

- **Open Device to View Files (File Explorer):** This opens File Explorer, handy for manually selecting a few favorite photos and copying or moving them to the folder of your choice. I explain how to copy and move files with File Explorer in Chapter 5. (Digital cameras and phones always store their photos in a folder called DCIM, so navigate to that folder to find your photos.)

- **Sync Digital Media Files to this Device (Windows Media Player):** Seen mostly on phones containing digital music, this opens Windows Media Player and lets you keep your device synced with the music on your PC. (I cover Windows Media Player in Chapter 16.)

- **Take No Action:** Stumped by all the choices? Choose this to stop the import process, go outside, and get some fresh air.

TIP

If you prefer the old photo importer from earlier Windows versions, you can still find it. Open File Explorer and click This PC from the pane along File Explorer's left edge. When you spot your camera on File Explorer's right side, right-click the camera's icon. When the pop-up menu appears, choose Import Pictures and Videos. The old Import Pictures and Videos program appears, ready to import your photos, just as it did in previous Windows versions.

TIP

If you choose the wrong option at this step, it's not too late to fix things. Click the Start button, click the Start menu's Settings icon, and choose the Devices category. When the Devices page opens, choose AutoPlay from the left pane. On the right, beneath your camera's name, click the drop-down menu. There, you can choose any of the choices listed above. (I choose Ask Me Every Time so I can choose the method that I prefer for that particular session.)

4. **Decide which photos to import.**

   The Photos app immediately searches your camera for new digital photos and videos, and then displays them, shown in Figure 17-2. The app sorts your photos by the month you snapped them.

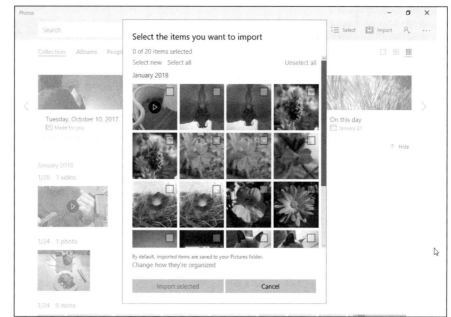

FIGURE 17-2:
The Photos app displays groups of pictures based on the time and date you took them.

To import only your new photos, click Select New; Windows quickly selects only the photos you haven't yet imported.

To import *all* of your camera's photos, click Select all.

Or, to cherry pick a few photos, just click the box next to the photos you want to import.

If you don't want to import a selected photo, click to remove the check mark from the unwanted photo's upper-right corner. To see more photos, use the scroll bar shown in Figure 17-2. (I cover scroll bars in Chapter 4.)

5. **Review your selected photos, and click the Import Selected button.**

Windows begins importing your selected photos, leaving the original copies on your camera. Windows places copies of your photos into your computer's Pictures folder, separating the photos into groups named after their year and month. For example, photos snapped in January 2018 will appear in a folder named 2018-01.

When Windows finishes importing your photos, the Photos app remains onscreen to display your newest pictures. Your newest photos always appear at the top of the app. As you scroll down the app's list of photos, you go back in time, seeing older photos organized by month and day. I cover the Photos app later in this chapter.

TIP

GRABBING YOUR CAMERA'S PHOTOS WITH A CARD READER

Windows grabs photos from your camera fairly easily. A *memory card reader,* on the other hand, not only speeds up the job but is also your only option when you've lost your camera's transfer cable. A memory card reader is a little box with a cable that plugs into your computer's USB port — the same spot used by your camera's cable.

To move your camera's pictures into your computer, choose File Explorer from the desktop and double-click the card reader's drive letter to see all the photos. (The photos live in a folder called DCIM.) From there, you can select the photos you want and cut and paste them to a folder in your Pictures folder.

Memory card readers are cheap (less than $20), easy to set up, fast at copying images, and super-convenient. (They're sometimes built in to the front of some desktop PCs.) Plus, you can leave your camera turned off while dumping the vacation photos, preserving battery life. When buying a card reader, make sure that it can read the type of memory cards used by your camera — as well as several other types of memory cards. (That ensures it will work with your next computer-related gadget.)

Taking Photos with the Camera App

Most tablets, laptops, and some desktop computers come with built-in cameras, sometimes called *webcams.* Their tiny cameras can't take high-resolution close-ups of that rare bird in the neighbor's tree, but they work fine for their main purpose: snapping a quick headshot photo for use as an account photo on your computer, Facebook, or other websites.

To take a photo through your computer's camera with the Camera app, follow these steps:

1. **From the Start menu, click the Camera tile to open the app.**

2. **If the app asks permission to use your camera and microphone or location, decide whether to click Yes or No.**

    As a security precaution, Windows may ask permission to turn on your camera. That helps prevent sneaky apps from spying on you without your knowing. If you're using the camera app, then click the Yes button to give it permission.

    The program might also ask for permission to access your precise location. That lets the program stamp your photo with its location information. That's handy to have when traveling, but it can be an invasion of privacy when at your house or that of a friend.

    After you decide whether to allow access to your location, the camera window turns into a giant viewfinder, showing you exactly what the camera sees: your face.

    If your computer or tablet includes two cameras (usually one in front and one in back), you can toggle between them by clicking the Change Camera icon, shown in Figure 17-3.

3. **Click the Camera icon to snap a photo or click the Video icon to begin recording a movie. (Click the Video icon again to stop recording.)**

When the camera detects a face, it places a square around the face, letting you know where the camera will focus. Yes, it's a little creepy.

TIP

The camera app saves all your snapped photos and videos in a folder named Camera Roll inside your Pictures folder. However, if you chose to use OneDrive when setting up your Microsoft account, your built-in camera's photos are also backed up on OneDrive. (I explain how to change OneDrive's behavior in Chapter 5.)

Toggle between cameras

Switch between Manual and
Automatic modes, or turn on
photo timer

Change settings

Switch to Video mode

Snap photo

View previously snapped photos

FIGURE 17-3:
Choose your
camera's options
and then click the
Camera icon for a
snapshot or the
Video icon for a
movie.

Viewing Photos with the Photos App

Microsoft constantly updates Windows 10 to add new features. But some features also disappear: The desktop's Photo Viewer, a Windows staple for nearly a decade, no longer appears on the Start menu.

When you want to view photos, Microsoft clearly plans for you to reach for the Windows 10 Photos app. It's a quick way to put your photos on display in different ways:

» **Collection:** When opened, the Photos app appears in Collection mode. It displays *all* of your photos, sorted by the order you snapped them. Although it leaves nothing out, it's often overkill unless you're ready to sit down and weed out the bad ones. (Right-click an unwanted photo and click Delete from the pop-up menu to ditch it for good.)

To quickly change the size of the displayed photo thumbnails, click one of the three little grid icons near the app's upper-right corner.

» **Albums:** The Photos app takes a more curated approach here, breaking down your photos into groups named after the day they were shot. It automatically weeds out duplicates, making for a short but sweet way to show off your highlights. To create your own album, select some photos, right-click any one

TIP

of them, and choose Add to Album from the pop-up menu. Then you can add those photos to an existing album or create your own new album.

>> **People:** The Photos app constantly scans your photos for faces. A click on the People link displays a headshot of every face it recognizes, grouped by person. Click that person's headshot to see every photo featuring their face. (If this sounds creepy, turn it off by clicking the Photo app's More icon, choosing Settings, and clicking the toggle switch in the People section.)

>> **Folders:** This simply lets you view your photos by their folders, which can be a handy way to view photos stored on a newly inserted thumbdrive.

The next four sections explain how to make the most of the Photos app.

Viewing your photo collection

When opened, the Photos app automatically grabs your photos and places them on the screen in large thumbnails, sorted by the date you took them. That makes it easy to show off the latest vacation photos on a tablet, phone, or even a computer that's hooked up to a TV or large monitor.

To launch the Photos app and start showing off your photos, follow these steps:

1. From the Start menu, click the Photos tile.

The Photos app quickly appears, shown in Figure 17-4. The Photos app searches for photos in your computer's Pictures folder, as well as your OneDrive folders, and displays them as one group, all in the order they were taken.

The Photos app also appears when you open a photo from the desktop's File Explorer. (I explain how to browse your files with File Explorer in Chapter 5.)

2. Scroll down to the photo you want to view or edit.

The Photos app displays your photos in one long stream, without folders. Called simply *Collection,* the scrolling display places your most recently shot photos at the top, with the oldest ones at the bottom.

Scroll down with a mouse by using the scroll bar along the app's right edge. On a touchscreen, just slide your finger up or down the screen to see newer or older photos.

3. Click a photo to see it fullscreen and then choose any menu option to view, navigate, manipulate, or share your pictures.

When a photo fills the screen, shown and labelled in Figure 17-5, sometimes the menus are hidden. You can bring the menus into view by either hovering your mouse near the photo's top edge or right-clicking (or tapping) the photo. When the menus appear, you can control the app and photos in a variety of ways:

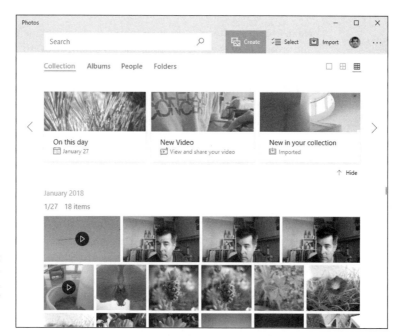

FIGURE 17-4:
The Photos app displays photos stored on your computer as well as on OneDrive.

Add photo to album or video   Delete   Edit   Print

Return   Zoom in or out   Rotate   Share   More

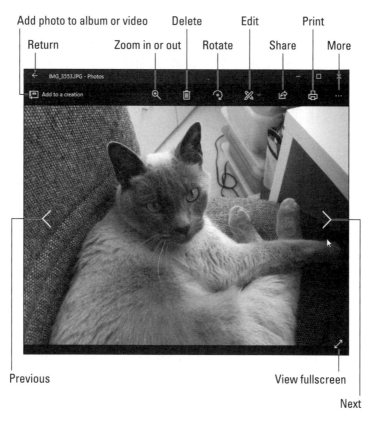

FIGURE 17-5:
Click any of these places to do different tasks while viewing a photo.

Previous   View fullscreen

Next

- **Next/Previous photo:** Move your mouse to the photo's left or right edge, and arrows appear along the edge. Click the right arrow to see older photos or click the left arrow to see newer photos.

- **Return to previous view:** Return to viewing thumbnails of your photos by clicking the left-pointing arrow in the photo's top-left corner. (You may need to click or tap the currently displayed photo before the little arrow appears.)

- **Add to a Creation:** Click this icon to add the photo to an existing album, turn it into a video slideshow (with optional music), or add it to an existing creation.

- **Zoom:** Click this button, and a sliding control appears, letting you zoom in or out of the photo.

- **Delete:** If you spot a blurred photo, click this icon to delete it immediately. Weeding out the bad photos makes it easier to relocate the good ones.

- **Rotate:** Clicking this icon rotates your photo clockwise by 90 degrees; to rotate in the opposite direction, click it three times.

- **Edit:** Clicking the Edit icon brings a new menu for editing the currently viewed photo. Click the X in the photo's upper-right corner to exit the editing menu.

- **Share the photo:** Click the Share button to share the photo with apps that can handle the job. (Chances are good that the Mail app appears, ready to email the photo to your destination.)

- **Print:** Click the little printer icon to send your photo to your printer.

- **See More:** A click on these three dots fetches a new drop-down menu. This menu lets you start a slideshow, copy the photo, save it in a new format, open it in a new program, set it as your computer's lock screen or background, and see details such as the photo's name, size, date taken, and resolution.

4. **To exit the Photos app, click the X in its upper-right corner.**

   The app clears itself from the screen.

Viewing photo albums

Everybody likes to take pictures, but only a meticulous few like to spend hours organizing them, weeding out the bad ones, and sorting them into easily accessible folders.

That's where the Photos app's robotically curated Albums view comes in handy. When you switch to Album view, the Photos app turns its robotic eye on all of your photos posted through OneDrive, weeds out the duplicates, finds a splashy one for the cover, and names it by the date of the photo session. When you open the Albums view, the app automatically turns your photos into a slideshow, complete with music, graphics, and titles.

To view the Photos app's albums, follow these steps:

1. **From the Start menu, click the Photos tile.**

   The Photos app quickly appears, shown earlier in Figure 17-4, to show its Collection mode: a string of photos sorted by the order you shot them.

2. **From the Photos app's top menu, choose Albums.**

   The Photos app sorts your photos into albums that represent the best of your session and displays them, shown in Figure 17-6.

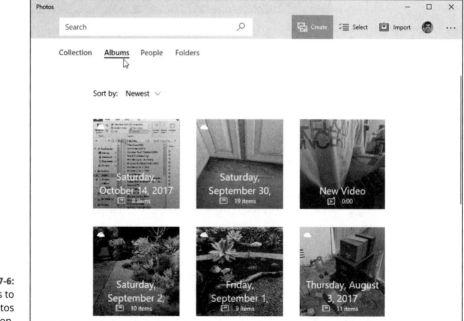

FIGURE 17-6:
Click Albums to see your photos sorted by session.

The app sorts each collection of photos by date. Click a date, and the Photos app shows you the best of that day's photos, shown in Figure 17-7.

FIGURE 17-7:
Click a date to see your best photos from that day's photo-shooting session.

3. **Click any photo to view it.**

   The Photos app fills the screen with the photo; to see more, click the Next or Previous arrows along the photo's left and right edges.

The Photos app takes its best guess as to which photos work best for each session. Taking mercy on the vacation-photo-saturated relatives sitting on your couch, the app leaves out some of your photos. That's usually a good thing, as it's smart enough to remove duplicates and blurry photos.

But if you want to change which photos should be included while viewing a particular album, click the Add Photos button along the app's top menu. When the dropdown menu appears, choose From My Collection to add your own photos. Or, to add photos taken from the Internet, choose From the Web. Windows displays check boxes next to the displayed photos, so you can pick and choose what should be included.

FIXING ROTATED PICTURES

TIP

In the old days, it never mattered how you tilted your camera when taking the photo; you simply turned the printed photo to view it. Many of today's computer screens don't swivel, so Windows rotates the photo for you — if you figure out how. Windows offers two ways:

- Click the Photos app's Rotate button, if it's visible. (The Rotate button only rotates photos clockwise, so you must click the button three times to rotate a photo counter-clockwise.)

- Right-click any photo that shows up sideways. Then choose Rotate from the pop-up menu to turn your green cliffs back into grassy meadows.

Viewing a slideshow

Windows 10 offers several ways to display your photos as a slideshow. They're a great way to show photos to friends crowding around your computer screen. Start the photos flowing across the screen in any of these ways:

>> When viewing your Pictures folder in File Manager, click the Manage tab and then click the Slideshow icon (shown in the margin) from along the folder's top.

>> When viewing a photo in the Photos app, click the Slideshow button from along the photo's top edge. When you click the More button, a slideshow option sometimes appears on the drop-down menu, as well.

>> While in Collection or Albums view, click the Create button from the menu bar along the program's top edge. To make Windows create an automatic slideshow for you, choose Automatic Video with Music from the drop-down menu. To create your own video slideshow, choose Custom Video with Music.

No matter which option you choose, Windows will fill the screen with your first picture, and then cycle through each picture selected for the show.

TIP

Here are more tips for successful on-the-fly slideshows:

>> Before starting the slideshow, rotate any sideways pictures, if necessary, so that they all appear right-side up.

>> The slideshow includes only photos in your currently viewed folder or that you've selected. It doesn't dip into folders *inside* that folder and show their photos, too.

>> Select just a few of a folder's pictures and click the Slideshow button to limit the show to just those pictures. (Hold down Ctrl while clicking pictures to select more than one.)

Copying digital photos to a CD or DVD

Your photos will be backed up automatically after you set up the Windows File History backup program, covered in Chapter 13. But if you just want to copy some photos to a CD or DVD, perhaps to share with others, stick around.

Head to the computer-or office-supply store and pick up a stack of blank CDs or DVDs. Most newer computers can handle any type of blank CD or DVD except for Blu-ray discs.

Then follow these steps to copy files in your Pictures folder to a blank CD or DVD:

1. **Open your Pictures folder from the File Manager app, select your desired photos, click the Share tab from the Ribbon along the top, and click the Burn to Disc icon.**

   Select the photos and folders you want to copy by holding down the Ctrl key and clicking their icons. Or, to select them *all,* hold down Ctrl and press the letter A. When you click the Burn to Disc icon, Windows asks you to insert a blank disc into your drive.

2. **Insert a blank CD or DVD into your writable disc drive's tray and push the tray shut.**

   TIP

   If you're copying a lot of files, insert a DVD into your DVD burner because DVDs can store five times as much information as a CD. If you're giving away a few photos to a friend, insert a blank CD instead because blank CDs cost less.

3. **Decide how you want to use the disc.**

   Windows offers two options for creating the disc:

   - **Like a USB Flash Drive:** Select this option when you intend for other computers to read the disc. Windows treats the disc much like a folder, letting you copy additional photos to the disc later. It's a good choice when you're backing up only a few pictures because you can add more to the disc later.

   - **With a CD/DVD Player:** Select this option to create discs that play on CD and DVD players attached to TVs. After you write to the disc, it's sealed off so you can't write to it again.

4. **Type a short title for your backup disc and click Next.**

   Type something short but descriptive. When you click Next, Windows begins backing up all of that folder's photos to the disc.

5. **Click the Burn or Burn to Disc button again if necessary.**

   If you selected With a CD/DVD Player in Step 3, click Burn to Disc to start copying your photos to the disc.

   If you didn't select any photos or folders in Step 1, Windows opens an empty window showing the newly inserted disc's contents: nothing. Drag and drop the photos you want to burn into that window.

Don't have enough space on the CD or DVD to hold all your files? Unfortunately, Windows isn't smart enough to tell you when to insert the second disc. Instead, it whines about not having enough room and doesn't burn *any* discs. Try burning fewer files, adding more until you fill up the disc.

6

Help!

IN THIS CHAPTER

» Enjoying the magic fixes in Windows

» Toning down Windows permission screens

» Reviving deleted files and folders and their older versions

» Retrieving a forgotten password

» Fixing stuck menus and frozen screens

Chapter **18**

The Case of the Broken Window

S ometimes you just have a vague sense that something's wrong. Your computer displays an odd screen that you've never seen before, or Windows starts running more slowly than Congress.

Other times, something's obviously gone haywire. Programs freeze, menus keep shooting at you, or Windows constantly nags you with an incomprehensible error message every time you turn on your computer.

Many of the biggest-looking problems are solved by the smallest-looking solutions. This chapter points you to the right one.

TRY THIS FIRST

Sometimes a vague sense of frustration keeps growing stronger. Your wireless Internet isn't working right. The printer won't connect. A website takes forever to load. A program just won't cooperate. Dozens of problems start with small irritations like these.

Oddly enough, sometimes the simplest fix is to restart your computer:

1. Right-click the Start button, choose Shut Down or Sign Out, and choose Restart from the pop-up menu.

Your programs begin closing by themselves. If a program asks you whether you want to save your work, be sure to save it. Then your computer turns itself off. A second later, it rises from the dead to leave you at the lock screen, ready for another round.

Whether restarting your computer gives *you* a much-needed cooling off period or it really fixes the problem, a restart often works wonders. Give it a try before spending too much time on the more strenuous fixes.

Toggling between Tablet and Desktop Mode

Much of the confusion surrounding Windows 10 involves one thing: *Tablet mode.* With Tablet mode turned on, Windows 10 works much better on touchscreen tablets. Your fingers can easily find the larger buttons and menus.

But when a *desktop PC* runs in Tablet mode, confusion reigns. You may spot these symptoms:

» Pressing the Start button won't bring the familiar Start menu to the screen's lower-left corner. Instead, clicking the Start button toggles between the full-screen Start screen and your most recently used app.

» The Search box, usually visible on the taskbar, doesn't appear. Instead, you see only Cortana's glowing blue circle, which must be clicked to summon the Search box.

» Apps and programs still run, but they always consume the entire screen.

» The traditional desktop is never visible; either a program or the Start screen always runs fullscreen on top of it.

>> In Tablet mode, the Start menu doesn't show you an alphabetically sorted list of tiles along the left edge.

Unless you know how to turn off Tablet mode on a desktop PC, Windows 10 won't make much sense.

To turn off Tablet mode and return to the regular desktop Start menu, follow these steps:

1. **Click or tap the Action Center icon (shown in the margin) near the taskbar's right end.**

2. **When the Action Center pane appears along the screen's right edge, click or tap the Tablet mode icon.**

   Your computer will toggle Tablet mode on or off with each press.

Press the Tablet mode toggle a few times so you can identify how the two very different Start menus behave in Windows 10. Then you'll know which switch to click when you're facing the wrong Start menu.

The Magic Fixes in Windows

For years, System Restore was the Windows go-to fix when your computer began running roughly. System Restore lives on in Windows 10, as I describe in this chapter's later sidebar, "Restoring from a restore point." But Windows 10 offers several other powerful tools that bring an ailing computer back to health.

The following sections explain each tool, when to reach for it, and how best to make it work its magic.

Resetting your computer

When dealing with a particularly sick computer, sometimes reinstalling Windows is the only cure. In the past, reinstalling Windows took a *lot* of time and effort. And after reinstalling Windows, you still needed to copy your files and programs back onto your computer. It could take hours — even if you had the backups.

Windows 10 aims to solve that problem. By pushing a few buttons, you can tell Windows to reinstall itself onto your computer. And while installing a fresh copy of itself, Windows preserves everybody's user accounts and personal files. For

Microsoft account holders, Windows preserves any apps they've downloaded from the Microsoft Store, as well as some of their most important computer settings.

Performing a reset saves settings from your wireless network connections as well as from your cellular connection, if you have one. The Reset tool also remembers any BitLocker and BitLocker-To-Go settings, drive letter assignments, and personalization settings, including your lock screen background and desktop wallpaper.

When your computer wakes up feeling refreshed with its new copy of Windows, you only need to reinstall your desktop programs. (The program politely leaves a handy list of those programs on your desktop, complete with website links, if available, so you know exactly what to reinstall.) Missing apps can easily be installed from the Microsoft Store: Open the Store app, choose Settings, and choose My Library to see your list of previously downloaded apps and install them again.

The Reset tool can go one step further, if you like, by wiping your computer completely clean of *everything*: user accounts, data, and personal files. Then Windows 10 reinstalls itself, just as if it were on a new PC. That lets you either start from scratch or simply give away your computer to a relative or charity without worrying about leaking your personal information.

To reset your ailing PC, follow these steps:

1. Click the Start button and choose the Settings icon from the Start menu.

The Settings app appears.

2. Click the Settings app's Update & Security icon. When the Update & Security window appears, click the Recovery option from the left pane. Then, in the Reset This PC section, click the Get Started button.

Windows displays the window shown in Figure 18-1, offering two ways to reset your computer.

If asked, insert your Windows disc, flash drive, or whatever else you used to first install Windows. Don't have a Windows installation disc or drive? Then click Cancel. You can't use the Reset option, unfortunately.

3. Choose an option and click Next.

The Reset tool offers two options:

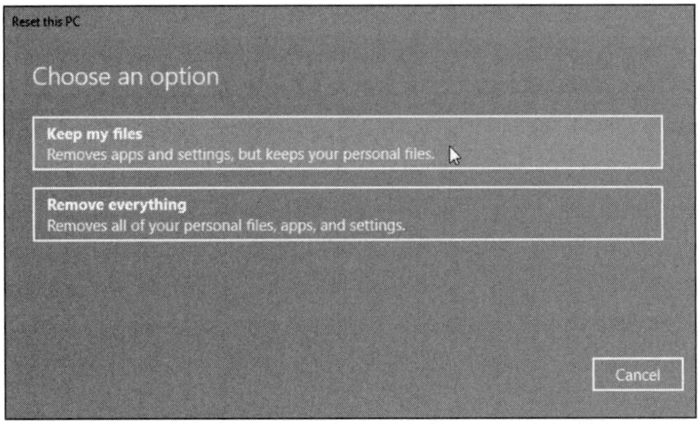

FIGURE 18-1:
Unless you have a very good reason, choose Keep My Files.

- **Keep My Files:** The most widely used choice, this reinstalls Windows, but preserves everybody's user accounts and files. The only things you lose are *desktop programs*, which must be reinstalled from their original discs or installation files. If you choose this option, jump to Step 5. (Windows 8 and 8.1 called this option Refresh instead of Reset.)

- **Remove Everything:** Only choose this when you want to wipe *everything* away from your computer, including everybody's user accounts and files, and reinstall Windows 10. Then you can start from scratch or safely give your computer to others. If you choose this, move to Step 4.

4. **Choose whether to just remove your files or to remove files *and* clean the drive.**

   Windows offers you several choices:

   - **Just Remove My Files:** Select this option only when your computer will stay within your family. Although this option is relatively secure, somebody with the right tools may be able to extract some previously erased information. (If your computer contains more than one drive, Windows asks whether you want to remove the files from both drives, or just the drive where Windows is installed.)

   - **Remove Files and Fully Clean the Drive:** Select this option when you intend to sell or donate your computer to strangers. This more time-consuming option removes your data and then scrubs the hard drive *extra* clean. That keeps out everybody but the most dedicated specialists who own expensive data recovery equipment.

   - **Which Drive:** A third option appears to people who have spread Windows across two disk drives, perhaps by storing their File History backups on a second drive. Choose All Drives to fully clean both drives; choose Only the Drive Where Windows Is Installed to preserve your File History backup.

When you click an option and click the Reset button, Windows removes everything from your computer, fully cleaning the drive, if requested, then reinstalls itself to leave your computer with a "like new" copy of Windows 10. At that point, you're finished, and your computer's ready to start afresh or be given away safely.

5. **Take note of what desktop programs (and, possibly, drivers) will need to be reinstalled, then click Next, and click the Reset button.**

Windows reinstalls itself on your computer, which takes anywhere from 15 minutes to an hour. When your computer wakes up, it should feel refreshed and ready to work again. Expect any or all of the following things to take place when resetting your computer:

>> When your computer wakes up and you sign in, you find a shortcut called Removed Apps waiting on your desktop. Click it, and your web browser displays a page with links to any available removed desktop programs and drivers that you need to reinstall — if you decide you miss them, that is. (And if you *do* miss them, you need the program's installation discs to reinstall them.)

>> Shortly after Windows wakes up, it visits Windows Update to download and install oodles of security patches, as well as updated copies of its bundled apps. Grab a good novel.

>> After resetting your computer, reinstall your desktop programs one by one, restarting your computer after each new install. That gives you the best chance to weed out any misbehaving programs that may have caused the problems that messed things up.

>> If you're connected to a network, you may need to tell Windows whether you're on a p*rivate* (Home) network or a *public* network.

WARNING

>> If you inserted a Windows DVD into your computer in Step 2, be careful when your computer restarts. As it restarts, your computer may ask you to "Press any key to boot from disc." *Don't* press any key; instead, wait a few seconds until the message disappears. Then Windows loads itself from your computer's newly refreshed *hard drive* rather than the Windows installation DVD.

>> If you've wiped your hard drive completely clean, you can use a File History backup, described in the next section, to restore the files that once lived in your Documents, Music, Pictures, and Videos folders.

Restoring backups with File History

The Windows backup program, File History, saves the files that *you've* created. It doesn't back up your apps and programs. After all, apps and programs can always be reinstalled. But many of the moments that inspired so many of your photos, videos, and documents can *never* be re-created.

To keep your files safe, File History automatically makes a copy of *every* file in your Documents, Music, Photos, and Videos folders. It copies all the files on your desktop, as well. And File History automatically makes those copies *every hour.*

File History makes your backups easy to see and restore, letting you flip through different versions of your files and folders, comparing them with your current versions. Should you find a better version, a press of a button brings that older version back to life.

REMEMBER

File History doesn't work until you turn it on, a process I describe in Chapter 13. Please, *please,* flip back a few chapters and turn it on now. The earlier you turn it on, the more backups you'll have to choose from when you need them.

To browse through your backed-up files and folders, restoring the ones you want, follow these steps:

1. **Click the taskbar's File Explorer icon (shown in the margin) and then open the folder containing the items you'd like to retrieve.**

For example, click This PC in the folder's left pane to see your most commonly used folders: Desktop, Downloads, Documents, Music, Pictures, and Videos. Open any folder by double-clicking its name.

2. **Click the Home tab on the Ribbon atop your folder; then click the History button.**

Don't see the menu-filled Ribbon atop the folder? Then click the little upward-pointing arrow in the folder's upper-right corner, next to the blue Question Mark icon. (That arrow shows or hides the Ribbon.)

Clicking the History button, shown in the margin, fetches the File History program, shown in Figure 18-2. The program looks much like a plain old folder. Figure 18-2, for example, shows what happens if you click the History button in any folder and then click File History's Home button: That button lets you see the most recent backups of your folders.

The File History program shows you what it has backed up: your main folders, your desktop, your contacts, and your favorite websites.

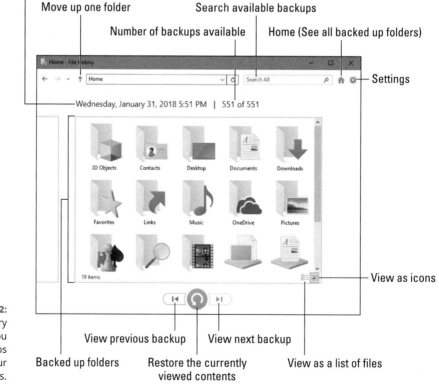

FIGURE 18-2:
The File History program lets you restore backups from any of your main folders.

Feel free to open the folders inside the File History window. You can also peek inside the files you find there to see their contents.

3. **Choose what you'd like to restore.**

   Point and click your way through the libraries, folders, and files until you spot the item or items you'd like to restore:

   - **Folder:** To restore an entire folder, open it so you're viewing its contents.

   - **Files:** To restore a group of files, open the folder containing them, so the files' icons are onscreen.

   - **One file:** To restore an earlier version of a file, open that file from inside the File History window. File History displays that file's contents.

   When you've found the file or folder you want to restore, move to the next step.

4. **Move forward or backward in time to find the version you'd like to restore.**

   To browse through different versions of what you're currently viewing, choose the left-pointing arrow along the bottom, as shown in Figure 18-3. To see a newer version, choose the right-pointing arrow.

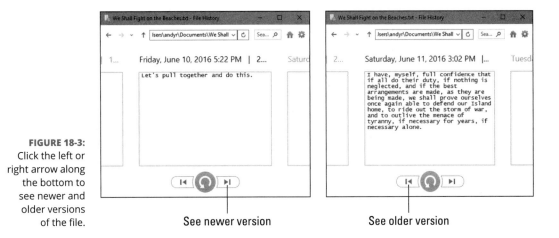

FIGURE 18-3:
Click the left or right arrow along the bottom to see newer and older versions of the file.

See newer version   See older version

   As you move forward and backward through time, feel free to click open folders or individual files, peeking inside them until you're looking at the version that you want to retrieve.

TIP

   Not sure whether a folder contains your sought-after item? Type a word or two from your document into the Search box in File History's upper-right corner.

5. **Click the Restore button to restore your desired version.**

   Whether you're looking at an individual file, a folder, or an entire library's contents, clicking the Restore button places that item back in the place where it used to live.

That brings up a potential problem, however: What happens if you try to restore an older file named Notes into a place that already contains a file named Notes? Windows warns you of the problem with the window in Figure 18-4, which brings you to Step 6.

6. **Choose how to handle the conflict.**

   If Windows notices a naming conflict with the item you're trying to restore, File History offers you three ways to handle the situation, as shown in Figure 18-4.

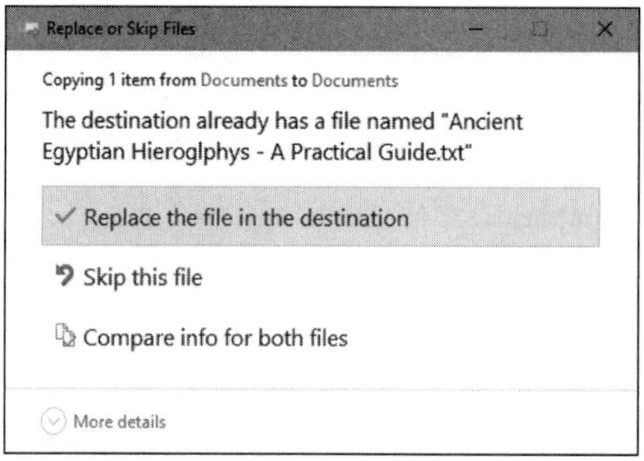

FIGURE 18-4:
Choose whether to replace the existing file, skip the file, or choose which file to keep.

- **Replace the File in the Destination.** Click this option only when you're *sure* that the older file is better than your current file.

- **Skip This File.** Click this if you don't want to restore the file or folder. This option returns you to File History, where you can browse other files.

- **Compare Info for Both Files.** Often the best choice, this option lets you compare the files' sizes and dates before choosing which one to keep, the replacement file or the currently existing file. Or, if you want, this choice also lets you keep *both* files: Windows simply adds a number after the name of the incoming file, naming it Notes (1), for example.

7. **Exit File History by closing the window.**

   You close the File History window just as you close any other window: Click the X in its upper-right corner.

Want to know more about File History? Read on:

>> In addition to backing up everything in your main folders and on your desktop, File History stores a list of your favorite websites, listed earlier in Figure 18-2 as Favorites. It also backs up the OneDrive files you've synced to your PC.

>> I explain how to use File History to move an old computer's files to a new computer in Chapter 20.

>> When buying a portable hard drive, flash drive, or memory card to create backups, don't skimp on size. The larger the hard drive you choose, the more backups you can save. File History comes in *very* handy.

TIP

TECHNICAL STUFF

RESTORING FROM A RESTORE POINT

The new Recovery programs in Windows work wonders in resuscitating an ailing computer, and they're more powerful than the older System Restore technology. But in case you've come to rely on the System Restore programs built into earlier Windows versions, Windows 10 still includes System Restore — if you know where to find it.

To send your computer back to a restore point when it was working much better, follow these steps:

1. **Right-click the Start button, type** System Restore **into the Search box, and choose Create a Restore Point from the pop-up menu. When the System Properties window appears, click System Restore.**

   The System Restore window appears.

2. **Click the Next button at the System Restore window.**

   The System Restore Point lists available restore points.

3. **Click a listed restore point.**

   You can see more available restore points, if available, by selecting the Show More Restore Points check box.

4. **Click the Scan for Affected Programs button to see how your chosen restore point will affect programs.**

   A handy touch, this feature lists programs you'll probably need to reinstall.

5. **Click Next to confirm your chosen restore point. Then click Finish.**

   Your computer grumbles a bit and then restarts, using those earlier settings that (hopefully) worked fine.

If your system is *already* working fine, feel free to create your own restore point, as I describe at the beginning of Chapter 13. Name the restore point something descriptive, such as Before Installing Tax Software. (That way, you know which restore point to use if things go awry.)

Windows Keeps Asking Me for Permission

Like earlier Windows versions before it, Windows 10 offers both Administrator and Standard user accounts. The Administrator account, meant for the computer's owner, holds all the power. Holders of mere Standard accounts, by contrast, aren't allowed to do things that might change the computer or its settings.

But no matter which of the two accounts you hold, you'll occasionally brush up against the Windows version of a barbed-wire fence. When a program tries to change something on your computer, Windows pokes you with a message like the one shown in Figure 18-5.

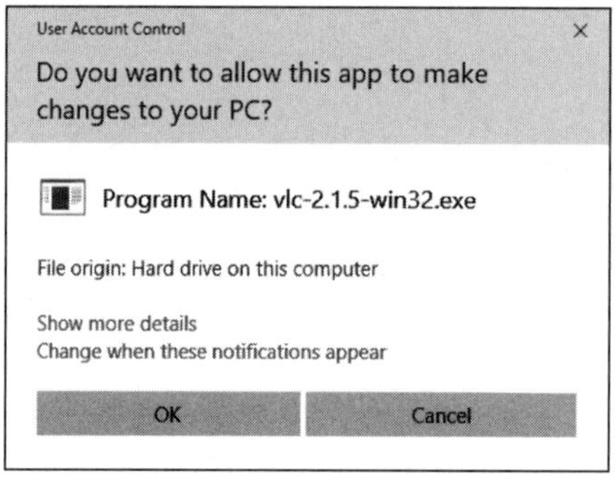

FIGURE 18-5:
The Windows permission screen pops up when a program tries to change something on your PC.

Standard account holders see a slightly different message that commands them to fetch an Administrator account holder to type in a password.

Of course, when screens like this one pop up too often, most people simply ignore them and give their approval — even if that means they've just allowed a virus to settle comfortably inside their PC.

So, when Windows sends you a permission screen, ask yourself this question: "Is Windows asking permission for something *I* did or requested?" If your answer is yes, give your approval so Windows can carry out your bidding. But if Windows sends you a permission screen out of the blue when you haven't done anything, click No or Cancel. That keeps potential nasties from invading your PC.

If you don't have time for this bothersome security layer, and you're willing to suffer the consequences, you can find out how to turn off user account permissions by reading Chapter 11.

I Need to Retrieve Deleted Files

Everybody who's worked on a computer knows the agony of seeing hours of work go down the drain: You mistakenly delete a file.

The Windows File History backup program, described earlier in this chapter, is a lifesaver here. But if you never turned on File History — an easy task I explain in Chapter 13 — Windows offers another way to retrieve your deleted files: the Recycle Bin.

The Recycle Bin works because Windows doesn't *really* destroy your deleted files. Instead, Windows slips those files into your Recycle Bin (shown in the margin), which lives on your desktop.

Open the Recycle Bin with a double-click, and you find every file or folder you've deleted within the past few weeks. I cover the Recycle Bin in Chapter 3, but here's a tip: To restore a file or folder from the Recycle Bin, right-click the file and choose Restore. The deleted item magically reappears in its former home.

Fixing Broken Apps

NEW

Microsoft's latest update to Windows 10 makes it much easier to repair groggy apps. If your app no longer seems in good health and you'd like to reset it and start from scratch, follow these steps:

1. **Click the Start button and choose the Settings icon from the Start menu.**

   The Settings app appears.

2. **Click the Settings app's Apps icon (shown in the margin). When the Apps window appears, click the Apps & Features link along the window's left edge.**

   The Apps & Features window appears, listing your apps alphabetically along its right side.

3. **Click the malfunctioning app's name and, when the menu drops down, click Advanced Options.**

4. **When the Advanced Options settings appear, click the Reset button.**

Windows deletes and reinstalls the app from scratch, taking any of your preference settings and sign-in details along with it. This isn't a big deal with say, the Calculator app. But more elaborate apps like Mail and Calendar may take some time to bring back up to speed with the right settings.

My Settings Are Messed Up

Sometimes you want to return to the way things were *before* you started messing around with them. Your salvation lies in the Restore Default button, which awaits your command in strategically placed areas throughout Windows. A click of that button returns the settings to the way Windows originally set them up.

Here are a few Restore Default buttons you may find useful:

>> **Internet Explorer:** When the age-old Internet Explorer program seems clogged with unwanted toolbars, spyware, or just plain weirdness, take the last resort of bringing back its original settings: In Internet Explorer, click the Tools icon (shown in the margin) and choose Internet Options from the drop-down menu. Click the Advanced tab and click the Reset button.

Resetting Internet Explorer wipes out nearly *everything,* including your toolbars, add-ons, and search engine preference. If you also select Internet Explorer's Delete Personal Settings check box, clicking the Reset button even kills your browser history and saved passwords. Only your favorites, feeds, and a few other items remain.

>> **Apps:** Released one year after Windows 10 arrived, the Anniversary update adds a reset button that restores malfunctioning apps back to their original working condition. I describe how in the previous section, "Fixing Broken Apps."

>> **Firewall:** If you suspect foul play within Windows Firewall, bring back its original settings and start over. (Some of your programs may need to be reinstalled.) Click the Start button and type Windows Defender Security Center into the Search box. When the Windows Defender Security Center appears, choose Firewall & Network protection from the left pane. On the right pane, click Restore Firewalls to Default. (Be careful with this one, as you may need to reinstall some apps and programs.)

>> **Media Player:** When the Media Player Library contains mistakes, tell it to delete its index and start over. In Media Player, press and release the Alt key, click Tools, choose Advanced from the pop-out menu, and choose Restore Media Library. (Or if you've accidentally removed items from the Media Player Library, choose Restore Deleted Library Items instead.)

>> **Colors:** Windows lets you tweak your desktop's colors and sounds, sometimes into a disturbing mess. To return to the default colors and sounds, right-click the Start button and choose the Settings app. Open the Personalization category, and choose Windows from the Apply a Theme section.

>> **Fonts:** Have you tweaked your fonts beyond recognition? Return them to normal by opening the desktop's Control Panel, clicking Appearance and Personalization, and then clicking Fonts. In the left pane, click Font Settings and then click the Restore Default Font Settings button.

>> **Libraries:** In Windows 10, libraries are hidden by default. (I explain how to turn them on in Chapter 5.) When turned on, libraries appear in every folder's Navigation Pane. But if one of your libraries is missing (say, the Music library), you can put it back. Right-click the word Libraries along the right side of any folder and choose Restore Default Libraries. Your default libraries — Documents, Music, Pictures, and Videos — all reappear.

>> **Network adapters:** This one-click solution removes and reinstalls your network adapters and returns your network to its original settings. To reset your network, click the Start button, choose Settings, and choose the Network & Internet category. Then click the Network Reset option near the bottom of the window's right column.

>> **Folders:** Windows hides a slew of switches relating to folders, their Navigation Panes, the items they show, how they behave, and how they search for items. To mull over their options or return them to their default settings, open any folder and click the View tab on the Ribbon menu along the top. Click the Options icon; when the drop-down list appears, click Change Folder and Search Options. The Folder Options window appears, which lists a Restore Defaults button on each of its tabs: General, View, and Search. (Click Apply after each change to make it stick.)

Finally, don't forget the Reset option in Windows, described at the beginning of this chapter. Although it's overkill for many problems, it resets most of your settings to the default.

I Forgot My Password

When Windows won't accept your password at the Sign In screen, you may not be hopelessly locked out of your own computer. Check all these things before letting loose with a scream:

>> **Check your Caps Lock key.** Windows passwords are *case-sensitive*, meaning that Windows considers *OpenSesame* and *opensesame* to be different passwords. If your keyboard's Caps Lock light is on, press your Caps Lock key again to turn it off. Then try entering your password again.

>> **Use your Password Reset Disk.** I explain how to create a Password Reset Disk for a Local account holder in Chapter 14. (The disk doesn't work for Microsoft account holders.) When you've forgotten the password to your Local account, insert that disk to use as a key. Windows lets you back into your account, where you can promptly create an easier-to-remember password. (Flip to Chapter 14 and create a Password Reset Disk now if you haven't yet.)

>> **Let another user reset your password.** Anybody with an Administrator account on your computer can reset your password. Have that person head for the desktop's Control Panel (see Chapter 12), click User Accounts and Family Safety, and click User Accounts. There, she can click the Manage Another Account link to see a list of every account. She can click your account name and click the Change the Password link to create a password you can remember more easily.

Note: If you've forgotten the password to your *Microsoft account*, none of the preceding suggestions will work. Instead, open any web browser and visit www.live.com. The site leads you through the steps to reset your password.

MY PROGRAM IS FROZEN!

TIP

Eventually, one of your programs will freeze up solid, leaving you in the cold with no way to reach its normal Close command. Should you find yourself facing this icy terrain, these steps will extricate the frozen program from your computer's memory (and the screen, as well):

1. **Right-click the Start menu and select the Task Manager option from the pop-up menu.**

   The Task Manager program appears, listing the names of currently running programs.

2. **Click the frozen program's name.**

   If you don't spot your program's name, clicking the More Details link reveals everything currently running on your PC.

3. **Click the End Task button, and Windows whisks away the frozen program.**

   If your computer seems a bit groggy afterward, play it safe by restarting it.

If none of these options works, you're in sad shape, unfortunately. Compare the value of your password-protected data against the cost of hiring a password recovery specialist. You can find a specialist by searching for *recover windows password* on Google (www.google.com).

My Computer Is Frozen Solid

Every once in a while, Windows just drops the ball and wanders off somewhere to sit under a tree. You're left looking at a computer that just looks back. None of the computer's lights blink. Panicked clicks don't do anything. Randomly tapping the keyboard does nothing, or worse yet, the computer starts to beep at every key press.

When nothing onscreen moves (except, perhaps the mouse pointer), the computer is frozen up solid. Try the following approaches, in the following order, to correct the problem:

» **Approach 1:** Press Esc twice.

   • This action rarely works, but it's a quick first salvo that can't hurt anything.

» Approach 2: Press the Ctrl, Alt, and Delete keys simultaneously and choose Start Task Manager from the menu that appears.

- If you're lucky, the Task Manager appears with the message that it discovered an unresponsive application. The Task Manager lists the names of currently running programs, including the one that's not responding. On the Processes tab, click the name of the program that's causing the mess and then click the End Task button. You lose any unsaved work in that program, of course, but you should be used to that. (If you somehow stumbled onto the Ctrl+Alt+Delete combination by accident, press Esc to quit Task Manager and return to Windows.)

- If that still doesn't do the trick, press Ctrl+Alt+Delete again and click the Power icon (shown in the margin) in the screen's lower-right corner. Choose Restart from the pop-up menu, and your computer shuts down and restarts, hopefully returning in a better mood.

» Approach 3: If the preceding approaches don't work, turn off the computer by pressing its power button. (If that merely brings up the Turn Off the Computer menu, choose Restart, and your computer should restart.)

» Approach 4: If you keep holding down your computer's power button long enough (usually about 4 to 5 seconds), it eventually stops resisting and turns off.

Chapter **19**

Strange Messages: What You Did Does Not Compute

rror messages in *real* life are fairly easy to understand. A blinking digital clock means you need to set the time. A parked car's beep means that you've left your keys in the ignition. A spouse's stern glance means that you've forgotten something important.

But Windows error messages may have been written by a Senate subcommittee, if only the messages weren't so brief. The error messages rarely describe what you did to cause the event or, even worse, how to fix the problem.

In this chapter, I've collected some of the most common Windows error messages, notifications, and just plain confusing attempts at conversation. Find a message that matches what you're experiencing and then read how to handle the situation as gracefully as Windows will allow.

Add Your Microsoft Account

Meaning: You must sign in with a Microsoft account to perform several tasks in Windows. If you don't have a Microsoft account, you see the message in Figure 19-1. As described in Chapter 2, Microsoft accounts let you reap the most benefits from Windows.

FIGURE 19-1:
To take advantage of some Windows features, you must create a Microsoft account.

Probable causes: You may have tried to buy an app from the Microsoft Store, access OneDrive from the Internet, or activate Family Safety controls, which all require a Microsoft account.

Solution: Sign up for a free Microsoft account, as I describe in Chapter 2.

Choose What Happens with This Device

Meaning: When the window in Figure 19-2 appears in your screen's bottom-right corner, click it to tell Windows what to do with the item you've just connected to your computer.

FIGURE 19-2:
Click to tell Windows how to react when you connect that device with your computer.

When you click the window in Figure 19-2, the window in Figure 19-3 appears in the screen's *top*-right corner.

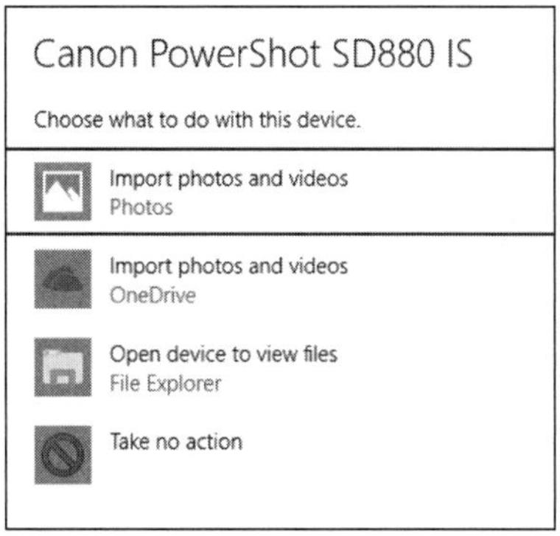

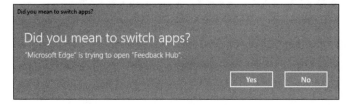

FIGURE 19-3:
Tell Windows what to do with the item you've just inserted into your computer.

Canon PowerShot SD880 IS

Choose what to do with this device.

Import photos and videos
Photos

Import photos and videos
OneDrive

Open device to view files
File Explorer

Take no action

Probable causes: You just slid a *flash drive* (a stick of memory) into your computer's USB port, attached a phone or camera, or connected another device to your computer.

Solution: Choose how you want Windows to react when you reconnect that device in the future. You can always change this decision by visiting the Settings app's Devices category and choosing AutoPlay from the left pane. Windows lists all of your devices in the window's right pane, as well as how Windows currently handles their arrival. Click any device, and a drop-down menu lists all of your choices. (I prefer the Ask Me Every Time option so I can choose the action I prefer at that particular moment.)

Did You Mean to Switch Apps?

Meaning: Your currently viewed app is trying to open another app. Windows shows you the message in Figure 19-4 to make sure the app's not trying to do anything evil.

FIGURE 19-4:
Click Yes unless you think the app is trying something sneaky.

Did you mean to switch apps?

Did you mean to switch apps?

"Microsoft Edge" is trying to open "Feedback Hub".

Yes   No

Probable Cause: You've clicked a link inside one app that requires another app to handle the job.

Solution: Unless you think the app is trying to install a virus or do something bad, click the Yes button to approve the job.

Do You Want to Allow This App to Make Changes to This Computer?

Meaning: Are you sure that this software is free from viruses, spyware, and other harmful things?

Probable cause: A window similar to the one shown in Figure 19-5 appears when you try to install downloaded software or a driver for one of your computer's parts.

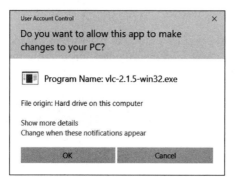

FIGURE 19-5:
Do you think this
software is safe?

Solutions: If you're sure the file is safe, click the OK, Yes, or Install button. But if this message appears unexpectedly or you think it may not be safe, click the Cancel, No, or Don't Install button. I cover safe computing in Chapter 11.

Do You Want to Save Changes?

Meaning: Figure 19-6 means you haven't saved your work in a program, the program is about to close, and your work is about to be lost.

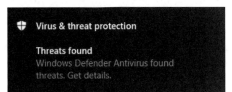

FIGURE 19-6:
Do you want to
save your work?

Probable causes: You're trying to close an application, sign out, or restart your computer before telling a program to save the work you've accomplished.

Solutions: Click the Save button to save your work and let the program close. I cover saving files in Chapter 6. Don't want to save the file? Then click Don't Save to discard your work and move on.

Threats Found

Meaning: When the built-in Windows antivirus program, Windows Defender, finds a potentially dangerous file on your computer, it lets you know with the message in Figure 19-7. Windows Defender then removes the file so that it can't harm your computer or files.

FIGURE 19-7:
Windows
Defender has
found and
removed a
potentially
dangerous file on
your computer.

Virus & threat protection

Threats found
Windows Defender Antivirus found
threats. Get details.

Like most notifications, this one always appears in the screen's bottom-right corner.

Probable cause: A potentially dangerous file — *malware* — probably arrived through email, a flash drive, a networked computer, or an evil website. Windows is removing the file so that it can't do any harm.

Solutions: Windows Defender is already removing the offender, but try to remember what action forced Windows Defender to clean up the problem. Then, if possible, try not to repeat that action. It wouldn't hurt to tell Windows Defender to give your computer a full scan, and to scan any storage device you just connected. (I explain Windows Defender in Chapter 11.)

How Do You Want to Open This?

Meaning: The window in Figure 19-8 appears the first time you open a new type of file on the desktop.

Probable cause: Windows apps and programs often fight over the right to open your files. To make sure that the right program is opening your file, Windows displays this message for you to confirm that the correct program is handling the job.

Solutions: If the right program is opening your file, click OK. Windows won't bug you the next time you open that type of file. The message reappears the next time you open a *different* type of file, however. If the wrong program is trying to open the file, choose the correct program from the message's list.

If Windows doesn't offer any valid suggestions, however, click the Look for an App in the Store option. (I cover this problem in Chapter 6.) To open that file, you may need to download or buy an app from the Microsoft Store.

We're Not Allowed to Find You

Meaning: An app is asking permission to know your current physical location, as shown in Figure 19-9, and Windows wants to know whether you want to allow that.

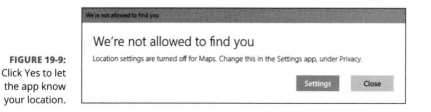

FIGURE 19-9:
Click Yes to let the app know your location.

Probable cause: An app needs your location to do something, perhaps to give you information about your immediate surroundings.

Solutions: If you trust the app and feel comfortable letting it know where you're currently sitting or standing, click Settings, which opens the app's Settings area. There, you can allow the app to access your location without it having to ask again. If you think the app is being too nosy, click Close or No. However, the app will probably ask for permission again the next time you open it.

Reconnect Your Drive

Meaning: The message in Figure 19-10 tells you that the Windows backup program, File History, has stopped working.

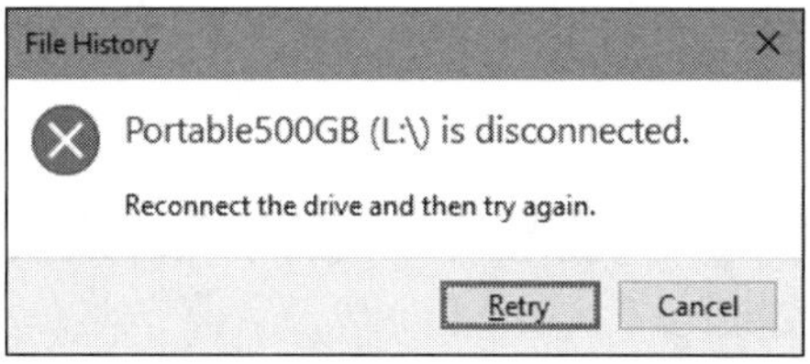

FIGURE 19-10:
Your backup drive or card isn't plugged in to your computer.

Probable cause: File History was saving your files on a portable hard drive, flash drive, or memory card that's no longer plugged in to your computer.

Solutions: This message appears most often on laptops and tablets after you've taken them on the road, leaving your backup drive at home. So, find your portable hard drive, flash drive, or memory card and plug it back into your computer. (If File History doesn't begin working again, revisit the File History section in Chapter 11 to make sure the settings are correct.)

Once you plug the drive back into your computer, File History thoughtfully makes a fresh backup of everything that hasn't yet been saved.

There Is No Email Program Associated to Perform the Requested Action

Meaning: The particularly cryptic message in Figure 19-11 means you're trying to send email from the desktop, but you haven't installed a desktop-based email program.

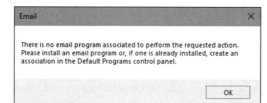

FIGURE 19-11:
You need to
install an email
program onto the
desktop.

Probable cause: Here's where the split between the traditional desktop programs and Microsoft's new apps becomes irritating. Microsoft doesn't allow Windows desktop programs to use the Mail app. If you click a desktop program's Send This or Email This option, this message appears until you install a *desktop*-based email program.

Solutions: Download and install a desktop email program. To keep things simple, you'll have to decide between using the Mail app or a traditional desktop-based email program. It's often difficult to run more than one email program on the same computer. I describe choosing and setting up email in Chapter 10.

You Don't Currently Have Permission to Access This Folder

Meaning: If you see the dialog box in Figure 19-12, it means Windows won't let you peek inside the folder you're trying to open. (The folder's name appears in the message's title bar.) A similar message appears when Windows won't let you peek inside a file.

FIGURE 19-12:
Find somebody
with an Adminis-
trator account to
open the folder
or file.

Probable cause: The file or folder belongs to somebody with a different user account.

Solutions: If you hold an Administrator account, you can open files and folders from other people's user accounts by clicking Continue. If you don't have an Administrator account, however, you're locked out.

Chapter **20**

Moving from an Old PC to a New Windows 10 PC

W hen you bring home your exciting new Windows 10 computer, it lacks the most important thing of all: The stuff from your *old* computer. How do you copy your files from that dusty old PC to that shiny new Windows PC? How do you even *find* everything you want to move?

Before Windows 10, Microsoft solved the problem by including a virtual moving van called Windows Easy Transfer. The Windows Easy Transfer program grabbed not only your old computer's files but its settings (your browser's list of favorite websites, for example).

Unfortunately, Microsoft discontinued Windows Easy Transfer in Windows 10, complicating the process of moving to a new PC. This chapter explains your current options for moving your information from your old PC to your new PC.

TIP

Here's a timesaver: If you're just *upgrading* your old Windows 8 or 8.1 PC to Windows 10, you can skip this chapter. When you upgrade, Windows 10 leaves your personal files, apps, and desktop programs in place.

Hiring a Third Party to Make the Move

Microsoft may have walked out on the automated PC file transfer business, but third-party vendors are happy to do the job. In fact, Windows XP, Windows Vista, and Windows 7 owners have no other choice — Microsoft doesn't offer *any* transfer solutions for those older Windows versions.

That leaves you two third-party options: computer upgrade software or taking your PC to a professional.

The following sections cover the pros and cons of each.

Buying Laplink's PCmover program

The PCmover software suite of programs from Laplink (`www.laplink.com`) transfers not only your old PC's files and settings but some of its programs, as well. That's more work than Microsoft's old Easy Transfer program ever attempted. The PCmover suite works on every Windows version from Windows XP to Windows 10. (It *doesn't* work with Windows RT, released on some inexpensive tablets.)

However, the powerful transfer programs come with a staggering array of potential complications, which isn't surprising: Moving from one PC to another is fraught with possible mishaps. (On the positive side, Laplink helps you move by offering free, 24-hour tech support in United States, Canada, Australia, and the United Kingdom.)

Your first job is choosing which PCmover software you need: PCmover Home or PCmover Professional. Both let you transfer information only from *one* old PC to *one* new PC. That's usually not a problem, but keep in mind that you can't give the program to a friend after you've transferred your files.

>> **PCmover Home:** This minimalist package moves files, settings, and user profiles to your new PC. However, it won't move apps and programs.

>> **PCmover Professional:** The more popular (and more expensive) option, this software copies apps and programs to the new PC, as well as files, settings, and user profiles.

Both programs copy your old PC's files, settings, and some programs to your new PC, as shown in Figure 20-1. However, neither package guarantees to copy *all* of your programs. Because of technical reasons, some programs can transfer, but others won't. (The reasons behind those potential problems come with their own fine-print section too detailed to list here.)

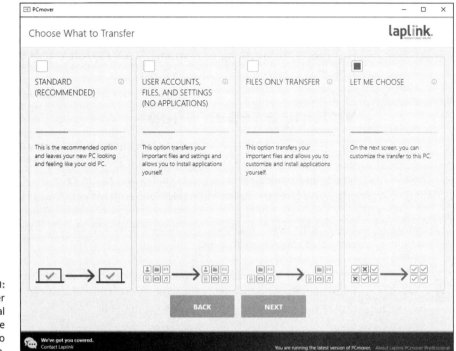

FIGURE 20-1:
PCmover
Professional
helps you move
from an old PC to
a new one.

If you plan to transfer your files over a network, you can buy and download your chosen PCmover program from Laplink's website. Most people, however, find a better deal by buying the PCmover Ultimate boxed program from Amazon (www.amazon.com). That package includes PCmover Professional *and* a transfer cable, and it costs less than the version on Laplink's website.

The PCmover programs are copy-protected, so you need a working Internet connection before you can begin using them. Also, depending on the amount of information on your old PC — and the way you connect your two computers — the transfer process can take several hours.

TIP

ZINSTALL'S WINWIN10 PRO

PCmover may be the least expensive third-party file transfer solution, but it's not the most comprehensive. Zinstall's WinWin software costs more than twice as much as the competition. Depending on your situation, though, it might do a more thorough job, especially when transferring desktop programs from your old PC to your new one.

For more information about Zinstall's products, visit the company's website at www.zinstall.com.

In short, the PCmover software works best for somebody who's not only patient but also experienced enough with computers to know how to talk with tech support people if something goes wrong. (Tech support people usually speak very, well, *technically.*)

Visiting a repair shop

Almost all local computer repair shops can move your old PC's information to your new PC. (Call first to see whether they want the PC alone, or the PC, monitor, keyboard, and mouse.) Repair shops that make house calls are even better because you won't have to unplug any cables and drop off your PCs at the shop.

Check with your neighbors — they've probably already found a favorite local computer shop or technician.

The prices at local computer repair shops vary widely, and they probably charge more than the price of buying file-transfer software. But if something goes wrong, *they're* the ones talking to tech support, not you.

TECHNICAL STUFF

MOVING THE MICROSOFT WAY

According to Microsoft, moving from an old PC to a new PC is easy. First, you log in with a Microsoft account on both your new and old PCs. Then you copy your old PC's Documents, Music, Pictures, and Videos folders to OneDrive, your online storage space.

When you step over to your new computer and sign in with that same Microsoft account, your settings travel automatically to your new PC. And, because Windows 10 includes OneDrive built-in, your old PC's files and folders are waiting for you.

However, Microsoft's method works only with PCs running Windows 8, Windows 8.1, or Windows 10; earlier Windows versions don't support Microsoft accounts as well. Copying files and folders to and from OneDrive can take a lot of time and effort, as well. When you move your files to OneDrive, Microsoft is banking that you'll simply keep everything stored there. As soon as you fill up your allotted OneDrive storage space, you'll need to pay Microsoft a monthly fee for more storage.

If you know how to find all of your old PC's files, and *if* they all fit onto your available OneDrive space, and *if* you're well-versed in file management chores with File Explorer, OneDrive might meet your needs. But that's a lot of "ifs." Simply put, Microsoft's method isn't the best for people who aren't experienced with computers or lack enough storage space on OneDrive.

A repair shop can probably transfer your files even if your old computer no longer turns on or has trouble running. Chances are good that your old computer's hard drive still works, and it still has all of your files. Techies at the repair shop can usually transfer your files from your old computer's hard drive directly to your new PC.

Even if you hate throwing in the towel and calling a professional, remember, you need to transfer your old PC's information only *once.* And, if the techie who does the job seems friendly and competent enough, grab a business card. It may come in handy down the road.

Transferring Files Yourself

You can transfer files yourself if you're moving from a Windows 8, 8.1, or 10 PC. You can do this with a combination of a Microsoft account and the built-in File History backup program in Windows. You tell the program to back up your old PC's files, and then you tell your new PC's program to restore those files.

However, you need a portable hard drive for this to work. Portable hard drives are fairly inexpensive, usually costing less than $100. But there's a bonus: When you're through transferring the files, the drive works perfectly for backing up your *new* computer.

To transfer files from an old Windows 8, 8.1, or 10 computer to a new Windows 10 computer, follow these steps:

1. **If you've already been using File History on your old PC, jump to Step 5. Otherwise move to Step 2.**

2. **Sign in with your Microsoft account on your old PC.**

When you sign in with a Microsoft account, Microsoft remembers many of your settings and services so that it can duplicate them on other PCs you sign in to.

3. **Plug the portable hard drive into your old PC and then set up File History to save your files onto the portable hard drive.**

File History comes built in to Windows 8, 8.1, and 10. I describe how to set it up and turn it on in Chapter 13. It could take anywhere from a few minutes to a few hours to back up your files for the first time.

While File History backs up your files, it shows the statement "Backing up your data."

When File History has finished backing up your files to the portable drive, those words change to say "Last Backup," followed by the date and time it finished backing up your files, as shown in Figure 20-2. At that point, move to Step 4.

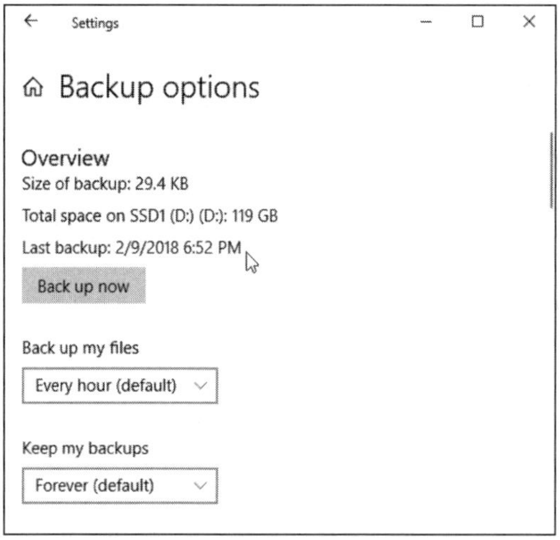

FIGURE 20-2:
The File History
window lists the
backup's date
and time.

4. **Sign in to your new Windows 10 PC with the same Microsoft account you used on your old PC. Then plug the portable hard drive into your new computer.**

   By signing in with your Microsoft account, your settings automatically transfer to your new PC. (Depending on your settings, the wallpaper on your new PC may change to match your old PC, letting you know that something is happening.)

5. **Open File History and direct your new Windows 10 PC toward your old File History backup.**

   On your new Windows 10 PC, click the Start button and type **File History** into the Search box. Then click Restore Your Files with File History. When the File History window appears, click Configure File History Settings.

   The Settings app's File History window appears, as shown in Figure 20-3.

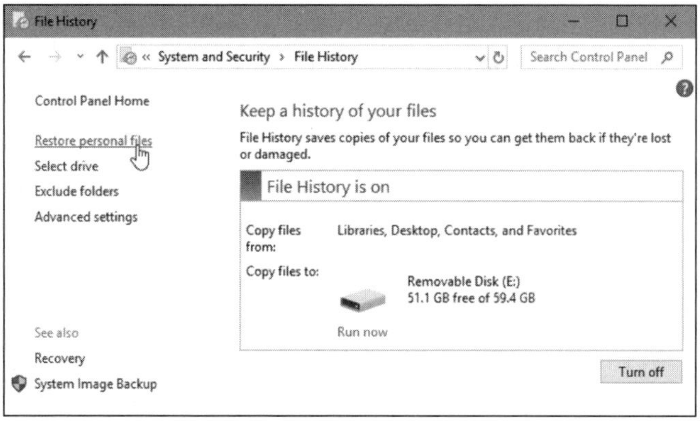

FIGURE 20-3:
Choose the
backup you'd
like to restore.

If you spot a check box labeled I Want to Use a Previous Backup on this File History Drive, click it. A window drops down, listing the backup you've made on your old PC. Click its name, and click the Turn On button.

Your new PC begins backing up its files for the first time, but these incoming files won't damage your old PC's backup.

6. **Choose Restore Personal Files from the File History window's left pane.**

The window shown in Figure 20-4 appears.

7. **Choose the files and folders to restore and then click the green Restore button.**

Click the Forward or Back arrows next to the big green button along the window's bottom until you find the date and time of the files you'd like to restore.

For example, if you used File History on your old PC for the first time in Step 4, click the Back arrow (on the left) until you're at the Number 1 backup.

If you've been using File History on your old PC all along, click the Forward arrow (on the right) to move to your most recent backup.

When you're viewing the files or folders you want to restore, click the green button found on the window's bottom edge, shown in Figure 20-4. File History begins copying your old PC's files and folders onto your new PC.

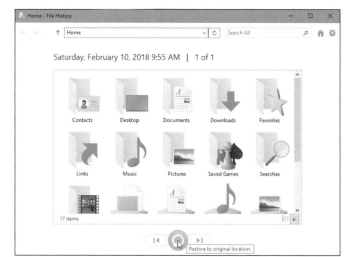

FIGURE 20-4:
Click the green button to restore the files and folders.

If there are no complications, your new PC should soon have the files and folders from your old PC.

>> If you've already been using File History on your old PC, all of your old PC's backups should still be available to you on your new PC.

>> Your new PC will continue to back up your new computer's files to your portable hard drive. Keep the hard drive plugged in permanently. (Or, if you bought a new laptop or tablet, plug it in frequently so your computer can keep your backups current.)

>> If you've just borrowed a friend's portable hard drive, you can unplug it at this point and give it back. But you should really have your own portable hard drive so you can begin backing up your new Windows 10 PC.

>> Your Microsoft account and File History can transport your settings and files to your new PC. However, you must still install all of your old desktop *programs* onto your new PC.

>> If you're moving to Windows 10 from a Windows 8 or 8.1 PC, you can find your apps waiting for you in the Microsoft Store app: Click your icon near the Store app's upper-right corner and choose My Library from the drop-down menu. There you can find and download your old apps to your new PC.

Chapter **21**

Help on the Windows Help System

D on't bother plowing through this whole chapter for the nitty-gritty. What you find here are the quickest ways to make Windows dish out helpful information when something on the desktop leaves you stumped:

» **Press F1 when on the desktop:** Press the F1 key from within Windows or any desktop program.

» **Start menu:** Click the Start button and click the Get Help tile.

 » **Question mark:** If you spot a little blue question mark icon near a window's top-right corner, pounce on it with a quick click.

In each case, Windows fetches help, either by going online, fetching built-in instructions, or leading you to a tutorial built in to Windows 10.

This chapter explains how to take advantage of the help Windows 10 has to offer.

Getting Started with Windows 10

The Windows 10 Tips app offers a short guided tour to Windows 10. It appeals mostly to the same people who enjoy reading book introductions that set the mood for what's coming.

 To open the app, click the Start button and click the Tips icon (shown in the margin) from the Start menu. The app fills the screen, shown in Figure 21-1.

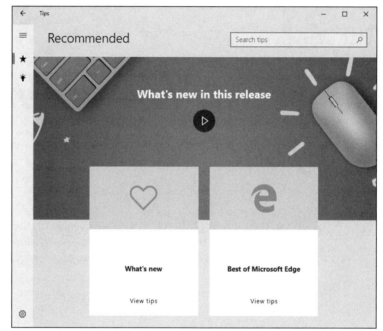

FIGURE 21-1:
The new Tips app offers a short introduction to Windows 10.

Like most apps, the Tips app lists icons along the left edge. Can't see the icons' labels? Then click the "hamburger" menu icon (the icon with three horizontal lines that's shown in the margin) in the app's upper-left corner. Clicking that icon in *any* app expands the app's left pane, letting you see labels next to the mysterious icons. You can also hover your mouse pointer over an icon and a pop-up reveals its name.

Click the What's New in Windows 10 link, shown in Figure 21-1, to see a quick explanation of the biggest changes in Windows 10's latest update.

Feel free to click any of the other categories along the left and browse the offered options. However, the Tips app serves as a very brief introductory guide to Windows 10. It's definitely not a problem solver.

In fact, the Tips app has its own problem: Many portions work only when you're connected to the Internet. If you're not connected, the app simply displays an error message.

Contacting Support

Windows 10 comes with a new app that hopes to simplify finding the type of help you need for your particular problem. Called simply, Get Help, the app works much like those phone robots that make you press different numbers on your phone until you're finally routed to the proper department.

To summon the Get Help app and begin routing yourself to somebody or something that can help you with your computer's particular problem, follow these steps:

1. **Click the Start button, and click Get Help (the icon is in the margin).**

    The Get Help program appears, shown in Figure 21-2, and fetches a Virtual Assistant (a robot) to answer your problem.

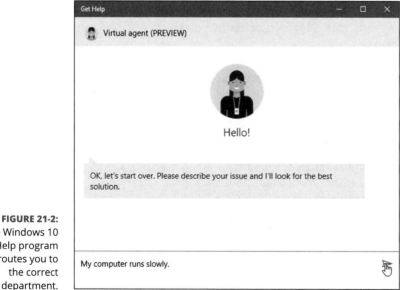

FIGURE 21-2:
The Windows 10 Get Help program routes you to the correct department.

2. **Type your question into the box along the app's bottom edge.**

   The robot searches Microsoft's Answers forum for any matches and presents the results. If any of the results answers your question, you're through! If you still have questions, click the Talk to a Person link.

3. **Choose your preferred method of support.**

   The Get Help app offers these ways to communicate with a person:

   - **Call Me Back; Schedule a Call:** These options provide variations on a common theme: paid support. I describe Microsoft's paid support options in this chapter's next section.

   - **Chat:** A good place to start, this begins as a free chat, where you type messages back and forth with a Microsoft representative. Depending on the severity of your computer's problem, though, it may move to a paid service.

   - **Ask the Community:** Perhaps your best bet, this involves posting your question in an online forum at answers.microsoft.com. I describe it in this chapter's last section.

I recommend trying the Chat option first. What seems like an insurmountable problem may be easily solvable if somebody walks you through the problem-solving steps. I cover the other two options, paid support and Ask the Community, in the next two sections.

Microsoft's paid support options

As of early 2018, Microsoft offers two main types of paid services, broken down into these categories:

» **Assure Software Support Plan:** For a $149 annual fee, Microsoft offers one year of help by online chat or phone (and personal training, if you live close to a Microsoft Store). For people who constantly take their PC to repair shops or call in-home tech support companies, the annual support plan may save some money.

» **Premium Software Support:** If you only need help with Microsoft's own software like Windows or Office, you can pay $99 for an hour's worth of online chat or phone support. That $99 is per *hour*, however. And the charge is for each session, which shows why the Assure Software Support Plan might be a better deal for problems that occur frequently.

If you've purchased your computers directly from Microsoft's online or retail stores, Microsoft offers extended service and warranty plans. By paying in advance, you can take advantage of Microsoft's support plans without having to pay a per-incident charge or hourly fee.

Microsoft changes its support plans often, though, so to hear the latest on Microsoft's paid support plans, open the Get Help app, choose Chat, and ask what support plans Microsoft currently offers.

If you live close to a Microsoft Store, you find better support by taking your computer to the store, where they can help you in person. To find the Microsoft Store nearest you, visit `www.microsoftstore.com`.

Microsoft's free support options

For free support, your best bet is the Microsoft Answers forum. It's an online gathering place for confused owners, knowledgeable tech enthusiasts, and an occasional Microsoft employee.

You visit the website, choose your category, type in your question, and wait. Sometimes a Microsoft employee will answer, but more often than not, somebody with a similar problem will chime in. The more people that respond, the more likely everybody will find a solution to a common problem.

Remember, though: The forums are for Microsoft products. If you're having problems with software from another company, you're limited to that other company's technical support.

To visit the free Microsoft Answers forum, follow these steps:

1. **Visit the Microsoft Answers website at** `answers.microsoft.com` **and choose Windows from the Categories section.**

2. **Choose your Windows version from the Browse by Version section.**

3. **Sign in with your Microsoft account.**

   The forum's website appears, shown in Figure 21-3.

4. **Search the forum for previously answered questions.**

   If something about your computer isn't working correctly, it probably isn't working for others, either. Type a few key words describing your problem in the Search box, located in the window's upper-right corner, and press Enter.

   When the website lists the results, spend some time browsing them to see if any solutions work for your computer's particular problem. If not, move to Step 5.

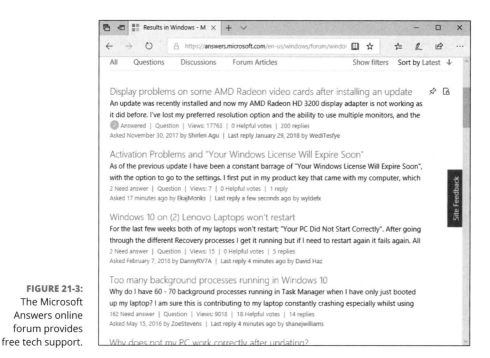

FIGURE 21-3:
The Microsoft
Answers online
forum provides
free tech support.

5. **Type in your question, and fill out a title, problem description, and category. Then click the Submit button.**

    To ask a question, click the Ask a Question link. The website presents a form, shown in Figure 21-4, for you to fill in a title and details about your computer's problem.

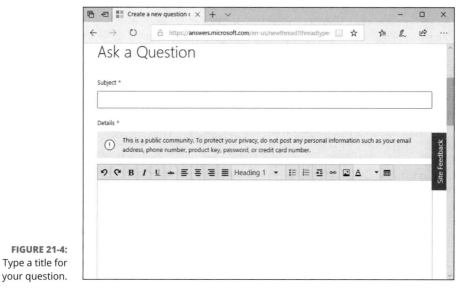

FIGURE 21-4:
Type a title for
your question.

Don't forget to fill out the Category drop-down lists at the bottom of the form. They let you choose your Windows version, as well as narrow down your question by topic. Those little chores help others find your question, and possibly provide answers, when they visit later on.

And then, you wait. When somebody responds, a notice appears in your email with a link to your posted message and the response. Click the emailed link to revisit the forum, where you can begin a correspondence that may solve your problem.

The Answers Desk is free, and although it's not guaranteed to provide an answer, it's definitely worthwhile.

TIP

For the best results, keep these tips in mind when posting a message on the Answers Forum:

>> Don't rant. Remember, most forum visitors aren't paid. Many of them are confused souls trying to piece together solutions, just like you. Many computer nerds also hang out there. They're actually interested in solving problems, and they're persuaded more by logic than emotions.

>> To attract the best responses, be as descriptive as possible. If you see an error message, list it in its entirety, without typographical errors. Type in your computer's exact make and model.

>> If possible, list the exact steps you take on your computer to reproduce the problem. If your problem is reproducible on other people's computers, it's always much easier to solve.

>> Most of the best answers don't come from Microsoft's paid technicians. They come from strangers who have your same problem, perhaps even the same make and model of computer, and who want to swap tips to make things better for you both.

>> Keep an eye on your e-mail Inbox, and respond to people who try to help. The information you're exchanging will live on for years. Even if you're not able to solve your immediate problem, you're leaving a trail that can help others solve that problem down the road.

7

The Part of Tens

IN THIS CHAPTER

» Returning to your previous Windows version

» Removing the Start menu tiles

» Avoiding the desktop

» Stopping the permission screens

» Finding Windows menus

» Capturing pictures of your screen

» Finding out your version of Windows

Chapter **22**

Ten Things You'll Hate about Windows 10 (And How to Fix Them)

You may find yourself thinking Windows 10 would be perfect if only . . . *(insert your pet peeve here)*.

If you find yourself thinking (or saying) those words frequently, read this chapter. Here, you find not only a list of ten of the most aggravating things about Windows 10 but also the best ways you can fix them.

I Don't Want Windows 10!

If your new PC came with Windows 10 pre-installed, there's little you can do: You're pretty much stuck with it.

But if you've recently upgraded your PC to Windows 10, here's how to return to the charms of your previous Windows version:

1. **Click the Start menu, click the Settings icon, and, when the Settings app appears, click the Update & Security category.**

2. **When the Update & Security page appears, click Recovery from the left pane.**

3. **From the right pane, find the Go Back to a Previous Version of Windows section and click the Get Started button.**

Your computer will grumble a bit before restarting. Eventually, after enough grumbling and restarting, you'll return to your older, more familiar version of Windows. Your files and programs should be waiting for you, as well.

After 30 days, however, this option disappears. Once that happens, you're stuck with Windows 10. Remember, though, Microsoft constantly updates Windows 10. It's grown increasingly easier to use during the past year. You might learn to like it.

Windows 10 Keeps Changing!

Microsoft sends two big updates to Windows 10 every year. (This book covers the latest update, released in April 2018.) Each update contains hundreds of changes; many are simply "under-the-hood" bug fixes, and others are subtle changes to the wording in menus, and others add big new features.

Even when Windows 10 doesn't change noticeably, its bundled apps do. Microsoft constantly tweaks its apps such as Mail and Calendar, Photos, Camera, Groove Music, and others. To see a list of changes, open the Microsoft Store app, click the three lines in its upper-right corner, and choose Downloads and Updates from the drop-down menu.

The Microsoft Store subsequently lists all your installed apps, and the last time they've been updated behind your back. (Click the Get Updates button at the page's top to download the app's latest versions.) Chances are that you'll see that many of your apps have been updated within the past week.

In short, Windows 10 changes constantly, and there's no way for you to stop it. Menus may change their names overnight; the Start menu sometimes sprouts new buttons in new locations. Some apps gain new features or names, others drop features. Some apps are dropped altogether.

Rapid change is the price you pay for Microsoft's "always up-to-date" vision for Windows 10; there's no way to lock it in place and say, "Stop changing!"

I Want to Avoid the Apps!

With the latest Windows 10 update, Microsoft continues its switch from the old-and-weary world of desktop programs to the mobile-friendly land of apps. After a year of updates, apps are more difficult to avoid than ever.

Some people love apps. They're designed for touchscreen tablets, as well as for phones, with limited screen real estate. They lack complicated menus and aim for touch-friendly simplicity. Other people hate apps, preferring to run programs on their desktop. After all, they've been doing it that way with a mouse and keyboard for two decades.

If you find Microsoft's focus on apps to be misguided and annoying, here's how to avoid them. Follow the tips in these sections to remove apps from the Start menu and your PC, keeping your focus on the desktop.

Pruning apps from the Start menu and your PC

Windows 10 stocks the Start menu's right edge with app tiles. Windows 8 and 8.1 owners may be accustomed to Microsoft's new app-loving lifestyle, but apps may be new and unwanted for Windows 7 upgraders.

Luckily, you can prune those tiles fairly easily. To remove a Start screen tile, right-click it and, when the pop-up menu appears, choose Unpin from Start. Repeat with all the other tiles until they're gone, gone, gone.

That removes the app tiles from the Start menu. But the apps still remain on the Start menu's All Apps alphabetical list. And it doesn't remove the apps from your PC.

To go one step further and *uninstall* the apps, follow these steps:

1. **Click the Start button and choose the Settings icon from the Start menu.**

   The Settings app appears.

2. **Click the Settings app's Apps category (shown in the margin). When the Apps window appears, click the Apps & Features link along the window's left edge.**

   The Apps & Features window appears, listing your installed apps along its right side, as shown in Figure 22-1.

3. **To remove an app, click its name, and click the Uninstall button that appears below its name. Then click Uninstall again when Windows asks whether you're sure you want to delete the app.**

   Windows deletes the app from your computer, removing it from the Start menu along the way. Not all apps can be deleted, unfortunately. If the Uninstall button is grayed out, that app can't be uninstalled.

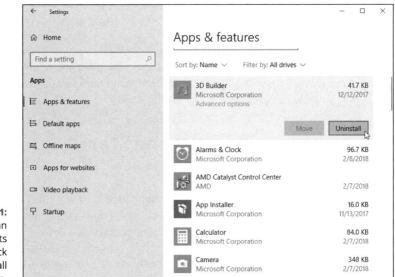

FIGURE 22-1: To remove an app, click its name and click the Uninstall button.

You can reinstall a mistakenly deleted app by visiting the Microsoft Store, searching for the app in the Store's Search box, and reinstalling it. (It's also listed when you click the "three dots" icon near the upper-right corner of the Microsoft Store and choose My Library from the drop-down menu.) I describe how to install apps from the Store in Chapter 6.

Telling desktop programs, not apps, to open your files

Some people don't mind apps, as long as the apps don't intrude on chores normally handled by their traditional desktop programs. But in Windows 10, apps often want to open your desktop files. Clicking a music file from the desktop's File Explorer, for example, normally fetches the Groove Music app rather than Media Player, which has held the reins for years.

To hand the chores back to your desktop programs, follow these steps:

1. **Click the Start button and click the Settings icon from the Start menu.**

   The Settings app appears.

2. **When the Settings app opens, click the Apps category (shown in the margin) and then click the Defaults Apps option from the left pane.**

   The Choose Default Apps screen appears.

3. **For each type of file, choose the program that should open it.**

   In the Music Player section, for example, click the currently listed program. When the Choose an App screen appears, showing apps and programs capable of playing music, choose the desktop player you want to handle the job.

Repeat for other program categories until you've replaced any Start menu apps with their desktop equivalents.

I Want to Avoid the Desktop!

A touchscreen tablet entices you to stick with apps for their finger-sized tiles and easy-to-touch icons. Smartphone owners have enjoyed the app lifestyle for years. Easily downloadable apps offer help for nearly every niche, from bird-watching to car repair.

A tablet's lightweight yet large screen makes it easy to read digital books, news-papers, and magazines. You can browse your favorite websites while away from your desk. The newly beefed-up Settings app in Windows 10 makes it easier than ever to avoid the desktop.

But staying nestled within the world of apps can be more difficult than it appears. No matter how hard you try to avoid the desktop and its pin-sized controls, you'll find yourself dragged there when you do any of the following things from the Start menu:

>> **Manage gadgetry:** The Devices category of the Settings app lists all the devices connected to your computer, from printers to mice to portable hard

drives. But it shows only their names; to change the *settings* of many of those devices requires a trip to the desktop's Control Panel and its Hardware and Sound category.

>> **Run Desktop Programs:** If you install or run any older programs designed for the desktop, you're back in the old-school land of the desktop and its mouse-central design.

>> **Manage files:** You can access your photos and music files from the Photos and Music apps, respectively. But if you need to visit your OneDrive files or do more advanced tasks — sorting files by creation date, for example — it's time to visit the desktop's File Explorer.

In short, the apps in Windows 10 handle most simple computing tasks, but when it comes to fine-tuning your computer's settings or performing maintenance work, you find yourself returning to the desktop or its Control Panel.

TIP

If you constantly return to the desktop for certain tasks, visit the Microsoft Store to search for an app that can handle the job. Microsoft stocks the store with more apps every day, and as the apps fill more niches, you'll find yourself relying on the desktop less often.

Until the apps catch up with the desktop, tablet owners might want to pop a portable Bluetooth mouse (covered in Chapter 12) into their gadget bags for those inevitable trips to the desktop and its tiny buttons and menus.

TIP

When running Windows on a tablet, make sure you're in Tablet mode: Slide your finger inward from the screen's right edge. When the Notifications pane appears, make sure the Tablet mode button is highlighted. If it's not highlighted, tap it to switch back to Tablet mode.

I Don't Want a Microsoft Account

Microsoft wants *everybody* to sign in with a Microsoft account. To Microsoft's credit, Windows 10 is much easier to use with a Microsoft account. Many services require one. Without a Microsoft account, you miss out on the handy OneDrive online storage space. Your *child* even needs to sign in with a Microsoft account if you want to track his computer usage.

But if you don't want a Microsoft account, you don't need one. Just sign up for a Local account instead. However, Local account holders limit themselves to the "old school" world of life on the desktop. For many people, the desktop works just fine.

A Local account lets you use your desktop and desktop programs, just as they've worked on Windows 7 and earlier Windows versions.

I explain how to create both Local and Microsoft user accounts in Chapter 14.

Windows Makes Me Sign In All the Time

The power-conscious Windows normally blanks your screen when you haven't touched a key for a few minutes. And, when you belatedly press a key to bring the screen back to life, you're faced with the lock screen.

To move past the lock screen, you need to type your password to sign back in to your account.

Some people prefer that extra level of security. If the lock screen kicks in while you're spending too much time at the water cooler, you're protected: Nobody can walk over and snoop through your email.

Other people don't need that extra security, and they simply want to return to work quickly. Here's how to accommodate both camps:

To keep Windows from asking for a password whenever it wakes back up, follow these steps:

1. **Click the Start button, and click the Settings icon.**

   The Settings app appears.

2. **Click the Accounts category from the Settings app, and click Sign-in Options from the left panel.**

3. **Click the Require Sign-In Options drop-down menu, and change it to Never.**

Taking these steps leaves you with a more easy-going Windows. When your computer wakes up from sleep, you're left at the same place where you stopped working, and you don't have to enter your password anymore.

Unfortunately, it also leaves you with a less-secure Windows. Anybody who walks by your computer will have access to all your files.

To return to the safer-but-less-friendly Windows, follow these same steps, but in Step 3, select the When PC Wakes Up from Sleep option. Your changes take place immediately.

TIP

If you hate signing in, you're a perfect candidate for Windows Hello. Instead of having to type in a name and password, you simply slide your finger over a fingerprint reader. Windows immediately greets you, and lets you in. I describe how to set up Windows Hello in Chapter 14.

The Taskbar Keeps Disappearing

The taskbar is a handy Windows feature that usually squats along the bottom of your desktop. Sometimes, unfortunately, it up and wanders off into the woods. Here are a few ways to track it down and bring it home.

If your taskbar suddenly clings to the *side* of the screen — or even the ceiling — try dragging it back in place: Instead of dragging an edge, drag the entire taskbar from its middle. As your mouse pointer reaches your desktop's bottom edge, the taskbar suddenly snaps back into place. Let go of the mouse and you've recaptured it.

Follow these tips to prevent your taskbar from wandering:

>> To keep the taskbar locked in place so that it won't float away, right-click a blank part of the taskbar and select Lock the Taskbar. Remember, though, that before you can make any future changes to the taskbar, you must first unlock it.

>> If your taskbar drops from sight whenever the mouse pointer doesn't hover nearby, turn off the taskbar's Auto Hide feature: Right-click a blank part of the taskbar and choose Taskbar Settings from the pop-up menu. When the Taskbar's settings page appears, turn off the toggle switch called Automatically Hide the Taskbar in Desktop Mode. (Another toggle keeps the taskbar from hiding in Tablet mode, as well.)

I Can't Line Up Two Windows on the Screen

With its arsenal of dragging-and-dropping tools, Windows simplifies grabbing information from one window and copying it to another. You can drag an address from an address book and drop it atop a letter in your word processor, for example.

However, the hardest part of dragging and dropping comes when you're lining up two windows on the desktop, side by side, to swap information between them.

Windows offers a simple way to align windows for easy dragging and dropping:

1. **Drag one window against a left, right, top, or bottom edge.**

   When your mouse pointer touches the screen's edge, the window reshapes itself to fill half the screen.

   Windows 10 also lets you drag windows to corners, which is your way of telling the windows to reshape themselves to fill one-quarter of the screen. By dragging a window into each corner, you can align four windows neatly on the screen.

2. **Drag the other window against the opposing edge.**

   When your mouse pointer reaches the other edge, the two windows are aligned side by side.

You can also minimize all the windows except for the two you want to align side by side. Then right-click a blank spot on the taskbar and choose Show Windows Side By Side. The two windows line up on the screen perfectly.

Try dragging windows to each position on the desktop, including the corners, so you'll be prepared when you need to view several files onscreen simultaneously.

It Won't Let Me Do Something Unless I'm an Administrator!

Windows gets really picky about who gets to do what on your computer. The computer's owner gets the Administrator account. And the administrator usually gives everybody else a Standard account. What does that mean? Well, only the administrator can do the following things on the computer:

>> Install programs.

>> Create or change accounts for other people.

>> Start an Internet connection.

>> Install some hardware.

>> Perform actions affecting other people on the PC.

People with Standard accounts, by nature, are limited to fairly basic activities. They can do these things:

» Run previously installed programs.

» Change their account's picture and password.

If Windows says only an administrator may do something on your PC, you have two choices: Find an administrator to type his or her password and authorize the action, or convince an administrator to upgrade your account to an Administrator account, a simple task I cover in Chapter 14.

I Don't Know What Version of Windows I Have

Windows 10 comes in several versions. Not sure exactly what version of Windows lives on your computer? Windows doesn't really shout it out, but a little probing forces it to reveal that information. Specifically, you need to look at the System window.

Follow this step to see what version of Windows is installed:

1. **Right-click the Start button, and choose System from the pop-up menu.**

   The Settings app opens to the System category's About section. Look in the right pane's Windows Specifications section to see what version of Windows lives on your PC. Chances are good that it's Windows 10 Home or Professional version.

If you're running an earlier version of Windows, follow these steps:

1. **From the Desktop, click the Start button.**

2. **Right-click the menu item named either Computer or My Computer and choose Properties from the pop-up menu.**

   When the System Properties window appears, read the information to discover your version of Windows, and whether it's 32-or 64-bit.

If your desktop doesn't have a Start button, you're running Windows 8.

My Print Screen Key Doesn't Work

Contrary to its name, the Print Screen key doesn't shuttle a picture of your screen to your printer. Instead, the Print Screen key (usually labeled PrintScreen, PrtScr, or PrtSc) sends the screen's picture to the Windows memory.

From there, you can paste it into a graphics program, such as Paint, letting the graphics program send the picture to the printer.

If you want to capture an image of the entire screen and quickly save it as a file, press ▓+PrtScr.

That shortcut tells Windows to snap a picture of your current screen and save it as a file. Windows saves those pictures in your computer's Pictures folder within a folder called *Screenshots.* Screenshot files are in the PNG format, a favorite with many graphics programs. (The screenshot doesn't include your mouse pointer.) Subsequent screenshots include a number after the name, as in Screenshot (2) and Screenshot (3).

When saved, your screenshot can head for your printer when you right-click the file and choose Print from the pop-up menu.

Some tablets can also take and save a screenshot if you hold down the volume down toggle and press the tablet's built-in Windows key. Other tablets require different key combinations, so check your tablet's manual to see how it takes screenshots.

When something on your computer screen looks confusing or broken, take a screenshot. Sending the screenshot file to a tech support person lets them see exactly what you're seeing, which increases his chance of fixing it.

Chapter **23**

Ten or So Tips for Tablet and Laptop Owners

For the most part, everything in this book applies to deskbound PCs, laptops, *and* tablets. Windows 10 offers some exclusive settings for the portable crowd, however, and I cover those items here.

Designed for travelers, it explains how to toggle Airplane mode in a hurry, connect to yet another Wi-Fi hotspot, and toggle an uncooperative tablet's autorotate feature.

If nothing else, please read the section on backing up your laptop or tablet before traveling. It's easier and more essential than ever.

Turning on Tablet Mode

When in Tablet mode, Windows 10 switches to its finger-friendly mode: The Start menu fills the entire screen. Your apps fill the screen as well. Because tablets are often smaller than desktop monitors, seeing one program at a time makes it easier to focus on the essential information.

When running in Tablet mode, Windows even adds extra space to a list of menu items, making it easier to poke the desired option with a fingertip.

However, Tablet mode isn't always easy to define. When you plug a keyboard into your tablet, for example, do you want to turn off Tablet mode and return to the desktop and its less-touch-friendly menus? The same question arises when you plug in a mouse.

The new convertible laptops that switch between a laptop and a tablet with a folding motion complicate matters. Windows 10 sometimes can't tell which mode you want.

Fortunately, it's easy to see whether or not you're in Tablet mode and to toggle the setting on or off.

To toggle Tablet mode on a touchscreen tablet, follow these steps:

1. **Slide your finger inward from the touchscreen's right edge.**

   The Action Center pane appears.

2. **When the Action Center pane appears, tap the Tablet Mode button.**

   The Action Center pane shows at least four toggle buttons along the bottom. The highlighted buttons are turned on; the others are turned off.

Some tablets may switch automatically depending on the devices plugged into it. When your tablet senses a change — perhaps you've removed it from a docking station — it sends you a message in the screen's bottom-right corner, asking whether you want to switch to Tablet mode. If you'd like to toggle to Tablet mode, approve the message, and Windows switches accordingly.

If your tablet toggles to Tablet mode at inappropriate times, give it a little supervision: Tap the Start button, tap the Settings icon, and, when the Settings app appears, tap the System category. The Tablet Mode section, found on the left side of the System page, gives you these options:

>> **When I Sign In:** Tap this, and a pop-up menu lets you choose how Windows should behave when you sign in to your account. Windows can automatically send you to your preference of desktop or Tablet mode. Choose the other option, Use When Appropriate for My Hardware, and your PC defaults to its manufacturer's recommendations, handy with some combination laptop/tablets.

>> **When This Device Automatically Switches Tablet Mode On or Off:** Here, a pop-up menu lets you fine-tune your computer's discretion in automatically toggling Tablet mode. If your tablet already chooses Tablet mode correctly, Choose Don't Ask Me Before Switching. If your tablet needs more supervision, choose Always Ask Me Before Switching.

>> **Hide App Icons on the Taskbar When in Tablet Mode:** This toggle lets you choose whether to see app and desktop program icons on your taskbar. Some tablet owners prefer to remove the icons to reduce clutter. (Tablet owners can always see which apps are running in the background by tapping the taskbar's Task View icon, shown in the margin.)

>> **Automatically Hide the Taskbar in Tablet Mode:** There's little need for a desktop in Tablet mode, so there's even less need for the taskbar, that once essential strip along the desktop's bottom edge. Choose this option to toggle it off when in Tablet mode. If you prefer the safety net of the taskbar, toggle this back on.

Choose any option, and the change takes place immediately; you don't need to click an OK or Yes button to approve the changes.

Switching to Airplane Mode

Most people enjoy working with their tablets or laptops during a long flight. Portable devices are great for watching movies and playing games while pretending to catch up on some work.

But most airlines make you turn off your wireless connection while the plane is in flight, referred to in airport lingo as *Airplane mode.*

To turn on Airplane mode, follow these steps:

1. **Click or tap the Action Center icon near the clock in the screen's bottom-right corner.**

The Action Center pane appears.

2. **Tap or click the word Expand above the row of buttons.**

   The Action Center pane normally shows four buttons along its bottom edge; tapping or clicking Expand reveals a row of hidden additional buttons.

3. **Click or tap your Airplane Mode icon (shown in the margin).**

   When the button is highlighted, Airplane mode is on, which turns off your tablet's radios: Wi-Fi, Bluetooth, and GPS.

To turn off Airplane mode and reconnect to the Internet, repeat these steps. This time, however, you toggle *off* Airplane mode, which reactivates your Wi-Fi, Bluetooth, and GPS.

TIP

Airplane mode not only puts your tablet and laptop in compliance with airline safety rules, but it conserves battery life, as well. Feel free to keep your computer in Airplane mode even when you're not on an airplane.

Airplane mode turns off not only your computer's wireless but its cellular gear, as well, if you have a cellular data plan. It's a handy way to shut *off* all your computer's radio activity with one switch.

Connecting to a New Wireless Internet Network

Every time you connect to a wireless network, Windows stashes its settings for connecting again the next time you visit. But when you're visiting a wireless network for the first time, you need to tell your computer that it's time to connect.

I explain wireless connections more thoroughly in Chapter 15, but here are the steps for quick reference:

1. **Turn on your laptop's wireless adapter if necessary.**

   Most adapters stay on continuously unless your computer is in Airplane mode. If so, turn off Airplane mode, as described in the previous section.

2. **Click your taskbar's wireless network icon, shown in the margin.**

   You can reach the taskbar's wireless network icon even when Tablet mode is turned on.

   Windows lists any wireless networks it finds within range.

3. **Connect to a wireless network by clicking its name and clicking the Connect button.**

At many places, clicking the Connect button connects your laptop to the Internet immediately. But if your laptop asks for more information, move to Step 4.

WARNING

Never connect to a wireless network listed as an *ad hoc* connection. Those connections are usually set up in public places by thieves hoping to rip off unsuspecting visitors.

4. **Enter the wireless network's name and security key/passphrase if asked.**

Some secretive wireless networks don't broadcast their names, so Windows lists them as Hidden Network. If you spot that name or Windows asks for the network's security key, track down the network's owner and ask for the network's name, known as its *SSID* (Service Set Identifier) and security key or passphrase to enter here.

When you click the Connect button, Windows announces its success. Be sure to select the check box labeled Connect Automatically. That tells your computer to remember the password and connect automatically the next time you come within range.

If you sign in with a Microsoft account, your Wi-Fi passwords travel with your account. If you log in to a Wi-Fi network with your laptop, you can automatically log in with your tablet, as well.

Toggling Your Tablet's Screen Rotation

Most Windows tablets are meant to be held horizontally. But when you pick them up, they automatically rotate to keep your work right-side up. Turn your tablet vertically, for example, and your desktop becomes long and narrow.

Autorotation comes in handy when you're reading a digital book, for example, because the longer, thinner pages more closely resemble a printed book. It's also a convenient way to rotate photos on a tablet when showing them off to friends. But when the screen rotates unexpectedly, autorotate becomes a bother.

TIP

Most tablets come with a rotation lock button along one edge. (The rotation button is usually near the power button for some reason.) Pressing that toggle button either locks the screen in place or lets it rotate freely.

You can also toggle autorotation directly from the desktop by following these steps:

1. **Click the Action Center icon near the clock in the screen's bottom-right corner.**

   On a touchscreen, slide your finger inward from the screen's right edge.

   The Action Center pane appears.

2. **Tap or click the word Expand above the four buttons.**

   The Action Center pane normally shows four buttons along its bottom edge; tapping or clicking Expand reveals the hidden buttons.

3. **Tap or click the Rotation Lock button.**

   When the button is highlighted, Windows stops the screen from rotating automatically. Tap it, and the highlight disappears, letting the tablet stay right-side up no matter how you move the tablet.

Repeat these steps to toggle autorotate on or off.

Adjusting to Different Locations

PCs don't move from a desktop, making some things pretty easy to set up. You need to enter your location only once, for example, and Windows automatically sets up your time zone, currency symbols, and similar things that change over the globe.

But the joy of a tablet or laptop's mobility is tempered with the annoyance of telling the thing exactly where it's currently located. This section supplies the steps you need to change when traveling to a different area.

Follow these steps to let your laptop know you've entered a new time zone:

1. **From the desktop, right-click the clock in the taskbar's bottom-right corner.**

   A pop-up menu appears.

2. **Click Adjust Date/Time.**

   The Settings app opens to the Time & Language category.

3. **Click the Time Zone option and then select your current time zone from the drop-down list.**

   That changes your time zone, which is all most travelers need. Extended-stay travelers may opt to change region-specific items — the region's currency symbol, for example, or the date, time, and number formats — or to add foreign characters to their keyboard.

   If you travel a lot, turn on the Set Time Zone Automatically toggle switch.

   If you're deeply embedded in a foreign zone, move to Step 4.

4. **Change your date and time formats, as well as regional and language preferences to match your current country's customs.**

   The Settings app's Time & Language category lets you change all of the regional settings in Windows:

   - **Date & Time:** This is the section you changed in Step 3. There's no need to revisit unless you erred in that step.

   - **Region and Language:** Choose this option, located just below the Date & Time option, to tell your apps what country you're visiting. (That lets the apps display local content that matches your location.) Choose the adjacent Add a Language button to add another language so you can read and type in that language.

   - **Speech:** Click here to fine-tune the speech recognition in Windows.

5. **Close the Settings app, if desired.**

   To exit the Settings app, click the X in its top-right corner.

Backing Up Your Laptop Before Traveling

I explain how to back up a PC in Chapter 13, and backing up a laptop or tablet works just like backing up a desktop PC. Please, please remember to back up your laptop before leaving your home or office. Thieves grab laptops and tablets much more often than desktop PCs. Your laptop and tablet can be replaced, but the data inside them can't.

Keep the backed-up information at *home* — not in your laptop's bag.

Theft is why I don't recommend storing any sort of backup memory card inside your tablet or in your tablet's carrying case. When the thief takes your tablet, he takes your backup, as well.

Microsoft's OneDrive, built in to Windows 10, lets you store your information on the Internet quite easily, providing an automatic backup. I explain how to set up OneDrive in Chapter 5.

Accessing the Mobility Center

Introduced in Windows 7, the Mobility Center lives on in Windows 10. It's a collection of frequently accessed settings for portable devices.

To access the Mobility Center, right-click the Start button and choose Mobility Center from the pop-up menu. The Mobility Center appears, as shown in Figure 23-1.

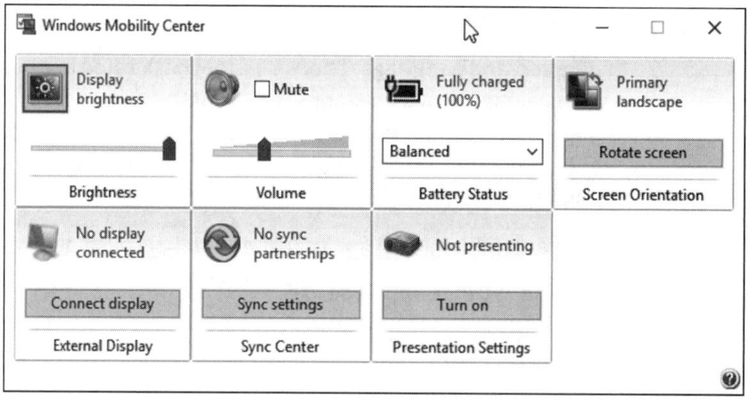

FIGURE 23-1: The Mobility Center places laptop and tablet settings in one easy-to-reach location.

Different manufacturers offer different settings, but almost all of them offer quick ways to toggle screen brightness, sound volume, rotation, battery plans, and ways to connect to monitors and projectors.

Turning Calculator into a Road Warrior Tool

When it burst onto the computing scene in the mid-eighties, Windows included a basic calculator with the usual arithmetic functions. With Windows 10, however, the calculator sports many new features that help not only math students, but world travelers.

Specifically, the calculator now includes a wide variety of converters, letting you calculate currency exchange rates, metric values, and a wide variety of other measurements.

To access Calculator's different conversion modes, follow these steps:

1. **Click the Start menu, type** Calculator **into the Search box, and press Enter.**

If you're running a tablet in Tablet mode, click the Cortana icon near the Start button to bring the Search box into view.

The Calculator app appears, shown in Figure 23-2.

FIGURE 23-2:
The Calculator app lets you convert foreign currency rates and metric system equivalents.

2. **Click the Menu icon in Calculator's upper-left corner.**

A menu drops down, listing all the modes the Calculator app can display.

3. **From the menu's Converter section, choose what you want to convert.**

Choose Currency, for example, to convert from dollars to Euros.

4. **Enter the amount you want to convert and the currency of your currently visited country.**

To convert $100 into Euros, for example, enter 100 into Calculator's type pad by clicking (or touching) the calculator buttons. Beneath that, use the drop-down menu to choose Euros, or the type of currency you'd like to convert. Calculator offers a wide variety of currency, from Afghanistan's Afghani to Yemen's Rial.

As soon as you choose the type of currency, Calculator looks up the current exchange rate, and lists how far that much money will go in the country you're visiting.

In another boon for travelers, Calculator converts volume, temperature, and speed measurements. It's worth a look when traveling in unfamiliar countries or when you've finished a trip and need to itemize receipts.

Index

R

reading email, 213–214

Reading List
  adding to in Microsoft Edge, 193
  removing items from, 198

Reading View (Microsoft Edge), 193

Reading View mode, 179

receiving files through email, 215–217

Recently Added section (Start menu), 35

Recommended Settings (Windows Media Player), 319

reconnecting drives, 379

Recycle Bin, 54, 60–61, 367

Recycle Bin icon, 60

Refresh (Microsoft Edge), 193

Region & Language category (Control Panel), 258

Remember icon, 5

removing
  appointments in Calendar app, 223
  apps, 255–256
  contacts in People app, 220–221
  email drafts, 213
  files, 105
  folders, 105
  items from Favorites, 198
  items from Reading List, 198
  items from Start menu, 41–42
  photos, 346
  printers, 249
  programs, 255–256
  Recycle Bin and, 60–61

renaming
  files, 103–104
  folders, 103–104
  photos, 167

repair shops, 384–385

repairing apps, 368

Repeat option (Windows Media Player), 328

Reply All button (Mail app), 214

Reply button (Mail app), 213–214

Reset tool, 358–359

resetting
  computers, 357–360
  Microsoft account passwords, 27
  passwords, 370

resizing windows, 86, 88, 89, 90

resolution
  for scanning, 183
  screen, 240–241

resources, Internet
  Adobe Reader, 249
  Apple iTunes, 95
  Avery, 175
  Avery Wizard, 181
  Cheat Sheet, 6
  Chrome, 194
  creating desktop shortcuts to, 146
  favorites for, 44
  Firefox, 194
  Google, 199, 331
  Laplink PCmover, 382
  Microsoft Answers Forum, 270
  Microsoft Privacy Center, 286
  Microsoft /Privacy Statement, 325
  OneDrive, 127
  Outlook, 214
  resetting Microsoft account passwords, 27
  SomaFM, 331
  Windows, 19
  Windows Insider's program, 1
  Zinstall, 383

restarting computers, 49, 356

Restore button, 32, 79

restore points
  creating, 264
  restoring from, 365

restoring
  backups with File History, 361–365
  from restore points, 365

retrieving deleted files, 367

returning to old Windows version, 361

revisiting favorites in Microsoft Edge, 197–198

About the Author

Andy Rathbone started geeking around with computers in 1985 when he bought a 26-pound portable CP/M Kaypro 2X. Like other nerds of the day, he soon began playing with null-modem adapters, dialing computer bulletin boards, and working part-time at Radio Shack.

He wrote articles for various techie publications before moving to computer books in 1992. He's written the *Windows For Dummies* series, *Microsoft Surface For Dummies*, *Upgrading & Fixing PCs For Dummies*, and many other computer books.

Today, he has more than 15 million copies of his books in print, and they've been translated into more than 30 languages. You can reach Andy at his website, www.andyrathbone.com.

Author's Acknowledgments

Special thanks to Dan Gookin, Matt Wagner, Tina Rathbone, Steve Hayes, Colleen Diamond, Ryan Williams, and Laura Bowman.

Thanks also to all the folks I've never met in editorial, sales, marketing, proof-reading, layout, graphics, and manufacturing who worked hard to bring you this book.

Publisher's Acknowledgments

Executive Editor: Steve Hayes

Project Manager: Colleen Diamond

Development Editor: Colleen Diamond

Copy Editor: Colleen Diamond

Technical Editor: Ryan C. Williams

Editorial Assistant: Matt Lowe

Sr. Editorial Assistant: Cherie Case

Production Editor: Tamilmani Varadharaj

Cover Photo: © Nikada/Getty Images